Islamic Philosophical Theology

STUDIES IN ISLAMIC PHILOSOPHY AND SCIENCE

Published under the auspices of
the Society for the Study of Islamic Philosophy and Science

Islamic Philosophical Theology

Edited by Parviz Morewedge

State University of New York Press
Albany

Published by
State University of New York Press, Albany

Printed in the United States of America

For information, address State University of New York Press, State University Plaza, Albany, N.Y., 12246

Library of Congress Cataloging in Publication Data
Main entry under title:

Islamic philosophical theology.

Bibliography: p.
Includes index.
1. Islamic theology—History—Philosophy, essays, lectures. I. Morewedge, Parviz.
BP166.1.I72 297'.2 79-14405
ISBN 0-87395-242-1

10 9 8 7 6 5 4 3 2

Contents

Introduction

THIS VOLUME contains a collection of essays by specialists in three areas of Islamic philosophical theology. Each paper is written in the style best suited to the topic in question, as is evident from Wilfred Cantwell Smith's theoretical analysis of the concept of "Faith" in Islam and its universal significance, and ʿAbdurrahman Badawi's historical and methodological remarks on his most recent findings of the Arabic version of Greek philosophical texts lost in their original. The result is a collection of what may constitute some of the best contemporary research in Islamic philosophical theology by many of its leading specialists. The occasion which led to the essays presented in this collection are two conferences: one on "Early Islamic Thought," organized by M. S. Mahdi in honor of Harry A. Wolfson, at Harvard University, 20–22 April 1971, and the other, the first international conference of the Society for the Study of Islamic Philosophy and Science SSIPS, on "Islamic Philosophy and Science" at Columbia University, 23–25 April 1971. Some of the papers dealing specifically with philosophy and science from the conference at Columbia University and an earlier conference at the State University of New York at Binghamton were collected and edited by George F. Hourani under the title *Essay on Islamic Philosophy and Science* and published by the State University of New York Press in 1975. Essays in the present volume deal with specific aspects of Islamic philosophic theology. Several other papers were commissioned to insure a balanced approaches to topics concerned with the major features of three aspects of Islamic philosophical theology: the integration of Greek philosophical and methodological contributions into Islamic theology; basic problems of classical Islamic theology and the contribution of major movements opposing the orthodoxy, such as Shīʿism; the philosophical, mystical contributions of the theologians and later movements that broke away from the classical Aristotelian tradition.

Since it is beyond the scope of this brief introduction to present an analysis of the papers, the following account is intended to outline their salient features.

I. THE GREEK PHILOSOPHICAL TRADITION AND ISLAMIC THEOLOGY

Evidently, one aspect of the study of Islamic philosophical theology facing the scholar in this field is a two-fold problem: how were the philosophical and methodological tools developed in Greek philosophy, integrated into the texts of the Muslim theologians, and how can we—on the basis of an examination of available Islamic sources—learn about some of the interesting aspects of the Greek philosophical texts which are no longer available in their original Greek Versions. ʿAbdurrahman Badawi, in an article entitled "New Philosophical Texts Lost in Greek and Preserved in Arabic Translations," offers an historical account of his recent discoveries of some of the Arabic versions of the texts of Alexander of Aphrodisias, and the paraphrases of some works of Aristotle by Olympiodorus and Themistius. In addition to commenting on topics of special interest to the theologians, such as the nature of the first cause and the clarification of the sources of *The Theology* of the pseudo-Aristotle in Arabic, this essay makes some corrections to previous historical scholarship in this special field and displays the relations between Arabic and Greek texts that can further our insight into a very significant area of the intellectual history of the West. The next two articles are devoted to clarifying the influences of the two major Greek traditions on Islamic theology, namely, the influences of the Platonic and the Aristotelian schools. F. E. Peters, whose previous writings include an investigation of Aristotle's works in Arabic, turns his attention to the development of Platonism among the Muslims in an article entitled, "The Origins of Islamic Platonism: The School Tradition." This work sheds light on several issues, including the role Proclus's philosophy played in this transmission, and offers support for the following claim: "What is certain is that Arabs knew, even within the confines of the school tradition, two different strains of Platonism: the Neoplatonic versions of Plotinus and Proclus, and an older Platonism brought in by the Roman schools during the second and the third century."

Ibrahim Madkour, whose work *L'Organon d' Aristote dans le monde arabe* of 1934 was among the first studies to investigate the role of Aristotelian logic in Islamic philosophy, singles out historical highlights in the use of Aristotelian logic among Islamic theologians, such as al-Ash arī, F. Rāzī, Suhrawardī, and others. His essay bears the title "La logique d'Aristote chez les Mutakallimūn."

In his contribution, "Aux débuts de la réflexion théologique de l'Islam," L. Gardet delineates the salient features of several issues playing a role in the development of the doctrines of the early Mutakallimūn in terms of Hellenistic influences. Theologians and topics covered include: the Jahmiyya, the forerunners of the Ashʿarī school, and the relationship of the doctrine of Jabariyya to Najjār and Burghūth (Muhammad b. ʿIsā).

II. CLASSICAL ISLAMIC THEOLOGY AND THE EARLY SHĪʿA MOVEMENT

Turning from the origins and the development of Islamic theology to central issues found in the classical works of Muslim theologians, we find that the following topics hold a position of prominence for investigators of Islamic theology proper: (i) the conceptual analysis of the key terms, their ordinary usage, and the significance they might have for the study of world religions, (ii) the investigation of interrelated controversies taken from philosophy proper, and (iii) the clarification of the extent of the theoretical contribution by early Shīʿa theologians who opposed the orthodoxy.

Central controversies between Mutakallimūn and the philosophers are investigated in the light of the Aristotelian tradition by Richard M. Frank in "*Kalām* and Philosophy, A Perspective from One Problem." Among the topics discussed by the author are the "understanding of the nature of the ultimate and unconditioned being," and analyses of modal concepts, which, in addition to presenting the usual treatment of physical causality, venture into related topics, such as the relationship between intentions and motives, the nature of the realization of our actions and the problems of Divine Actions. On the basis of the detailed arguments presented, Frank points out that "the *kalām* and the *falsafa* reflect in their opposition and diversity two distinct traditions: the one Islamic (and like Islam itself, closely related to the preceding monotheistic tradition) and the other pagan. Rather than by abstract intellect, they are bound and committed by these traditions and their canonical sources to the understanding of which they both employ the tools of philosophical reasoning in which they share, in part, a common heritage."

In this section, W. C. Smith presents a conceptual analysis of one of the key terms in Islamic theology, the notion of *Taṣdīq,* to which Harry A. Wolfson invited our attention a decade ago. In the essay entitled, "Faith as *Taṣdīq,*" Smith compares the notion of "faith in Islam" with faiths current in the modern West, using historical, philosophic, and philological analyses. Singling out for consideration and contrast the two concepts of faith in the West (one derived from the Judaeo-Christian tradition, and another the objective critical concept, which has gained ground since the Enlightenment), the author traces the historical and logical aspects of this important concept in Islam. His findings include analyses of the relationship between various meanings of *Taṣdīq,* e.g., *Taṣdīq* in relationship to the concept of "truth," *Taṣdīq* meaning to "recognize a truth, to appropriate it, to affirm it, to confirm it, to actualize it. And the truth, in each case, is personalist and sincere." Further analysis leads to an extension of the notion of *Taṣdīq* to knowledge and to moral truth.

In a comprehensive article, "The Shiite and Khārijite Contribution to Pre-Ashʿarite *Kalām,*" W. Madelung investigates for the first time two significant aspects of the Shīʿite and Khārijite contributions to the "two most prominent problems of *kalām:* the unity of God versus the multiplicity of His attributes and divine determinism versus human free will." In addition to specifying the doctrines of various theoreticians of these movements, Madelung's penetrating analysis brings out the subtlety in the philosophical issues embedded in the aforementioned controversy, e.g., the physical nature of space and time in relationship to the divine, epistemological issues of God's knowledge as well as the ethical problems of free will and responsibility.

III. THE DEVELOPMENT OF PHILOSOPHICAL AND MYSTICAL THEOLOGY

One of the major areas of Islamic philosophical theology still in need of further research is the development of philosophical and mystical tendencies, a development which may constitute the most original contribution to the history of ideas. Within this domain are many topics of special interest, such as philosophical theses relevant to the areas of ethics, logic, and metaphysics; the peculiar relationship between the philosophical and the mystical views of several writers; and the formation of a comprehensive perspective on the contribution of later philosophers, such as Mullā Ṣadrā.

In his article, "Reason and Revelation in Ibn Ḥazm's Ethical Thought," George F. Hourani indicates how Ibn Ḥazm answers "the most fundamental questions of modern philosophical ethics: the meanings of ethical concepts; the sources of our knowledge of them and of values in practice; the theory of moral motivation." In terms of the traditional context of the analysis of reason and revelation, the author extracts from Ibn Ḥazm's writings theories of interest to contemporary analytic philosophy, including theories of obligation, opinion, and analogy. Apart from presenting analyses of problems that arise out of these and similar concepts, the author argues that ". . . the center of his concern was to uphold the autonomy of God as the sole source of value judgments, against the rationalist objectivism of the Mu tazila. Reason cannot independently decide questions of right and wrong: this is his most urgent message. But reason is competent and necessary wherever description or explanation of facts is called for, and must be used actively in the service of obedience to revelation, the sole path to salvation."

The next two essays deal with the same topic, viz. Ibn Sīnā's proof of God's existence. In his article, "Avicenna's Proof of the Existence of God as a Necessarily Existent Being," Herbert A. Davidson argues that Ibn Sīnā's celebrated proof is a cosmological one. Davidson develops his thesis on the basis of ample references to the works of Aristotle and later western philosophers. In an essay entitled "A Third Version of the Ontological Argument in the Ibn Sīnian Metaphysics," Parviz Morewedge demonstrates the presence of at least one form of the ontological argument for God's existence in Ibn Sīnā's metaphysical writing, and shows that a phenomenologically sophisticated proof of God's existence may be constructed from various Ibn Sīnian texts and the ontological proofs found in the works of Augustine, Descartes, Spinoza and others. The paper concludes with a criticism of all these versions of the ontological argument.

In his essay "Al-Jāmī's *Treatise on Existence,*" Nicholas Heer presents a critical edition, a translation of, and a comprehensive commentary on an important text of the celebrated fifteenth-century mystical poet Jāmī, in which a complex doctrine of universals is criticized by Jāmī. Heer's penetrating analysis reveals the primary purpose of Jāmī's deductive treatise to be a defense of the theological doctrine of the concept of absolute existence with a ṣūfic notion of God. It is noteworthy that Jāmī, primarily known as a ṣūfī poet like many other Muslim intellectuals, integrates an interest in purely philosophical arguments with proving a theological doctrine.

Special acknowledgment is due to William E. Gohlman and Kazem Tehrani for preparing the final manuscript. Each contributor has been permitted to make use of his preferred system of dating and of transliteration; each is responsible for the validity of his own arguments. I alone am responsible for the organization and collection of these essays.

Parviz Morewedge
Department of Philosophy
Baruch College of
the City University of New York

I.
The Greek Philosophical Tradition and Islamic Theology

New Philosophical Texts Lost in Greek and Preserved in Arabic Translations

ʿAbdurrahman Badawi
University of Libya

ONCE AGAIN I am most happy to tell about my discoveries in the field of philosophical texts lost in their Greek originals but preserved in Arabic translations. Two years ago, I came across a number of these texts, which I have since edited for publication in the new series of the collection *Recherches* published under the auspices of the Institute of Oriental Letters of Beirut, with the title: *Commentaires sur Aristote perdus en grec.*

The collection comprises several treatises of Alexander of Aphrodisias, the paraphrase by Olympiodorus of the *Meteorologica* of Aristotle and the paraphrase of the *De Animalibus* of Aristotle by Themistius.

A. The treatises of Alexander of Aphrodisias are the following:

1. *On Time.*
2. *On the Establishment of the First Cause.*
3. *Refutation of Those Who Affirm That Vision is Produced by the Rays Emanated at Their Emission From the Eye.*
4. *On Matter,* privatio *and* generatio: *and Solution of a Problem Raised by Some of the Ancients, by Which They Invalidated the Concept of* generatio *in the* Physics *of Aristotle.*
5. *On Matter and That It Is Caused and Effected.*
6. *On Sound.*
7. *On Contraries and That They Are the First of Things.*
8. *On the Fact that Generation and Augmentation are Brought About in the Form, not in the Matter.*
9. *On the Conversion of Premises.*
10. *On Human Capacity.*
11. *On the Intellect.*
12. *On the Fact that Matter Is Different From Genus, and on What They Have in Common and in What Things They Differ.*

Of these, only the last two exist in a Greek original; the others are lost. The treatise *On the Intellect* was published by Ivo Bruns in his edition:[1]

Alexandri Aphrodisiensis, Praeter commentaria scripta minora: De anima liber cum mantissa, in Berlin in 1887, as the first part of volume two of the *Supplementum Aristotelicum.* In fact, the treatise περί νοῦ forms a chapter in the so-called *Mantissa* published by the same editor as a second book of the περί ψυχῆς, which in reality is only one book, as is certified by Arabic sources.[2] The περί νοῦ must be considered as an isolated treatise, and Ivo Bruns had no reason to publish it as the second book (liber alter) or even as a mantissa.[3]

Our manuscript, Tashkent MS 2385, is much more correct than the manuscript of the Escorial, MS Asiri 794, and that of Istanbul, MS Garullah 1279, ff. 58b–60b, on the basis of which the Arabic text of the *De Intellectu* of Alexander was published by J. Finnegan in Beirut in the *Mélanges de l'Université St.-Joseph,* in 1956. For the reader's convenience, I have reproduced the Greek text before the Arabic text, in order to make comparison easier.

The other treatise whose original Greek text is still existing, that is, the *Treatise on the Fact that Matter Is Different From Genus, and on What They Have in Common and in What Things They Differ* was published by Ivo Bruns in the second part of his edition: *Alexandri Aphrodisiensis . . . scripta survivia,* Berlin 1892, pp. 77–79. It is n. 28 of the so-called *Quaestiones naturales,*[4] on Φυσικων σχολιχων ἀπορίων καὶ λυσέων, book one, and is entitled: ὅτι μή ὕλη γένος.

I have discussed the problems raised around the *De Intellectu* of Alexander fully in my forthcoming book *L'Histoire de la Philosophie en Islam.* In the light of the Arabic text, all these problems can be solved or shown to be false. First of all, the Latin translation of the Alexandrian term Θὕραθεν by the word *adeptus,* which so much puzzled M. Etienne Gilson in his long study: "Les sources greco-arabes de l'Augustinisme avicennisant,"[5] can be understood by the aid of the Arabic original. In fact, the Arabic translation, on the basis of which the Latin translation was made, designates the *intellectus adeptus* or *acquisitus* by the words: *al-mustafād min al-khārij* المستفاد من الخارج and the expression *min al-khārij* is the translation of the Greek word Θὕραθεν.

The Greek Θὕραθεν is rendered by three words: *mustafād min al-khārij* (acquired from outside); and the Latin translator, following the Arabic translation, rendered literally the three Arabic words. For the sake of brevity, one can omit the last two words; *min al-khārij* من الخارج, and use only the first one: *mustafād* (acquired), on the condition that the other two words are always understood. This phenomenon is quite frequent in Islamic philosophy: for instance, one says: *ʿālam al-kawn* عالم الكون, (world of generation), and he means: *ʿālam al-kawn wa al-fasād* (world of coming to be and passing away); another example, one says: *ḥads* حدس, and it is understood: صائب (= exact), etc., etc. So whenever we come across the word *adeptus,* or *acquisitus* in these Latin translations of Arabic texts, we must suppose that it is always understood: *adeptus* or *acquisitus from outside.*

So, there is nothing surprising in the translation of the Greek word Θύραθεν by *adeptus* or *acquisitus,* because the literal sense is always understood: *from outside.* Therefore, M. Gilson is not right that the Arab translators of Alexander have arabicized him: "ils ont arabisé Alexandre" (*op. cit.* p. 21), in introducing a foreign body into the text of Alexander, that is to say, the *intellectus adeptus* or *acquisitus;* rather Edward Zeller was right in saying that it is Alexander of Aphrodisias that we find the source of the doctrine of the *intellectus acquisitus.*[6]

Another problem raised by Etienne Gilson is what he calls: des enigmes insolubles: for example, "la désignation curieuse de 'philosophie tabernaculorum' (ed. Théry, p. 82) p. 113, e, traduit en réalité le grec: τοίς ἀπὸ τῆς Στοᾶς, ed. I. Bruns." But the explication is very easy. In fact, these Greek words were translated by Isḥāq ibn Ḥunain thus: قوم من أصحاب المظلّة (*qawm min aṣḥāb al-miẓallah* = a group of Stoics), because the word Στοᾶς was translated literally and according to its etymology by أصحاب المظلّة (= men of the portico = τοίς ἀπὸ τῆς Στοᾶς). But the Latin translator translated the Arabic words literally, without giving the usual designation: Stoici. Another issue pointed out by Gilson is the confusion between *intellectus agens* and *intelligentia agens.* But the Arabic translation uses one word: عقل to designate the two words: *intellectus* and *intelligentia.*

Regarding the eventual use of the Arabic text for a new edition of the Greek original, we are certain the Arabic text is of little help or of no help at all. Surely, the Arabic translation, as we have edited it, is very faithful to the Greek original; but there is an embarrassing note by the translator Ḥunain ibn Isḥāq which runs as follows: "In this place there is a lacuna in the Greek text which we have collated with this copy." First of all, this note was present neither in our manuscript nor in that of the Escorial, but only in that of Gārullah and in the Latin translation. Secondly, compared with the Greek text edited by Ivo Bruns, there is nothing missing in the Arabic translation. Thirdly, does this note (Ḥunain's) refer to another copy of the Greek text other than that used for the translation; or may it be understood otherwise? The problem cannot be solved except by the first hypothesis, that is to say, that the translation was made from one manuscript, and the revision was made from another manuscript which had this lacuna. This supposition supports the Greek text published.

In comparing the Arabic translation with this Greek text, we have noticed that the translation, as we have edited it according to Tashkent MS 2385 and sometimes with the help of the other manuscripts, is complete and correct. All the remarks made by J. Finnegan on the relations between the Greek text and the Arabic translation are due solely to his misreading and misediting of the Arabic text, and also to the fact that the manuscripts he used are not very correct. This remark applies to many judgments improperly made about Arabic translations of Greek texts and on Latin translations from the Arabic, as I have several times proved. May I advise scholars in this field to be more cautious in their judgments, or to suspend judgment until a correct text is published?

Let us proceed now to a discussion of the other treatises, all lost in Greek.

1. The treatise *On Time* was translated by Ḥunain ibn Isḥāq, and from his Arabic translation it was translated into Latin by Gerald of Cremona. Al-Bīrūnī, in his book *On India* (English translation, I, p. 320) mentioned the Arabic translation.

In this treatise Alexander of Aphrodisias refutes the opinion of those who profess that time is neither the Sphere, nor is it the movement of the number of the movement of the Sphere. He discusses the problems concerning the instant, the relation between the Universal Soul and Time, the unity of time, and the truth of the allegation that time is the cause of destruction. He adheres everywhere to the Aristotelian doctrine of time.

2. The second treatise is entitled: *On the Establishment of the First Cause, a Discourse Abstracted by Alexander from the Book (called) Theology, on the Establishment of the First Cause.*

Ibn Abī Uṣaybiʿah[7] mentions this treatise as: مقاله فيما استخرجه من كتاب ارسطوطاليس الذي يدعى بالرومية ثولوجيا ومعناه الكلام في توحيد الله تعالى : *Treatise on What He Extracted from the Book of Aristotle called in Greek* Theologia, *Which Means Discourse on the Unity of God.* The title is briefer in Ibn al-Nadīm,[8] and this is followed by Ibn al-Qifṭī: كتاب الثاؤلوجيا ، مقالة :[9] *Book of Theology, One Treatise.*

In this treatise, Alexander wants to prove the following features of the First Cause: (a) it is one, (b) it exists prior to the plurality of things, (c) there is no plurality whatsoever in it, and (d) it is the cause of every plurality. Oneness cannot be said properly except of the First Cause. The oneness in other things is an effect. The True One is not formed by generation, because generation comes from the One.

It is in fact a commentary on two passages of the *Theology* attributed to Aristotle: (a) p. 112, lines 16–20, (b) p. 134, lines 5–10 of our edition (Cairo, 1955).

Curiously enough, the exposition of theology by Abd al-Laṭīf al-Baghdādī, in his book *On Metaphysics (fī ʿilm mā baʿd al-ṭabīʿah)* which we have edited as an appendix to our edition of *The Theology* of Pseudo-Aristotle,[10] is very similar to this treatise of Alexander, but more developed; it is entirely plausible that al-Baghdādī used our treatise as a basis for his exposition.

So the problem of its attribution to Alexander of Aphrodisias becomes very complicated, and may be similar to that of the other treatise on *The*

Spiritual Forms[11]—which was found afterwards to be extracted from Proclus' *Elements of Theology.* In the title of our treatise it is not said that *Theologia* belongs to Aristotle; and this is an important fact in the discussion of the problem of authenticity. For the moment, we leave this problem open.

3. The third treatise:*Refutation of Those Who Affirm That Vision is Produced by the Rays Emanated at Their Emission From the Eye,* in which Alexander proves that vision is not produced by movement of something, and therefore it cannot be the result of the incidence of rays on things, or the movement of the image towards the eye, or both.

The treatise is mentioned by all Arabic sources: Ibn al-Nadīm, al-Qifṭī (p. 54, last line), and Ibn Abī Uṣaybiʿah (I, p. 70, lines 14–15).

4. The fourth treatise: *On Sound* is not mentioned by these three sources. But this silence proves nothing because, as we have proved in our introduction to *Arisṭū ind al-Arab,* many extant treatises already published are not mentioned by these three sources and yet are genuinely from the hand of Alexander of Aphrodisias, as is proved and attested to by other sources, especially Greek sources. It is, however, very short and of little value.

5. The fifth is *On Matter and That It Is Effected.* The title in Ibn Abī Uṣaybiʿah is a little more developed: *On Matter and That It Is Caused and Effected.*[12] It is not mentioned by Ibn al-Nadīm or al-Qifṭī.

Here Alexander wants to prove that First Matter is caused and effected, and is capable of receiving forms without movement or alteration. Because matter is *in potentia,* therefore, it needs something *in actu* in order that it can be realized, and this thing *in actu* is the *First Cause.* But the *passio* (πἄσχεἰν) of the first matter (ὕλη) is different from that of the second, in the sense that the first receives form without alteration or destruction, whereas the second matter cannot receive form without alteration or destruction.

6. The sixth is *On* materia, privato, *and generatio: and Solution of a Problem Raised by Some of the Ancients, by Which They Invalidated the Concept of* Generatio *in the* Physics *of Aristotle.*

It is mentioned by Ibn Abī Uṣaybiʿah[13] under this title, but it may be the same as the one entitled: *al-raddʿalā man qāla innahū lā yakūnu shay'un illa min shay'*[14] mentioned by Ibn al-Nadīm, followed by al-Qifṭī.[15] The question discussed in this treatise may be the question mentioned by Aristotle in chapter 8 of the first book of the *Physics* (191 a 23–33).

Here Alexander develops the arguments laid down by Aristotle against this opinion of the Ancients (ἀϱχαίων ἀποϱία), without elucidating the names of these Ancients. He explains what is generation, matter, *privatio,* and that generation applies necessarily to matter.

7. The seventh treatise deals with another problem raised by a passage in the *Physics* of Aristotle, where he states that all the Ancients agree that contraries are the principles of all things. Here is the text of Aristo-

tle: "All thinkers then agree in making the contraries principles. . . . It is plain then that they all, in one way or another, identify the contraries with the principles. And with good reason. For, first principles must not be derived from one another nor from anything else, while everything has to be derived from them. But these conditions are fulfilled by the primary contraries, which are not derived from anything else because they are primary, nor from each other because they are contraries."[16]

Alexander considers this passage "very obscure" because Aristotle says: "contraries must not be derived from one another," and he says afterwards that "contraries are derived from one another." This is contradictory; for this reason, Alexander examines it seriously, and finds the solution in the following way: Aristotle, when he says that the first contraries are not derived from others, means that if they were derived from others, they would not have been first; and when he says that the contraries must not be derived from one another, he means that the contrary cannot be like its own contrary, for instance the form cannot be like its *privatio,* that cold cannot be warmth, nor warmth coldness.

When Aristotle says afterwards that contraries derive from one another, he means by that the bearer of contraries, that is to say the matter (ὕλη), because matter changes from one contrary to its contrary.

By that it has become quite clear how contraries can derive from one another, and how they cannot derive from one another. In fact, matter remains and the quality changes. If this is so, it is not then impossible that the first contraries change into one another in that way.

In the end, he explains Aristotle's view saying that contraries are permanent.

8. The eighth treatise is entitled: *On the Fact that Generation and Augmentation are Brought About in the Form, not in the Matter.* It was translated by Abū Uthmān al-Dimashqī, from whose Arabic translation the treatise was translated into Latin by Gerard of Cremona. This Latin translation still exists, and though it is incomplete, it is preserved in four manuscripts,[17] under the title: *De eo quod augmentum et incrementum fiunt in forma et non in yle.*

The title is a little different in the Escorial manuscript n. 794: في أن النشؤوالنحاء انما يكونان في الصورة instead of في ان الزيادة والنحاء. We did not find this title or the other in our sources.

In this treatise Alexander wants to solve a problem raised by a passage in Aristotle's *De Generatione et Corruptione,* where he states that growth and augmentation are produced in the form, and not in the matter. Some people have denied that and said that growth occurs both in form and in matter likewise.[18]

Alexander solves this problem in the following way: matter changes little by little in growth, because some part passes away and another thing comes from outside. But matter does not pass away wholly, because if it did, form would not remain as it is. Matter resembles quantity, and form resembles quality. As the quantity of a thing changes it does not remain as it is; but as to its quality, which is form, it remains as it is. Augmentation is a movement, and movement cannot be produced except in a motionless thing. Therefore, augmentation is not produced except in the form alone.

Notwithstanding the similarity of title between this treatise and the treatise number V published by Ivo Bruns (p. 13), the two texts are very different. There are some ideas and phrases in common, but that is all. For this reason, we should consider our treatise as a separate and independent one, and that its Greek original is lost.

9. The ninth treatise of Alexander is *On the Conversion of Premises.* It is translated by Abū Uthmān al-Dimashqī. This, the most elaborate of our treatises, deals with the question of the conversion of premises, in connection with the problem of the reduction of the modes of the so-called imperfect figures, that is to say: the second and third figures, to the perfect or first one. It deals likewise with the conversion of modal propositions.

Alexander begins by summarizing the rules of the syllogism and the different kinds of categorical syllogisms, after which he speaks about topical and sophistical syllogisms. He refers the reader to his commentary on the *Analytica Priora.*[19] Then he deals with the specific problem of the conversion premises: what premises can be converted, and how to convert them. This discussion is in relation to chapters 8, 9, and 10 in the second book of *Analytica Priora.* This treatise is mentioned by Ibn Abī Uṣaybiʿah (I, p. 70).

10. The 10th treatise of Alexander is *On Human Capacity.* The treatise, mentioned by Ibn Abī Uṣaybiʿah (I, p. 70), deals with the problem of human capacity. Since man is the cause of the things he does, he alone, apart from other natural beings, is provided with the faculty of deliberation.

The Paraphrase of the *Meteorologica* of Aristotle by Olympiodorus

Besides these treatises of Alexander of Aphrodisias, we have found in the same manuscript two other Greek texts which I want to discuss now.

The first, the paraphrase of the *Meteorologica* of Aristotle by Olympiodorus, is a simple and clear exposition of Aristotle's *Meteorologica.* Translated by Ḥunain ibn Isḥāq, the famous translator, and corrected by his son Isḥāq, it resembles what is conventionally called a medium commentary among Ibn Rushd's commentaries. It follows faithfully the original text of Aristotle, free from discussions or solutions of problems.

We know, on the other hand, that Olympiodorus wrote commentaries on the *Meteorologica* of Aristotle. The Greek text was edited by Wilhelm Stüve, *Olympiodori in Aristotelis Meteora Commentaria.* Edidit Gulielmus Stüve, Berolini, Typis et imprensis Georgii Reimeri, 1900 (MGM). This edition comprises 382 pages of a large format.

These commentaries are completely different from the Arabic paraphrases about which we are speaking. In the method adopted in these Greek commentaries, Olympiodorus gives a summary of the text of Aristotle, and then comments on it. The entire work is divided into chapters without titles, each of which is a summary followed by its commentary.

In the preface to his edition (p. x), Stüve declares that the *Commentaries* of Olympiodorus on the *Meteorologica* of Aristotle did not come down to us in a complete text. There are many lacunae in the text, and two sections are lost entirely: that is, the last part of book II, which comprises chapters ϰθ, λ, λα, λβ, and the beginning of chapter λγ, which correspond to pages 388a11 to 390b23 of the text of Aristotle. So, several chapters are missing.

The Greek text of these commentaries is preserved in seven manuscripts, but the edition of Stüve is based on 2 only: Eislini anus 166, and Vaticanus 1387. The other five are: Laurentianus 85, 1 (Oceanus); Laurentianus 86, I; Parisinus 1892; Parisinus Suppl. Gr. 556; and Escorialensis φ-1-9.

It is well established by historians[20] and scholars that the author of these commentaries is Olympiodorus, the Neoplatonist author of many commentaries on some works of Plato and Aristotle. He lived in Alexandria in the sixth century of the Christian era, was a pupil of Ammonius Hermeiou as he says himself in his commentary on *Gorgias* (p. 153, edited by A. Jahn, in Jahn's *Jahrbücher* Supplement b., p. 385), and was the master of Elias and David the Armenian. He depends on Ammonius in his commentaries on Aristotle, and on Damascius in his commentaries on Plato.

The *Commentaries* on the *Meteorologica* are of a high standard; the *Paraphrase* of the same is a simple, clear, and running exposition, with many divisions and subdivisions. He furnishes this *Paraphrase* with many examples, and makes use of the latest discoveries in the field of meteorology. In fact, Olympiodorus is regarded as the last representative of the scientific current in Alexandria.

We have no reason to doubt the propriety of attributing this *Paraphrase* to Olympiodorus. If the Greek sources which we have till now consulted do not mention this *Paraphrase,* that fact has no bearing on its authenticity, because many of his works are not mentioned by these sources; moreover, it is unlikely that such a paraphrase was falsely attributed to a second-class commentator such as Olympiodorus. Therefore, we think that there is no justification for questioning its authenticity.

The Paraphrase of the *De Animalibus* of Aristotle, by Themistius

The second is the paraphrase of *De Animalibus* of Aristotle, by Themistius. We know that Themistius (circa 317–388 of the Christian era) had written many paraphrases of Aristotle. He did not find it useful to make commentaries (ἐξηγήσεις) on the works of the Stagirite, because there were too many. Therefore, he thought it better to write paraphrases, in which he condensed the ideas and expounded them clearly. He declares in the preface to his paraphrase of *De Anima* of Aristotle: "I have expressed the ideas more clearly, sometimes I developed them, and other times I have abridged them."

We knew till now six of these paraphrases, namely the *Analytica Secunda, Physica, Parva naturalia,* (which in fact is by Sophonias, not Themistius), *De Anima,* and *De Coelo* in their original Greek text, and the *Metaphysica* in a Hebrew translation based on an Arabic translation of which we have discovered a part, which we have edited and published in our book: *Arisṭū ʿind al-ʿArab* (pp. 12-21, and 329–333). To this list we must now add this paraphrase of *De Aminalibus* of Aristotle, which we have discovered and edited in the volume to appear shortly.

This paraphrase of *De Animalibus,* divided into 20 books, covers the three books of Aristotle on animals, that is to say: (a) *Historia Animalium,* (b) *De Partibus Animalium,* and (c) *De Generatione Animalium.*

It is highly possible that this paraphrase of *De Animalibus* by Themistius is the one referred to by Yaḥyā ibn ʿAdī, the translator in the catalogue of his private library. It is reported by Ibn al-Nadīm in the *Fihrist,* when he says apropos the *De Animalibus* of Aristotle: "this book has a paraphrase—so I have read in the catalogue of the library of Yaḥyā ibn ʿAdī, written by his hand."[21] Ibn al-Nadīm reports also, on the authority of Ya'hyā ibn ʿAdī, that Nicolaus had also written a *résumé* of the *De Animalibus,* which Abū Alī ibn Zurʿah had begun to translate into Arabic and collate (*ibid.*).

But the paraphrase of *De Animalibus* by Themistius, about which we are now speaking, was translated by Isḥāq ibn Ḥunain, as is stated in our manuscript. It is in a clear, beautiful style, as are all translations made by the most distinguished translator from Greek into Arabic in the third century of the Hijrah, the ninth of the Christian era.

As I have already done to the other philosophical texts lost in Greek and preserved in Arabic translations, I am translating them now into French, in order to make them accessible to a wider range of readers.

So we are in possession of a very valuable set of texts lost in Greek and preserved only in their Arabic translation; and this fact in itself constitutes a valuable contribution of Islamic philosophy to the philosophical heritage of Greece and of all humanity, and at the same time, a valuable contribution to the development and elaboration of philosophic thought during the ages.

Notes

1. Pp. 106-113.
2. Ibn al-Nadīm: *al-Fihrist,* Cairo, 1348 H., p. 354; al-Qifṭī: *Tārīkh al-ḥukamā',* p. 54, l. 20, Leipzig, 1903, ed. J. Lippert: Ibn Abī Uṣaybi'ah, *'Uyūn al-'anbā' fi Ṭabaqāt al-Aṭibbā'* Cairo, 1882, I, p. 70, 1, 12.
3. Mantissa: a worthless addition, makeweight.
4. Ed. Venice, 1536; Munich, by Speagel, 1842; Latin translation with *de facto,* Hieron. et J. Bapt. Bagliono interpreter, Venice, 1541, with *de anima,* Herveto interprete, Basel, 1548.
5. In: *Archives d'Histoire doctrinale et littéraire du Moyen Age.* 4a année (1929-30) pp. 5-149.
6. Ed. Zeller: *Die Philosophie der Griechen,* 4th ed., III, 1, p. 826, note 2: "in diesen Bestimmungen Alexanders liegt die Quelle für die bekannte Lehre der arabischen und scholastischen Philosophie vom intellectus acquisitus."
7. *Ṭabaqāt al-Atibbā',* I, pp. 70-71.
8. *Fihrist,* p. 352.
9. *Tārīkh al-ḥukamā',* p. 55, 1, 1-2.
10. *Plotinus apud Arabes,* Cairo, 1955, pp. 199-208.
11. See our: *Arisṭū ind al-'Arab,* Cairo, 1947, pp. 291-292.
12. But two words exist at the end of the treatise.
13. *Ṭabaqāt al-Aṭibbā',* I, p. 70, 1, 27-28.
14. *Fihrist,* p. 354.
15. *al-Qifṭī,* p. 54.
16. Aristotle: *Physica,* I, 5, p. 188a 18-19, p. 188a 26-29. English translation by R. P. Hardie, K. R. G. Gaye, Oxford, *The Works of Aristotle,* vol. II, without date.
17. Numbers: (a) 16602 (folli 119a-119b); (b) 6443 (ff. 193a-194); (c) 6325 (ff. 231b-232b) in Bibliotheque Nationale in Paris; (d) 996 (497) f. 53 in the library of Caius College, Cambridge. See G. Thery: *Autour du Décret de 1210:* II, *Alexandre d'Aphrodise,* pp. 97-100, Paris 1926.
18. We do not find this assertion textually in *De Generatione et Corruptione.* I, chap. 5; but the reference may be to I, 5, p. 321b22-24; "Now, that any and every part of the tissue *qua* form should grow—and grow by the accession of something—is possible, but not

that any and every part of the tissue *qua* matter should do so." (English translation by Harold H. Joachim, Oxford, n.d., p. 321 b.

19. Αλεξανδρου 'Αποϱίων χαι Αυσέων, p. 13, in *Alexandre Scripta Minora reliqua, supplementum Aristotelium,* II, part 11, Berlin, 1892, edidit Ivo Bruns.

20. Zeller: *Philosophie der Griechen,* III, 2917 f.: Skowrowski, *De auctoris Herenni et Olympiodori scholis,* f. 12sqq; Praechter, ed. *Grundriss der Geschichte der Philosophie,* I, 190, p. 385 sqq.

21. Ibn al-Nadīm: *al-Fihrist,* p. 251, ed. Flugel; and 252, ed. Cairo.

The Origins of Islamic Platonism: The School Tradition

F. E. Peters
New York University

THERE WERE many varieties of Platonism in Islam. One of the earliest of the Muslim theologians, Jahm ibn Ṣafwān (d. 746), was promulgating a view of God totally different from that of his contemporaries and yet remarkably like the negative theology current in later Greek Neoplatonism. Two centuries later an avowed Platonist, Muḥammad ibn Zakariyyā al-Rāzī (d. 925), was drawing upon even more complex sources, including the philosophical and scientific tradition of the Sabians of Harran. The Sabians in turn appear to represent the survival of an occult Platonism long defunct within the Christian Byzantine Empire. Later, the Ismāʿīlīs, the Ṣūfīs, and the eastern partisans of "philosophy of illumination" all bear witness, in varying degrees, to a persistent and vital Platonic legacy in Islam.

How a Platonic strain survived from the Athens of Proclus to the Harran of Thābit ibn Qurrah and the Isfahan and Shiraz of Suhrawardī's disciples is a question that has not even begun to be answered. The Sabians and the Dayṣāniyyah remain almost as obscure as they were in the last century. Where progress has been made, however, is in the investigation of the public, scholastic Platonism that passed through known literary channels from the academics of late antiquity to the academic *falāsifah* of Islam, the Platonic school tradition.

Platonism survived on its merits, but the high literary and scholastic quality of much of that tradition has enabled us to chart the path of its survival, for methods, texts, and curricula all passed into Islam through the hands of Syrian intermediaries, who were themselves both schoolmen and sophisticated translators. The Arabs observed the passage of philosophy from Hellas to Islam and carefully recorded its progress, but not always with the same degree of understanding.

The history of the translations of Aristotle into Arabic can be clearly read in the Arab bibliographers and historians and in the preserved manuscripts. Our chief source, Ibn al-Nadīm, was exceptionally well informed on the Aristotelian corpus, its Greek commentators, and its Syriac and Arabic translations, both Islamic and pre-Islamic. But to turn from his convincing paragraphs on Aristotle to his entry upon Plato is to desert understanding for mere information, some of it scarcely digested. And even after all of that information is collated and evaluated, it remains difficult to say just how much of Plato, whether in integral translations or in epitomes, the medieval Muslim actually possessed.[1]

No Arabic version of a Platonic dialogue has been preserved. And yet Ibn al-Nadīm, writing in the late tenth century at the height of Islam's reception of Hellenism, knew, principally on the basis of a written memoir by the Christian scholar Yaḥyā ibn Adī (d. 974), of translations of the *Republic* (Ḥunayn), the *Laws* (Ḥunayn and Yaḥyā),[2] the *Sophist* (Isḥāq ibn Ḥunayn), the *Timaeus* (Ibn al-Biṭrīq and Ḥunayn), and finally the *Letters,* though no translator is mentioned in their case.[3] But as soon as we approach more closely to the works themselves, we find ourselves in the presence of epitomes rather than translations. We do have a translation of the *Timaeus* credited to Ḥunayn, but it was not done from the text of the entire dialogue. Instead it is an Arabic version, done by Ḥunayn, as he himself tells us (*Risālah* #124), of Galen's *Synopsis of the Platonic Dialogues.* The Arabic is extant and has been published,[4] and it includes not merely a resumé of the *Timaeus* but considerably smaller fragments of paraphrases of the *Republic* and the *Laws.* That the complete work also embraced the *Parmenides* we know from a reference in the preserved section, as well as Ibn al-Nadīm's explicit statement in the *Fihrist* (p. 246/Dodge, p. 593).

We cannot progress much beyond this. There is a summary of the *Laws* transmitted by al-Fārābī, which significantly omits the important Book X.[5] Nothing comparable is extant on the *Republic,* but the references and citations of that work scattered through Arabic literature suggested that here too the *falāsifah* had available a resumé, probably the one based on Galen's epitome of the dialogues as translated by Ḥunayn ibn Isḥāq.[6]

Since so many of the Arabs were working from paraphrases of Plato rather than from integral texts of the dialogues, it is unlikely that they felt the same need for the elaborate apparatus of textual commentary that so impressively supported their work on Aristotle. The likelihood is confirmed by Ibn al-Nadīm, who mentions (p. 246, 11 ff./Dodge, p. 593) only the commentary of Olympiodorus on the *Sophist* and possibly the *Theaetetus,* the first translated by Isḥāq ibn Ḥunāyn and the latter by unknown hands (the *Fihrist* says that Olympiodorus was the translator), even though the work was copied, presumably used, in the school of Yaḥyā ibn Adī. There was, in addition, Proclus's work on the myth in the *Gorgias* and his commentary on the *Phaedo,* a small part of which was translated by Ibn Zurʿah (*Fihrist*, p. 252/Dodge, p. 608).

From other sources we can add some further details. At least some Arabs were reading Proclus's commentary on the *Timaeus* (see n. 36 below) and on the *Republic*.[7] Further, a work of Plutarch on the *Timaeus* is mentioned by Ibn al-Nadīm in his section on Plato (p. 246, 11, 18–19/ Dodge, p. 593). It does not reappear in his later entry devoted to Plutarch (p. 254/Dodge, p. 611), though he does list here a treatise *On the Soul*. Both citations probably refer to the same essay, Plutarch's *On the Production of the Soul in the* Timaeus, a work also known to Muḥammad ibn Zakariyyā al-Rāzī.[8] Finally, as Ibn al-Nadīm also attests, the Arabs knew and used Theon of Smyrna's propaedeutic *The Order of Plato's Books and the Titles of his Works* (p. 255/Dodge, p. 614).[9]

Following directly upon his almost tabular treatment of Plato is Ibn al-Nadīm's presentation of the biography of Aristotle and the elaborate and informed history of the Aristotelian translations (pp. 246–252/ Dodge, pp. 594–606). This emphasis was not a peculiarity of the *Fihrist;* whatever the actual content of their philosophical heritage, the Arabs saw Aristotle as the chief of the file of Hellenic sages. He was better known and more highly esteemed than any other Greek thinker in Islam; and Fārābī, the most considerable Muslim Platonist, was being measured not against Plato but against Aristotle when he was flatteringly called "the second master."

The *Fihrist's* review of the post-Aristotelian philosophers (pp. 252–255/Dodge, pp. 602–614) reveals the same perspective. The list includes Theophrastus, Proclus "the Platonist," Alexander of Aphrodisias, Porphyry, Ammonius (Hermieu), Themistius, Nicolaus, Plutarch (of Chaeronea), Olympiodorus, Hippocrates, Epaphroditus, "another Plutarch,"[10] John Philoponus, and a final jumble of names, drawn from another source and including Gregory of Nyssa and Theon of Smyrna, "whose periods and order of sequence are not known." In the entire group only Proclus and Theon are identified as Platonists; the rest are seen almost exclusively through the focus of an Aristotelian exegetical tradition.

Even in the rudimentary sequence of Hellenic philosophers presented by Ibn al-Nadīm, there is one striking near-omission: the founder of the very type of Platonism that consistently shows itself in the systems of the Islamic *falāsifah,* Plotinus.[11] Ibn al-Qifṭī, who does devote a few lines to Plotinus (p. 258), identifies him as an Aristotelian commentator. He knows that some of Plotinus's works were translated into Syriac, but he is forced to admit ignorance on whether or not they subsequently appeared in Arabic versions. We are somewhat better informed: the Arabs did study Plotinus, but inevitably as a pseudepigraphon of Aristotle, or anonymously, or under what appears to be a pseudonym, "the Greek elder" (*al-shaykh al-yūnānī*).[12]

The abridgement of *Enneads* 4–6 in Arabic, under the title of *The*

Theology of Aristotle but paraphrasing the same Plotinian passages as that work, has come to light over the last thirty years. A work spuriously attributed to al-Fārābī has turned out to be a Plotinian abridgement. It was edited by Paul Kraus and published in 1941,[13] and over the following years Franz Rosenthal has collected the Plotinian passages by the supposed *shaykh yūnānī.*[14] All the evidence has found its place in Rosenthal, and in Geoffrey Lewis's English translation, opposite the parallel Greek passages, in the second volume of the new critical edition of Plotinus by Henry and Schwyzer;[15] but neither the new material nor a careful study of the old has brought the question of the identity of the "editor" or the question of his motives any closer to a solution.

If it can be conceded that someone abridged and rearranged the latter half of the *Enneads* without, at the same time, holding him responsible for the attribution of the results to Aristotle or to anyone else, then Plotinus's student and confessed editor, Porphyry, is a not unlikely candidate.[16] Even the Arabic text of the *Theology,* while it explicitly attributes what follows to Aristotle, adds "with the commentary of Porphyry of Tyre, translated into Arabic by ʿAbd al-Masīḥ ibn Nāʿimah of Emesa and corrected . . . by al-Kindī." The superscription points in two directions; first toward an original commentary by Porphyry on the *Theology* and/or *Enneads,* a commentary that may have been nothing more than that reworking of the *Enneads* which is the *Theology,* and, second, in the direction where Ibn al-Qifṭī had already pointed, to a Syrian Christian milieu, the kind that produced Ibn Nāʿimah,[17] as the possible locale for the conversion of Porphyry's abridged Plotinus into the later spurious Aristotle.

Something will be said later on the possible motives for such a transformation, but it should be remarked here that it could have been an honest mistake. Porphyry's introduction to the Aristotelian logic, which was widely diffused in Syriac, was already an integral part of the *Organon;* and so a similar Porphyrian reworking of an Aristotelian theology would not have appeared unlikely to the sixth or seventh century reader.

Why the philosophers under Islam were so transparently Neoplatonists and were, at the same time, so oblivious to the true nature of their Platonism that they could not identify its author is one of the abiding mysteries of *falsafah.* To say that they simply did not care defies both the evidence of the *Fihrist,* which was obviously attempting to trace out some kind of philosophical lineage for the Arab thinkers, and our own knowledge of the historical attitudes of the later philosophical schools. The lecturers at Athens and Alexandria knew whence they had come. The Academy had adopted Aristotle into its curriculum, but it never lost sight of the fact that it was a Platonic school. Truth lies in Platonic orthodoxy, Plotinus had taught (*Enn.* 2:9,6). His Greek successors did not forget the lesson; but the Arabs, who had just as much of a claim to the Platonic tradition as Damascius or Olympiodorus, did not recognize their affiliations.

In talking about the late scholastic tradition we mean nothing more than the history of the Platonic schools. At the beginning of the third century A.D. the schools of Epicurus, Zeno, and Aristotle were moribund, if not dead; after A.D. 200 there existed among the Greeks of the Empire only the Platonic schools at Alexandria and Athens and their lesser reflections at Apamea and Pergamum;[18] and in the end, on the eve of the Muslim invasion, there was only Alexandria. The final masters at Alexandria, and their solitary Platonic contemporary at Athens, were, however, deeply concerned with the study of Aristotle.

Somewhere within this paradox rests the explanation of the Arabs' confusion about their own philosophical identity. The Athenian Academy traded its mixed Platonism of the second and third century for the insights, first of Plotinus and then of Porphyry, Iamblichus, and Proclus, a combination that proved dangerous and finally deadly to Athenian Platonism. The pains of this transformation were lost on the Arabs, though they had perhaps inherited, without understanding it, the dissimulations that enabled the Alexandrian Platonists to outlive their Athenian colleagues.

Dissimulation is a charge that can likely be sustained against the Platonists of Alexandria; but for the Muslims and Christians under Islam the alleged subterfuges of an Ammonius or an Olympiodorus had yielded to mere ignorance, to the point where the Arabs could, though Platonists, somehow consider themselves Aristotelians, could believe that the *Enneads* really did constitute the "theology of Aristotle,"[19] and that Porphyry's greatest achievement was his explication of the *Categories*. And beyond Porphyry the mystification was almost total.

The Arabs knew almost nothing of Iamblichus. He turns up twice in Ibn al-Nadīm's history of the Aristotelian corpus, as a commentator on the *Categories* (p. 248/Dodge, p. 599) and on the *De interpretatione* (p. 249/Dodge, p. 599). But in the first case, and likely in the second as well, the citation is derived secondhand through Simplicius.[20] Ibn al-Nadīm knew something more about Iamblichus, but just as in the case of Plotinus, it was under a different name: Iamblichus, the commentator of Aristotle, is the identifiable "Amlichus," while Iamblichus, the author of *On the Mysteries of the Egyptians*, is transformed into the mysterious Anebo ("Anabun"), the priest to whom Porphyry directed the original letter that had in turn provoked Iamblichus's response (*Fihrist*, p. 300, l. 18/ Dodge, p. 705).

The reference to "Anabun" occurs within Ibn al-Nadīm's bibliographical survey of the works of Muḥammad ibn Zakariyyā al-Rāzī: "A Criticism of the book of Anebo against Porphyry concerning a commentary on the teachings of Aristotle on theology."[21] We do not, of course, possess the Greek of Porphyry's *Letter to Anebo,* though the Arabs certainly did, at least in part;[22] but neither its Greek reconstruction,[23] nor the analysis of Iamblichus's response[24] guides us even remotely in the direction of the *Metaphysics.* It is equally unlikely that they point in the direction of the *Theology of Aristotle,* which some of the Arabs connected with the name of Porphyry, since the *Letter to Anebo* was written long before Porphyry arranged the essays of Plotinus into what was to be the *Enneads,* and so prior to any possibility of commenting upon them.

Among other things Porphyry's *Letter* dealt with the delicate relationship between speculative theology and practical theurgy.[25] Porphyry was in doubt on the question, but Iamblichus's response was unequivocal: theurgy is superior to theology. Nor was that all. The theology of the Easterners, the Egyptians, Chaldaeans, Magi, etc., was superior to that of the Greeks. Greek theology was first the writings of Plato, summed up in the *Timaeus* and the *Parmenides,* to which he would add the works of the poets from Homer onward. The net of Eastern theology was thrown equally wide; but for Iamblichus and most of his successors it was constituted, in effect, by the *Chaldaean Oracles.*[26]

Neither of these themes, the extension of Greek theology beyond the purely philosophical tradition and beyond the Hellenic *paideia* itself, was the innovation of Iamblichus. The emphasis and conviction were, however, new; and from Iamblichus onward non-Greek *theologia* and a marked interest in *theourgia* were characteristics of Athenian Platonism until Justinian closed the Academy in 529. There were theurgists too within Islam; but no one of them, with the possible exception of Muḥammad ibn Zakariyyā al-Rāzī, belonged to the school tradition that was the Muslim's principal inheritance from later Platonism. The Arab scholatics were immune to the Iamblichan virus.

How the Iamblichan version of Platonism passed into the still conservative Academy of the fourth century is gradually becoming clearer.[27] There are gaps in our knowledge of the Platonic *diadochoi* from the days of Plotinus, when the holders of that dignity were a pair of undistinguished scholars (*Vita. Plot.* 20), to the accession of Plutarch toward the end of the fourth century. Between times, Iamblichus and his immediate students had set up shop at Apamaea in Syria and Pergamum in Anatolia. One of Iamblichus's spiritual heirs, Maximus, was in the immediate circle of the Emperor Julian,[28] while two others, Piscus and a younger Iamblichus, who was named after but not related to the other Iamblichus, took up residence at Athens. Neither of them was demonstrably in the Academy, but Iamblichus (II), who lived in the fifth century, was a rich and influential citizen of the city.

No immediate connection can be established between Iamblichus (II) and his contemporary Plutarch, the grandson of a chief priest of Eleusis and the Platonic *diadochus* in the Academy in the early fifth century. But Plutarch was a "new" Platonist in the style of Plotinus, Porphyry, and Iamblichus, —and of Priscus and Iamblichus (II)—and his influence is immediately perceptible in his students Syrianus and Proclus.[29] The Greek sources, chiefly Marinus's *Life of Proclus* and Damascius's *Life of Isidore,*[30] enables us to trace the Platonic "successorship" at Athens, now firmly in Neoplatonic hands, uninterruptedly from Plutarch, who died in 432, down to Damascius a century later.

The Arabs knew nothing of this. Of Proclus and of Damacius's colleague Simplicius they possessed considerable textual evidence, but it was unaccompanied by any sense of the position of these philosophers in the evolution of later Platonism. Indeed, Athens appears to have disappeared completely from their historical perspectives. In the two earliest treatments devoted by Arab authors to the history of later Greek philosophy, those of Fārābī and Masʿūdī,[31] the fortunes of philosophy are tied not to Athens but to Alexandria and Rome. The Greek source, upon which they were relying was clearly Peripatetic—Andronicus of Rhodes figures prominently in the account—and late as well, since it alleges that the Christian Emperor Theodosius closed down the Roman branch and so confined the study of philosophy to Alexandria alone. There is no mention of Athens, nor indeed of Platonism.

The Arabs, it appears, were far more interested in Proclus than they realized.[32] Ibn al-Nadīm's entry under his name (*Fihrist,* p. 252/Dodge, pp. 607–608) identifies him as a Platonist, as the "successor" of Plato,[33] and the author of an imposing list of works, including the *Elements of Physics* and the *Elements of Theology,* a commentary on the *Golden Sayings* of Pythagoras,[34] and in a more precisely Platonic context, a book on the myth (*mathal*) in Plato's *Gorgias.*[35]

The list is interesting but hardly complete. Our Greek versions of Proclus's *Commentary on the Timaeus* end at 44e3 of the text. In Aya Sofya 3725 there is, however, an Arabic version of the *peri ethon* in which Galen cites *Timaeus* 89e4–90c7, a passage near the end of the dialogue, and the Arab editor immediately added Ḥunayn's translation of Proclus's commentary on that passage. The evidence appears unmistakable that Proclus's exegesis covered the entire *Timaeus* and that the Islamic philosophers possessed it in an Arabic version.[36]

Ibn al-Nadīm also mentions, somewhat obliquely, that Proclus was the author of a treatise refuted by John Philoponus. This is the 18 questions or proofs *On the Eternity of the World,* which is known in Greek only from its citation in Philoponus's imperfectly preserved refutation.[37] Not one but two versions of the original have turned up in Arabic, neither of them complete, but extremely valuable nonetheless. The older version, translator unknown, is preserved in two Istanbul manuscripts,[38] while the later is the work of Isḥāq ibn Ḥunayn.[39]

There are other small texts that may or may not be Arabic versions of Proclus;[40] but by far the most considerable piece of Proclus known to the Arabs was the treatise "On the Pure Good" and called, in its Latin version, the *Liber de causis.*[41] The two current editions of the Arabic text, both done on the basis of the same Leiden manuscript (Golius 209), are badly out of date since the discovery of new texts.[42] The material in the *De causis* is surely from Proclus, as Aquinas had already observed, and derived from the *Elements of Theology.* But for the Arabs, or at least for most of those who addressed themselves to the question, the work was attributed to Aristotle.[43]

The question of who extracted the *De causis* from the *Elements of Theology* and circulated it under the name of Aristotle is as unsettled as that surrounding the *Theology,* whether it was a Greek or a Syrian Christian before the coming of Islam, or whether it was done in Islamic times, by al-Fārābī in the East or the Jew Dāwūd in the west. The evidence is still accumulating. There is a resumé of the *De causis,* attributed to Aristotle, by the physician and *faylasūf* ʿAbd al-Laṭīf al-Baghdādī (d. 1231)[44] and in addition, what has been identified as a translation of Propositions 15–17 of the *Elements* by Abū ʿUthmān al-Dimashqī (*fl. ca.* 914),[45] but which cannot, in the present state of our knowledge, be said to be a translation of the integral text of the *Elements.*

In sum, the Arabs knew Proclus as a late Platonist and absorbed his metaphysics, as they had Plotinus's, as an indistinguishable part of the Neoplatonist synthesis of Plato and Aristotle. His work on Pythagoras probably appeared to be a rather harmless gnomonology, while the Proclus who admired Pythagoras the *Wundermann,* who commented upon the "theology" of the *Chaldaean Oracles,* the mystery adept and theurgist, was ignored by the Islamic tradition.[46] Of theurgy the Arabs had perhaps some sense, but not through the ordinary scholastic channels described by Ibn al-Nadīm.

One of Proclus's fellow students at Athens under the brief tenure of Syrianus as scholarch (432–437?)[47] was Hermias, and from him descended the final series of Platonic philosophers at Alexandria, down to the time in 616 when Stephen deserted that city for the university in Constantinople. At Athens itself Proclus's immediate successors, Isidore and Zenodotus, were not distinguished. We are aware of them solely from Damascius' *Life of Isidore,* an important historical source denied to the Arabs; no trace of their own work is left. There were, in addition, difficulties with the Christian authorities. Even Proclus, who could be prudent when need be on the subject of his paganism, was forced to go into exile for a year (*Vita Procl.* XV), and his successors were less careful until Justinian finally closed the Academy in 529 and confiscated its property.[48]

There followed the curious and interesting sojourn of the seven Athenian philosophers, including the current *diadochus* Damascius and his student Simplicius, at the court of Khusraw I at Ctesiphon. Their stay there was exceedingly brief, less than a year perhaps, before their return to Byzantine territory under the terms of the peace treaty of 533, and so it is probably dangerous to draw too many conclusions from it. But Khusraw's intellectual credentials are well attested from other sources.[49] The *Denkart* (p. 413, Mādan) has him pressing the pursuit of truth through analogical reasoning, while both Procopius (*Anec.* 18, 29) and Agathias (2,2) testify to his interest in Greek philosophy, particularly Plato and Aristotle, whose works he had translated for himself,[50] so that, according to Agathias, "not even the *Timaeus* escaped him."

The Arabs' view of Khusraw was not very different. Ibn al-Nadīm, citing (p. 239/Dodge, p. 575) the Iranian savant Abū Sahl al-Faḍl ibn Nawbakht on the subject, describes the reign of Khusraw as the time of a renewal of scholarship. He likewise took note (p. 316/Dodge, p. 740) that the Byzantine Emperor sent philosophers to the Shah to ask about matters of wisdom. If this is a reference to Damascius, Simplicius et al., it hardly does justice to the motives for the philosophers' coming to Ctesiphon. But those scholars were not the only ones who crossed the border. In the same year that the Platonists returned to Byzantine territory, Justinian asked for and received a delegation of Nestorian Christian scholars to participate in a theological conference in the capital.[51]

Khusraw, it would seem, was served by philosophers whose chief preoccupations were Aristotelian, either of the Christian variety, like those of Paul the Persian, who as a Christian was interested chiefly, if not exclusively, in the Aristotelian logic,[52] or of a chastened Platonic paganism like that of Simplicius, who upon his return to Athens after 533 devoted himself exclusively to commenting upon Aristotle. Despite the remark of Agathias, there is no trace of a Pahlevi *Timaeus,* unless it existed, as was frequently the case with the latter day Greek Platonists, under the cover of a discussion of the proofs for the eternity of the cosmos in the *Physics* and *De coelo.*

On his return from Persia Damascius was well into his seventies,[53] but Simplicius still had an active career before him, likely at Athens, though not as a teacher. Lecturing had ceased forever in the Academy, and Simplicius became a library scholar, whose chief monument is in his commentaries on Aristotle.[54] Of these the Arabs appear to have known only those on the *Categories* and the *De anima,* the latter of which was in Syriac and may have constituted, on the basis of the *Fihrist's* description (p. 251/Dodge, p. 605), a *reportatio* of his teacher Ammonius's lectures on the subject.[55] They did not possess the extensive commentaries on the *Physics* and the *De coelo,* though the Arabs were well instructed on the controversies that unfolded there.

At different points in these latter two commentaries, Simplicius took up the task of refuting an Alexandrian contemporary, the Christian John Philoponus, who had earlier written two works on the subject of the eternity of the world: *On the Eternity of the World against Proclus,* written in 529, and *Against Aristotle,* a treatment in six books of Aristotle's views as expressed in the *Physics* and the *De coelo.* We do not possess the Greek text of the latter work of Philoponus and must reconstruct it from Simplicius; the Arabs, who did not have the pertinent commentaries of Simplicius, could still read the work of Philoponus, and it had, in fact, an enormous influence in Islam.[56]

How Philoponus and Simplicius, both students at Alexandria of Ammonius, who had in turn matriculated with Proclus at Athens, came to be debating Aristotle and not Plato in the first half of the sixth century carries us back to Ammonius himself. Like his father Hermias, Ammonius had gone to Athens for his philosophical education. Both men, father and son, eventually returned to Alexandria to teach and write, Hermias on Plato,[57] and Ammonius chiefly on Aristotle. The work was published in his own name and those of his students. Asclepius and John Philoponus. The interest in Aristotle is not strange in someone trained in a Platonic tradition who had been studying Peripatetic work at least since the days of Plotinus and Porphyry, but the *publication* of almost exclusively Aristotelian material is curious and abrupt. And among its results was the fact that the Arabs, who had a limited literary access to late antiquity, regarded Ammonius and his successors almost entirely as Aristotelian commentators.

Ibn al-Nadīm's brief notice on Ammonius (p. 253/Dodge, p. 610) is drawn from Isḥāq ibn Ḥunayn's *History of Physicians.* It identifies him as an Aristotelian exegete who lived some time after Galen. In addition to the commentaries on the *Categories* and *Topics,* whose Greek originals are no longer extant, the *Fihrist* cites the titles of three other works: "An Exposition of Aristotle's Doctrines about the Creator,"[58] "Aristotle's Intentions in his Books,"[59] and "Aristotle's Proof of Oneness."

It would be interesting indeed to be able to read the first of these. Did the student of Proclus trim his theological sails, as has been conjectured, for monetary considerations, and so turn aside the mounting Christian pressure that led to the closure at Athens?[60] There is even some evidence that Ammonius may have undergone a forced conversion.[61] Whatever occurred, it did not prevent Ammonius from continuing to lecture on Plato; though he, or his students, published his courses on Aristotle, Ammonius kept up his Platonic interests in the classroom. Some of his immediate students, even Damascius and Olympiodorus, could still report on Ammonius's views on Plato; but for the Arabs, who had only his books, or reports about his books, Ammonius was an Aristotelian commentator.

Ammonius's (d. ca. 520) students dominated both Athens and

Alexandria during the next generation: the Athenian *diadochus* Damascius, who was unknown to the Arabs, and his student Simplicius at Athens; Olympiodorus, Asclepius, and John Philoponus at Alexandria.[62] Olympiodorus produced a number of Platonic commentaries, but only one of them, that on the *Sophist,* was extant or known in Arabic,[63] together with his commentaries on the Aristotelian *Meteorology* and *De anima.*

Olympiodorus, who was almost certainly not a Christian, appears to have moved nonetheless to a more accommodating position with Christianity;[64] but there is no mention of a Christian in the *Fihrist* until the next of Ibn al-Nadīm's entries, that on John Philoponus, "a bishop over some of the churches of Egypt, upholding the Christian sect of the Jacobites," (pp. 254–255/Dodge, pp. 612–613). The same passage closes with what became a standard Arab confusion on the dates of John: "he lived during the days of ʿAmr ibn al-ʿĀṣ," that is, until the Muslim conquest of Egypt.[65]

John "the grammarian" (*al-naḥwī*), as the Arabs called him and as he styled himself (*grammatikos*) in his own works,[66] was a well-known figure in Islam as an Aristotelian commentator,[67] a medical writer and historian,[68] and, considerably more obscurely, as a Christian theologian.[69] Over the years John's career turned away from his earlier scholastic work under Ammonius.[70] His redaction of his professor's notes on the *Physics* dates from 517; but by 529, the same year that Justinian closed the Academy for its flagrant paganism, Philoponus was working in a far more Christian vein. In that year appeared his *On the Eternity of the World against Proclus,* followed shortly by the complementary *Against Aristotle,* a twofold attack on the current Neoplatonic position on the eternity of the cosmos.

The attack on Aristotle was frontal, but in refuting Proclus's reading of the *Timaeus* Philoponus had some support from earlier Platonism. Proclus himself names two men who read the *Timaeus* as advocating creation in time, Plutarch of Chaeronea and Atticus (*In Tim.* I,276,30); and Philoponus can adduce Atticus's predecessor as *diadochus,* Calvisius Taurus, who headed the Academy under Hadrian and Antoninus Pius. All these citations may, however, go back only as far as Porphyry's own commentary on the *Timaeus.* The Muslims, who shared Philoponus's view of creation in time, were highly interested in the controversy and could follow it closely through Arabic versions of the *Timaeus* (albeit in an *epitome*), the *De coelo* and *Physics,* Proclus's *Arguments* and his commentary on the *Timaeus,* and Philoponus's refutation. But they knew of and cared nothing for the rest of Philoponus's career after 530, his progressive involvement in theology and his final bout with tretheism.[71]

In the Arabs' version of the history of philosophy, Olympiodorus's Christian students Elias and David have no place.[72] The last known scholarch at Alexandria, Stephen, was summoned to Constantinople sometime about 616 to assume a teaching post there.[73] His portrait among the Arabs is thin but congruent with the Greek sources. Stephen's commentaries on the *Categories* and *De interpretatione* were extant in Arabic, as were some medical writings. There is a further odd tradition (*Fihrist,* p. 244/Dodge, p. 586) of "Stephen the ancient" who translated certain works on the Art (of alchemy) for the Umayyad prince Khālid ibn Yazīd (*d. ca.* 705). Another part of the tradition (*Fihrist,* p. 242/ Dodge, p. 581) derives Khālid's instruction in alchemy from savants summoned from Alexandria, one of whom was the Syrian Marinos who had studied with Stephen. Whether this is the same Stephen is uncertain, though the attribution of alchemical works to him is widespread in Greek.[74]

This is the end of the *falsafah* tradition of late antiquity. Stephen, who served Heraclius, touches the chronological limits of Islam. The Arabs who followed pieced together their knowledge of that tradition from the philosophical texts available to them and from a far less easily identified set of historical perspectives. Both, however, betray their origins in a clear way: clustered around the works of Aristotle are the names of the great commentators from the Platonic school tradition at Alexandria, from Ammonius in the fifth century to Stephen in the seventh. From there it is possible to trace the connection back to Porphyry in the fourth century, as the man who introduced the textual exegesis of Aristotle into the curriculum of the Platonic schools.

Considerable nuances can be added to this on the basis of the texts that have actually been preserved. There are, of course, Aristotle and Plato, the former in integral Arabic versions and the latter in resumé, a situation which once again points to Alexandria, where from Ammonius onward the publishing emphasis was on the Aristotelian lectures and where the scholars lectured on *texts.* Oddly, there are at present no textual remains of the great Alexandrian commentators discussed so knowingly by Ibn al-Nadīm. It is difficult to believe that the exegetical works of Simplicius, Olympiodorus, Ammonius, et al. were *not* once preserved in Arabic; but if they were translated, transcribed, and studied, the texts themselves have since disappeared without a trace, over and above the texts of Plato and Aristotle.

What has been preserved is of a somewhat different orientation: the work of two Peripatetic paraphrasts. Nicolaus of Damascus and Themistius, and a number of treatises by the Aristotelian Alexander of Aphrodisias. Were these three men important in the curriculum at Alexandria in the fifth and sixth centuries? We do not know.[75] The second group of Greek philosophical texts derives not from the Aristotelizing Alexandrian school tradition but from the Neoplatonists. As has been seen, the Arabs did in fact possess texts of Plotinus and Proclus, though they were transmitted, from some unknown point in time, under false attributions to Aristotle. Finally, there was available in Islam a body of philosophical material from the pre-Plotinian period of Platonism, chiefly Galen and Plutarch of Chaeronea.

Some of these anomalies are easily understood. Alexandrian Platonism made its peace with Christianity, ignominiously perhaps, with Ammonius, subtly with Olympiodorus, and overtly with John Philoponus. Thus it survived into the seventh century, long enough to transmit its scholastic attitudes to the Arab *falāsifah*,[76] and to commit its ostensibly Aristotelian curriculum to the pages of the *Fihrist*. It has been suggested that one of the fruits of Alexandrian prudence was precisely the sliding of Plotinus and Proclus into the safety of an Aristotelian curriculum under assumed names.[77] The abbreviation of the *Enneads* may well have been the work of Porphyry, done for the best—or worst—of academic motives, but its circulation as the "Theology of Aristotle" is not necessarily the doing of the same person. That this person or persons were cautious or frightened Platonists of the sixth century is an attractive possibility, particularly since that century produced just another such psuedepigraph, the corpus of Proclan theology masquerading as the literary output of a Christian contemporary of Saint Paul, Dionysius of Areopagite.

An Aristotelian curriculum, superficially purged of the Platonic theology that was its normal complement in the philosophical schools of later antiquity, may have had another point of origin. The Arabs' knowledge of the history of philosophy ran thin, as has been seen, at a point some time before the lifetime of Plotinus. Their views of the later Alexandrians were founded on the connection of those scholars with the Aristotelian texts of the standard curriculum. They were less well informed on the Alexandrian school itself, except to acknowledge that there were teachers in Baghdad ca. 900 who somehow traced their intellectual lineage back to Alexandria.

The men who did most of the translating into Arabic did not, however, belong to that same line of philosophers. They were physicians trained at the medical school of Jundishāpūr, and as interested in Galen as they were in Aristotle. And when we look once again to late antiquity we note that the details of the Arabs' version of the history of medicine begin to grow dim at somewhat the same point as their philosophical perspectives, that is, the lifetime of Galen (d. 199). There are important figures later than Galen. Oribasius and Paul of Aegina, for example, who are mentioned in the *Fihrist;* but the author does not know precisely where to locate them in the history of medicine. Their names, like those of the Alexandrian Platonists, came, it would appear, from the title pages of their translated works which stood at the heart of Alexandrian medicine. It was Galen too who insisted on the importance of a philosophical education for the physician. And it was Galen, we may suspect, who gave to that physician his picture of the history of philosophy, a portrait whose final resting place was, by way of John Philoponus, Isḥāq ibn Ḥunayn's *History of Physicians.*[78] In the *Fihrist* the chronology for both Porphyry and Ammonius, the latter explicitly derived from Isḥāq, is measured against Galen's lifetime. And when Ibn al-Nadīm does refer to his chief post-Galenic historical source, the *Philosophical History* of Porphyry (see below), it is by way of his philosophical friends at Baghdad and not from the Jundishāpūr medical tradition.

When we put aside the bibliographical notices and turn to Islam's *falāsifah,* the same anomalies reappear. All of the *falāsifah,* from al-Kindī to Suhrawardī and his successors, were to some extent operating within the Platonic tradition, at least in the sense of the syncretizing of Plato and Aristotle that had been current in philosophical circles since the early days of the Roman Empire. Among those philosophers, Muslim and Christians, al-Fārābī stands somewhat apart. He was the most self-consciously Platonizing of the *falāsifah,* both in his understanding of Plato and his familiarity with the texts. Fārābī's Platonism has been closely investigated,[79] and it is at once abundantly clear that neither his interest in Plato nor his approach to the dialogues confirms to our understanding of the patterns of the final, Neoplatonic stages in the Platonic tradition.

Al-Kindī, the earliest of the *falāsifah* and one whose work seems to antedate, since it antedates the translations of Ḥunayn, the full impact of Alexandrian medical scholaticism upon Islamic Philosophy, is a historically predictable Muslim Neoplatonist of the Proclan variety;[80] Fārābī, however, was drawing from other sources. There is, for example, his elaborate reworking of the Platonic politics of the *Republic* and the *Laws.* There were, to be sure, peculiarities in Fārābī's reading of this latter dialogue, due perhaps to the historical circumstances of his own theological position within Islam;[81] but the mere fact that he could read both dialogues as political treatises and not merely as a discussion of the immortality of the soul and a primer in theology unmistakably distinguishes Fārābī from almost all of his immediate pre-Islamic Platonic predecessors.

Plato may have had his own difficulties with the practical value of political activity for the philosopher, but in his own day the polis was still the unique focus of moral activity for men, and the concern with morality that he shared with his master, Socrates, combined to produce an elaborate and earnest political theory. Later Platonism had little recollection of either Socrates or the polis,[82] and it read the dialogues with quite different emphases. Its eyes were directed not toward the political associations of the City of Man, but turned upward to the *kosmos noetos* whither man's divine and immortal soul strove to return.

For Plotinus the conditions of that return were still understood in terms of an intellectualist *theoria,* although very few of his successors shared that conviction. Porphyry and Iamblichus debated the primacy of speculative wisdom through the pages of the *Letter to Anebo* and *On the Mysteries.* Iamblichus's qualms about *theoria* were not, of course, based upon a belief in the value of moral activities, political or otherwise. The preferred Iamblichan praxis was theurgy, not human action aimed at the acquisition of virtue but the manipulation of the "virtues" (*aretai, dynameis*), frequently occult, of physical beings.

A confidence in the achievements of theurgy remained a characteristic of Athenian Neoplatonism. Equally characteristic was an almost total disinterest in political and even ethical theory. Such a theory was, however, possible, even within the confines of a Proclan metaphysic and theurgic "morality." Proclus never constructed such, but we are provided with a convincing example of Neoplatonic politics in the body of work circulating in Greek and Syrian theological circles of the sixth century under the name of Dionysius the Areopagite.[83] Pseudo-Dionysius's City of Man is a true Proclan *eikon;* it is the Christian polity of the Church, the grades of ecclesiastical officers (bishops, priests, monks) whose task is to understand and give instruction in the complex of sacramental symbols which lead the soul upward to the angelic hierarchy and finally to God himself.

There is remarkably little moral activity in the strict sense contained in the *Corpus Aeropagiticum*; all action is either subsumed into metaphysics or handed over to Pseudo-Dionysius's peculiar brand of sacramental theurgy.[84] Fārābī's polities, on the other hand, were not invariable *eikones* of a transcendent, intelligible cosmos but historical possibilities shaped by human, and so moral, choices.[85] But while psuedo-Dionysius's reliance on Proclus is beyond reasonable doubt, Fārābī's own political antecedents remain obscure. His own brief adversions to his philosophical formation (Us. 2, pp. 135 ff.) betray only traditional Aristotelian concerns.

Whatever else Fārābī's Aristotelian training may have included, it is unlikely that he, or many other people, were reading the *Politics,* a work that seems to have disappeared from the ancient philosophical curriculum even before that curriculum reached the Arabs. But the now commonplace judgment that the political treatises of Plato replaced the *Politics* of Aristotle in the later school curricula is doubly misleading. There was, as has been seen, little interest in *anyone's* political theory in the later Platonic schools. And while it is true that Aristotle's *Politics* excited little interest in late antiquity, it is equally true that there were circulating among the Arabs treatises that purported to be Aristotle's thinking on political subjects.

Modern scholars have not been overly impressed by the claims to authenticity of the body of *Letters* bearing the name of Aristotle in Greek, Arabic, Latin, and Hebrew during the Middle Ages. But the Arabs accepted their share of the windfall as authentic; and while some of the letters are unabashedly Hermetic, at least some are political in content.[86]

The *Letters,* many of them addressed to Alexander, are neither very philosophical nor analytical, but belong somewhere in the middle ground between politics and ethics inhabited by the *Fürstenspiegel.*[87] That territory we know was cultivated by later Peripatetic scholars, and there is nothing intrinsically improbable in Aristotle's communicating with his own former student on the subject of politics. A case has recently been made for the authenticity of one such letter, the Arabic *On Governance* (*Fī-siyāsah*), possibly the *Alexander* or *On Colonies* mentioned by the Greek bibliographers, which, if it is authentic, reflects some radical departures in Aristotle's thought.[88]

Whether authentic or not, the Aristotelian correspondence in Arabic had no visible effect on the political theories of Fārābī. They ended instead, frequently ground exceedingly fine, in the somewhat shapeless pages of the Arabic gnomonologies, like most of al-Mubashshir ibn al-Fātik and Ḥunayn ibn Isḥāq. Fārābī certainly knew of the Aristotelian correspondence, though not perhaps at first hand;[89] but he either ignored or was ignorant of the political letters, when it came to his own theories. Similarly, the studies to date on Miskawayh's *Tahdhīb alp-akhlāq* have turned up no references to Aristotle's political and ethical correspondence.

Fārābī's political theorizing is as unmistakably Platonic in its premises as the Pseudo-Dionysius's was Proclan; it rested firmly on his reading of the *Republic* and the *Laws,* two works of considerably varying importance in later Platonism. We can now reconstruct with some accuracy the Platonic curriculum favored by the Neoplatonists.[90] It proceeded from I *Alcibiades* through the series *Gorgias* (politics), *Phaedo* (catharsis of the philosopher), *Cratylus* (names), *Theaetetus* (concepts), *Sophist* and *Statesman* (physics), *Phaedrus* and *Symposium* (theology), to end with the treatment of the Good as the Final Cause in the *Philebus.* The characterizations are not, of course, Plato's but probably go back to Iamblichus, who bore the chief responsibility of arranging the dialogues in a curricular order and assigning a specific interpretation to each.[91]

The *Timaeus* was by no means neglected. The series described above constituted what might be described as the "long course"; it was summarized in its essence by the two dialogues which the later Academics embraced as the summa of Platonism, the *Timaeus* and the *Parmenides.*[92] Each dialogue had its own proper exegesis; and even within the longer curriculum of ten dialogues—out of the thirty-five in the Thrasyllan canon—a further selection was imposed: not all the parts of each dialogue were studied. The exegesis of the *Sophist, Statesman,* and perhaps the *Phaedrus* was restricted to their myths, the *Theaetetus* to its central digression, and the *Symposium* to the speech of Diotima. The *Republic* and the *Laws,* which were not even in the curriculum, suffered a similar compression: interest in the *Republic* fastened on the myth of Er, and that in the *Laws* on Book 10.

The contrast with Fārābī is striking. He worked over the whole of the *Republic,*[93] and Book 10 is precisely the one he ignored in his own treatment of the *Laws.* The epitome of Plato's philosophy reproduced by Fārābī tells a similar story:[94] it is a survey of a Platonic curriculum considerably different from the one in fashion among the Neoplatonists.[95] It is closer to the first of two Platonic bibliographies reproduced by Ibn al-Nadīm (p. 246/Dodge, pp. 592–593) and explicitly credited, for both its titles and its order, to the second century Platonist Theon of Smyra. In its order, this latter differs from the Thrasyllan tetrarchies, an arrangement the Arabs knew about but which they, or Theon, attributed to Plato himself. The manuscript is garbled in places; but the list in the *Fihrist* appears to begin with two translated titles, *Al-Siyāsah (Republic?)* and *Al-Nawāmīs (Laws),* and then proceeds through a series of transliterated Greek titles from the *Theages* down to what seems to be the *Politicus.* Unlike the case of the Aristotelian corpus, Ibn al-Nadīm knows little of the translation history of each dialogue. He notes Arabic translations for the *Siyāsah,* the *Nawāmīs,* and the *Sophist,* and at another point Galen is said to have made an abridgment of the *Parmenides.* There is no mention in the list of the *Apology, Philebus, Symposium, Lysis, Epinomis,* and *Letters,* all of which appeared in the Thrasyllan canon, while the *Philebus* and the *Symposium* were central in the Neoplatonic curriculum.

This series is followed immediately by another which is based on Ibn al-Nadīm's own knowledge, and which may represent the identifiable Plato circulating in Islam: the *Timaeus,* "Relationships,"[96] "a book of Plato to the Cretan on the laws," "Oneness,"[97] "his dialogue on the soul, the intelligence, substance, and properties," "Sense Perception and Pleasure,"[98] the *Timaeus* again, the *Theaetetus;* "the Education of Young Men,"[99] and the *Letters.* The difference between Theon's list, reproduced almost literally by Ibn al-Nadīm, and that actually available to the *falāsifah* is striking. Equally striking is the fact that neither list corresponds to the curriculum of the Neoplatonic Academy.

Nor is there much in common between Fārābī and the fifth century Academy. His First Cause as not the utterly transcendent Neoplatonic One, but an intelligent Creator. There is no trace of theurgy in Fārābī; his prophecy is naturalistic rather than mystical, derived to a great extent from the Peripatetic Alexander of Aphrodisias.[100] And there is, finally, Fārābī's extraordinary interest in politics.

In a sense none of this requires explanation. Fārābī was a Muslim; and his God is the activist Creator of the *Qur'ān,* whose message was, no less than that of Jesus, an ethical one. Islam was a political as well as a religious community, but it was almost completely innocent of any sacramental basis for a theurgy in the style of the Pseudo-Dionysius. And yet Fārābī's theories, for all their originality, are explicitly and consistently derived from Greek archetypes. Some of his reading was obviously Plato, but no scholastic philosopher came to Plato in private. He approached the dialogues with the exegetical attitudes and apparatus that comprised Platonism, the Platonic tradition.

By the time it reached Fārābī that tradition had been evolving for over a millennium, from Aristotle's original revisions of his master's teachings to Christianity's own expropriation of the version of those teachings current in the sixth century. From what point in that tradition were Islamic *falāsifah* like Fārābī drawing their perspectives? In a number of recent publications Richard Walzer has drawn attention to the mounting evidence that the Arabs in general and Fārābī in particular had access to a form of pre-Plotinian Platonism,[101] and most likely that form in vogue among the so-called "Middle" Platonists of the early Roman Empire.

It is difficult now to assess that possibility since the eventual triumph of Plotinian Neoplatonism in the Academy reduced those earlier representatives of the tradition to a mere shadow. Much of what can be retrieved goes back to a source well known to the Arabs, Porphyry of Tyre.[102] Porphyry was regarded by the Arabs chiefly as the author of the *Eisagoge*[103] and as an Aristotelian commentator; although his connection with the exegesis of Plato was not known,[104] there were grounds for suspecting it. The *falāsifah* had in their hands Porphyry's *Philosophical History* in four books, the entirety in Syriac and half, perhaps the first half, in Arabic (*Fihrist,* p. 245/Dodge, p. 590). Ibn al-Nadīm had himself seen Book 4 in Syriac (p. 253/Dodge, p. 610). If so, he saw the life of Plato, since Porphyry's work ended, according to a well-known Middle Platonic perception of history, with Plato.[105]

Parts of Porphyry's *History* have been retrieved,[106] including the long life of Pythagoras reproduced by Ibn abī Uṣaybiʿah (1, pp. 38–41). All the Porphyrian motifs are present in the fragments, the concern for a scientific chronology,[107] the important position assigned to Pythagoras,[108] and the connection between Pythagoras and Plato, an association first underlined by Aristotle and one which became increasingly important as the Middle Academy was drawn into the Pythagorean revival of the early Empire.

The *Philosophical History* provided Arab authors with biographical details on the early Greek philosophers; but from a doctrinal point of view Porphyry's *Concordance of the Philosophy of Plato and Aristotle* had a far more profound effect in Islam, or so it appears.[109] It was not, however, the first such work: Plotinus's teacher Ammonius Saccas was preaching just such a concordance a century before Porphyry.[110] The Arab bibliographers do not mention by name a *Concordance* by either man; indeed they did not know the name Ammonius Saccas at all. So while the probabilities remain that Porphyry's work was the direct source of such syncretizing among the *falāsifah,* and of Fārābī's *On the Agreement of the Opinions of the Two Sages,*[111] for example, it is not to be excluded that the influence of Ammonius was also at work, if only indirectly.

Porphyry's positions were not, of course, identical with those of the long dead scholars of Middle Platonism; he was, after all, a student of Plotinus, even though the Arabs were unaware of that affiliation; and it was precisely his somewhat dimly perceived Neoplatonism that bothered the *falāsifah.* His *Points of Departure for the Intelligibles,* known in the Arabic tradition as *On the Intellect and the Intelligible,*[112] was a kind of Neoplatonic handbook based, like the *Theology,* on the *Enneads.* It included among its other arguments a defense, against Middle Platonists like his former teacher Longinus, of the absolute transcendence of the One and a discussion of the mode of union between the intellect and the objects of its intellection.[113]

The notion that the mind somehow became its object in the act of intellection was a commonplace in Peripatetic circles, but the manner of its "becoming" was a matter of some dispute. In his *Points of Departure* Porphyry argued for an ontological unity between intellect and the intelligible. Among the Arabs, who drew a great deal of their psychological theory from Alexander of Aphrodisias, Ibn Sīnā resolutely rejected that interpretation (*Shifā': De anima* 5,6; *Ishārāt,* pp. 178–180), which he explicitly attributed to Porphyry's *Points of Departure.*[114] Ibn Rushd, who seems to have had trouble with that same work, though on different grounds,[115] spoke unfavorably of Porphyry. He did, however, regard him as a Peripatetic, albeit a strange one.

The remaining Porphyrian psychological texts in Arabic are not easy to identify. There are passages in Tawḥīdī (*Muqābāsāt,* p. 234 Sandubi) and Shahrastānī (Ed. Cairo, Pt. 3, pp. 53–63, 88–94: *Letter to Anebo*), and what appears to be part of an Arabic version of his *On the Soul Against Boethius* in an Istanbul manuscript.[116] They probably did not exercise a great deal of influence in a tradition that preferred to take its psychology from Alexander or Themistius, or from sources wrapped in the anonymity of pre-Plotinian Platonism.

Some of that latter material may have come to the Arabs, as it has to us, through the hands of Porphyry. But they had more direct access. Plutarch was available in Arabic,[117] and the *falāsifah* had a detailed and sophisticated knowledge of Galen, the student of Gaius and Albinus. Further, Galen's connection with Platonism was somewhat better understood than Porphyry's. His epitome of Plato's dialogues was in circulation in Arabic, for example, and bore his name upon it.[118] But for the Arabs Galen was also part of the Aristotelian tradition: his commentary on the *De interpretatione* was preserved (*Fihrist,* p. 249/Dodge, p. 599), his association with Alexander of Aphrodisias stressed,[119] and one major account of his life emphasizes his Peripatetic teachers.[120] The reason is not far to week: at least some of the biographical information on Galen in Arabic came from John Philoponus (*Fihrist,* p. 289/Dodge, p. 681).

There is no mention in the Arab bibliographers of the fourth or fifth century work often ascribed to Galen in the manuscripts, the *Philosophical History.* What they did possess, however, is one of the sources of that work which bore, in Greek and Arabic, and equally incorrectly, the name of Plutarch, the *Placita Philosophorum.*[121] The Arabic version was by Qusṭā ibn Lūqā and was widely read in Islam.[122] The pseudo-Plutarch, like the pseudo-Galen after it, was a doxography rather than a history; it collected opinions of philosophers and arranged them under topic headings, chiefly in the physical branches of philosophy.

The Arabs had in their hands another such Neoplatonic doxography, this one unknown in the Greek sources: (pseudo-) Ammonius's *The Opinions of the Philosophers.* This was first known from citations in Bīrūnī and Shahrastānī, but now the text itself has been discovered in an Istanbul manuscript.[123] It appears to stand closer to the *Placita* than to that other form of handbook wisdom transmitted from antiquity into Islam, the gnomonology. There was an abundant sampling of the wit and wisdom of the Greeks available in Arabic; and it was incorporated into works like Ḥunayn's *Anecdotes,* Mubashshir's *Epitome of Wisdom,* and Abū Sulaymān's *Garden of Wisdom.*[124]

The diffusion of these scholastic handbooks in Islam has made it difficult in the extreme to trace to their sources opinions held by the *falāsifah* on Plato or anyone else. The historical knowledge of a Kindī or a Fārābī could derive from an integral text of the author in question, an epitome, or a doxography. Simplicius, writing in the sixth century in Athens, still had pre-Socratic texts in his hands, but not many of his contemporaries elsewhere possessed the same kind of library resources. And it is even less likely that the Arabs did.

To return to Galen: he was not one of the authors who came to Islam through the selective hands of Porphyry. The Arabs read deeply in his works, both medical and philosophical.[125] There was, moreover, a strong pre-Islamic Syriac tradition in Galen. When Ḥunayn ibn Isḥāq turned to the task of translating Galen's works, he had before him the considerable labors of Sergius of Reshayna (d. 536).[126] Sergius had received his medical and philosophical education at Alexandria and was the translator not merely of Aristotle and Galen but of the Pseudo-Dionysius (the Areopagite) as well.[127] Sergius stood, then, in an especially interesting relationship to the Syrian intellectuals who three centuries later mediated the passage of Hellenism into Islam: a physician and a philosopher, a knowledgeable student of Galen, of Aristotle, and of Proclan Neoplatonism, albeit under concealment of a Christian theology.[128] And if those other pseud epigraphs, the *De causis,* or the *Theology of Aristotle,* are substituted for the *Corpus Areopagiticum,* the combination is not very different from that which prevailed in Islamic *falsafah.*

The Arabs could have come to their Middle Platonic attitudes through the historically minded Porphyry or more directly in the works of Galen. There was, in addition, a third possibility, whose outlines and importance remain somewhat obscure. As far back as 1912 attention was being directed behind the accommodating attitudes of Ammonius and Olympiodorus to the earlier Alexandrian Platonist Hierocles.[129] Before coming to Alexandria to take up the teaching of philosophy there in the opening decades of the fifth century, Hierocles had studied at Athens under Plutarch. By that time Alexandria was already a well established center of Christian theology. Two centuries earlier the Christian Origen had studied philosophy with the most eminent Platonist of *his* day, Ammonius Saccas; and just one generation before Hierocles, Alexandrian Platonism had produced a notable Christian bishop for Egypt, Synesius (d. 413).[130]

The religious and intellectual climate of Plutarch's Athens was very different, or so it appears in the enthusiastic pages of Marinus's *Life of Proclus.* As has already been seen, Plutarch was the first of the scholarchs in the Academy to profess the Neoplatonic reading of Plato, that is, the themes outlined by Plotinus and developed, sometimes in quite perverse directions, by Porphyry and Iamblichus. And yet Hierocles, on the basis of the very scanty remains of his work preserved by Plotinus, did not go down the same path. Most striking, perhaps, is the absence in his thought of that centerpiece of Neoplatonic metaphysics, the One above being, action, and name. For Hierocles the High God was the demiurge, the creator who by an act of his will brought the world into existence from nothing.

This view of God as well as other elements in Hierocles's philosophy—his insistence, for example, on human freedom in the face of an all-powerful *heimarmene*—is very alien to contemporary Athenian attitudes. They are, on the other hand, quite close to Christian theories on the nature and operations of God. Praechter thought he saw in Hierocles an example of Christian influences on Hellenic philosophy, exercised, doubtless, through the Christian intellectual establishment at Alexandria during Hierocles's tenure there. A closer scrutiny of Hierocles has revealed another possibility, however: that Hierocles represents the latest known survival of the teaching of Ammonius Saccas, Plotinus's teacher at Alexandria.[131]

Ammonius's own teachings are scarcely better known than those of Hierocles, but it does seem possible to trace a line of descent from Middle Platonic circles like those of Gaius and Galen into Ammonius at

Alexandria at the beginning of the third Christian century. Thereafter the Platonic focus is resolutely on Plotinus. But Plotinus was not the only student of Ammonius, nor the most faithful to his master's teachings. The Neoplatonist Origen[132]—not the Christian theologian of the same name—was one, as was Longinus at Athens. Both betray traces of Ammonius's point of view; and the same teachings can be found in Gregory of Nyssa—whom the Arabs translated (*Fihrist,* p. 255/Dodge, p. 614), and whose education went back, via Basil, to Athens;[133] and finally, and most obviously, in another student at Athens, Hierocles.

What was this Ammonian teaching? By placing Origen, Gregory, and Hierocles side by side one can reconstruct Ammonius's portrait of a creator God, a single transcendent hypostasis rather than Plotinus's hierarchy, creation by will, the co-creation of spirit and matter, the positing of the Platonic *eide* as thoughts in the mind of God, and, finally, a belief in the essential agreement (*symphonia*) of Plato and Aristotle.

Most of these are commonplace doctrines in Middle Platonism, which were later replaced by Plotinus's way of construing the dialogues. What the modern resurrection of Ammonius Saccas reveals is that Plotinian Neoplatonism was not the only version of the Platonic tradition after 300; that there survived into the fifth century, principally at Athens and then, in the person of Hierocles, at Alexandria, another variant version of the tradition, at once closer to the Platonism of Gaius and Albinus[134] and at the same time more congruent with Fārābī's understanding of a creator God. There were clearly survivals of Middle Platonism in late antiquity, some of them lodged perhaps in the ill-studied metaphysics of the Alexandrian scholars of the fifth and sixth centuries.[135] And until more is known of the metaphysics of Ammonius, the son of Hermias, and of Olympiodorus, for example, it is impossible to judge Islamic access to those survivals.

If we cannot as yet get at Alexandrian metaphysics, there are other possibilities of disengaging the continuing existence of a variant, non-Proclan Platonism after Hierocles. The *Corpus Areopagiticum* represents Christian theology's first major confrontation with Proclus. The results were not favorably received in all quarters. Almost as soon as the *Corpus* began to circulate, it was accompanied by *scholia* which undertook to explain and defend it.[136] The work of exegesis, composed ca. 530, was the work of the Christian theologian, John of Scythopolis. The effect of John's *scholia* was to reduce the Pseudo-Dionysius to positions more closely approximating those of Middle Platonism, and this presumably for the benefit of Christian theologians for whom such pre-Plotinian conservatism was a more acceptable form of Platonic theology. The *scholia* have not been much studied,[137] and John appears, in any event, to be relying heavily on doxographical information for his Platonic positions. But so too were the Arabs; and for them, as for John, normative

Platonism was still that which emerged in the schools of the second Christian century.

All of this is surmise. What is certain is that the Arabs knew, even within the confines of the school tradition, two different strains of Platonism: the Neoplatonic version of Plotinus and Proclus, and an older Platonism taught in the Roman schools during the second and third century. The first was rendered all but anonymous by the body of pseudepigraphy with which someone, pagan Greek, Christian Syrian, or Muslim Arab, felt it necessary to conceal the traces of Neoplatonic metaphysics. The second points insistently to Galen and may have come to the Arabs either directly from Middle Platonic sources, or indirectly from a strain of Middle Platonic conservatism which may have survived within the Neoplatonism of the fifth and sixth centuries at Alexandria.

Notes

1. For a general orientation, see s.v. "Aflāṭūn," in *Encyclopaedia of Islam,* new ed. [by Richard Walzer] 1: 235-36; Roger Paret, "Notes bibliographiques sur quelques travaux récents consacrés aux premières traductions arabes d'oeuvres grecques," *Byzantion,* 29-30 (1959-60): 425-36; and ʿAbdurraḥmān Badawi, *La Transmission de la Philosophie Grecque au Monde Arabe,* Paris: J. Vrin, 1968, pp. 34-45.

2. We learn from the better known Aristotelian versions that when the second translator is one of the Baghdad Peripatetics it is likely a question of a revised edition rather than a completely new translation.

3. Ibn al-Nadīm, *Kitāb al-Fihrist,* ed. Gustave Flügel (Leipzig, 1871), p. 246; Bayard Dodge, *The Fihrist of Al-Nadīm,* New York: Columbia University Press, 1970, pp. 592-93.

4. Paul Kraus and Richard Walzer, *Galeni Compendium Timaei Platonis corumque Dialogorum Synopsis quae exstant Fragmenta.* In "Corpus Platonicum Medii Aevi, Plato Arabus," vol. 1, London: Warburg Institute, 1951.

5. Francesco Gabrieli, ed. and trans., *Alfarabius Compendium Legum Platonis.* In "Corpus Platonicum Medii Aevi, Plato Arabus," vol. 3, London: Warburg Institute, 1952.

6. See Paret, "Notes bibliographiques," pp. 428-30.

7. If Walzer's supposition is correct, that the fragment of the *Eudemus* in al-Kindī comes from Proclus, *In Timaeum;* see Richard Walzer, *Greek into Arabic,* Oxford: Bruno Cassirer, 1962, p. 42. But Walzer himself has raised the possibility that it may derive from a work of Porphyry in the same dialogue; cf. n. 104 below.

8. See Schlomo Pines, *Beiträge zur Islamischen Atomenlehre,* Berlin, 1936, pp. 69, 73, n. 2.

9. To which Ḥunayn's similar "That which Ought to be Read Before Plato's Books" is related. It was, at any rate, one of the most common of the scholastic *topoi* in late antiquity.

10. Identified by Dodge, p. 613, n. 167, as Plutarch of Athens, a highly unlikely possibility.

11. The name "Plotinus" does occur in the nondescript list of names reproduced by Ibn al-Nadīm (p. 255, 1, 16/Dodge, p. 614) from some Aristotelian commentary.

12. The most recent detailed reviews of the problem connected with that work are Josef Van Ess, "Jüngere orientalische Literatur zur neuplatonischen Überlieferung im Bereich des Islam" in *Parousia: Festgabe für Johannes Hirschberger,* Frankfurt, 1965, pp. 334-9; Badawi, *Transmission,* pp. 46-59; Paret, "Notes bibliographiques," pp. 437-9; cf. F. E. Peters, *Aristoteles Arabus: The Orientatal Translation History of the Aristotelian Corpus,* Leiden: E. J. Brill, 1968, pp. 72-4.

13. Paul Kraus, "Plotin chez les Arabes," *Bulletin de l'Institut d'Egypte* 23 (1941): 263-95.

14. Franz Rosenthal, "Al-Shaykh al-Yūnānī and the Arabic Plotinus Source," *Orientalia* 21 (1952): 462-529; 22 (1953): 370-400; and 24 (1955): 42-66.

15. P. Henry and H. R. Schwyzer, *Plotini Opera,* Paris and Brussels, 1959. The Arabic texts have been collected into a new edition by ʿAbdurrahmān Badawi, *Plotinus apud Arabes,* Cairo, 1955.

16. See Wilhelm Kutsch, "Ein arabisches Bruchstück aus Porphyrios *peripsukhès* und die Frage des Verfassers der 'Theologie des Aristoteles,'" *Mélanges de l'Université Saint-Joseph* 31 (1954): 265 ff., and Richard Walzer, "Porphyry and the Arabic Tradition," in *Fondation Hardt: Entretiens sur 'Antiquité Classique,* vol. 12, Vandoeuvres and Geneva, 1966, pp. 296-7.

17. Walzer, *Greek into Arabic,* pp. 68, 112. See also Carl Brockelmann, *Geschichte der arabischen Litteratur,* 2 vols., Weimar and Berlin, 1890 & 1902; 2d ed. 2 vols., Leiden, 1943-49; Suppl. 3 vols., Leiden, 1937-42. In Brockelmann, note especially 1st ed., 2: 22 and Suppl. 1: 364-65.

18. The fact is equally apparent in the list of scholarchs put together in F. Ueberweg and K. Praechter, *Grundriss der Geschichte der Philosophie: Die Philosophie des Altertums,* Basel and Stuttgart, 1957, pp. 663-66, and in the latest general treatment of the period, A. H. Armstrong, ed., *The Cambridge History of Later Greek and Early Medieval Philosophy,* Cambridge: At the University Press, 1967, which is, in effect, a history of later Platonism.

19. But not everyone, apparently. Badawi, *Transmission,* pp. 58-9, has drawn attention to a commentary on Suhrawardī by Shīrāzī in which both men, author and commentator, deny the attribution of the *Theology* to Aristotle and credit it instead to Plato.

20. Walzer, *Greek into Arabic,* p. 72.

21. Pines, *Atomenlehre,* p. 88, n. 1.

22. A fragment from the letter has turned up in Arabic in a doxographical passage of Shahrastānī on Porphyry; cf. Francesco Gabrieli, "Plotino e Porfirio in un eresiografo musulmano," *La Parola del Passato* 1 (1946): 338 ff., and Franz Altheim and Ruth Stiehl, *Die Araben in der Alten Welt,* Berlin, 1964, 1: 252 ff.

23. Chiefly from Christian sources: A. R. Sodano, *Porfirio: Lettera ad Anebo,* Naples, 1958.

24. Édouard des Places, *Jamblique: Les Mystères d'Egypte,* Paris: Association Guillaume Budé, 1966.

25. On the role of theurgy in later Platonism: Martin P. Nilsson, *Geschichte der Griechischen Religion,* 2d ed., Munich: C. H. Beck'sche Verlagsbuchhandlung, 1961, 2: 450-4, and Clemens Zintzen, "Die Wertung von Mystik und Magie in der neuplatonischen Philosophic," *Rheinische Museum* 108 (1965): 71-100.

26. A collection of oracular utterances put together from miscellaneous sources by a certain Julian who lived during the reign of Marcus Aurelius; cf. Wilhelm Kroll, *De Oraculis Chaldaicis,* Breslau, 1894; reprint. Hildescheim, 1962.

27. See especially H.-D. Saffrey and L. G. Westerink, *Proclus: Théologie Platonicienne,* Paris: Association Guillaume Budé, 1968, 1: xxv-xlviii, and É. Évrard, "Le maître de Plutarque d'Athènes et les origines du néoplatonisme athénien," *L'Antiquité Classique,* 29 (1960): 108-33.

28. Maximus, for all his well-known theurgic eccentricities, was also, on the authority of Simplicius, a commentator on the Aristotelian *Categories.* The interest in Aristotle, already attested to by Plotinus, Porphyry, and Iamblichus, obviously survived, even in the unlikely person of Maximus.

29. The Aristotelian works were also cultivated (cf. n. 28). Proclus read both Aristotle's *De anima* and Plato's *Phaedo* with Plutarch. At Plutarch's death he undertook a two-year study of the Aristotelian curriculum under the direction of Syrianus (*Vita Procli,* 22-23).

30. Marinus's *Life* has been available in the edition of J. Boissonade since 1814. Damascius's work is not preserved and must be reconstructed from the excerpts in Plotinus and Suda: Clemens Zintzen, *Damascii Vitae Isidori Reliquiae,* Hildersheim: Georg Olms, 1967; cf. Rudolf Asmus, "Zur Rekonstruktion von Damascius' Leben des Isidorus," *Byzantinische Zeitschrift* 18 (1909): 424-80; 19 (1910): 265-84.

31. Fārābī, quoted by Ibn abī Uṣaybiʿah 1:135, and Masʿūdī, citing one of his own works in *Tanbīh,* pp. 121-2; cf. Max Meyerhof, "Von Alexandrien nach Baghdad: Ein Beitrag zur Geschichte des philosophischen und medizinischen Unterrichts bei den Arabern," *Sitzungsberichte der preussischen Akademie der Wissenschaften,* Berlin, 1930, 23: 393-4, 406-7, and Franz Rosenthal, *Das Fortleben der Antike im Islam,* Zurich and Stuttgart: Artemis Verlag, 1965, pp. 74-6.

32. "Baruḳlus," *Encyclopaedia of Islam,* new ed., vol. 1, s.v. (by Richard Walzer) and van Ess, "Jüngere Literatur," pp. 339-47. Many of the basic texts have been published by ʿAbdurraḥmān Badawi, *Neoplatonici apud Arabes,* Cairo and Wiesbaden, 1955.

33. And Ḥunayn adds, in a fragment preserved from his translation of Proclus, *In Tim.* (cf. n. 36 below), that Proclus was the preeminent interpreter of Plato's works; cf. E. Pfaff, *Corpus Medicorum Graecorum,* Supp. 3: xlii.

34. The translation was begun by Thābit but never completed. On the *Golden Sayings* translated by Ḥunayn, see Franz Rosenthal, "Some Pythagorean Documents Transmitted in Arabic," *Orientalia,* 10 (1941): 104 ff. and 383 ff., and *idem. Fortleben,* pp. 165-8. On Plato and Socrates as students of Pythagoras, see *Fortleben,* p. 63, from Ṣāʿid al-Andalūsī.

35. The work is lost in Greek but the title in the *Fihrist* confirms the suspicion (cf. *In Remp.* 2: 178, 11, 5-6) that Proclus's commentary was confined to the myth.

36. Cf. Paret, "Notes bibliographiques," p. 446, n. 3.

37. H. Rabe, *Iohannes Philoponus: De aeternitate mundi contra Proclum,* Leipzig: Teubner, 1899.

38. Franz Rosenthal, "From Arabic Books and Manuscripts VII: Some Graeco-Arabica in Istanbul," *Journal of the American Oriental Society,* 81 (1961): 9-10.

39. Badawi, *Neoplatonici,* pp. 33-42; cf. *idem.* "Un Proclus perdu et retrouvé en arabe," in *Mélanges Massignon,* Damascus, 1956, 1: 149-151; G. Anawati, "Un fragment perdu

du *De Aeternitate Mundi* de Proclus," in *Mélanges Diès,* Paris, 1956, pp. 21-5; and for a comparison of Philoponus's Greek fragments and the new Arabic, Richard Walzer, *Oriens,* 10 (1957): 393-4.

40. Such are the *Physical Problems* and the passage on the "Good" published by Badawi in *Neoplatonici,* pp. 43-9 and 257-9. The editor has identified them both as Proclan, but their authorship is far from certain.

41. For a general survey of the state of the question see Peters, *Aristoteles Arabus,* pp. 56-7; and H.-D. Saffrey, "L'Etat actuel des recherches sur le *Liber de Causis* comme source de la métaphysique au Moyen Âge," *Miscellanea Mediaevalia,* Berlin, 1963, 2: 267-81.

42. Otto Bardenhewer, Freiburg, 1882, and Badawi, *Neoplatonici,* pp. 3-33.

43. Unless the treatise attributed to Proclus under the title of "On the First Good" (*Fihrist,* p. 252/Dodge, p. 607) is meant to be the *De causis.* In the same passage Ibn al-Nadīm mentions a Proclan "Theology." Proclus is, however, credited in the Greek sources with a commentary on the *Philebus,* a work we know the Neoplatonists read as a proof-text on the Final Good.

44. Badawi, *Neoplatonici,* pp. 248-56.

45. Published from Damascus MS. Zahiriyah 4871 by ʿAbdurraḥmān Badawi, *Arisṭūʿinda 'l-ʿArab,* Cairo, 1947, pp. 248-256; cf. Shlomo Pines, "Une version arabe de trois propositions de la 'Stoikheiosis Theologike' de Proclus," *Oriens,* 8 (1955): 195-203, and B. Lewin, "Notes sur un texte de Proclus en traduction arabe," *Orientalia Suecana,* 4 (1955): 101-108. Since then a number of new MSS. have been identified.

46. Ṣāʿid al-Andalūsī did, however, link a Proclus with the Alexandrian alchemical tradition, and in his *Ṭabaqāt al-umam* the name is found in the company of Hermes and Zosimus.

47. So Saffrey and Westerink, *Théologie Platonicienne,* vol. 1, pp. xvi-xvii.

48. See now Alan Cameron, "The Last Days of the Academy at Athens," *Cambridge Philological Society,* 114 (1969): 7-29.

49. On the intellectual atmosphere under Khusraw see F. E. Peters, *Aristotle and the Arabs: The Aristotelian Tradition in Islam,* New York: New York University Press, 1968, p. 48, n. 49.

50. Though not necessarily in Pahlevi. Mani, for example, composed almost entirely in Syriac, the lingua franca of the Sasanian Empire.

51. See Arthur Vööbus, *History of the School of Nisibis,* Louvain: Secretariat du CSCO, 1965, pp. 152-3.

52. There is a considerable confusion here among three men, all named Paul. Two of them were bishops of Nisibis, but the third was Khusraw's court philosopher, who is reputed to have written in Pahlevi. Two of his reworkings of the Aristotelian logic are preserved in their Syriac translations; see Vööbus, *ibid.,* pp. 170-1, and Peters, *Aristotle and the Arabs,* p. 48.

53. See Cameron, "Last Days of the Academy," pp. 21-22.

54. The commentary on the *Encheiridion* of Epictetus almost certainly antedates his departure for Persia; cf. Cameron, *ibid.,* pp. 13-21.

55. The *Fihrist* says that Simplicius "made this for Athawalis," probably a corruption of "Ammonius." Cf. n. 57 below.

56. For its history see H. A. Davidson, "John Philoponus as a Source of Medieval Islamic and Jewish Proofs of Creation, *JAOS* 89 (1969): 357–91, and, on Simplicius's attitude toward Philoponus, Cameron, "Last Days of the Academy," pp. 223. Fārābī devoted a special work to the subject, *Against John the Grammarian,* trans., from a still unpublished MS., by Muhsin Mahdi in *Journal of Near Eastern Studies,* 26 (1967): 233–60.

57. The preserved commentary on the *Phaedrus* is really his transcription of Syrianus's lectures on the subject; on the custom of students reproducing such, see M. Richard, "ἀπὸ φονῆς'," *Byzantion,* 20 (1950): 265–272. The Arabs do not seem to have been aware of this scholastic phenomenon, except unconsciously in the case of Simplicius's commentary on the *De anima* (cf. n. 55 above). Thus they possessed far more Ammonius and less Philoponus than they imagined.

58. Perhaps the work referred to by Simplicius, *In De Coelo,* 271: 13–21, and *In Phys.,* 1363: 8–12.

59. This is clearly an academic textbook well within the *eisagoge* tradition (cf. Peters, *Aristotle and the Arabs,* pp. 79–87) and may actually represent the preliminary material in Ammonius's commentaries on either the *Eisagoge,* not mentioned in the *Fihrist,* or on the *Categories;* see L. G. Westerink, *Anonymous Prolegomena to Platonic Philosophy,* Amsterdam, 1962, pp. xxviii–xxxii.

60. See H.-D. Saffrey, "Le Chrétien Jean Philopon et la survivance de l'école d'Alexandrie au VIe siècle," *Revue des Études Grecques,* 72 (1954): 396–410.

61. Westerink, *Anonymous Prolegomena,* pp. xi–xii; cf. Cameron, "Last Days of the Academy," pp. 14–15.

62. And perhaps even Boethius. The suggestion that Boethius was a student of Ammonius in Alexandria advancd by P. Courcelle, *Les Lettres grecques en Occident,* 2nd ed. (Paris, 1948), pp. 288 ff. has not, however, been universally accepted; see H. Liebschütz in A. H. Armstrong, ed., *Later Greek Philosophy,* pp. 553–4.

63. And perhaps also the *Theaetetus.* The name in the *Fihrist,* p. 246, l. 19 is obscure. Flügel read it as the *Sophist;* Dodge, p. 593, as the *Theatetus.* On Olympiodorus's interesting information on the contemporary (*ca.* 560) Academy, see Cameron, "Last Days of the Academy," pp. 11–12, and Westerink, *Anonymous Prolegomena,* pp. xiv–xv.

64. The pertinent text is in I Alc., 223–224; see Westerink, *Anonymous Prolegomena,* pp. xvi–xvii.

65. See Meyerhof, "Von Alexandrien nach Baghdad," p. 398, n. 2.

66. His other title, *Philoponus,* which refers to his pious militancy on behalf of Christian causes, was also known to the Arabs; see Meyerhof, "Von Alexandrien nach Baghdad," *loc. cit.* On the guild of the *philoponoi* in sixth century Alexandria, see H. J. Margoulias, *Byzantinische Zeitschrift,* 57 (1964): 133–135.

67. *In Cat., Anal. Pr., Anat. Post., Phys.* (A.D. 517), *De Gen. et Corr.,* all of which were *reportationes* of Ammonius's lectures with John's additions, as indicated in the Greek manuscript tradition. Philoponus's commentary of the *Eisagoge,* which was widely used among the Syrians, had oddly left no trace in Islam.

68. Isḥāq ibn Ḥunayn's *History of Physicians,* a fundamental source for the *Fihrist's* treatment of the history of medicine, drew heavily upon John; see Franz Rosenthal, "Isḥāq b. Ḥunayn's *Tārīkh al-Aṭibbā'*," *Oriens,* 7 (1954): 75.

69. Ibn al-Nadīm describes him as a student of "Sawari," perhaps Severus, the Patriarch of Antioch in 512–538, who much earlier, before 488 at any rate, had studied

rhetoric at Alexandria and was, like John, a Monophysite; cf. n. 72 below. The *Fihrist* also cites a *Refutation of Nestorius* under John's name.

70. See É. Évrard, "Les convictions religieuses de Jean Philopon et la date de son Commentaire aux *Météorologiques*," *Bull. Acad. Royale de Belgique*, Cl. de Lettres, 5 (1953): 299-357, and *idem*, "Jean Philopon, son Commentaire sur Nicomaque et ses rapports avec Ammonius," *Revue des Études Grecques*, 78 (1965): 593-8.

71. See T. Hermann, "Johannes Philoponus als Monophysit," *ZNTW*, 29 (1930): 209-64, and H. Martin, "Jean Philopon et la controverse trithéite du VIe siècle," *Studia Patristica*, 5 (1962): 519-25.

72. Nor do the Christian Platonists of Alexandria: Aeneas, Zacharias, the bishop of Mytilene, and his brother Procopius. The Gaza intellectuals of the early sixth century generally appear to be more interested in rhetoric than philosophy, but they were, nonetheless, heirs to a genuine philosophical tradition. Its origins were in Alexandria, where Aeneas studied with Hierocles; Zacharias was a fellow student there of the Monophysite theoretician Severus of Antioch, and his *Life of Severus* (M. Kugener, ed., *Patrologia Orientalis* 2, Paris, 1907), 1-115, provides most of what we know about university life in Alexandria in the late fifth century. On the Gaza Platonists see I. P. Sheldon-Williams, "The Reaction Against Proclus. Gaza," in A. H. Armstrong, ed., *Later Greek Philosophy*, pp. 483-8, and Basile Tatakis, *La Philosophie Byzantine*, Paris: Presses Universitaires de France, 1949, pp. 27-39.

73. On Stephen see R. Vancourt, *Les derniers commentateurs alexandrins d'Aristotle* (Lille, 1941), pp. 26-42, and Westerink, *Anonymous Prolegomena*, pp. xxiv-xxv.

74. See F. Sherwood Taylor, "The Alchemical Works of Stephanos of Alexandria," *Ambix*, 1 (1937): 116-39; 2 (1938): 39-49. The translations done for Khālid, certainly not by Stephen, were allegedly (*Fihrist*, p. 242/Dodge, p. 581) the first done from a foreign language into Arabic during the Islamic period.

75. The most intimate connection between Alexander and the Neoplatonists is the attested fact that Plotinus studied his work (*Vita Plotini*, 14).

76. So, in detail, Meyerhof, "Von Alexandrien nach Baghdad."

77. H.-D. Saffrey, "Le Chrétien Jean Philopon," pp. 409-10.

78. Edited by Franz Rosenthal in *Oriens*, 7 (1954): 61-80; cf. Rosenthal, "Graeco-Arabica in Istanbul," pp. 10-11.

79. Most recently by Richard Walzer, "Al-Farabi and his Successors" in A. H. Armstrong, ed., *Later Greek Philosophy*, pp. 652-66; cf. his earlier essay "Platonism in Islamic Philosophy," reprinted in *Greek into Arabic*, pp. 236-52.

80. So Walzer, *Greek into Arabic*, p. 202.

81. Cf. Leo Strauss, "How Fārābī Read Plato's *Laws*," in *Mélanges Massignon*, 3 (Damascus, 1957), 319-44.

82. R. F. Hathaway, "The Neoplatonist Interpretation of Plato: Remarks on its Decisive Characteristics," *Journal of the History of Ideas*, 7 (1969): 19-26. Another peculiarity of the Islamic tradition was its veneration of Socrates, the moralist. The *Fihrist* lists among Kindī's works (p. 260/Dodge, p. 623) a number devoted to Socrates. They are included in a group assigned to politics (*siyāsah*), but on the basis of their titles they appear to be extracted from the *Phaedo*. The later Platonists read that dialogue not as a testimonial to Socratic ethics but as a treatise on psychology.

83. On the still unresolved question of the author's identity, whether a Neoplatonist like Damascius attempting to take cover under Christianity, or a Christian like Sergius of Reshayna bent on Platonizing Christianity, see most recently R. F. Hathaway, *Hierarchy and the Definition of Order in the Letters of Pseudo-Dionysius,* The Hague, 1969, pp. 12–30; and on "Dionysius's" political theory, *ibid.,* pp. 38–46.

84. R. F. Hathaway, *Letters of Pseudo-Dionysius,* p. xviii, no. 11; I. P. Sheldon-Williams, "The Pseudo-Dionysius," in A. H. Armstrong, ed., *Later Greek Philosophy,* p. 459.

85. Cf. the various types of polity described in his *Opinions of the Citizens of the Best State,* F. Dieterici, ed., Leiden, 1895.

86. M. Plezia, *Aristotelis Epistularum Fragmenta cum Testamento* (Warsaw, 1961); for the Arabic tradition: J. Bielawski, "Lettres d'Aristote à Alexandre le Grand en version arabe," *Rocznik Orientalistyczny,* 28 (1964): 7–34, and M. Grignaschi, "Les *Rasāʾil Arisṭāṭālīs ila-l-Iskandar* de Salīm Abu-l-ʿAlā et l'activité culturelle à l'époque omayyade," *Bullétin des Études Orientales* (1967): 7–83.

87. Typically preserved in ethical *majmūʿāt* like those in MSS. Fatih 5323, Aya Sofya 2890 and 4260, and Köprülü 1608.

88. See S. M. Stern, *Aristotle and the World State,* Columbia, S.C.: University of South Carolina Press, 1970. There is no integral edition of *On Governance*—that of J. Lippert, Halle and Berlin, 1891 is an abridged version—but both Plezia and Bielawski (cf. n. 86) are working on the text.

89. Walzer, *Greek into Arabic,* p. 140, n. 4.

90. The evidence, drawn chiefly from Iamblichus, Proclus, and Olympiodorus, is analyzed by Hathaway, "The Neoplatonist Interpretation of Plato," pp. 19–26, and by A.-J. Festugière, "L'Ordre de lecture des dialogues de Platon aux Ve/VIe siècles," *Museum Helveticum,* 26 (1969): 281–96.

91. See Karl Praechter, "Richtungen und Schulen im Neuplatonismus," in *Genethlikon* C. Robert, Berlin, 1910, pp. 128 ff.

92. Each understood, of course, in its appropriate way. A history of *Timaeus* exegesis could doubtless be written from Proclus, *In Timaeum,* and Proclus himself did just that for the *Parmenides* in his *Platonic Theology;* cf. Saffrey and Westerink, *Théologie Platonicienne,* vol. 1, pp. lxxv–lxxix.

93. His somewhat younger contemporary, the philosopher al-ʿĀmirī (d. 992), gives an elaborate resume of the debate on justice and injustice in Books I and II of the *Republic;* cf. A. J. Arberry, "Some Plato in an Arabic Epitome," *Islamic Quarterly,* 2 (1955): 86–90. The text occurs in his *On Seeking and Causing Happiness,* M. Minovi, ed., Wiesbaden, 1957–58.

94. Franz Rosenthal and Richard Walzer, eds., *Alfarabius de Platonis Philosophia* (London, 1943), and is translated, in its original composite setting, by Muhsin Mahdi, *Alfarabi's Philosophy of Plato and Aristotle,* New York, 1962.

95. Cf. Paret, "Notes bibliographiques," p. 426, n. 1.

96. Identified by Flügel as the *Cratylus.*

97. Flügel and Dodge connect this title with the phrases that follow and identify the whole with the *Timaeus.* It is just as likely that "Oneness" is a reference to the *Parmenides* and that the following phrases are indeed a description of the *Timaeus.*

98. Identified by Flügel as the *Philebus.* The normal Neoplatonic exegesis of that dialogue identifies it, however, as "On the Good."

99. Identified by Dodge as the *Laches,* but one of Flügel's guesses, *Alcibiades,* appears sounder.

100. Walzer, *Greek into Arabic,* pp. 206–19.

101. Most explicitly in *Greek into Arabic,* p. 209, and in "Porphyry and the Arabic Tradition," pp. 26-27.

102. On Porphyry as the transmitter of Middle Platonic texts into Neoplatonism see H. Dörrie, "Die Schultradition im Mittelplatonismus und Porphyrios" in *Fondation Hardt: Entretiens sur l'Antiquité Classique,* vol. 12, Vandoeuvres and Geneva, 1966, pp. 1-25; and on the Arabic Porphyry, Walzer, "Porphyry and the Arabic Tradition," pp. 275-297, and *idem,* "Furfūrīyūs," *Encyclopaedia of Islam,* new ed.

103. On the *Eisagoge* in Islam see Ibrahim Madkour, *L'Orgamon d'Aristote dans le Monde Arabe,* 2nd ed., Paris, 1969, pp. 70–5.

104. Unless Walzer's surmise in "Porphyry and the Arabic Tradition," p. 280, that the fragment of the *Eudemus* in al-Kindī goes back, via Proclus, *In Remp.,* to Porphyry's commentary on the myth of Er is sound.

105. Cf. Walzer's remarks, *op. cit.,* p. 81.

106. The Greek fragments were published by A. Nauck, *Porphyrii Opuscula Selecta,* 1886; rpt. Hildesheim, 1963, and the Arabic tradition of the same work studied by Franz Rosenthal, "Arabische Nachrichten über Zeno den Eleaten," *Orientalia,* 6 (1937), pp. 30 ff., and Franz Altheim and Ruth Stiehl, *Porphyrios und Empedokles,* Tübingen, 1954, pp. 7-26.

107. See Jean Pépin, "Porphyre, exégète d'Homère," in *Fondation Hardt: Entretiens sur l'Antiquité Classique,* vol. 12, Vandoeuvres and Geneva, 1966, pp. 331–4.

108. A middle Platonic theme introduced—or reintroduced—into the school by Numenius; see H. J. Waszink, "Porphyrios und Numenios," *ibid.,* pp. 35-78.

109. See Walzer, "Porphyry and the Arabic Tradition," pp. 286–94.

110. W. Theiler, *Forschungen zum Neuplatonismus,* Berlin, 1966, pp. 2-3.

111. F. Dieterici, ed., *Alfarabi's Philosophische Abhandlungen* (Leipzig, 1890) and Albert Nader, ed., *Abū Naṣr al-Fārābī: Kitāb al-jamʿ bayna ra'yay 'l-ḥakīmayn,* Beirut, 1960; cf. Majid Fakhry, "Reconciliation of Plato and Aristotle," *Journal of the History of Ideas,* 26 (1965): 469–78.

112. *Fihrist,* p. 253/Dodge, p. 620, describes it as extant in an "old translation," that is, in a pre-Ḥunayn version.

113. See A. C. Lloyd, "Porphyry and Iamblichus," in A. H. Armstrong, ed., *Later Greek Philosophy,* pp. 286–7, and, for Porphyry's psychology, H. Dörrie, "Mittelplatonismus und Porphyrios," pp. 167-187.

114. The attribution is doubted by A. M. Goichon, trans., *Ibn Sīnā. Livre des Directives et Remarques,* Beirut and Paris, 1951, p. 448, n. 2, but without good reason; cf. W. Kutsch, "Ein arabisches Bruchstück aus Porphyrios," in *Avicenna Commemoration Volume,* Calcutta, pp. 266–7. Ibn Sīnā had his difficulties with the *Eisagoge* as well, but in the end he went along with what had become in his eyes a standard interpretation of Aristotle: see Madkour, *L'Organon,* p. 73.

115. Simon van den Bergh, trans. *Averroes' Tahāfut Al-Tahāfut* (London, 1954) 1: 154 and 2: 100; cf. *ibid.,* 2: 63.

116. Wilhelm Kutsch, ed., in "Ein arabisches Bruckhstück aus Porphyrios," pp. 268–9.

117. See Badawi, *Transmission,* pp. 114–5.

118. The evidence for an Arabic version of Galen's *Epitome* must now include the section on the *Phaedo;* see Shlomo Pines, *An Arabic Version of the Testimonium Flavianum and its Implications,* Jerusalem, 1971, pp. 73–82.

119. The Arabs also knew that the two men were not in agreement on some fundamental issues. They could read in Arabic three of Alexander's refutations of Galen; see Albert Dietrich, "Die arabische Version einer unbekannten Schrift des Alexander von Aphrodisias über die Differentia specifica," in *Nachrichten der Akademie der Wissenschaften in Göttingen* (1964, p. 96, 11; p. 97, 16; and pp. 99–100, 28.

120. Al-Mubashshir, *Mukhtār al-ḥikam,* pp. 288–93 (Badawi), dating from 1048–1049. The shorter biographies in the *Fihrist* (pp. 288–9/Dodge, pp. 680–1) may have preserved, however, in a garbled form, the name of Albinus as Galen's teacher; cf. Doge, p. 680, n. 59.

121. Ed. from Damascus MS. Zahiriyah 4871 by ʿAbdurraḥmān Badawi, *Arisṭū fī al-nafs,* Cairo, 1954. There are, however, additional MSS.; cf. Rosenthal, "Some Graeco-Arabica in Istanbul," pp. 7–9, and James Kritzeck, "Une Majmu a philosophique à Princeton," *Mélanges de l'Institut Dominicain d'Études Orientales,* 3 (1956): 379.

122. See Peters, *Aristotle and the Arabs,* p. 124, n. 84. Only the brief excerpts in Shahrastānī were incorporated into the *testimonia* in Diels, *Doxographi Graeci,* but see how Hans Daiber, *Die arabische Übersetzung der Placita Philosophorum,* Dissertation Saarbrücken, 1968.

123. Aya Sofya 2450, 4, fols. 107–135; cf. A. Altmann and S. M. Stern, *Isaac Israeli,* Oxford, 1958, p. 70.

124. See Peters, *Aristotle and the Arabs,* pp. 124–9.

125. For the Arabic Galen see Richard Walzer, "Djālīnūs," *Encyclopaedia of Islam,* new ed., s.v. and the literature cited there.

126. Ibn Abī Uṣaybiʿah. I: 204; cf. Anton Baumstark, *Geschichte der Syrischen Literatur,* Bonn, 1922, pp. 167–9.

127. Sergius's Syriac version of the *Corpus Aeropagiticum,* which is still unedited, is the most considerable testimony to Neoplatonism extant in Syriac; cf. L. Sherwood, Sergius of Reshaina and the Syriac versions of Pseudo-Dionysius," *Sacris Erudiri,* 4 (1952): 174–84. On the possibility that Sergius himself might be "Dionysius," see Hathaway, *Letters of Pseudo-Dionysius,* pp. 23–5.

128. Hathaway, *op. cit.,* p. 24: "Taken as is, if one juxtaposes the *Corpus Areopagiticum* with Sergius' Aristotelian treatises, one would roughly reproduce the outlines of the Athenian [philosophical] curriculum." But in another combination Sergius's translation of Galen and Aristotle would seem to reproduce the Alexandrian medical curriculum.

129. Karl Praechter, "Christlich-neuplatonische Beziehungen," *Byzantinische Zeitschrift,* 21 (1912): 1–27.

130. Synesius, the student of Hypatia at Alexandria, did not actively pursue philosophy, however; see H. I. Marrou, "Synesius of Cyrene and Alexandrian Neoplatonism," in Arnaldo Momigliano, ed., *The Conflict between Paganism and Christianity in the Fourth Century,* Oxford, 1963, pp. 126–50.

131. See W. Theiler, "Ammonius der Lehrer des Origenes," in *idem, Forschungen zum Neuplatonismus,* Berlin, 1966, pp. 1–45; cf. E. R. Dodds, "Numenius and Ammonius,"

in *Fondation Hardt: Entretiens sur l'Antiquité Classique,* vol. 5, Vandoeuvres and Geneva,? p. 26, and H. Dorrie, "Ammonius der Lehrer Plotins," *Hermes,* 83 (1955): 459.

132. See K. O. Weber, *Origenes der Neuplatoniker. Versuch einer Interpretation,* Munich, 1962.

133. See Jean Daniélou, "Grégoire de Nysse et le néo-platonisme de l'École d'Athènes," *Revue des Études Grecques,* 80 (1967): 39 ff.

134. Cf. Theiler, "Ammonius," pp. 8–9.

135. Cf. G. C. Lloyd, "Athenian and Alexandrian Neoplatonism," in A. H. Armstrong, ed., *Later Greek Philosophy,* p. 315.

136. Edited in Migne, *PG* 4 under the name of Maximus Confessor.

137. Cf. Urs von Balthasar, "Das Scholienwerk des Johannes von Skythopolis," *Scholastik,* 15 (1940); 16–39, and I. P. Sheldon-Williams, "The Reaction Against Proclus," in A. H. Armstrong, ed., *Later Greek Philosophy,* pp. 474–7.

Aux débuts de la réflexion théologique de l'Islam[1]

Louis Gardet
University of Toulouse

TRES VITE, trop vite peut-être, le *ʿilm al-Kalām,* "apologie défensive" ou, si l'on veut, "théologie" de l'Islam, s'est forgé ses termes techniques. Dès le IV siècle de l'hégire, les écoles constituées sont en place, avec les durcissements et systématisations inhérents à toute formation "scolastique." Ces écoles évolueront au cours des siècles, tantôt s'enrichissant et s'ouvrant à des problématiques nouvelles, tantôt se refermant sur elles-mêmes. Ce sont elles, et leurs plus notables représentants qui furent surtout étudiés jusqu'ici. Et certes, la tâche n'est pas achevée: publications de textes, recherches des influences et de leurs connexions, le *ʿilm al-kalām* classique sollicitera longtemps encore les travaux des spécialistes.

Mais c'est peut-être le *ʿilm al-kalām* en sa fraîcheur d'invention, en ses toutes premières prises de position et ses premiers affrontements, qui reste le plus mal connu. Les textes font défaut. Dans l'ensemble, ce n'est qu'à travers les traités postérieurs d'hérésiographie que ces tendances initiales nous sont parvenues, et donc à travers les raccourcis et systématisations d'école. Plusieurs chercheurs—nous aurons à les citer en cours de route—se sont mis à la tâche. Nous pensons que leurs travaux pourront éclairer bien des solutions "classiques," et nous amener à réviser des jugements trop sommaires. Mais la difficulté est grande de resituer dans leur contexte authentique et selon leurs authentiques virtualités ce que nous appellerions volontiers les affrontements du "pré-*kalām.*"

Comme il nous serait profitable de pouvoir cerner de près l'histoire sémantique et culturelle des "termes techniques" (*iṣṭilāḥāt*)! Faut-il, une fois de plus, regretter l'absence de documents suffisamment élaborés et cohérents?

En ce qui concerne les écoles muʿtazilites, l'œuvre du qāḍī ʿAbd al-Jabbār nous permet maintenant de pallier en partie à ce manque. Mais il s'agit tout de même d'une rédaction relativement tardive (V° siècle H.):

elle ne saurait suppléer aux œuvres originales des maîtres. Et fort démunis restonsnous s'il s'agit des tendances les plus anciennes, agréées ou récusées par l'*iʿtizāl* peu importe, mais qui ne s'y intègrent pas. Dans quelle mesure les ouvrages de seconde main, écrits par les Ashʿarī, Baghdādī, Ibn Ḥazm, Shahrastānī... ont-ils su en conserver le dynamisme? Est-il possible, à partir de paragraphes décousus, et groupés déjà selon des problématiques plus tradives, d'en ressaisir le cheminement, les limites sans doute, mais aussi certaines perspectives qui restaient ouvertes, et que fermera la mise en place des écoles constituées?

Les jahmiyya *et l'influence hellénistique*

Je prendrai deux exemples. D'abord celui des *jahmiyya,* que je me bornerai à rappeler brièvement; puis celui de trois penseurs, précurseurs de l'ashʿarisme, sur lesquels j'insisterai davantage.

C'est la suggestive étude du Dr. Richard Frank sur Jahm Ibn Ṣafwān et ses disciples[2] qui me permettra d'être bref à leur sujet. Il s'agit d'un courant qui fit très vite figure d'hétérodoxie. Jahm Ibn Ṣafwān avait pris part à une révolte contre les Umayyades; il fut condamné à mort et exécuté par le bras séculier en 128 H./746. Fut-il un fondateur d'école? Ou plus exactement une référence accolée à la tendance qu'anima Bishr b. Ghiyāth (m. 218 H./833)? En tout cas, je crois opportunes les remarques du Dr. Frank sur le possible ou probable *background* néoplatonicien des *jahmiyya,* et, à cette lumière, son analyse de leurs notions de *shay* ("chose" au sens de "substance"), de *qudra* ("pouvoir" d'agir), d'*istiṭāʿa* ("capacité" à agir), Les prises de position de l'école par rapport aux habituelles mises en question du *kalām,* et même du pré-*kalām,* en sortent éclairées. Le déterminisme existentiel des grands *falāsifa,* des Fārābī et des Ibn Sīnā, plus maîtres de leurs formules conceptuelles, auraient comme répondant, chez les *jahmiyya* créationnistes, le *jabr,* la "contrainte" divine; cependant que la réduction du Dieu de la prédication coranique à l'Un plotinien, "pensée qui ne pense pas," conduirait à un rigoureux dépouillement notionnel (*taʿṭil*),—bien plus rigoureux que cette "exinanition des attributs divins" en l'essence divine, reprochée aux muʿtazilites.

Autrement dit: nous serions en présence d'une influence plotinienne s'exerçant dans les cadres d'une axiomatique non hellénistique.—c'est une vue du monde directement aristotélico-plotinienne (et à influences stoïciennes) que les *falāsifa* reçurent de leurs prédécesseurs grecs. L'impact de leur foi en ses références musulmanes, si capital qu'il ait été, se surajoute à cette vue du monde plutôt qu'il ne l'infirme. C'est selon une mise en problème tout autre, celle même opérée par l'apologie défensive du *ʿilm al-kalām,* que s'insinue le néoplatonisme des *jahmiyya.* Il ne s'exprimerait pas (ou assez rarement) par des formules directement traduites du grec; il s'abriterait sous le couvert d'*iṣṭilāḥāt* élaborées par les premières discussions sur les statuts du croyant, du pécheur, du non croyant, telles que les menèrent les sectes et tendances politico-religieuses d'après Ṣiffīn. Sommes-nous sûrs que ces "termes techniques" ne traînèrent pas par la suite une coloration hellénistique dont les *jahmiyya*—et d'autres avec eux, sans doute,—les auraient revêtus? Ce n'est pas un système d'équivalences approchées qu'il faudrait établir. Il faudrait détecter, sur la pensée philosophico-théologique de l'Islam, une double ligne d'influences grecques: l'une directe (les *falāsifa*), l'autre réassumée par un mode de penser plus spécifiquement sémitique, et une vision du monde plus exclusivement inspirée par les textes du Coran. Si nous arrivions à préciser et délimiter la seconde—à laquelle Louis Massignon fait allusion plus d'une fois dans sa *Passion d'al-Ḥallāj*—je pense que nous aurions progressé, philosophiquement parlant, dans la connaissance des procédés d'investigation et de discussion qui furent à l'honneur aux premiers temps du *kalām.*

De ce point de vue, je me permettrai de contredire un peu, ou du moins de nuancer la conclusion du Dr. Frank. En raison du néoplatonisme qu'on y décèle, nous dit-il, la doctrine des *jahmiyya,* en son origine et en son esprit, est tout-à-fait incompatible avec l'esprit fondamental de l'Islam sunnite, non seulement les tenants de l'école ḥanbalite, mais aussi la plupart des docteurs en *kalām.*[3] —Les ḥanbalites, oui. La plupart des *mutakallimūn?* Je serais moins affirmatif. Je serais porté à croire que des influences grecques se sont exercées, selon ce mode indirect que j'essayais de cerner tout-à-l'heure, sur bien des lignes primtives du *kalām,* et sur les premières définitions des *iṣṭilāḥāt.* A mon sens, ce ne serait pas l'accueil de ces influences qui aurait fait des *jahmiyya* une école constamment attaquée et récusée, mais d'une part le drame politique qui aboutit à la condamnation et à l'exécution de Jahm, d'autre part l'*insuffisant* intégration de l'apport grec par Bishr b. Ghiyāth. Ce dernier fut sans doute le vrai fondateur de l'école, et la référence à Jahm n'est peut-être qu'une dénomination venue des adversaires. Avons-nous affaire à un néoplatonisme mal dominé? Ce qui, au surplus, eût empêché Bishr d'accueillir certaines vues de la Stoa, susceptibles de contrebalancer Plotin. Tant que nous ne pourrons juger des *jahmiyya* qu'à travers des réfutations qui entendent les condamner, il faudra bien nous en tenir à de simples hypothèses.

Quoi qu'il en soit, si nous arrivions à déceler, comme je le croirais possible, un apport hellénistique au second degré en la plupart des élaborations du *kalām* primitif, on en devrait conclure que la problématique aussi bien ash arite que ḥanafite-māturīdite en reçut l'héritage, même non reconnu comme tel. Cette problématique est directement musulmane, mais ce n'est peut-être pas à l'Islam seul qu'elle dut certaines perspectives. Nous aurions là un cas complexe de ces interactions inévitables en toute histoire culturelle. Il éclairerait l'opposition des "pieux Anciens" ḥanbalites aux écoles et systèmes du *kalām*, quels qu'ils soient. Il permettrait également de mieux saisir sur quel plan se déroulèrent les réfutations de la *falsafa* tentées par le *kalām* postérieur,—et pourquoi et dans quelle mesure les futures tendances ashʿarites, dites "modernes" par Ibn Khaldūn, se laissèrent tant de fois imprégner par les arguments, voire les réponses de cette *falsafa* qu'elles se devaient de combattre.

Quelques précurseurs de l'ashʿarisme

Je dois avouer que je ne suis aucunement prêt à apporter aujourd'hui de nouvelles preuves décisives de ces influences grecques que je pressens dans les toutes premières prises de position du *kalām*. Certains travaux y préludent: ainsi, l'analyse que fit Nyberg du *kumūn* de Naẓẓām. Le *kumūn,* pris dans une vue créationiste du monde, n'est pas les σπερματικοὶ λόγοι des stoïciens. Ne leur doit-il pas cependant l'impact qui en commanda l'intuition? D'autres exemples pourraient être donnés.

Mon actuel propos est moins ambitieux. Je voudrais revenir sur quelques essais de réponse du *kalām* primitif au sujet du problème de l'acte humain. Ils me semblent appeler en effet des compléments de recherche, philosophique d'une part, historique de l'autre. Ils furent tantôt utilisés, tantôt discutés ou réfutés par les écoles constituées et leurs systématisations quelque peu durcies. Peut-être, ce faisant, certaines avenues ouvertes ont-elles tourné court, cependant que les discussions s'enlisaient en des dialectiques *ad hominem* que submergera, à partir des XV°—XVI° siècles environ, le genre des "manuels" figés. C'est ici qu'il faudrait pouvoir cerner historiquement à partir de quelle date et dans quelle mesure les premiers essais de réponse ont pu être guidés par une intégration de concepts et de termes influencés par des traductions venues du grec, et s'insérant dans une problématique spécifiquement musulmane. Mais ce serait un second temps de recherche.

Pour expliquer le choix de ce thème, je me permettrai une référence personnelle. Au cours de séjours dans le *dār al-Islām,* et de causeries ou de séminaires que j'ai été amené à donner dans les Universités du Caire, d'Alger, de Rabat, plus récemment en certains cercles ou Collèges de Karachi, j'ai été frappé de voir combien une telle question reste encore vivante aux yeux des professeurs, et même de jeunes musulmans soucieux de philosophie. Par derrière les problématiques occidentales, et concurremment avec elles, c'est volontiers qu'ils s'interrogent sur les élaborations du *ilm al-kalām.* Et mon sentiment, plus d'une fois, fut que ces élaborations se présentent à eux comme des réponses contrastées et antinomiques, disons de apories, dans la mesure où elles ont subi le durcissement notionnel et systématique des manuels. En gros: liberté humaine affirmée aux dépens de la Toute-Puissance divine (muʿtazilites): Toute-Puissance divine affirmée aux dépens du fondement ontologique de la liberté humaine (ashʿarites). Les positions intermédiaires sont peu ou mal connues, peu ou mal comprises, sauf des spécialistes. Et l'actuel regain de faveur du muʿtazilisme, centré sur la défense de la raison et de la libre initiative de l'homme, risque de se solder par une minimisation du vrai problème métaphysique,—ce qui serait d'ailleurs une singulière infidélité à l'égard des maîtres anciens de Baṣra et de Baghdād.

Pour en revenir au temps du pré-*kalām,* je prendrai préférentiellement mes exemples auprès de trois auteurs des II—et III—siècles de l'hégire. Ils ne sont ni *qadariyya,* ni *murjiʾa,* ni vraiment *jabariyya*—les trois lignes de force habituellement recensées—mais semblent préfigurer sur plus d'un point ce que seront les attitudes d'esprit d'Ashʿarī lui-même et de ses premiers disciples. Ils traversent ainsi l'histoire des écoles musulmanes au temps des *Maqālāt.* Les manuels ashʿarites de l'âge suivant les mentionnent ici ou là, mais ne feront que recopier les sommaires indications du maître; et il faut reconnaître que les hérésiographes futurs ne se soucièrent guère de leur dresser une fiche précise d'identité. On peut se demander cependant si maintes thèses ashʿarites ne prirent pas naissance dans l'utilisation de leurs formules,—je dis bien utilisation de formules, avec tout le durcissement qui en peut résulter.

Il s'agit d'une part de Ḍirār b. ʿAmr et des *ḍirāriyya,* d'autre part de Najjār et de Burghūth identifié ou non avec Muḥammad b. Ḥarb (et, à la suite de Burghūth, d'Aḥmad al-Kushānī). La réunion de ces docteurs en *kalām* des premiers siècles sous une même accolade peut surprendre. Sans doute est-il possible que Najjār ait été un élève de Ḍirār, et est-il à peu-près sûr que Burghūth et Kushānī doivent être considérés comme disciples de Najjār. Mais dans les classifications par écoles et sectes, Ḍirār (dont l'acmé se situe vers 180 de l'hégire) est souvent présenté comme un précurseur des maîtres de l'*iʿtizāl* baṣrien, ou comme un "mauvais muʿtazilite," diront certains. Najjār, lui, sera recensé tantôt comme murjiʾite, tantôt comme "jabarite réformé." Mentionnons pour mémoire l'erreur de Jurjānī qui le classe, dans son *Sharḥ al-mawāqif,*[4] parmi les muʿtazilites. Et Shahrastānī fera de ces deux Anciens et de Burghūth, bien qu'à des titres divers, des *jabariyya.*

A vrai dire, ce sont les détails historiques de leurs biographies, et leurs engagements de fait, aussi bien politiques que doctrinaux (les premiers commandant souvent les seconds), qui seuls pourraient dirimer ces questions d'appartenance. Il faut souhaiter que pour chacun d'eux. Ḍirār, Najjār ou Burghūth, puisse être menée une étude aussi pertinente que celle du Dr. J. Van Ess sur *Les Qadarites et la Gailānīya de Yazīd III.*[5]

Mais présentement, ce que j'ai en vue, ce ne sont point encore les diverses silhouettes politico-doctrinales. A titre de simples préliminaires, je voudrais souligner certaines formules qu'Ashʿarī ou Shahrastānī et d'antres avec eux atrribuent à ces anciens maîtres à propos du problème de l'acte human. En les serrant de près, ces formules me semblent se référer, ou pouvoir se réféerer, à des notions qui échappèrent en fait aux *iṣṭilāḥāt* ashʿarites, ou que ces dernières durcirent en les logicisant à l'extrême.

Ḍirār b. ʿAmr

L'enjeu principal concerne les rapports réciproques à établir entre les deux dénominations *fāʿil* (agent) et *khāliq* (créateur). La réponse de Ḍirī, telle que la résume Ashʿarī,[6] est bien connue. Les manuels postérieurs se contenteront de la recopier. On peut la présenter ainsi: quand um sujet humain accomplit unc action délibérée, le terme *fāʿil* doit s'appliquer pour cette action même, en toute réalité et vérité (*ḥaqīqan*), et à Dieu et à l'homme; mais le terme *khāliq,* pour cette action toujours, désigne Dieu seul. Autrement dit: l'action humaine est créée par Dieu, bien que l'homme en soit, tout comme Dieu, l'"agent." Ḍirār en ceci s'oppose donc à la réponse muʿtazilite la plus habituelle, qui fait de l'homme le créateur (*khāliq*) de son acte. Et comme par ailleurs il déclare "acquis" (*muktasab*) par l'homme l'acte humain créé par Dieu, on peut voir en cette dernière expression une source de la fameuse "acquisition" (*kasb* ou *iktisāb*) ashʿarite.

Il y a filière historique, sans doute. Mais la perspective reste-t-elle la même? L'insistance mise par Ḍirār à souligner l'existence "en réalité" de deux agents (*fā ʿilān*) ne suggère-t-elle pas que, pour lui, l'*iktisāb* est autre chose qu'un simple rapport établi par le Vouloir divin entre l'homme et et l'acte dont il est le "lieu" (*maḥall*)? Telle sera, on le sait, la définition la plus courante en ashʿarisme. Ḍirār il est vrai, comme bien des muʿtazilites, fait de l'homme un ensemble d'accidents, sans recours à une notion de substance (*jawhar*).[7] Mais *jawhar,* en ces premiers temps du *kalām,* n'évoquaitil pas une réalité spirituelle non créée? Nous savons par ailleurs, a propos du *tawallud* ("engendrement" des causes secondes), que seul Ḍirār parmi les *ahl al-ithbāt,* note Ashʿari,[8] soutiendra que l'homme puisse agir (*yafʿala*) sur un autre sujet que lui-même. Une efficace "réelle" est donc reconnue à l'action humaine.

Nous avons ainsi: d'une part l'affirmation que l'homme et Dieu sont "vraiment" agents l'un et l'autre, bien qu'à des titres divers; d'autre part que Dieu seul "crée" et que l'homme "acquiert" l'acte accompli. Faut-il rapprocher cette opinion de la réponse proposée plus tard par les tendances ḥanafites-māturīdites? Rappelons sommairement cette dernière: Dieu crée la "racine" de l'acte, *aṣl,* en son fondement disons ontologique, mais c'est la volonté de l'homme qui lui donnera une *ṣifa,* une attribution ou qualification morale. Dès lors, le *kasb,* au lieu d'être un simple rapport dans le "réceptacle" (*maḥall*) humain, devient lui aussi une qualification, une *ṣifa* dépendant du sujet. En cette thèse, il y a bien, comme chez Ḍirār, deux agents coopérant en quelque sorte à la production de l'acte libre. Et je pense, quant à moi, que certaines ouvertures du *kalām* primitif, et de l'*iʿtizāl* avec hui, resurgiront en ces tendances dites ḥanafites-māturīdites, bien plus directement que dans les élaborations ashʿarites. Mais il faut noter aussitôt une différence qui semble fondamentale: pour les ḥanafites-māturîdites, à chacun des deux agents revient bien un effet sur l'acte, mais non sur la totalité de l'acte. En écartant tout rapprochement indu, surtout historique, disons que c'est un peu le "*duo trahentes navim*" de Molina. Rien n'indique qu'il en aille ainsi chez Ḍirār. Le sens le plus obvie des rares textes que nous avons de lui, ou qui lui sont attribuès, nous porterait à penser qu'à ses yeux chaque agent opère bien en réalité (*fāʿil ḥaqīq*) le tout de l'acte, mais selon deux aspects ou rapports différents, l'agir humain acquisitif étant subordonné à l'agir divin créateur.

On peut regretter que ces phrases sur la production de l'acte libre ne soient pas, dans nos textes, mises en regard de la notion de cause, que cette dernière soit désignée par *sabab* ou par *ʿilla.* Ne s'y trouve-t-il pas cependant comme une ouverture sur l'affirmation et la hiérarchisation de la Cause première incréée et de la cause seconde créée? C'est là où je voulais en venir, et ce serait certainement un acquis à inscrire au compte de ce tout premier *kalām,* si une telle suggestion s'avérait exacte. Pour les muʿtazilites, l'homme est absolument "créateur de ses actes" par un pouvoir créé en lui par Dieu, une fois pour toutes. Pour les ashʿarites, Dieu est à la fois seul créateur et seul agent. Pour les ḥanafites-māturīdites, c'est une part de l'acte, si l'on peut dire, qui revient en propre à Dieu, et une autre part à l'homme. Il est assez fréquent d'ajouter que, dans l'histoire culturelle musulmane, seuls les *falāsifa* disciples des Grecs ont reconnu tout ensemble la réalité de l'efficace des causes secondes, et leur subordination intrinsèque à la Cause première. Mais dès lors que la création, chez les philosophes hellénistiques, est une émanation nécessaire et voulue, non un acte libre de Dieu, cette subordination des causes va s'inscrire selon un déterminisme existentiel. On ne saurait dire en conséquence que Dieu meut (librement) les causes secondes à agir chacune selon son être, contraint ou libre. Pour les *falāsifa,* et spécialement pour Ibn Sīnā, les causes subordonnées sont une émanation nécessaire de la causalité universelle; la question du fondement ontologique de la liberté humaine ne se pose plus.

Ce serait donc le pré-*kalām* créationniste, plus que la *falsafa* émanatiste, qui aurait entrevu le mystère de l'action divine, de la motion divine dans l'agir humain. Bien sûr, les élaborations philosophiques restent, du moins en ce que nous en savons, assez sommaires. Disons qu'elles pouvaient s'avancer ou vers une analyse métaphysique, ou vers le durcissement de prises de position dialectiques. Ainsi en est-il des termes d'*iktisāb* et de *muktasib* dont se sert Ḍirār pour définir le rôle de l'agent humain dans l'acte libre. Il n'apparaît point, nous l'avons vu, qu'il s'agisse dans sa pensée d'un rapport directement et immédiatement créé par Dieu. C'est l'homme qui, accomplissant cet acte en tant que cause créée et subordonnée, se l'approprie.

J'espère n'avoir pas reporté indûment sur Ḍirār la ligne de réponse qui sera, quelques siècles plus tard, et dans un tout autre climat culturel, celle de la philosophie de l'être. Tout ce que je veux dire, c'est qu'il y avait sans doute, en ce *kalām* primitif, des virtualités que l'urgence des prochains débats dialectiques entre écoles ennemies ne pemettra guère d'actualiser. Est-il possible d'y détecter une part, directe ou indirecte, d'influence grecque? L'étude du Dr. Frank nous indiquait comment l'émanatisme plotinien a pu devenir, dans la vue créationiste des *jahmiyya,* une négation de l'acte libre de la créature. Il n'est pas écarté qu'un effort pour maintenir, dans la même vue créationniste, l'efficace de l'homme sur son acte, ait rencontré de près ou de loin des éléments d'explication venus cette fois non plus de Plotin, mais d'Aristote. Je me borne à poser ici la question. L'utilisation directe d'Aristote par les *falāsifa,* dans la perspective de leur déterminisme existentiel, n'était peut-être pas le seul apport possible de la théorie des causes, et de la transcendance de la Cause première motrice, qui meut sans être mue.

Najjār et Burghūth

Quelques mots maintenant sur Najjār et ses disciples, spécialement Burghūth: désignés par Shahrastānī comme sous-branches des *jabariyya*. Tout comme Ḍirār, ils ont certainement influencé l'*iʿtizāl* de Baṣra, mais à part l'erreur historique de Jurjānī, nul ne songerait à faire de Najjār un muʿtazilite. On sait que ʿAllāf et Naẓẓām réfutèrent plusieurs de ses thèses.

Il est assez probable, nous l'avons noté, que Najjār fut un un élève de Ḍirār, et Burghūth un élève de Najjār. Je ne dirais cependant pas que les vues de Najjār soient aussi consonantes à celles de Ḍirār que le suggère le Dr. W. Montgomery Watt.[9] Au sujet des actes humains, il semble qu'une question de vocabulaire distingue nettement Ḍirār d'une part, Najjār et Burghūth de l'autre. Nous avons vu le premier appliquer le terme de *fāʿil* ("agent") à Dieu et à l'homme, mais selon une diversité analogique d'acception,—ce qui pourrait conduire à une vue également analogique de la Cause increéée et des causes créées. *Faʿala* se diversifiait radicalement chez Ḍirār en *khalaqa* (créer) et *kasaba* (acquérir). Est-ce la difficulté de maintenir cette diversité foncière dans les cadres d'un vocabulaire unifié? Najjār et Burghūth, eux, se refuseront à désigner l'homme par des termes qui s'appliquent à Dieu. Dès lors, précise

Baghdādī résumant leur pensée, non seulement *khāliq,* mais *fāʿil* également, ne sauraient convenir à l'homme. Notions ici l'argumentation de Burghūth, que nous a conservée Ashʿarī,[10] et qui est fondée sur l'usage coranique des termes en question. Il s'agit moins d'un argument d'autorité *stricto sensu* que d'un argument d'ordre sémantique, de nominalisme sémantique si l'on veut. Il n'est pas sans annoncer la démarche d'un Ibn Ḥazm par exemple.

Déjà donc apparaît au temps de Najjār et de Burghūth ce souci d'établir jusque dans le détail du vocabulaire une dissemblance absolute entre Dieu et l'homme, qui sera certainement l'un des axes de l'ashʿarisme. Face à Dieu, seul Créateur et seul Agent en rigueur de termes, l'homme est celui qui acquiert son acte, le *muktasib.* On comprend qu'Ashʿarī ait pu voir là, plus nettement encore que chez Ḍirār, un précédent à sa notion de *kasb* ou d'*iktisāb,* telle qu'il la définit.[11] Rien n'indique cependant que Najjār et surtout Burghūth n'aient fait de l'*iktisāb* qu'un simple rapport d'attribution directement créé par Dieu comme l'acte lui-même. Pour Najjār, si Dieu est créateur de l'acte, l'homme a bien "pouvoir sur le *kasb*", *qādir ʿalā l-kasb.*[12] Quant à Burghūth, il voit dans l'acte d'obéissance au Commandement de Dieu un acte de volonté humaine, qui semble bien être, comme le dit le Dr. Montgomery Watt, un "pouvoir spontané" d'obéir. Ne serait-ce pas la raison d'une modification dans le vocabulaire technique? Alors que depuis Jaʿfar b. Ḥarb et le rāfiḍite Hishām b. al-Ḥakam, le corrélatif d'opposition (*muqābal*) se prend entre *ikhtiyār* ("libre choix") et *iḍṭirār* ("contrainte nécessitante"), Burghūth, de préférence, substitue *ṭawʿ* ("obéissance") à *ikhtiyār.*

On peut dire que l'emploi d'*ikhtiyār* ne préjuge absolument pas de la réponse au problème ontologique de la liberté humaine. Le déterminisme existentiel des *falāsifa,* aussi bien que le volontarisme divin des ashʿarites, s'y réfèrent. Si nous comparons des textes d'Ibn Sīnā et de Ghazzālī par exemple,[13] il faut reconnaître que leurs analyses, fort bien menées, mettent en lumière les rapports de la volonté et de l'intellect humains dans l'acte de choix. Mais tout reste pris chez Ibn Sīnā dans un déroulement de causes secondes qui procèdent nécessairement de la Cause première; et si Ghazzālī voit bien que c'est le jugement de l'intellect qui va commander la décision, il en conclura que cette dernière ne saurait donc être pleinement "libre" en l'homme, puisque nécessitée par le "motif de préférence." "Motif de préférence,"-c'est le *murajjih,* dont un ashʿarite aussi "moderne" que Fakhr al-Dīn al-Rāzī fera encore l'argument "décisif" contre la réalité de la liberté humaine.[14] De ce point de vue, certaines approches muʿtazilites sauvegardaient sans doute mieux les rapports intelligence-volonté dans l'acte libre.[15] Il reste qu'*ikhtiyār* sera pris avant tout d'un point de vue phénoménologique, ainsi chez Bāqillānī. Quand Jaʿfar b. Ḥarb parle d-*ikhtiyār,* on peut penser qu'il s'agit bien d'un acte conçu et voulu par l'homme. Le même terme, chez Bāqillānī et la plupart des ashʿarites, s'opposrea simplement aux actes incontrôlés, tel un tremblement incoercible de la main.[16]

De ce point de vue, le choix de *ṭawʿ* par Burghūth reste significatif. La racine n'évoque plus l'obtention d'un bien (*khayr*), mais une obéissance qui suppose, pour être obéissance, d'être acceptée comme telle par le sujet. Au surplus, dans le lexique du *kalām*, *ṭaw an* ne peut pas ne pas évoquer la dixième forme de la racine, *istiṭāʿa*, traduite ordinairement par "capacité," et qui prêta à tant de discussions. La plupart des manuels ashʿarites lui consacreront un chapitre, et les rapports entre *kasb* et *istiṭāʿa* sont lin d'être toujours clairement élucidés. En fait, le problème de l'*istiṭāʿa* fut, chez Ashʿarī et ses disciples, un héritage, subi plutôt que voulu, du tout premier *kalām*. Je ne reviendrai pas sur les définitions données au gré des écoles, j'en ai traité ailleurs.[17] Mais si variées qu'aient été les acceptions de ce mot, il semble bien que la notion première soit celle de "pouvoir" au sens de liberté d'accomplir.

Ici cependant, Ḍirār d'une part, Najjār et ses disciples de l'autre, se différencient non moins nettement que sur la notion d'acte et d'agent. Pour Ḍirār, l'*istiṭāʿa* à la fois précède et accompagne l'acte. Les muʿtazilites le suivront sur ce point. Pour Najjār, elle ne saurait être antérieure à l'acte. Selon une vue ponctuelle et discontinue des choses, qui restera dominante en *kalām*, l'*istiṭāʿa*, dit Najjār, surgit en l'instant précis où commence l'acte, et l'accompagne au long de son accomplissement. Les ashʿarites repredront, en l'urgeant, cette analyse: ils préciseront en effet que l'*istiṭāʿa* est un accident, et que l'accident ne "dure" pas; dès lors. Dieu, à chaque moment de l'acte, crée une *istiṭāʿa*, une "capacité d'agir," sans cesse renouvelée.

Nous avons ainsi: 1) chez Ḍirār, une notion de "capacité" qui semble bien un réel pouvoir d'agir, et fait de l'homme un agent qui s'approprie l'acte, non toutefois un "créateur"; 2) chez Najjār, une "capacité" qui recommence pour chaque acte, mais qui donne à l'homme—qui ne saurait être appelé *fāʿil*—"pouvoir sur le *kasb*," sur l'acquisition de l'acte; 3) chez les ashʿarites enfin, une "capacité" san durée ni réalité intrinsèque dans le sujet même qui agit. C'est là un exemple, entre bien d'autres, de ce dont l'ashʿarisme est redevable an *kalām* primitif, en même temps que de la mutation subie par les nitions en jeu.

Nous pourrions multiplier ces références. Ce ne sont que de simples approches; je les présente non sans hésitation. Sur les deux points que nous, avons effleurés: rapport des causalités divine et humaine, et analyse de l'acte humain libre, n'y eut-il pas, chez les prédécesseurs de l'ashʿarisme, dans la mesure où l'on peut considérer comme tels Ḍirār ou Najjār (et Burghūth), des possibilités d'élaborations et de distinctions qui devaient rester lettre morte?

A supposer qu'il en fût ainsi, cela devrait nous conduire à certaines révisions historiques. Traditionnellement, l'école ashʿarite se considérera comme un "juste milieu" entre *qadariyya,* partisans du libre arbitre absolu, et *jabariyya,* partisans de la "contrainte" divine. Or voici que Shahrastānī se borne à recenser parmi les *jabariyya* Jahm, Ḍirār, Najjār, Burghūth. Mais si l'hypothèse du néoplatonisme des *jahmiyya* s'avère exacte, il faut en inférer que le *jabr,* entendu comme refus de toute liberté humaine, n'est point au centre de leur système, et devrait s'expliquer par un difficile équilibre entre émanatisme et créationnisme. Quant à Ḍirār, Najjār et Burghūth, nous l'avons vu, leur "jabarisme" (ou prétendu tel) serait peut-être bien plus favorable à la réalité ontologique de la liberté humaine que la "via media" ashʿarite. Ce serait vrai surtout de Ḍirār et de sa théorie des "deux agents"; on comprend dès lors que son influence se soit exercée, mais selon des lignes fort différentes, aussi bien sur les muʿtazilites de Baṣra que sur la réaction d'al-Ashʿarī. Par ailleurs, les "termes techniques" dont s'ornent les vocabulaires se retrouvent en ashʿarisme comme en muʿtazilisme ou dans le māturīdisme postérieur. A travers les oppositions dialectiques, qui furent violentes, se manifeste ainsi, sur le double plan argumentatif et axionmatique, une unité du *ʿilm al-kalām,* quelles que soient les écoles considérées. L'opposition globale à son égard des lignes ḥanbalites ou ẓāhirites prend, par là même, un relief nouveau.

Quelle est la portée de ces suggestions? Pour en cerner la part de vérité ou d'erreur, deux lignes de recherches me sembleraient devoir être poursuivies:

1) Etudier de près la formation des *iṣṭilāḥāt,* et détecter si et comment des influences hellénistiques, que nous dirions volontiers au deuxième degré, se sont exercées; et comparer les vocabulaires si différents du *ʿilm al-kalām* à ses débuts et de la *falsafa.* Y eut-il, comme nous le suggérions, deux voies d'accès, l'une directe, l'autre indirecte, de la philosophie grecque dans la culture musulmane?

2) Dans toute la mesure du possible, cerner, en sa complexité historique et contingente, la silhouette politico-doctrinale de ces tout premiers *mutakallimūn,* qui nous restent si mal connus. L'étude déjà citée du Dr. Van Ess sur Ghaylān nous indique la voie à suivre. Sur un plan, plus doctrinal cette fois qu'historique, j'y joindrais l'étude du Dr. Madelung sur Abū Ubayd al-Qāsim et sa notion de foi,[18] ou celle du Dr. Montgomery Watt sur les rapports entre les débuts de l'imāmisme et le mu tazilisme.[19] Nous aurions grand intérêt à mieux connaître le contexte précis ou s'est formée la pensée d'un Hishām b. al-Ḥakam par example. D'autres travaux encore seraient à recenser.

Je souhaite que ces quelques aperçus, trop partiels et fragmentaires, j'en suis le premier persuadé, puissent être "revus et corrigés," et donner lieu à de nécessaires mises au point.

Notes

1. Ces pages sont la reprise corrigée d'une communication donnée au Colloque "On Early Islamic Thought, in honor of Professor Harry A. Wolfson", Harvard, avril 1971; elles inspirent par ailleurs l'un des chapitres d'un ouvrage paru en 1972, *Etudes de Philosophie et de Mystique comparées* (coll. "Histoire de la Philosophie," éd. Vrin, Paris).

2. Richard M. Frank *The Neoplatonism of Ǧahm Ibn Ṣafwān,* ap. *Le Muséon,* t. LXXVIII, 3-4, Louvain 1965, pp. 395-424.

3. *Ibid.,* p. 424.

4. Ed. du Caire 1325 H./1907, t. VIII, p. 148.

5. Ap. *Studia Islamica,* XXXI, Paris 1970, pp. 269-286.

6. *Maqālāt al-Islāmiyyīn,* éd. Md. Muḥyī al-Dīn ʿAbd al-Ḥamīd, Le Caire 1369 H./1950, t.I, p. 313.

7. *Ibid.,* t.II, p. 25.

8. *Ibid.,* t.II, p. 83. Rappelons qu'Ashʿarī s'appuie volontiers sur ceux qu'il appelle *ahl al-ithbāt* comme sur des prédécesseurs valables.

9. *Free Will and Predestination in Early Islam,* London 1948, p. 106.

10. *Maqālāt, éd. cit.,* II, p. 198.

11. Et de même pour les notions de *tawfīq, hudā, khidhlān,* etc.

12. Cf. *Maqālāt.* II, p. 248. Et Jurjānī (*Sharḥ al-mawāqif,* loc. cit.) reprochera à Najjār, ainsi qu'à Isfarā'inī d'ailleurs, d'avoir soutenu que "deux causes" (l'homme et Dieu) agissent simultanément, et sous le même rapport, sur la totalité de l'acte. Ce qui est impossible, ajoute-t-il, car deux causes, selon l'adage grec, ne sauraient produire un seul effet.— Est-ce vraiment "sous le même rapport" que Najjār envisage cette action des "deux causes"?

13. Voir entre autres, pour Ibn Sīnā, Kitāb al-Shifā', Ilāhiyyāt, Le Caire 1960, t. II, pp. 387-388, et *Risāla fī l-ʿishq,* éd. Mehren ("Traités Mystiques" III), Leyde 1894, pp. 9-14; pour Ghazzālī, *Iḥyā' ʿulūm ad-dīn,* éd. du Caire 1325 H./1933, t.IV, pp. 219-220.

14. *Muḥaṣṣal,* éd. du Caire, s.d., p. 141.

15. V.g. ʿAbd al-Jabbār, *al-Mughnī* VI (*al-Irāda,* 2), éd. du Caire, pp. 81 et ss.

16. Cf. *Kitāb al-tamhīd,* éd. R. J. McCarthy, Baghdād-Beyrouth 1957, p. 308.

17. Cf. *Les grands problèmes de la théologie musulmane: Dieu et la destinée de l'homme,* éd. Vrin, Paris 1967, pp. 65-67.

18. *Early Sunnī Doctrine concerning Faith as reflected in the* Kitāb al-Īmān *of Abū ʿUbayd al-Qāsim b. Sallām (d. 224/839),* ap. *Studia Islamica* XXXII, Paris 1970, pp. 233-254.

19. *Sidelights on Early Imāmite Doctrine,* ap. *Studia Islamica* XXXI, pp. 287-298.

La logique d'Aristote chez les Mutakallimūn

IBRAHIM MADKOUR
Academy of Arabic Language

NOUS AVONS déjà essayé, il y a plus de trente ans, de faire l'histoire de l'*Organon* dans le monde arabe. Nous avons expliqué comment il fut traduit, interprêté, et appliqué en arabe. Nous avons également attiré l'attention sur le rôle qu'il a joué dans les différentes écoles musulmanes. Les philosophes l'ont bien adopté avec la plupart des additions qui lui avaient été ajoutées auparavant. Les théologiens s'en sont servis pour défendre leurs crédos. Les juristes en ont fait usage pour établir leur méthode legislative.[1] Plus récemment, nous avons traité longuement l'influence de la logique d'Aristotle sur la grammaire arabe.[2] Aujourd'hui, nous voulons nous arrêter un peu au rôle qu'il a joué dans la dogmatique musulmane.

I. Au fond, une dogmatique n'a rien à voir contre la logique elle-même. Au contraire, elle peut lui fournir une arme solide pour défendre ses idées et ses principes. C'est ainsi, pendant six siècles environ au moyen âge, que l'on a considéré la logique comme base de toute spéculation. Elle fut la première branche de la philosophie qui pût fraterniser avec la théologie chrétienne.[3] Certains tableaux du moyen âge sont assez significatifs sous ce rapport. St. Augustin (+430 A.D.) s'y montre avec la théologie scolastique, tenant en main l'arc de la controverse. On y voit aussi Boëce (+524 A.D.) et la théologie démonstrative avec son triangle représentant les trois figures du syllogisme.[4] En un mot, l'Eglise qui surveillait la pensée en Occident durant le moyen âge autorisa l'étude de l'*Organon.*

Il en est de même de la théologie musulmane. Nous savons que l'*Organon* fut traduit en arabe d'assez bonne heure. Déjà au huitième siècle, on connaissait quelques unes de ses parties et presque à la fin du neuvième siècle il était entièrement traduit, y compris ses commentaires anciens. C'est par l'intermediaire de ces commentaires que certains principes de la logique stoicienne on été transmis au monde musulman. La quatrième figure du syllogisme attribuée à Galien n'a pas manqué, elle-aussi, de trouver son chemin vers la culture arabe. Une fois traduit, l'*Organon* fut résumé et commenté par des auteurs arabes. Parmi eux, se trouvent des mutakallimūn dont on peut citer Ibn Karnīb (+dixième siècle) et Abou Zaid al-Balkhī (+934 A.D.).[5] Le fameux Kindī (+873 A.D.) peut être considéré à la fois un philosophe et un théologien, il était un moʿtazilite avant d'être philosophe.

II. En fait, pendant cette période du mouvement traducteur s'est formée la première grande école théologique musulmane, à savoir, l'école moʿtazilite. C'est elle qui a fondé la théologie musulmane (*al-Kalām*). Avides de science, ses grands chefs voulaient tout savoir; ils s'intéressaient aux différentes cultures orientales et occidentales. Ils ont bien connue Aristote et ses grands écrits. Parlant de lui, Jāḥiẓ (+868) l'appelait le logicien (*Ṣāḥib al-Manṭiq*).[6] Il n'y a pas de doute qu'à certains égards ils s'en sont inspirés. Certes, ils se sont opposés à quelques uns de ses principes physiques et métaphysiques, mais jusqu'à présent, rien ne prouve qu'ils ont critiqué sa logique. Siyūṭī (d. 1505) en a déjà parlé, cependant il n'a fait que donner des citations générales qui ne signifient pas grand chose.[7] A sa suite, M. Nashar est revenu à la question sans rien préciser.[8]

Les premiers Moʿtazilites étaient de grands dialecticiens qui cherchaient à defendre leur dogme contre les athés (*al-zanādiqa*), les hérétiques (*almolḥidīn*), les dualists et les polythéistes (*al-mochrikīn*), mazdéistes, manéchéens et sabéens. Ils nous font penser aux premiers apologistes du christianisme.

Mais leur défense est une des plus énergiques que l'on ait jamais connu dans l'histoire des sectes religieuses. Parmi eux, on peut citer; un Wāçil ibn ʿAṭā' (+747), un Naẓẓām (+845), un ʿAllāf (+849) et Jāḥiẓ. Ils ont tous fait preuve d'un talent marqué dans la discussion et la controverse, talent grâce auquel ils ont pu lutter contre leurs adversaires nombreux. Aussi apelle-t-on en général les Moʿtazilites des dialecticiens (*al-jadaliyyīn*)[9] et chaque dialectique a son art.

Ils ont composé beaucoup de dissertations et de traités pour réfuter les opinions adverses. Hélàs, peu de chose de leurs écrits nous est arrivé et on ne trouve aue des fragments de leurs discussions dans les grandes ouvrages littéraires arabes, tels que: *al-Bayān wa l-Tabyīn* de Jāḥiẓ, *al-Kāmil* d'al-Mubarrad (+898), *Kitāb al-Aghānī* d'al-Iṣfahānī (+966) et *al-Amālī* d'Abū ʿAlī al-Qālī (967). Nous devons mentionner également *Kitāb al-Intiṣār* qui est proprement un écrit polémique. Son auteur, al-Khayyāṭ (+910), est un grand Moʿtazilite du dixième siècle qui réfute les accusations injustes d'Ibn al-Rawandī (dixième siècle).[10] Nous avons récemment publié la majeure partie d'*al-Mughnī* qui est une grande encyclopédie moʿtazilite. Son auteur, ʿAbd al-Jabbār (+1024) est, lui-aussi, un polémiste de premier ordre.[11]

Cependant, la dialectique des premiers Moʿtazilites s'appuie essentiellement sur l'éloquence et l'ingéniosité. Elle se sert de certains termes logiques, mais elle est avant tout une dialectique oratoire qui doit toute sa force aux expressions choisies et à l'interprétation des faits naturels. Ibn Khaldūn (+1406) avait déjà remarqué avec raison que les premiers théologiens n'ont pas beaucoup tiré profit de la logique aristotélicienne.[12]

De notre côté, nous avons constaté que la dixième siècle est une transition entre deux périodes distinctes dans l'histoire de la dogmatique musulmane. Il est marqué deux phénomènes très importants. D'une part, l'école ashʿarite commence à prendre la place de l'école moʿtazilite. D'autre part, à la dialectique oratoire aue nous venons d'indiquer se substitute une dialectique savante et ordonnée.[13] Nous n'avons pas à nous occuper ici de la doctrine des ashʿarites, nous voulons simplement dire un mot de leur méthode dialectique.

III. Ashʿarī (+935) avait un talent polémique aussi développé que celui des premiers Moʿtazilites, et auquel il a ajouté une technique ces derniers n'ont pas connue. C'est par le contact des philosophes contemporains et par les écrits logiques d'Aristote qu'il a appris cette technique. La syllogistique aristotélicienne est devenue entre ses main une arme solide de la polémique religieuse. Son *Ibāna,* qui est sans doute son dernier écrit, nouse renseigne suffisamment sur sa méthode dialectique.[14] Il discute dans ce livre les opinions de ses adversaires moʿtazilites. Il distingue toutes les faces d'une même question, donne sur chaque point les arguments contraires, et finit par choisir entre l'affirmation et la négation. Chose digne de remarque la dialectique ashʿarite offre beaucoup d'analogie avec celle des scolastiques latins, sans doute parce qu'elles ont subi toutes deux des influences identiques.[15] Comme les latins, Ashʿarī procède par division et classification, essaie de tout ramener à la forme du syllogisme et fait appel à l'autorité religieuse. Une de ses expressions fréquentes est celle-ci: "si l'on dit . . . nous disons" (*fa'in qīl qolto*). Cette formule, par laquelle il envisage toutes les hypothèses possibles relatives à un problème donné et qui fait époque dans la scolastique arabe, ressemble, dans une large mesure, à la méthode *sic et non* très connue dans la scolastique occidentale. Ashʿarī adopte en outre un procédé dont les dialecticiens latins font souvent usage et qui consiste à multiplier le nombre des arguments; par exemple, pour démontrer la possibilité de voir Dieu dans l'au-delà, il donne une dizaine d'arguments.[16] Enfin, habile dialecticien, il réfute ses adversaires par leurs propres arguments, c'est la *al-ilzām* des Arabes ou l'*argumentum ad hominem* des Latins. A côté de cette technique, il excelle dans les analyses des mots et il suit la méthode qu'Aristote avait pratiquée dans ses études sur les synonymes et les homonymes.

Ses disciples ont suivi son exemple et ont développé son art dialectique. Ils ont, peut-être, fait mieux que lui l'usage de la logique aristotélicienne.

Déjà Bāqillānī (+1013), le second fondateur de l'école ashʿarite, ouvra son *Tamhīd* par une sorte de théorie de la connaissance et traite du raisonnement (*istidlāl*).[17] Nous savons qu'il a été envoyé par ʿAḍoḍ al-Dawla (+983) à Constantinople pour discuter avec les Chrétiens sur place des problèmes religieux.[18] Ibn Khaldūn a remarqué que Bāqillānī avait posé, le premier, les principes rationnels de la spéculation et de la démonstration théologique.[19]

Al-Jowaynī, Imām al-Ḥaramein, (+1088) en a fait autant, il s'occupe, lui-aussi, de la théorie de la connaissance et du raisonnement dans l'introduction de ses grands livres qui nous sont arrivés, à savoir: *Kitāb al-Irshād* et *Kitāb al-Shāmil.*[20] C'est une tradition établie et suivie par presque tous les auteurs postérieurs. Il nous a laissé également un écrit encore manuscrit, qui s'appelle "*al-Jadal*" (la Dialectique) et qui porte une marque évidente de la logique aristotélicienne.[21]

Son grand élève, al-Ghazālī (+1111), en particulier, a mis la logique au service de la théologie d'une manière plus savante et très fine. Il est par excellence le plus grand dialecticien de l'Islam: son combat contre les philosophes et auquel il consacre son *Tahāfot al-Falāsifa* est un des rares exemples de la polémique philosophique et religieuse. Sa dialectique est basée sur une connaissance profonde de l'aristotélisme et des idées philosophiques. Il s'intéresse à la logique, lui consacre plusieurs écrits et l'applique non seulement à la théologie, mais aussi à la jurisprudence.[22] Dans sa lutte contre la philosophie, il met la logique hors cause, car elle s'occupe des lois générales de la pensée et sur lesquelles nous sommes tous d'accord.[23] D'ailleurs, la logique n'est pas une affaire propre aux philosophes, c'est aussi une partie du *Kalām* que les théologiens appellent *Kitāb al-Naẓar (livre de la spéculation)* ou *Kitāb al-Jadal (livre de la dialectique).*[24] Il essaie, lui-même, de faire un tableau de ce qu'il appelle "*al-Mawāzīn alʿaqliyya*" (les balances rationnelles) qu'il prétend avoir tiré du Coran. Ces "Mawāzīn" ne sont rien d'autre que le syllogisme aristotélicien dans ses différentes formes; catégorique, conditionnelle et hypothétique.[25]

Inutile de remarquer que l'histoire de l'école ashʿarite est encore à faire, nous ne pouvons le tracer ici en entier, nous nous contentons de citer les grands noms de cette école. Il n'y a pas de doute que Shahrastānī (+1153) en est un, c'est un contemporain de Ghazālī qui était versé dans l'histoire des sectes et des systèmes théologiques et philosophiques. Par son *Milal wa Niḥal,* nous l'avons connu depuis longtemps. Pour avoir une idée de sa méthode dialectique, il suffit jeter un coup d'œil sur son livre précieux, *Nihāyat al-Iqdām fī ʿIlm al-Kalām.* On y trouve une dialectique très serrée, savante et bien ordonnée. Elle use beaucoup de la terminologie aristotélicienne, et particulièrement en logique que Shahrastānī connait à fond. Elle emploie à outrance le syllogisme conditionnel et hypothétique.[26]

Après Shahrastānī, vient Fakhr al-Dīn al-Rāzī (+1208) qui est, pour nous à bien des égards, une image parfaite de Ghazālī, avec peut-être moins d'originalité et moins de profondeur. Sa dialectique est fondée, comme celle d'Ashʿarī, sur la multiplicité des arguments, et dominée par un esprit philosophique comme celle de Ghazālī. Il procède, comme ses devanciers, par définition et division. C'est surtout par des propositions disjonctives qu'il épuise les termes de chaque alternative, montre les idées sous leurs différents aspects, tourne et retourne l'objet dans tous les sens. Il emploie constamment cette methode dans son *Asās al-Taqdīṣ*, quie est un de ses grands écrits polémmiques.[27] Comme Baqillʿānī et Jowaynī, il donne dans son *Moḥaṣṣal Afkār al-Mutaqaddimīn wa l-Muta'akhkhirīn* une introduction portant sur la théorie de la *Muta'akhkhirīn* connaissance et traitant quelques données logiques.[28]

Rāzī, semble-t-il, est le dernier grand représentant de l'école ashʿarite. Ses successeurs sont pour la plupart des compilateurs qui suivent fidèlement la doctrine et la méthode de leurs devanciers, ou des auteurs qui se contentent d'abréger les ouvrages précedents. Parmi les premiers, on peut citer ʿAḍoḍ al-Dīn al-Igī (+1354), auteur d'*al-Mawāqif* qui a eu un grand succès dans l'enseignement théologique musulman durant les cinq siècles derniers. C'est une vaste compilation qui contient à la fois de la théologie et de la philosophie, y compris la logique.[29] Chose curieuse, après la grande attaque de Ghazālī, la philosophie n'a trouvé asile que chez théologiens et quelques mystiques. Parmi les seconds, nous pouvons mentionner Laqānī (+1631), auteur d'*al-Jawhara* qui est un traité de dogmatique en vers.[30] Tous ces auteurs poussent davantage l'emploi du syllogisme dans la démonstration théologique. Ils tiennent à prouver chacun des attributs divins par un syllogisme spécial.

IV. L'influence de la logique aristotélicienne sur la théologie musulmane, qui se fait sentir à partir du dixième siècle, ne se cantonne pas dans l'école ashʿarite; elle la dépasse et elle agit sur d'autres écoles. On peut la constater chez les Moʿtazilites postérieurs, tels que Khayyāṭ et ʿAbd al-Jabbār dont nous avons déjà parlé.

Un grand traditionaliste (*Salafī*) du onzième siécle, Ibn Ḥazm (+1062) a subi la même influence. On dit à tort qu'il a critiqué et contredit la logique d'Aristote.[31] Comme l'a fait observer Goldziher, on peut affirmer qu'il n'y a rien de pareil chez lui et qu'au contraire il semble estimer beaucoup la logique aristotélicienne.[32] Sa dialectique s'appuie sur des règles d'Aristote, aussi bien que celle des autres théologiens musulmans. Dans son grand ouvrage, *al-Fiṣal fil Milal wa l-Aḥwā' wa l-Niḥal,* il se sert, pour ainsi dire, d'Aristote, le logicien, pour réfuter Aristote, le métaphysicien.[33] Sa dialectique redoutable tire souvent sa force d'une fermeté méthodologique.

Il y a enfin une autre école sunnite, soeur de l'école ashʿarite et sur laquelle nous sommes mal renseignés. Un bon livre de son fondateur,

Abū Manṣūr al-Māturīdī (+944) vient de paraître, il s'appelle *Kitāb al-Tawḥīd.* Dans ce livre, Māturīdī esquisse quelques lignes concernant les sources de notre connaissance et les différentes sortes d'arguments que nous employons.[34] Dans son exposé, il emploie quelques termes philosophiques et logiques, par exemple, la quiddité, l'essence, la substance et l'accident. Ses grands successeurs, comme Abū al-Muʿīn al-Nasafī (+1114) dont les écrits théologiques sont encore manuscrits et Najm al-Dīn al-Nasafī (+1142), auteur d'*al-Aqāʿid*[35] adoptent la même dialectique que les Ashaʿrites et se servent beaucoup de la logique aristotélicienne.

V. Ibn Khaldūn est, croyons-nous, le premier qui ait reconnu l'influence de la logique sur les études théologiques musulmanes. Il fait remonter cette influence à Imām al-Ḥaramein qui, d'après lui introduit pour la première fois la méthodologie aristotélicienne dans les sciences dogmatiques de l'Islam.[36] Dans un article savant de *l'Encyclopedie de l'Islam,* MacDonald reproduit exactement cette thèse.[37] Nous avons déjà montré la part d'Imām al-Ḥaramein dans l'établissement de la méthode dialectique et dans son application aux recherches théologiques. Mais nous croyons avoir suffisamment démontré qu'Ashʿarī est le vrai initiateur de cette méthode qui s'est developpé dans son école par la suite.

Il y en a qui sous-estiment aujourd'hui le rôle joué par la logique d'Aristote dans le monde arabe ou qui le nient completement.[38] C'est sans doute sous l'influence d'un certain traité d'al Siyūṭī publié dernierement et auquel nous avons fait mention auparavant. Mais au fond ce traité ne prouve rien, car il porte surtout sur *ʿIlm al-Kalām* (la théologie), il donne des citations qui s'y opposent et qui interdisent même son enseignement. Siyūṭī cite en effet encore une phrase attribuée à Shāfiʿī (+820), disant que "les musulmans ne se sont mise en désaccord que lorsqu'ils abandonné la langue arabe et aimé la langue d'Aristote".[39] Mais là aussi, Shāfiʿī ne vise que des problèmes théologiques, il fait allusion plutôt à la grande querelle de son temps concernant la création du Coran (*Miḥnat Khalq al-Qor'ān*). Je n'ai pas besoin de faire remarquer qu'à son époque, l'*Organon* d'Aristote était à peine connu.

D'ailleurs Siyūṭī, lui-même, avoue qu'il n'aime pas la logique et qu'il ne l'a jamais bien connu. Il en a même eu une forte deception, il lui est arrivé de croire qu'il est une autorité en matière du droit musulman, mais ses contemporains ne l'ont pas accepté. Car il ne connaissait pas la logique qui est une condition indispensable pour avoir doit à ce titre.[40] Dira-t-on donc que c'est par vengeance que Siyūṭī a fait ce procès? D'ailleurs, le fait d'imposer cette condition, pour être une autorité juridique, signifie que la logique continue jusqu'au seizième siècle à jouer son rôle dans la culture arabe.

En réalité, comme nous l'avons déjà dit, Ghazālī dans son attaque contre la philosophie tenait à sauver la logique. Mais la postérité ne l'a pas suivi fidèlement. Déjà au treizième siècle deux grands traditionalistes, Ibn al-Ṣalāḥ (+1245) et son élève al-Nawāwī (+1277) ont interdit l'enseignement de la logique.[41] Bien d'autres ont soutenu au contraire le point de vue de Ghazālī. Siyūṭī cherche donc à appuyer Ibn al Ṣalāḥ et à prouver l'interdiction qu'il avait lancée.[42] Un logicien algérien de seizième siècle, al-Akhḍarī, auteur, du *Sollam*, a tranché la question. Pour lui, l'enseignement de la logique est permis à tous ceux qui ont un esprit mûr et une connaissance suffisante du Coran et du Ḥadīth.[43] C'est grâce à cette solution que la logique n'a pas été aussi persécutée que les autres branches de la philosophie. Elle a pu être enseignée jusqu'à nos jours, dans les écoles et les mosquées.

VI. Dire que la logique d'Aristote a joué un grand rôle dans le monde arabe n'implique pas qu'elle a toujours été adoptée purement et simplement. Au contraire, elle a soulevée des objection et a subi des attaques, pas moins sévères que celles des Stoïciens et des sceptiques grecs. Deux grands-penseurs musulmans, en particulier, s'en chargent; l'un mystique, Suhrawardī (+1190), communément nommé *al-Sheikh al-Maqtūl,* l'autre traditionaliste déclaré, Ibn Taymiyya (+1328), le polémiste acharné.

Ce n'est pas banal qu'un mystique illuministe s'occupe du rationalisme. Mais n'oublions pas que Suhrawardī est un mystique philosophe qui garde une place pour la pensée discursive à côté de la pensée intuitive. C'est par l'illumination, dit-il d'ailleurs, qu'il est arrivé à redresser la discussion. Suhrawardī critique la logique d'Aristote d'une manière assez habile, il accepte sa ligne générale, en rectifiant quelques-unes de ses parties. C'est une critique qui cherche d'après lui à former une logique "plus ordonée, plus précise et moins difficile à saisir."[44]

Sans entrer trop dans le détail, nous signalons seulement deux points. Le premier, Suhrawardī remarque que la théorie aristotélicienne de la définition est difficile à appliquer, car elle se base sur l'essence et la quiddité qui sont des notions métaphysiques.[45] Comment peut-être découvrir les caractères essentiels d'un objet et les avoir tous? Pour définir, il suffit de donner quelques caractéristiques qui expliquent l'objet le distinguent des autres. Par ce moyen, nous pouvons nous servis facilement de la définition dans les différentes sciences.[46] Suhrawardī voit par là le rôle méthodologique de la définition et sa place a un point de vue tout à fait modern.

Le deuxieme, il connait les quatres formes de la proposition admises par Aristote, mais il préfère l'universelle affirmative et nécessaire, tout en reconnaissant l'utilité des négatives et des particulières.[47] Il appelle cette universelle "la décisive" (*al-battāta*) et cherche à convertir toutes les autres formes en elle, c'est elle qui sert dans la science.[48] Il connaît également les quatre figures du syllogisme, mais d'accord avec Aristote il n'admet pas la quatrième. Pour lui, comme pour le philosophe grec, la première est la plus parfaite, il s'efforce de convertir les deux autres en elle.[49] A part son idée de la définition, Suhrawardī ne s'éloigne pas trop du Stagirite.

Au contraire, le débat d'Ibn Taymiyya est plutôt destructif, il a pour but de se débarrasser complètement de la logique et des logiciens. Ce grand dialecticien est très véhément et il accable son adversaire par une série d'objections. Il analyse son sujet de différentes façons et à chacune de ses faces il donne des coups mortels. Pour réfuter les logiciens, il compose un livre de 550 pages qui a été reproduit sommairement par Siyūṭī, un siècle et demi plus tard.[50] Ce livre porte sur la définition et la démonstration qui représentent, aux yeux d'Ibn Taymiyya, toute la logique. Il suit en cela, sans doute Ghazālī qui avait divisé la logique en deux parties distinctes, la définition et la démonstration.[51] Nous devons remarquer que cette réfutation ne vise pas uniquement Aristote, mais aussi ses disciples arabes, en particulier Ibn Sīnā et Fakhr al-Dīn al-Rāzī.[52] Elle est aussi liéé intimement à la théologie, parce qu'elle rejette les définitions et les démonstrations qui ne conviennent pas aux dogmes de l'Islam. Pour Ibn Taymiyya, la révélation est au-dessus de la raison.

S'attaquant à la définition, il soulève plusieurs objections. Sans nous arrêter à un certain verbiage, nous en donnons seulement deux. Ibn Taymiyya remarque d'abord que la définition véritable (*al-ḥadd al-ḥaqīqī*) est difficile à faire.[53] Cette remarque à été faite par d'autres, Suhrawardī l'a déjà dite. Ibn Taymiyya ajoute ensuite que cette définition est basée sur une distinction fausse de l'essentiel (*al-dhātī*) et de l'accidentel (*al-ʿaraḍī*). Les logiciens, eux-mêmes, confondent l'essence avec l'accident (*al-ʿaraḍ*) inséparable. Rejetons donc la définition véritable et contentons-nous de la definition nominale (*al-ḥadd al-lafẓī*).[54]

Ibn Taymiyya consacre la majeure partie de son livre à la théorie de la démonstration. Il commence par la proposition, élément principal du syllogisme, et par une dialectique artificielle elle refuse sa forme universelle.[55] Si cette forme est refusée, il n'y a plus moyen d'avoir un syllogisme productif. D'ailleurs le syllogisme ne nous apprend rien de nouveau, car sa conclusion est continue dans ses prémisses.[56] Là, notre dialecticien touche à la vieille objection soulevée contre Aristote et son syllogisme. Sans mentionner le paralogisme, "*Muṣādara ʿala al-maṭlūb*" (Pétition de principe), il en donne le sens. De plus, pourquoi exige-t-on deux prémisses pour former un syllogisme? D'une seule on peut tirer une conclusion.[57] Ibn Taymiyya avoue qu'il a appris cette idée d'un penseur chiʿite du dixième siècle, Ḥasan Ibn Mūsā al-Nobakhtī. Enfin il réfuse le syllogisme, l'analogie et l'induction qui sont les trois sortes du raisonnement reconnues par Aristote et ses disciples arabes. Il cherche à les remplacer par d'autres moyens de demonstration auxquels nous ne nous arrêtons pas.[58]

La logique d'Aristote a subi plusieurs critiques dans l'antiquité et dans les temps modernes. Celle d'Ibn Taymiyya est sans doute la plus longue et la plus détaillée. Il faut noter néanmoins qu'elle contient beaucoup de répétitions et de digressions. Elle n'est pas toujours fondée; elle est plutôt dogmatique que rationnelle. Elle cherche à sauver la dogmatique musulmane des fausses définitions et démonstrations, et par là elle est très troublante. Cependent après elle et malgré elle, la logique aristotélicienne continue, comme nous l'avons dit, à être enseignée dans le monde arabe.

Pour terminer, nous devons signaler que si les arabes ont adopté la méthodologie aristotélicienne, ils ont eu une méthodologie propre à eux, aussi bien en jurisprudence qu'en théologie. Dans le domaine du droit musulman (*al-fiqh*), ils ont fondé une nouvelle science, "*ʿIlm Uṣūl al-Fiqh*" (science des principes du droit). Cette science est une méthodologie très riche et assez originale. On y trouve des analyses assez intéressantes, des lois et des méthodes d'induction que l'on peut comparer à celles d'un Bacon ou d'un J. S. Mill.[59]

Dans leur polémique continuelle entre sectes et entre partisans des différents systèmes juridiques, les musulmans ont été amenés à élaborer une "science des règles de la recherche et de la discussion" (*ʿIlm ādāb al-baḥth wa l-monāẓara*). Cette science remonte au onzième siècle; elle à été fondée par al-Bazdawī (+1090) et developpée par la suite.[60] Elle a pour but, comme l'indique son nom, de fixer certaines régles qui servent dans la discussion pour échapper à sa longeur ou à sa briéveté. Elle s'occupe de la définition, de la division et du raisonnement.[61] Elle cherche surtout à éviter les sophismes et les jeux des mots. Voilà encore une parenté entre la science arabe de *Jadal* et la vieille *Topique* grecque d'Aristote.

Notes

1. Ibrāhīm Madkour, *L'Organon d'Aristote dans le monde arabe,* Paris, 1934, 1969.
2. Ibrāhīm Madkour, *Majallāt majmaʿ al-lugha al-ʿArabiyya,* le Caire, 1953, 7: 338.
3. A. Franck, *Esquisse d'une histoire de la logique,* Paris, 1838, pp. 217-218.
4. E. Renan, *Averroès et l'averroisme,* 8th ed., Paris, 1925, p. 321.
5. Ibn al-Nadīm, *al-Fihrist,* le Caire, 1930, p. 350.
6. Jāḥiẓ, *al-Ḥayawān,* ed. by Sasy (Cairo, n.d.), 1:85, 27:18, 222:162, 4:52, 5:147, 156; 7:72.
7. Al-Siyūṭī, *Ṣawn al-Monṭiq wa-l-kalām ʿan fann al-monṭiq wa-l-kalām,* ed. by Nashar, le Caire, 1947, p. 18.
8. Nashar, *Manāhij al-Baḥth ʿind mufakkirī al-Islām,* le Caire, 1947, pp. 68-69.
9. Masʿoudī, *Morūj al-dhahab*, Paris: 1861-77, 2:401.

10. al-Khayyāṭ, *al-Intiṣār,* ed. by Nyberg, le Caire, 1925.

11. Abd al-Jabbār, *al-Mughnī,* le Caire, 1957.

12. Ibn Khaldūn, *Muqaddima,* Beyrouth, 1874, p. 406.

13. Madkour, *L'Organon,* pp. 252-253.

14. Ashʿarī, *al-Ibāna ʿan oṣūl al-diyāna,* le Caire, 1900.

15. Sur la méthode dialectique des Latins, voir Hauréau, *Histoire de la philosophie scolastique,* Paris 1872-80, p. 288; Picavet, *Hist. des philosophies médiévales,* Paris, 1907; pp. 11, 62.

16. Ashʿarī, *al-Ibāna,* p. 13.

17. Bāqillānī, *Kitāb al-Tamhīd,* Beyrouth, 1957, p. 6-14.

18. Ibn ʿAsākir, *Tabyīn Kādhib al-Muftarī fī mā nusiba ilā al-ʿAshʿarī,* Damas, 1928, p. 217.

19. Ibn Khaldūn, *Muqaddima,* p. 406.

20. Jowaynī, *al-Irshād,* le Caire, 1950, pp. 8-15; *al-Shāmil fī uṣūl al-Dīn,* Alexandrie, 1969, pp. 97-105.

21. Mme Fawqiyya Ḥusein, *al-Jowaynī,* le Caire, 1964, pp. 92-113.

22. Ghazālī, *Maqāṣid al-Falāsifa,* le Caire, 1913, *Miḥakk al-Naẓar,* le Caire, s.d.; *Miʿyār al-Ilm,* le Caire, 1927, *al-muṣṭafā,* le Caire, 1902.

23. Ghazālī, *Maqāṣid,* p. 8.

24. Ghazālī, *Tahāfot al-Falāsifa,* le Caire, 1903, p. 5.

25. Ghazālī, *al-Qisṭās al-Mostaqīm,* le Caire, 1934.

26. Shahrastānī, *Nihāyatu-l-Iqdām,* London, 1934.

27. Rāzī, *ʿAsās al-Taqdīs,* le Caire, 1910, pp. 41-42, 110-11.

28. Rāzī, *Muḥaṣṣal Afkār al-Mutaqaddimīn wa-l-Mutaʾakhkhirīn,* le Caire, 1865.

29. Al-Igī, *Mawāqif,* le Caire, 1948.

30. Laqānī, *Al-Jawhara,* le Caire, 1865.

31. Van Arendonk, s.v. "Ibn Ḥazm", dans *Encyclopédie de l'Islam,* tome 2, 408.

32. Goldziher, *Die Zahiriten,* Leipzig, 1884, p. 157.

33. Ibn Ḥazm, *al-Fiṣla,* le Caire, 1928, pp. 6, 8.

34. Maturīdī, *Kitāb al-Tawḥīd,* Beyrouth, 1970, pp. 3-7.

35. Nasafī, *al-ʿAqāʿid al-Nasafiyya,* le Caire, 1948.

36. Ibn Khaldūn, *Muqaddima,* p. 406.

37. MacDonald, s.v. "Kalām" dans *l'Encyclopedie de l'Islām,* tome 2, 716.

38. Nashār, *Manāhij al-Baḥth,* p. 68-69.

39. Siyūṭi, *Ṣawn al-Monṭiq.*

40. Siyūṭī, *Ṣawn al-Monṭiq,* pp. 1-3.

41. Ibn al-Ṣalāḥ, *Fatāwa Ibn al-Ṣalāḥ,* le Caire, 1930.

42. Siyūṭī, *Ṣawn al-Monṭiq,* p. 8.

43. Al-Akhḍarī, *al-Sollam,* le Caire, 1896, p. 5.

44. Suhrawardī, *Ḥikmat al-Ishrāq,* dans *le commentaire de Shīrāzī,* Tehran, pp. 15-16.

45. *Ibid.,* pp. 59-63.

46. *Ibid.,* p. 52.

47. *Ibid.,* p 71.

48. *Ibid.,* p. 84.

49. *Ibid.,* p. 100.

50. Ibn Taymiyya, *ar-Radd ʿala al-Manṭiqiyyīn,* Bombay, 1949; Siyūṭī, *Jahd al-Qarīḥ fī Tajrīd al-Naṣīḥa,* ed. par Nashar, le Caire, 1947.

51. Ghazālī, *Miḥakk,* pp. 4-6.

52. Ibn Taymiyya, *ar-Radd,* pp. 141, 390, 450.

53. *Ibid.,* p. 9.

54. *Ibid.,* p. 51-52.

55. *Ibid.,* pp. 107-124.

56. *Ibid.,* pp. 122-147.

57. *Ibid.,* pp. 173, 338.

58. *Ibid.,* p. 364 et suiv.

59. Madkour, *L'Organon,* pp. 256, 262-265; Nashar, p. 84-100.

60. Ibn Khaldūn, *Muqaddima,* le Caire, 1967, 3.1168.

61. Marʿashī, *Kitāb al-Waladiyya,* Le Caire, 1911; Ḥusein Walī, *al-Mūjaz fī ilm adab al-baḥth.*

II.
Classical Islamic Theology and the Early Shīʿa Movement

Kalām and Philosophy, A Perspective from One Problem*

RICHARD M. FRANK
The Catholic University of America

Philosophy like science is
  an activity of mind
  a state of mind
    for framing questions
    the right question for
    the right answer
But the framing
  of questions
  requires itself a framework
    so that the round can be
    round and
    found so and
    the square square and
    believed so
    maʿa sukūni n-nafs.
Some philosophers consider
  theologians
    squares within
    their round-framed
    eternal universes
But philosophers too are
  conceived as they conceive
    within their frames
    discourse within framed universes
    they cannot reasonably escape
    taqlîdan.

*The following was originally presented as the opening paper in the *Conference on Early Islamic Thought in Honor of Harry A. Wolfson,* 20–22 April 1971 at Harvard University.

Some like Ash'arites
  find speculation obligatory
  since cannonized tradition
    so reports
    ḫabaran mutawâtiran.
Some like Mu'tazilites
  beginning in unquestioned questioning
    find it the only way and path
    methodos and *šar'*
    to know what is
    al-ḥaqq.

I DO NOT, in this short presentation, wish to enter into a debate over the nature of the *kalâm* but would make, here at the outset, a few observations on how it appears within the framework of the foregoing remarks which touch, I think, the essence of the question of philosophy and the *kalâm.* The question is not philological.

Let us for the moment take the *kalâm* to be what it, at least sometimes calls itself: *'ilm 'uṣûl ad-dîn.* As with the *disputatio* of medieval Scholasticism, the *munâẓara* was one of the chief techniques of learning and research for the *kalâm* (as for the *figh* too); and it is this, again as in the case of Scholasticism, that gave it its characteristic form of literary expression. One ought not, without some further evidence, simply from this literary convention, conclude that the *munâẓara* was the aim and end of *kalâm* and that it was essentially, as its opponents insisted, no more than a "verbal exercise in the defense of professed religion."[1] Under any circumstances "the science of the fundamental elements of the professed religion" of Islam contains, as in the nature of things it must, a large number of constructions and theses that have to do with philosophical problems—that explicitly or implicitly take up and elaborate positions on major philosophical questions.

Now, some hold that philosophy is done through the exegesis of philosophical texts, but this is not the essence of philosophy. Its being is, as I suggested earlier, an act and process of questioning; and the history of philosophy is the history of the questions: how they have been posed and how treated. The questions are discovered to us in the texts; we take up the activity of philosophy in the study of the texts and continue it as an exegesis, as it were, in discourse with the texts. The texts of the *kalâm,* however, do not tell us of the texts (the schools and traditions) from which the specific form of its own speculation arose, insofar as these are not included in the texts recognized as canonical by the consensus of Muslims. From one standpoint this is reasonable and as it should be, because the speculative activity of the *kalâm* is essentially the exegesis of these texts, sc., the *koran* and the *sunna.* In brief, it is reasonable to the extent that the *kalâm* means to be a theology. To be sure, it is not a theology in the strictest sense in which the Christian tradition has defined this science, for Islam offers to the faith of the believer no proposition that would articulate a mystery that professes to be utterly removed from the grasp of unaided human reason. The *kalâm* does, nonetheless, articulate in analytic form what it sees as the essential and fundamental content of Islam's belief, constructing in the form of a dialectical discourse (*kalâm:* διάλεξις) the speculative framework according to which it understands the rational content and coherence of the principles and elements of this belief. The original and originating problem for Islam, and so for the *kalâm,* is that of the questions raised and implied in the texts of the revelation and the canonical tradition.

Viewed from another perspective, viz., from that of the sociological context of the earlier *kalâm,* one notes that it addressed itself specifically to those segments of the Muslim community whose chief concern was the revelation and the faith of Islam. It is reckoned among the religious sciences and it was primarily by those who were dedicated to those sciences (the *'ulamâ'*) and in their *majâlis* that the *kalâm* was elaborated, learned, and transmitted. Within this ambience, and to this audience, and in a matter that so intimately involved the revealed faith of the community, no Muslim could cite the teaching or opinion of any non-believer, pagan or Christian, as authority. The earliest mutakallimûn do not, thus, tell us of the sources of their speculative discipline; but they do themselves raise and treat the basic philosophical and theological questions. They become for us texts within the history of the philosophical tradition, and therefore we ask how they understood the questions, the meaning of their formulations, and the sense of their argumentation and exposition. That the *kalâm* does not manifest, like Scholasticism, an explicit interest in ancient philosophy and cite its texts, chapter and verse, is not of itself sufficient ground to conclude that the mutakallimûn did not know and did not understand the sense and significance of those texts. (They are not cited by Basil, Athanasius, Gregory of Nyssa, the Pseudo-Denys, or Maximus the Confessor, either.) That the vocabulary and expression of the *kalâm* are not Aristotelian or Neoplatonic, that, in fact, its basic physics and metaphysics are deliberately non-Aristotelian and non-Platonic does not necessarily indicate that the theology of the *kalâm* lacks philosophical profundity and so fails of its expressed theological aim. The question must be answered through an examination of the mutakallimûn's treatment of the questions.

Here I should like to examine one central question whose analysis will at once illustrate something of the philosophical thought of the *kalâm* and manifest its attitude towards the philosophy of the Greeks and the *falâsifa.* The conflict of the *kalâm* and the *falsafa* arises early. We read that abû l-Hudhayl studied the works of the philosophers and that an-

Naẓẓâm, when Ja ʿfar b. Yaḥyà l-Barmakî told him that he did not even know how to read Aristotle properly, began to go through the work point by point.[2] Ibn al-Qifṭî reports, in an oft cited passage,[3] that, when invited by the wezir to carry on a discussion with a number of theologians (*ahl al-kalâm*), Yaḥyà b. ʿAdī declined saying: "They do not understand the underlying principles of what I say and I, for my part, do not understand their terminology. I fear lest I find myself in the position of [abû Hâšim] al-Jubbâ'î in his *Kitâb at-Taṣaffuḥ;* the work is a criticism of the teaching of [the *de Caelo*[4] of] Aristotle and a refutation of it according to what he fancied he understood of it, but in fact he did not understand its logical foundations and consequently the refutation has no validity."[5] A similar charge was leveled against an-Nâšî', who wrote specifically against the Aristotelian logic.[6] The essential conflict, however, does not center in the obstinacy of the mutakallimûn in their refusal to recognize and take up the use of logic, for this, from one standpoint, at least, was simply the logical consequence of their rejection of the Aristotelian categories, which were inseparable from logic as it was taught by its proponents in Islam. The fact is that the *falsafa* and the *kalâm* share a number of basic concepts inherited from common, ancient sources, and that the *kalâm* rejects *falsafa* precisely because it understood quite clearly the ultimate and basic structure and meaning of Greek philosophy as represented in the Aristotelian and Neoplatonic schools, which were those that had survived.

If we abstract from the encumbrance of details whose significance may better be assessed later, we can say that both traditions reason from the conditioned, whose existence is contingent upon the fulfillment of its condition, to the existence of a single and unique ultimate ground or cause, whose being is absolutely unconditioned. For the *kalâm,* there are several forms of this demonstration, but their specifics need not concern us here. For both *falsafa* and *kalâm,* the whole matter to this point rests upon an ontological analysis of the eternal and the temporal; and in this the two traditions share, at least in part, an understanding that is in all senses classical: the conditioned, whose being is contingent upon the realization of its conditions, is characterized as the possible that exists instead of its contrary. The conditionality or non-necessity of its being is entailed by the possibility of the contrary. It is thus that for the *kalâm* "the essential characteristic of a pair of contraries is that it is possible for the one to exist in the stead of the other."[7] They are commonly defined as those "whose union is impossible in the same substrate at the same moment."[8] All of this is, if you wish, unadulterated Aristotelian doctrine[9] and is found also in al-Kindî,[10] al-Fârâbî,[11] and the rest of the tradition.

Conversely, the eternal: τὸ ἀΐδιον, τὸ ἄναρχον, *al-qadîm, al-'azalî,* is essentially that whose being is necessary or whose nonbeing is impossible. This too is a common conception in the Aristotelian tradition.[12] In the *kalâm,* the term *al-qadîm* (for which the verbal equivalent is, from an early date, *lamyazal*[13]) is taken in the same sense by nearly all authorities. Following the customary usage, i.e., the principles of definition used by the philologists (*ahl al-luġa*), they will commonly define it as the ἄναρχον: that whose being has no beginning (*mâ lâ 'awwala li-wujûdihî*),[14] but the implication that the eternal exists necessarily is clearly and explicitly understood. *Al-qidam* (to be eternal) is, from the outset, considered an attribute of God alone,[15] and al-Jubbâ'î and the traditions descended from him, despite the heated argument over the matter, consider it the one attribute in terms of which all the others are to be understood.

What a being has by being, what it is (*li-nafsihî/li-ḏâtihî*) belongs to it unconditionally (*yastaḥîlu min ʿindi gayrilû*); and while the actuality of the essential properties of the possible are contingent upon its existence (*bišarṭi l-wujûd*), God's existence is His essential attribute, for the attribute is that His being has neither beginning nor end.[16] It belongs to Him to exist per se (*yastaḥiqqu l-wujûda li-ḏâtihî,*[17]) so that His existence is necessary (*wâjib*),[18] and "He is distinguished from all other being by the necessity of His being."[19] The nonexistence of the eternal is therefore impossible.[20] God, thus, with His essential attributes, can have no contrary (*ḍidd*),[21] for to have a contrary entails the possibility (non-necessity) of being and of not being[22] and, in *kalâm* terms, is to be subject to the efficient causality of another[23] and consequently to be generated in existence.[24] The necessary (eternal) can, in brief, have no contrary; "the necessity of a thing is indicative of the impossibility of its contrary."[25] Here again we find ourselves in the presence of classical philosophical doctrine, common also to the *falsafa.* Al-Fârâbî devotes an entire chapter of the *Kitâb Arâ' ahl al-Madîna al-Fâḍila*[26] to showing that God (*al-'awwal,* in his terminology) has no contrary, arguing on the basis of an analysis of the term *ḍidd* that is essentially parallel to that of the mutakallimûn. The first being or cause can have no contrary since to have a contrary entails the possibility of nonexistence and whatever can possibly not exist cannot be eternal (*'azalî*). For al-Fârâbî, contraries are forms of the possible and temporally generated.[27]

Thus far the two traditions—the *kalâm* and the *falsafa*—share a common set of conceptions, ultimately inherited from a common source. Enlightening as the investigation may be, I shall leave aside from the present study the consideration of the divergent uses to which these concepts are put by the two traditions in their treatment of the question of the generation of material being, and the temporality or eternity of matter itself. Their opposition on this matter is ultimately only a symptom of a prior and more primary disagreement.

The center and source of the conflict between the *kalâm* and *falsafa* can be summarized thus: the common doctrine of the Aristotelian tradition, adopted by the *falâsifa,* holds that all nature inclines to and seeks completeness in the fulfillment of its act and being; its act (ἐνέϱγὲια) is the expression of its being (οὐσία); the more perfect a being, i.e., the more fully it *is*, the less it has within itself otherness and becoming (δύναμις). The most perfect being will, consequently, be absolute in its completeness, stability, and perfection of being, having a oneness that is beyond all otherness: ἐνέϱγὲια beyond all δύναμις. The highest being, which is the unconditioned source of all conditioned being is, therefore, beyond and above all deliberation and choice, for in choice and deliberation is entailed otherness: potentiality and the imperfection of becoming. Thus, where common Islamic belief, expounded by the *kalâm*, affirms a doctrine of creation according to which the world (i.e., everything other than God Himself) exists by a radically free and gratuitous act of the creator, the "philosophers" and *falâsifa* will say that God cannot, by His very nature, exist without the world; His causation is an essential property of His being so that the actuality of His causation is posited with His existence and to deny either is to deny the other.

The crux of the question, then, lies in the understanding of the nature of the ultimate and unconditioned being: the nature of its being and activity (its οὐσία and ἐνέϱγὲια) and so of its causality and of the possibility of the possible as it is related to the ultimate ground of its possibility and its actuality. For the mutakallimûn, the speculative understanding of the nature of both God and the world rests ultimately on an analysis of the nature of causality. It is not simply that it is through the consideration of the nature of the contingent and possible *as* contingent and possible that one concludes that there must be a first and ultimate ground of the being of the world, but that the nature of the world and of human existence and activity will depend upon the nature of the ultimate cause as that is determinant of the contingency of the contingent and the possibility of the possible. In order to illustrate how the *kalâm* understands this problem and deals with it, I should like to use the example of the Baṣra School of the Muʿtazila that is descended from abû l-Hudhayl al-ʿAllâf and abû ʿAlî al-Jubbâ'î, since their doctrine, one might say, represents the extreme of the *kalâm's* explicit opposition to the Greeks and the *falâsifa*.

If we take it that a thing (and for the early and classical *kalâm*, all being other than God is corporeal[28]) may have or might have had a contrary perfection or state (*ḥâl, ṣifa, ḥukm*),[29] then there must be a specific cause or determinant (*ʿilla/maʿnà*) whose actuality in it determines or specifies its being in that particular state. For example, "it is possible that a body move to the right when it might have to the left instead, given one and the same state [sc., *wujûd:* existence] and one and the same condition [sc., *taḥayyuz*];[30] therefore there must be something to determine the state specifically [*muḥaṣṣiṣ*] and this can only be the existence of a determinant cause [*maʿnà*]."[31] This phrasing is valid for a large area of the early *kalâm* as one recognizes readily from the terms. In the more refined analysis of abû Hâšim, this is that if a perfection of a being is not due directly and immediately to its very being what it is (*li-nafsihî* or *li-mâ huwa ʿalayhî fî nafsihî*) so that its being-so is, in the terminology, *ḥâl nafsîya,* then it is due to the entitative presence (*wujûd*) or inherence (*ḥûlûl*)[32] of a determinant act or perfection (*maʿnà*) that is the cause (*ʿilla*) of the state, which is then termed *ḥâl maʿnawîya.* This act, perfection, or determinant (*maʿnà*) is, however, an entity (*šay' mawjûd*) which comes to be (*ḥadaṯa*) and exists (*wujida*) in the corporeal substrate (*maḥall*);[33] its being or nonbeing itself requires an explanation. It is the sufficient cause (*ʿilla*) of the perfection or state (*ḥâl, ṣifa, ḥukm*), *ʿilla* (cause) and *maʿlûl* (caused: viz., *al-ḥâl*) being so correlated that the presence or absence of the one implies or entails that of the other. But the actuality (*wujûd*) of the determinant cause and the possibility (*ṣiḥḥa*) of its existence must likewise be grounded and explained.[34]

Besides the *ʿilla* there is another form of causality of which we have experience, viz., that one thing is generated or arises from (*tawallada ʿan*) another when its coming-to-be is directly correlated to the coming-to-be of the other (*bi-ḥasbihî*).[35] That is, "when a thing comes to be in consequence of another and in direct correlation to it (*ʿaqîba ġayrihî wa-bi-ḥasbihî*), then the latter must be what produces it" (*muwallid lahû*)[36]; and this is called the "cause" (*sabab*). The relationship here, again, is simply one of the sufficient cause, wherefore ʿAbd al-Jabbâr insists that "though the being of the effect (*musabbab*) is necessary given the existence or actuality of the cause (*ʿinda wujûdihî*), the latter is not, strictly speaking, that which necessitates its being."[37] That is, the existence of the *musabbab* is already determined with that of the *sabab* and that which necessitates it is, strictly speaking, that which determined the being of the *sabab.* This form of causality does not, consequently, yield an insight into the origin of the being of the caused but simply pushes the question back one step. It does not reveal the cause of its being over and against its non-being at the point where its possibility is grounded as a possibility of existence and not a necessity. No sequence of such causes of which we have experience can afford any insight for an adequate understanding of the being of anything, since every term, including the first, is contingent; there is no first term where the being of the possible is initiated out of its pure possibility. This is particularly clear in the systems with which we are here concerned since the Muʿtazila hold that all being of which we have experiential knowledge is corporeal.

If the consideration of physical causality of the programmed sequence of sufficient causes and fulfilled conditions represented in the causation of the *ʿilal* and *'asbâb* does not offer an adequate model for an explanation of the grounding of the possible that exists, i.e., does not give an adequate account of its being and the possibility of its being in the origin of its being (i.e., of its original possibility and the ground of its actuality in being), we do have available an insight into another causal nexus which would seem, perhaps, to offer some understanding of the origin of the initial term of a sequence, viz., the grounding within us of our own acts, where our initial act does sometimes stand as the first cause (*sabab*) in a sequence of events. The causality of the *'asbâb* gives us a view only of sufficient and fulfilled conditions which are themselves the necessary result of the fulfillment of other conditions and if one had ultimately to project such a sequence backwards to the existence of a first, self-sufficient and unconditioned *sabab* or *ʿilla,* he would find no true initiation of being and no truly possible; there could be no becoming but only the eternally necessary.[38] By contrast, in the case of the acts that are ours and truly depend upon us (that are *min jihatinâ* ἐφ' ἥμιν), we seem to be witness to a real and true beginning in which the indifferent possibility of the possible depends for the real possibility of its being on our unconstrained free choice. Here, as in no other situation, one sees an apparent beginning in which the contrary might have taken place—*yaṣiḥḥu wuqûʿu l-ḫalâfi dûna l-'awwal*[39]—in which the sequence of sufficient and fulfilled conditions for a specific event takes its initiation out of an indeterminant possibility. The matter, however, requires further inquiry in order to verify and clarify the apparent insight.

ʿAbd al-Jabbâr, following abû Hâšim, argues that we have a direct and fundamentally unquestionable knowledge[40] of the correlation between our intention and motive, and the realization of our act. We know, with the certainty of experience, the invariant consistency (*istimrâr*)[41] of the correlation of the actuality of our intention and motive and the realization or nonrealization of particular acts, as also we know the difference between the human agent and inanimate beings in regard to the possibility of acting. This, he notes, is universally admitted by all intelligent men, regardless of how they interpret and explain the correlation.[42] Man projects the future as futurable (possible). We know both the fact of the correlation, and the possibility of the act of intending a particular act, and the possibility of the occurrence of the act in accordance with this intention (in contrast to the absence of the possibility of these things in the case of lifeless bodies—*jamâd*—which, for whatever causal function they may have, can play no more than the role of *sabab* within a series of *'asbâb*).[43] The observed invariance of the relationship between our intention and the occurrence of the act would indicate that there is a necessary correlation (*taʿalluq*) between them.[44] For al-Jubbâ'î, followed by abû Hâšim and the Qâḍî, this knowledge is essentially irreducible; "there is no prior principle to which it can be reduced" (*lâ 'aṣla lahû yuraddu 'ilayhî*), rather it is founded ultimately and certainly on the consideration of immediate experience.[45]

The question, however, of whether the act really depends upon us—

i.e., is really *min jihatinâ* (ἐφ' ἡμιν)—is another matter and one the fact of which is not given in direct and unquestionable experience.[46] In some, indeed in many, instances it appears clear that the act takes place by a kind of (psychological) compulsion (*'iljâ'*) or constraint (*ḥaml*); the act is *mulja' 'ilayhi* and so is, in a sense, necessary[47] in that free and deliberate choice is excluded;[48] that is, the possibility of the realization of the contrary is precluded. For abû Hâšim and ʿAbd al-Jabbâr, this kind of compulsion is defined generally as the situation in which the motivation (*ad-dâʿî*) becomes overpowering so that any motivation to the contrary is effectively excluded or suppressed.[49] In other instances, however, we *experience* a situation which is free (*muḫallan bayna l-fâʿilihî wa-fiʿli*), one in which there is neither compulsion (*'iljâ'*) nor impediment (*manʿ*).[50] The knowing agent, who has the power of efficient causality (*qudra*) and is aware of his motives, acts in accord with the intention that he forms,[51] and, given a free situation, it belongs to him to do what he wills.[52] "He acts as a free agent who chooses his act in accord with his own particular aims,"[53] choosing without constraint or compulsion among several alternatives.[54]

In the case of the deliberate act, thus, we witness the initiation of an act whose possibility, as a real but nonetheless indifferent possibility of being and not being, resides in the power of efficient causality (*qudra*—ἐξουσία) out of which and through which the agent may realize his act in accord with deliberate choice. Through an intuition of our free act (*taṣarrufunâ*) that is realized in accord with a motive that is likewise ours (whether this motive be knowledge, conviction, consciously uncertain opinion, or erroneous belief), we have a clear and unambiguous indication that in such a case we are the true initiators of the act;[55] i.e., the efficient causality that initiated the act resides in us and is freely disposed by us. The factors that underlie the realization of the act (the motives, intention, power of efficient causality, etc.) do not function as causes (*'asbâb* or *ʿilal*) that directly determine the coming to be of the act merely by their presence and actuality in specific parts of the material body which is the agent. Their material presence is in specific organs and parts of the corporeal complex (*jumla*), inhering in which they are the causes (*ʿilal*) of states (*'aḥwâl*) that qualify the whole (*jumla*),[56] but these states do not necessitate the act. Specifically, knowledge and *qudra* do not necessitate the act, but as *ʿilal* produce the states that, as constitutive of the being of the agent, are the conditions under which the free act may be produced. The power of efficient causality (*qudra*) inheres in the substrate and effects a state of the composite, its being-*qâdir;* but "it does not necessitate its object (*maqdûr* sc., the act); rather it is determinant of the state in virtue of which the agent has the power of causation to realize his act by his own free choice" (*iḫtiyâr*).[57] The givenness of the being of the agent entails not the actuality of his action but its possiblity as a deliberate act. His activity (ἐνέργεια) does not flow directly and necessarily from the constitution of his being (οὐσίᾳ);[58] if it did, there would be no agent in any real sense.[59] The act (*fiʿl*), by definition, cannot be determined by some necessitating factor (*muḍṭarran li-ʾamrin mûjib*) for its actuality in being depends upon the *qâdir* insofar as he is *qâdir*[60] (i.e., not on the material substrate as such), and the power of efficient causality is not *determinatum ad unum.* It does not necessitate the agent's acting at all,[61] but rather extends characteristically to acting and not acting[62] and to a plurality of contrary and alternative objects (*maqdûrât*).[63] Accordingly, it is the ground of the possibility of the act as a possibility of being and not being. It is the ground of the possibility of the initiation of being, and the agent's essential freedom of deliberate choice is thus implicit.[64]

This is true even in the case in which there is apparent psychological compulsion. Even though compulsion (*ʾiljâʾ*) is defined in common usage as determinant constraint (*iḍṭirâr*),[65] and even though the situation appears to be one of determinant necessity,[66] it is yet the *qâdir* who is compelled to the act[67] and whatever the compulsion, the agent yet acts through choice (*iḫtiyâr*).[68] His power of efficient causality, as such, extends to alternative possibles and his motives, whatever their strength, remain subject to change. His motives, i.e., his assessment of the situation (whether his understanding of the situation be objectively true or false), are essentially alterable and subject to reconsideration, and in contrast to the power of efficient causality, have no direct determinant effect on the act, either in its possibility or its actualization.[69] They cannot, therefore, function as a determinant cause (*ʿilla mûjiba*).[70] The compulsive act is in this way distinguished from acts not subject to our choice in any way; . . . those which do not take place in accord with any motivation of ours are not subject to our *qudra,* and cannot be considered our acts.[71]

In sum, according to the Baṣra School, we have, in examining the free act, access to an understanding of the character of the causality involved therein, and through this, in turn, an intuition of the essential difference between the nature of the causality of the agent (*al-fâʿil al-qâdir*) and that of material and physical determinant causes (*al-ʿilal wa l-ʾasbâb*). [72] The act is a true initiation of being that is not predetermined absolutely in the being of the agent, but is freely initiated by his choice out of the ground of its pure possibility of being and nonbeing. Here, and here alone, we witness (*nušâhid*) the initiation of being (*ḥudûṯ ʾiḥdâṯ*); and consequently it is here alone that we gain a direct insight into the possibility of the possible, as that possibility is grounded in the possibility of the initiation or noninitiation of its being. It is here that we know that its being is not necessary in its ground but rather is indifferent to being and nonbeing. Thus ʿAbd al-Jabbâr says that "were the matter not as we have stated it, it would be impossible to know that it were possible that what is in motion might, instead of being as it is, be at rest; for the sole basis of this assertion is that if it were not for the free choice of him who moves, he would remain at rest."[73] That is, apart from this insight, we have no knowledge that all being is not necessary.

The possibility of the agent's acting resides in his power of efficient causality (specifically, in his being-*qâdir*);[74] it is out of this power of efficient causality and through it that he initiates and produces the being (*'aḥdaṯa*) of the act, so that the possibility of its being as well as the actuality of its being is grounded in the agent's power of efficient causality. Though some beings cannot exist and thus are not subject to causation, it remains, nevertheless, true that the possibility of being (*ḥudûṯ* and *wujûd*) of the possible is the possibility of the initiation of its being,[75] so that one must conclude, in the words of the Qâḍî, that "if one could not imagine at least one single agent having the power of efficient causality, it would be impossible to characterize even one thing as possibly existent (*bi-ṣiḥḥati l-ḥudûṯ*).[76] "It belongs to that which is not subject to the power of causation that its existence is impossible, just as it belongs to what is subject to the power of causation that its existence is possible."[77]

Abû Hâšim asserts in the *Jâmiʿ aṣ-ṣaġîr*[78] that the only valid argument for the temporal generation of material bodies (and therefore for the dependence of the world on the creator) is that based on the "four premises", attributed to abû l-Hudhayl al-ʿAllâf.[79] This demonstration, however, as he understands it (like the other proofs allowed by the other masters of the school) is valid as a proof of the creation of the world by a *ṣâniʿ* (= ποιητής) in that it presupposes the causality of the free agent and his relation to his act: that the initiation of being (*al-'iḥdâṯ*) is an act (*fiʿl*) and that the act is freely and deliberately produced by the agent out of his powers of efficient causality. To know simply that a thing is temporally generated (*muḥdaṯ*) and no more does not include anything beyond "the becoming of its being" (*tajaddud wujûdihî*), so that one may "know that the thing is temporally contingent and not know that the generation of its being is an act (*fiʿl*), as is the case with the *aṣḥâb aṭ-ṭabāʾiʿ* and others."[80]

It is within this framework that one may understand the Muʿtazila's rejection of the Ašʿarite demonstration of creation by "particularization" or "specification" (*taḫṣîṣ* in Avicenna's terminology, *tarjîḥ*).[81] This argument ʿAbd al-Jabbâr outlines in three forms:[82] 1) that a things comes to be in one moment rather than in another requires something that determines its being to the particular instant (*muḥditun yuḫaṣṣiṣuhu bi-'aḥadi l-waqtayn*); 2) that it exist out of nonbeing requires something that determines its existence (*'amrun yaqtaḍî wujûdahû*); and 3) that it exist in a moment in which it might instead not exist implies that there must be something that causes its existence (*mûjid*).[83] Particularization, in this sense, is, for ʿAbd al-Jabbâr and his school, a valid argument for the entitative reality of causes: *ʿilal* (sc., *maʿânî, ʾaʿrâḍ*) or *ʾasbâb;*[84] but precisely because it is a valid argument for the reality of this kind of causation, it offers no insight into the initiation of being and so cannot be used to establish and elucidate that causation which is involved in the production of being out of its pure and indifferent possibility of being and not being,[85] for, in the words of the Qâḍî, "It is not excluded that temporal beings be characterized by a temporal coming-to-be in the manner that they have stated [in the *taḫṣîṣ* argument], even if one does not affirm the existence of a free agent that is the cause of their being."[86] What he says, in essence, is that, apart from our experience and knowledge of the act of the free agent and his exercise of his autonomous power of efficient causality through deliberate choice, we simply cannot know the possibility of being as a possibility of indifference[87] and so can have no proof of the existence of God as a Creator.[88] One is, so to speak, already beyond all recall and exit down the path of the "philosophers."

The system's understanding of the causality involved in the initiation of being through the free agent seeks, as we have already noted several times, to exclude the function of the kind of causation implied in the *ʿilla* or *sabab.*[89] The problem which the masters of the Baṣra School quite clearly saw as inherent in using this kind of "natural" causation as the model for all causation, sc., the eternity and necessity of God's (and thereby all) action, cannot, however, be avoided simply by establishing that the initiation of being is an act grounded in, and realized through, an agent whose power of efficient causality (*qudra*) is not, per se, determined to a single object. ʿAbd al-jabbâr raises the question over and over again in a number of contexts and from the frequent citations of his predecessors in the school makes it clear enough that both the problem and his treatment of it are traditional within the school. The basic issue with its principal elements is brought together in outline in the eleventh part of the *Muġnî,* where he asks specifically "whether it is possible that God create or initiate creation on account of a cause (*ʿilla*) or not."[90] In traditional form he begins by discussing the term itself, saying that the fundamental sense established in common usage is that of the "reason" for which one does something and that this is the foundation of its juridical use as the reason for the juridical qualification (*ḥukm*) of a thing or an act. In contrast to these senses, the mutakallimûn apply the term in a special, technical sense (*iṣṭilâḥ*) that does not correspond exactly with that established in everyday usage (*al-luġa*), viz., as "necessitating cause" (*as-sabab al-mûjib*).[91] In conclusion he says, "Since the term is used in diverse ways, we prefer to say that 'God created creatures for a reason (*ʿilla*) that is none other than His creating them,' adding that 'He created creatures not on account of any necessitating cause' (*lâ li-ʿillatin mûjiba*), in order that the statement be unambiguously clear."[92] The primary and crucial question is, he notes, "the manner of God's choosing" to create (*wajhu l-iḫtiyār*).[93]

Several problems are raised that reflect on the one hand reasoning that is in part typical of the *falâsifa* and on the other significantly parallel to that of the Aš'arite arguments from *taḫṣîṣ*.[94] "(1) If God did not create creation on account of an *'illa,* then why should He have created what He did create rather than something else? (2) Why should He have created at one time rather than at another? (3) Why should one temporally contingent being exist rather than its contrary if there were no *'illa* on account of which one of them were specifically determined to existence?"[95]

The position taken by the Baṣra School is that God is a free agent, (*fâ'il qâdir*) and that as such He acts on the basis of motives (*dawâ'î*).[96] God's motivation for the initiation of creation can, since He is all-knowing and altogether self-sufficent, unable to derive any benefit or suffer any diminution from another,[97] only be the goodness (*ḥusn*) of His act.[98] This thesis, that the agent may act for no other reason or motive than the goodness of his act, is crucial to more than one area of the school's theology and is argued, consequently, at some length in an earlier section of the *Muġnî,*[99] for, as the author notes, if this thesis is not true, then either God cannot act at all or His act is eternally necessary and determined. Even so, the problem regarding the determination and specification of creation is raised anew on virtually the same grounds:[100] If God acts for the sole reason of the goodness of His act, and His knowledge of the goodness of the act is eternal, then why should He initiate creation at one particular moment rather than from eternity or any other instant? Again, why, since His knowledge of the goodness of what He did not create is similar to His knowledge of what He did create, should He create this universe rather than another? If, finally, there is really no determinant cause, then one should conclude that either 1) God must have acted from eternity (*fîmâ lam yazal*), or 2) He could not have created save what He did actually create, or 3) He cannot create at all.

The question, thus starkly posed, is one of the freedom and spontaneity of God's act as opposed to the thesis of the determinant necessity of creation and at the core of the *kalâm's* conflict with the *falsafa* and the pagan tradition that the latter enshrines, the Mu'tazilite masters return to their analysis of the relation between the being of the agent and his act. The act does not flow immediately and necessarily from the being of the agent (from his being-*qâdir* and being-*'âlim*). In the words of 'Abd al-Jabbâr, "the agent's knowledge of a thing's goodness does not entail the inevitable necessity of his doing it; rather, it entails only that he may choose it for this reason and that his choice, on this basis, is good. . . ."[101] The fact is, God need not have created anything at all but could have remained forever inactive.[102]

This problem is recurrent and is raised from a number of perspectives and in various contexts—for example, when it is argued that "since God creates creation initially on the sole basis of his generosity (*jûd*) and mercy . . . and since these attributes are eternally actual in Him, He must then be eternally creating."[103] This argument from the attribute of generosity (God's being *jawâd*) is explicitly raised by Avicenna.[104] The debate must have arisen quite early, for the Baṣra School, almost from the outset, systematically shunned any position or formulation that might tend to imply necessity or constraint on God's action, any restraint on the absolute freedom of his act within the framework of the ethical system.[105] Thus al-Jubbâ'î sees the implication of the eternal necessity of God's action in the thesis of the "*aṣḥâb al-aṣlaḥ*" (those who hold that God must of necessity do what is absolutely most salutary for His creatures),[106] as do abû Hâšim and his successors.[107] The same fundamental position of the *mulḥida* they find entailed in the related thesis that the *taklîf* was necessary (*wâjib,* i.e., morally obligatory), given the creation of man.[108] Likewise, to cite a final example, the same sense underlies the vehement opposition of the school, even from its founder, abû l-Hudhayl, to the thesis held by the Aš'arites and the School of al-Mâturîdî and others, including some of the Ḥanbalites,[109] that God's will is an essential and eternal attribute whereby He wills eternally everything He knows will come to be.[110]

This outline, I think, is sufficient to illustrate the philosophical and theological acuity of the Mu'tazila, at least in this one complex of problems. It remains to place this briefly within the historical context.

The radical formulation of the notion of creation within the disciplined framework of speculative thought is essentially a Christian innovation and was first elaborated, in part at least, in conscious opposition to the common doctrine of the classical world, for which such a notion was fundamentally alien and uncouth. Already with Methodius (d. 311) we find outlined an argument, of seemingly Stoic ancestry, for the creation of the universe (for the temporal origin of all material being) that is essentially parallel to that commonly used in the classical and early *kalâm.*[111] The same basic argument is common in Patristic writing.[112] As I indicated earlier, however, concerning the *kalâm,* the center and crux of the problem does not lie here, but rather in the understanding of the idea of causation and the initiation of being. From the outset it was common doctrine for the Christians that God creates the world by willing it, not in a βούλησις that, after the conception of Plotinus, Porphyry, or Proclus, is devoid of all deliberation (προαίρεσις), but in a willing that is a free and deliberate act. This notion was already partially elaborated with Pentaenus and Clement.[113] An adequate conceptual understanding of the idea of creation, however, and the elaboration of the questions involved, took some time to work out, especially since the conceptual machinery that was currently at hand had been created and refined over centuries to give rational articulation to the assumption of an eternal and necessary universe. It seems to have been St. Athanasius (d. 373) who gave the problem what was to be its classical solution for the Patristic writers of the Greek tradition, bringing its elements into the clear focus of a systematic exposition.[114] In his treatment of the matter one can see quite clearly the primary elements of the teachings of the main traditions of the *kalâm*. "Created being arose through an act of willing . . . and all creation came to be through an act of volition."[115] Ποίημα (*fiʿl*), which is of an agent (ποιῶν, *fâʿil*), he distinguishes from what is produced by the very nature (φύσει) or by the essential being (τῇ οὐσία, *li-nafsihi, li-ḏâtihî*) of the cause and so by necessity of its being.[116] He insists that the agent (ποιῶν), unlike the natural cause, is essentially different from the act he produces,[117] a thesis that becomes common doctrine for the main schools of the *kalâm*.[118]

Against the pagan thesis, variously formulated, that by its very being the first cause must produce its effect necessarily and eternally, since its ἐνέργὲια is determined in and with its being (οὐσίᾳ, αὐτῷ τῷ εἶναι), Athanasius states that God need never have created anything at all "because the act is outside the agent . . . and He would be an agent and termed so even if His works never existed."[119] The activity of the agent is not determined by his being, and the possibility of the possible as the possible act of the agent is a possibility of indifference (ἐπίσης).[120] It is here, in this conception of the relation between οὐσίὰ and ἐνέργὲια, and not in the philosophy of the Greeks, that one finds the background of the distinction between God's essential attributes (*ṣifât aḏ-ḏât* or *ṣifât an-nafs*) and the attributes of action (*ṣifât al-ʾafʿāl*) common to both the Muʿtazila and the Ašâʿira.[121]

The Christian conviction that the universe is neither necessary nor divine originated in religious faith, founded and embodied in the scriptures. So too the Muʿtazilite teaching that I have outlined here is, in a true sense, founded in an understanding of the proposition that God is *faʿʿâlun limâ yurîd*,[122] which it means to elucidate. But although the original insight arises within the context of religious faith, the formulation and critical exposition of the matter are carried out in a process of philosophical reasoning. From its earliest beginnings philosophy, at least in some of its major areas of concern, has been associated with religion in one way or another, offering critical reflection on various common beliefs but not altogether independently of them. Indeed, some of the central doctrines of Greek philosophy—the Platonic conception of the soul, for example—are rooted originally in religious belief far less sophisticated than the Hebraic concept of a creator who is altogether independent of his creation. Ancient philosophy early asserted its intellectual independence but ever remained, as it had to, the expositor of a world that was rooted in pagan antiquity. In the later Hellenistic world, the debate between Greek paganism and Christianity became ever sharper, especially following the abortive attempt of Julian to reestablish paganism as the religion of the Empire. Ancient paganism found itself more and more on the defensive in the face of the growing predominance of Christianity, and traditional philosophy came more and more to be put into service as the apologist for the traditional conviction that the universe is divine and eternal.[123] Some philosophers well sensed that they were defending a whole cultural tradition with its own native sense of the nature of the world and the divine that had been so magnificently articulated over the many centuries that separated the pre-Socratics from the thinkers of the late Hellenistic period. It had become more or less common doctrine by this time that the world depends upon a first cause: the Demiurge, the One, Patêr, Hyparxis, or what have you, and in the debates between the Patristic writers and the traditional philosophers, one sees clearly enough the later opposition of the *kalâm* and the *falsafa.*

The *kalâm* is an Islamic science, formed according to an Islam topology, and worked out in terms of a fundamentally materialistic view of the world within the framework of an atomistic physics that rejects many of the Aristotelian and Neoplatonic categories and conceptions common to the Patristic tradition. What I wish to point out here is simply that the two great speculative traditions of Islam, the *kalâm* and the *falsafa,* reflect in their opposition and diversity two distinct traditions: the one Islamic and, like Islam itself, closely related to the preceding monotheistic tradition, and the other pagan. Rather than by abstract intellect, they are bound and committed by these traditions and their canonical sources, to the understanding of which they both employ the tools of philosophical reasoning in which they share, in part, a common heritage. Metaphysically both are theological. Aeneas of Gaza in his dialogue has Theophrastus, a representative of the Academy, long the most steadfast and intransigent defender of classical paganism, express his delight at the questions of the Christian, Axitheos, concerning the creation of the world and the soul, saying that philosophy is clean fallen away in Athens and that "it is years since anybody has asked me anything new."[124] Likewise Zacharias of Mytilene, in his dialogue *de Opificio Mundi*[125] speaks of the ancient philosophers in a way that deliberately reflects Socrates' comments concerning Homer in the beginning of the *Republic* X. So perhaps may the mutakallimûn look upon their philosophical contemporaries:[126] وما ياتيهم من ذكر من الرحمن محدث الا كانوا عنه معرضين

Notes

The following abbreviations are used below for the works of the Qāḍī ʿAbd al-Jabbār al-Hamadānī:

M = *al-Mugnī fī abwāb at-tawḥīd wal-ʿadl* (various editors under the direction of Ibrahim Madkour), Cairo, 1962–).

MQ = *Mutašābihāt al-Qur'ān* (ed. A. M. Zarzur), 2 vols., Cairo, 1969.
Muḥ = *al-Majmūʿ al-muḥīṭ bit-taklīf* (ed. U. S. Azmi), Cairo, n.d.
SU5 = *Šarḥ al-uṣūl al-ḫamsa* (ed. A. Ousman), Cairo, 1384/1965.

1. "*Mujāhadatun ʿani d-dīni bil-lisān*": al-ʿĀmirī, *K. al-iʿlān bi-manāqib al-Islām*, ed. by A. Gorab, Cairo, 1387 (1967), p. 99; cf. also Josef van Ess, "The Logical Structure of Islamic Theology," in *Logic in Classical Islamic Culture,* ed. by Gustave E. von Grünebaum, Wiesbaden, 1970, p. 24, nn. 16 f. and references. That speculation (*an-naẓar*) and reason (*al-ʿaql*) are the basis of the acceptance of the revelation and the speculative sciences, therefore, in a real sense, the foundation of the religious sciences, is a thesis that is taken quite seriously by the Muʿtazila but also al-Ašʿarī. Cf., e.g., his discussion of the uṣūl in *ar-Risāla ilà ahl aṯ-ṯagr bi-Bâb al-Abwâb, Ilahiyat Fakültesi Mecmuesi* 8 (1928), pp. 80 ff., by which he quite unambiguously means the *ʿaqlīyāt;* Ibn Fûrak, *Bayân muškil al-'aḥādīṯ,* ed. by R. Köbert, Rome, 1941, pp. 15 ff., and al-Māturīdī (Cf., e.g., *Kitāb at-Tawḥīd,* ed. by Fathallah Kholeif, Beirut, 1970, 287 ult. ff.).
2. Ibn al-Murtaḍà, *Ṭabaqāt al-Muʿtazila,* ed. by S. Diwald-Wilzer, Wiesbaden, 1961, 50.
3. *Tā'rīḫ al-ḥukamā',* ed. by J. Lippert, Leipzig, 1903, 40.
4. That this is the work in question is made clear on p. 39.
5. The rendering of this passage by A. Périer in *Yahyà ben ʿÁdī* (Paris, 1920, pp. 63f.) is very inexact and erroneously refers to abū Hāšim as Hisām.
6. Cf. Josef van Ess, *Frühe muʿtazilitische Häresiographie, zwei Werke des Nâšī' al-Akbar,* Beurit, 1971, 3 f. and Muhsin Mahdi, "Language and Logic in Classical Islam," in *Logic in Classical Islamic Culture,* 80 f.
7. Cf. *Muḥ,* 148, 8f.
8. Cf. *M* 16, 389, 20f. and cf. the identical definition by ʿAbbād b. Sulaymān in al-Ašʿarī, *Maqālāt al-Islāmīyīn,* ed. by Hellmut Ritter, Istanbul, 1929–30, 367; the older definition of abū l-Hudhayl, sc., that the existence of the one entails the nonexistence of the other and vice versa (cf. *ibid.*) fell generally into disuse with the later Baṣra School through the refinement of the conception of accidents to which the definition was bound; cf., e.g., *M* 11, 444, 12 ff. See *M* 6/2, 153, 6 f.; 13, 247, 7–9; and al-Bāqillānī, *at-Tamhīd,* ed. by Richard J. McCarthy, Beirut, 1957, 361.
9. Cf. e.g., *de Gen. et Corr.,* 331a14; *Physics,* 193b13; *de Caelo,* 286a31ff.
10. *Rasā'il,* ed. by M. ʿA. H. abū Rīda, Cairo, 1369/1950, 1:374 f.; cf. also Richard Walzer in Oriens 10 (1957), 213.
11. *Arā'ahl al-madīna al-fâḍila,* ed. by Albert Nader, Beirut, 1959, 52 f. and *as-Siyāsa al-madanīya,* ed. by Fawzi Najjar, Beirut, 1964, 54, 9ff. and below.
12. Cf., e.g., *de Caelo,* 282a21 ff. Alexander of Aphrodisias states quite succinctly that τὸ ἐξ ἀνάγκης ὄν ἔν ἀεὶ ἐστί, τὸ γὰρ ἐξ ἀνάγκης τοῦ ἀϊδιου δηλωτικόυ. *Quaestiones* III, 5: *Scripta Minora* II, ed. by I. Bruns, Berlin, 1892, p. 87, 26 f.
13. Cf. e.g., ʿAbbād b. Sulaymān, cited in al-Ašʿarī, *Maqālāt,* 497 f. and Ibn Kullāb, *ibid.,* 517.
14. E.g., al-Jubbā ī, cited in *M* 5, 233, 1 f.; cf. cf. also al-Ašʿarī, *op. cit.,* 180, 4 f. = 517, 10f. and Ibn Fûrak, *op. cit.,* 19 (825). ʿAbd al-Jabbār states that "our masters say 'the eternal is a being that has forever been' even though 'has forever been' implies time. . . . All that is meant by this is that it has no becoming (*tajaddud*) to its being, in

order to distinguish it from that whose being has a beginning." (*M* 11, 19 f.); cf. also *ibid.*, 432, cited below and see *SU5.* 107, 16 and 561, 14f.; abū Rašīd an-Nīsābūrī in a fragment edited by M. abū Rīda (Cairo, 1969) under the title *Fīt-Tawḥīd,* most likely to be identified with his *Ziyādāt aš-Šarḥ,* p. 225, 9f. and 246, 4ff.; Ibn al-Muṭahhar al-Maqdisī, *K. al-Bad'wat-ta'rīḫ* 1, ed. C. Huart, Paris, 1899, 87 and al-Bāqillānī, *K. al-Inṣāf,* Cairo, 1369/1950, 87 and *at-Tamhīd,* § 449 and generally *M* 4, 233 f., 239, and 7, 111, 18f.

15. Note the discussion in Ibn Ḥanbal, *Radd ʿalà l-Jahmīya, Ilahiyat Fakültesi Mecmuasi* 5–6, 1927, 322f., translated in M. S. Seale, *Muslim Theology,* London, 1964, 116 and Ibn abī Yaʿlà, *Ṭabaqāt al-Ḥanābila,* ed. M. al-Faqi, Cairo, 1371/1952, 2, 298 f.; see also Richard M. Frank, "The Divine Attributes according to the Teaching of abū l-Hudhayl al-ʿAllāf," *le Muséon* 82 (1969), 470, n. 66 and 472, n. 72; and cf. Zacharias of Mytilene, *de Opificio Mundi, PG* 85, 1112A f., concerning the ἰδιώτατεν γνώρισμα (= *'aḫaṣṣ al-'awṣāf*).

16. NB. *SU5* 107 ff. and cf. also *M* 7, 85 ff.

17. Cf. *Muḥ,* 188, 4 ff.; note that the term *istaḥaqqa* denotes not so much "merit" or "deserve" but that quality which belongs to a thing as a property of its essential nature (*ḥaqīqa*), as when one says *min ḥaqqi š-šay'i'an*. . . . Cf., e.g., *M* 8, 77, 16; abū Rašīd, *op. cit.,* 224ff. and cf. generally M 4, 250 f.

18. *K. al-Masā'il,* ed. A. Biram, Berlin, 1902, 44; this is, of course, implicit in Ibn Kullāb's statement that God "is existent without an act of existence and a being (*šay'*) without a cause (*maʿnà*) [on account of which He is a being]," al-Ašʿarī, *Maqālāt al-Islāmīyīn,* 170, 1. NB. also, the citation of al-Ašʿarī in al-Juwaynī, *aš-Šāmil,* ed. A. an-Naššār, et al., Alexandria, 1969, 196f. and v. also 251 ff. Cf. also ʿAbd al-Qāhir al-Bagdādī, *Uṣūl ad-dīn,* Istanbul, 1346/1928, 88, 10ff. and 112f.

19. Cf. *M* 11, 432, 13 ff. and 4, 250 f.

20. Cf. besides the references given above, generally abū Rašīd (text given by abū Rīda), 191–200, and esp. 224–230, and al-Juwaynī, *op. cit.,* 194 ff., also al-Ašʿarī, *K. al-Lumaʿ*, §§6, 33, and 36; *Risāla ilà ahl aṯ-ṯağr* 82, 13 f.: al-Bāqillānī, *at-Tamhīd,* §§52 (p. 29, 5) and 53; *SU5,* 107, 7 and 108, 15.

21. Cf., e.g., *SU5,* 108, 16 ff. and 516 f.; *Muḥ,* 147 f. and 185 f. (q. v. for the elaboration of the question). Cf. also al-Māturīdī, *K. at-Tawḥīd,* 23, 8–12, and generally al-Juwaynī, *op. cit.,* 195 ff.

22. Cf., e.g., *Muḥ,* 185, 20.

23. Cf., e.g., *M* 8, 69, 5.

24. Cf. e.g., *M* 9, 41, 7 ff.; *Juḥ,* 194, 5 ff.; and also al-Bāqillānī, *at-Tamhīd,* 253 (where one finds the expression *al-muḥdat li-nafsihī* [the per se contingent] contrasted to *al-qadīm li-nafsihī* [the per se eternal] and also al-Māturīdī, *at-Tawḥīd,* 23, 8 ff. (esp. 13 ff.) and 387.

25. *Muḥ,* 194 f.: *wujūbu š-šay i dāllun alà stiḥālati ḍiddih.*

26. Pp. 27 f.

27. *As-Siyāsa al-madanīya,* 57, 12 ff.

28. Cf., e.g., abū-Hudhayl, cited by al-Hayyāṭ *K. al-Intiṣār,* Beirut, 1957, 19 ff., and 20, 16 ff.; al-Kaʿbī, cited by al-Māturīdī, *op. cit.,* 82, 21; Ibn al-Muṭahhar al-Maqdisī, *op. cit.,* 1, 152 f; *Muḥ,* 36, 20 f.; al-Ašʿarī, *Risāla ilà ahl aṯ-ṯağr* 96, 10 f.; al-Bagdādī, *op. cit.,* 33;

al-Juwaynī, *al-Iršād,* ed. M. Moussa and A. Abd el-Hamid, Cairo, 1950, 17; and al-Māturīdī, *op. cit.,* 233, 4 ff., 385, 17 f. *et alibi pass.*

29. These terms which, though interchangeable in many contexts, are not strict equivalents, are not used in this sense by al-Aš'arī and those who deny the *aḥwāl.*

30. On this cf. *SU5,* 96f.

31. *Muḥ,* 41, 15-17.

32. The term *ḥulūl* is not used of God's *ṣifāt ma'nawīya* by Ibn Kullāb and his Aš'arite followers even though they say that these attributes are *qā'ima bihi.* For the Baṣra School of the Mu'tazila God's will is *ṣifa ma nawīya* but is "in no substrate" (*lā fī maḥall*).

33. N.B. that the terms *wujida* and *ḥadaṯa* (to be and to come-to-be) and their derivatives are not used of the *aḥwāl* or *ṣifāt* (which are not entities) but rather *tajaddada;* on the distinction cf. R. Frank, "Abū Hāšim's Theory of 'States', its Structure and Function." in *Acts of the Fourth Congress of Arabic and Islamic Studies,* pp. 93 f.

34. It is to be noted that within the system and terminology of abū Hāšim and his followers, the relation between *'illa* and *ma'lūl* does not ground and explain any genuine being or coming-to-be, since the *ma'lūl* as a state (*ḥāl*), is not existent but only *mutajaddid.* In this the relationship differs from that between the *sabab* and *musabbab,* on which see below.

35. Cf. *M* 9, 159, 16 f.: *li'anna 'aṣla l-'ilmi bi'anna š-šay'a yatawalladu 'an ġarihī huwa ḥudūṯuhū bi-ḥasbi ḥudūṯihī.*

36. *M* 12, 78, 2. (In line one here *bihī* following *tuḫtaṣṣ*)

37. *M* 9, 49, 19 f.

38. Cf. *M* 11, 94, 8 f.

39. *Muḥ,* 77, 6 f.: see also below.

40. *Ḍarūratan* (necessary): this is not immediate and innate (*bil-badīha*) but a knowledge, established through habitual experience, observation, and reflection, that cannot be reasonably called into question; cf. *M* 8, 6, 13 ff. (here read *wal-iḫtibār* for *wal-iḫtiyār* in p. 6, 11, 16, 18 and in the following pages).

41. Cf. *M* 8, 6, 8 and *Muḥ,* 77, 16; on the consistency of observed phenomena as the basis of knowledge, cf. also *Muḥ,* 42, 8 ff., 187, 13-18 *et alibi pass.* The same principle is used by the Aš'arites and al-Māturīdī.

42. *M* 8, 8, 15 ff.

43. Cf. *M* 8, 7, 5 ff.

44. *M* 8, 11 ff.

45. *M* 8, 23, 16 ff.

46. *M* 8, 11, 16 ff.

47. *M* 14, 278, 11 f.: *qad ḥaṣala fīhī min ba'ḍi l-wujūḥi ma'nà l-'ījābi min kulli wajh.*

48. Cf. *M* 8, 173, 1; 15, 347, 14 ff. Some followers of the school feel that in such a case the necessity (*ījāb*) is complete; cf. *M* 8, 176, 9 f. and 12, 352 f.

49. Cf. *SU5,* 40, 12 ff.; *M* 11, 486, 17ff.; 16, 288, 10 ff.; *MQ* 2, 712, 9 ff.; and for abū Hāšim, *M* 8, 166, 14 ff.; and in general see *M* 6/1, 186 ff. and especially *M* 11, 394 ff.

and *MQ* 2, 711 ff. For this reason moral praise and blame cannot be assigned in the case of acts done under psychological composition; cf., e.g., *M* 8, 171 ff.; 14, 135 ff. *et alibi.*

50. For *at-taḫliya* as the absence of *'iljā'* and *man'* in the presence or availability of the prerequisite factors (*al-muḥtāj'ilayhī,* i.e., physical capability, knowledge of how to perform the act, needed implements, etc.) cf., eg., *MQ* 2, 715.

51. Cf. the citation of abū Hāšim in *M* 8, 14, 7–11.

52. *M* 8, 119, 14: *'al-qādir ma'a s-salāmati wal-taḫliya min ḥaqqihī' an yaf'ala mā yurīduhū. At-taḫliya* is commonly used as the opposite of *al-man'*.

53. *M* 11, 396, 8 f.: . . . *'alà ḥukmi l-muḫtāri lil-fi'li li agrāḍin mujtami'atin taḫuṣṣuhu.*

54. This is implied in *at-taḫliya;* cf. *M* 14, 201 f.; cf. also *M* 11, 486 f. *et alibi.*

55. Cf. *M* 11, 314, 3 f. On this whole argument cf. abū Rašīd, abū Rīda's text, 344, ff. and in general the whole section pp. 296–364.

56. Cf., e.g., *M* 8, 92, 1: 97 f.; and 12, 33, 1 ff., *et alibi.*

57. *M* 9, 50, 4 f.; cf. also *M* 8, 54, 7 f. Cf. also abū Rašīd, *K. al-Masā'il* (MS. Berlin, 5125 = Glaser, 12) foll. 147V°—148V° and see also the citation of abū l-Ḫudhayl in al-Hayyāt *K. al-Intiṣār,* reprinted by A. Nader, Beirut, 1957, 18, 2f.

58. Cf. *M* 9, 23, 3 ff. and also 88.

59. Cf. *M* 11, 94, 11 and 96, 15 f., cited below. Cf. also Alexander of Aphrodisias, Εἰ τοῦ ἐφ' ἡμῖν τὸ ἀντικείμενον μή ἐφ' ἡμῖν, οὐδ' αὐτὸ τὸ ἐφ' ἡμῖν ἐφ' ἡμῖν ἔσται, *Scripta Minora* II, 50 f.

60. Cf. the definition in *M* 6/1, 5 ff.; 8, 91, 20 and 169 ff.; 16, 50; *Muḥ,* 230, 20 ff., *et alibi;* and for abū Hāšim's comment on the definition of the term as it is given by the lexicographers cf. *M* 9, 89, 10 ff.

61. Cf. *M* 14, 207–210 and also 4, 330 ff., *et alibi.*

62. Cf., e.g., *M* 8, 110, 6 ff.; 9, 39, 17 ff. and 72 ff. I shall not here attempt to unravel the distinctions between not acting (*'an lā yaf'al*), leaving the act undone (*at-tark*), and performing the contrary (*fi'l aḍ-ḍidd*), for the matter is much debated and very complex.

63. Cf., e.g., *M* 9, 43, 17 ff.; 13, 206, 5 ff.; 11, 4 f.; 16, 229, *et alibi.*

64. Besides the above references, cf. also *M* 9, 90, 12 f. Note also within the present context that, according to 'Abd al-Jabbār, though we may see some necessary link between the act of the will and the realization of the act, it still cannot be said that the realization of the act is necessitated, as within an *illa* or *sabab* (*M* 8, 18, 10 ff.), for the act of the will (*al-irāda*) is itself an act performed by the agent through his *qudra,* according to his intention and motives; this is the basis of the argument set forth in *M* 8, 39, 12 ff., viz., that intention is formed freely (at least where there is no psychological compulsion) while *irāda* is an act based on this intention. Cf. also the remark concerning motivation and indetermination in *M* 11, 216, 19.

65. Cf. *M* 8, 167, 6 f. and 11, 394, 12 ff.

66. Cf. *M* 8, 62, 14–21 and *MQ* 2, 712, 8f.

67. Cf. *M* 6/2, 267, 17 f.

68. Cf. *M* 8, 59, 15 f. and 11, 397 f.

69. Cf. *M* 8, 62, 4 and below.

70. Cf. *M* 11, 96, 6 ff. and 8, 62, 18–21. Note that likewise there is no question of the "nature" of the substrate; cf. *M* 12, 128, 8–20 and generally also *M* 8, 60, 13 ff. and 166 f.; 9, 30 f.; 11, 96, 6 ff. and *MQ* 2, 712 f. The same is true of the act that is apparently spontaneous or fortuitous (*wāqiʿ ʿalà l-ittifāq*); cf. *M* 8, 46, 16 ff.

71. Cf., e.g., *M* 12, 63, 19 ff.

72. *M* 14, 293: انما يضاف الفعل اليه من حيث كان قادراً عليه من قبل ويفارق ما يجب من حال العلل

73. *M* 8, 9, 19–21.

74. Cf., e.g., *M* 9, 33, 8 f.; 8, 54, 7 f.; 7, 13, 9f., *et alibi pass.*

75. Cf., e.g., *M* 8, 72, 5 f. and 109, 3 f.; 9, 134, 23 f.; 11, 94, 15 ff., *et alibi.* Note that the matter of the impossibility of being (*istiḥālat al-wujūd*) and what is *mamnūʿ* as opposed to what is *maʿjūz ʿanhū* is quite complex in the texts.

76. *Muḥ,* 365, 13 f.

77. *M* 8, 116.

78. Cf. *Muḥ,* 38, 23 ff. and 71, 15 ff.; this is alluded to by Ibn Suwār in his *Maqāla fī ʾanna dalīl Yaḥyà n-naḥwī ʿalà ḥudūṯ al-ʿālam ʾawlà bil-qabūl min dalīl al-mutakallimīn,* cf. A. Badawī, *Neoplatonici apud Arabes,* Cairo, 1955, 245, 19 f.

79. *SU5,* 94, 9 ff.; the same attribution is made by abū Rašîd (abū Rīda's text), 101; see also the remarks attributed to abū-Hudhayl in aš-Šarīf al-Murtaḍà, *al-Amālī* (ed. M. Ibrahim, Cairo, 1373/1954) 1, 181, 18 ff.; v. also *M* 8, 286, 7 ff.

80. *M* 6/1, 6, 8 ff. (where read *tjdd* for *tḥdd* in 1.9). It is for this reason that the Baṣra School holds that al-Ašʿarī cannot reasonably affirm that there is any free causation of being, since he denies (as they see it) the autonomy of the human agent and his power of efficient causality, which is the sole locus wherein we have any experiential access to an understanding of the causality of the agent; cf., e.g., *Muḥ,* 230 f., where al-Ašʿarī is mentioned by name (a rare occurrence in the writings of the Qāḍī).

81. On this argument cf. H. A. Davidson, "Arguments from the Concept of Particularization in Arabic Philosophy," *Philosophy East and West* 18 (1968), 299 ff.

82. *M* 8, 33, 10 ff.

83. That the *mūjid* is an agent (fāʿil = ποιῶν) is implicit in the concept both for the Ašʿarites and the Muʿtazila; *iḥdāṯ* is determined only through choice; cf., e.g., *M* 9, 50, 4 f. and 8, 54, 7 f. and below n. 118.

84. Cf. for example the usage in *Muḥ,* 41, 15 f., 42, 12–15, *et alibi,* as well as the citations above concerning the *ʿilal* and *asbāb.*

85. Davidson, *op. cit.,* notes the differing use of the argument by the Muʿtazila and the Ašāʿira but does not deal with the underlying reason.

86. *M* 8, 33 f.

87. Cf., e.g., *M* 6/1, 137, 10 ff. and also *M* 8, 9 and references above. Abd al-Jabbār states (*M* 8, 34, 1) that this matter has been treated fully in an earlier chapter; unable to locate this, I judge that it probably was found in one of the first three sections of the work, now lost. At any rate, one sees clearly enough that the Baṣra School of the Muʿtazila are in basic agreement with Maimonides in his objection to the Ašʿarite arguments based on *taḫṣīṣ,* cited by Davidson, *op. cit.,* 307.

Thus too ʿAbd al-Jabbār rejects most of the earlier arguments for the free agency of the human agent (*fāʿil*) as either begging the question or implying the intuition of the free and autonomous causality of such an agent (*M* 8, 25 ff.). For his rejection of the Ašʿarite arguments based on the experienced difference between *al-fiʿl aḍ-ḍarūrī* and *al-fiʿl al-muktasab* (e.g., al-Ašʿarī, *K. al-Lumaʿ*, §§ 91 f.), cf. *SU5,* 368 f., *M* 8, 34 and especially 282 ff., and their argument from the objective moral qualifications of voluntary acts (e.g., *al-Lumaʿ*, §§ 85 f.), cf. *M* 8, 285 ff.

88. Cf. *M* 8, 16, 10–14 and p. 17, 3 ff.

89. Besides the references given above, cf. also *M* 11, 456–459.

90. *M* 11, 91.

91. The semantic parallel in the use of this term in the *fiqh* and the *kalâm* to those of the term *maʿnà* is fully evident.

92. *M* 11, 93, 5–7. For al-Māturīdī's refusal of the term *ʿilla,* cf. *at-Tawḥīd,* 33, 5 ff. and 30, 9–12.

93. *M* 11, 93, 9 ff. There is no need within the present perspective to dwell upon much of the argument presented here (pp. 93 ff.) concerning God's acting because of an *ʿilla.* The following should be noted, however: the first line on p. 93 belongs at the bottom of the page, following *lattaṣala ḏālika;* also read *ynqḍ* on p. 95, 1.

94. The present passage (95, 3 ff.) is a particularly clear example of how the objections and responses in the form *'in qīla . . . qīla lahū* are used to progress systematically through the separate elements of the problem; the passages introduced by 'in qāla (pp. 93 f.) are reasonings set forth in support of the counter positions previously given.

95. *M* 11, 95, 13–15: يخلّق الخلق لعلة فلم صار بان يخلق ما خلقه اولى من غيره ولم صار بان يخلقه في
اخر ولم صار ذلك الحادث بالوجود اولى من ضده ولا علة يختص احدهما لاجلها بالوجود ان لم
وقت اولى من وقت

96. Cf. *M* 11, 96, 13 ff. (in the last line of p. 96 read *bit-taʿalluqi l-fiʿl* in place of *yataʿallaqu bil-fiʿl*); 15, 157 ff., *et alibi passim.*

97. On God's being *ganīy* (αὐτάρκης), cf., e.g., *M* 6/1, 139 f.; 16, 66, 7 ff.; *Muḥ,* 213 f., *et alibi.*

98. On some of the implications of this, cf. *M* 11, 72 ff.; that the initial act of creation cannot be morally obligatory, cf. *M* 14, 110 ff.; there is moral obligation (*wujūb*) on the part of God but there is no *mūjib* (cf. *M* 14, 14, 10 ff. and Frank, in *Studia Islamica* 33, 14 ff.).

99. *M* 6/1, 210 ff.

100. *M* 11, 97 f.; cf. the parallel objection raised in another context, *M* 11, 61, 10 ff., and generally 59, 10 ff.

101. *M* 11, 98, 7 ff.; cf. also *M* 11, 65, 8 ff.: "The agent's knowledge of a thing's goodness does not entail the necessity of his doing it but entails only that he may choose it. Further it is not excluded that an agent do at one time rather than at another something that he is not compelled by necessity to do." Cf. also *M* 6/1, 221 f.

102. *M* 11, 99, 5 ff.; cf. also *M* 14, 209 ff. and esp. 112, 12 ff. The initiation of creation is a

purely gratuitous act (*tafaḍḍulan*); cf., e.g., *M* 11, 68 ff., 126, 134 ff.; 14, 67 ff. *et alibi*, as well as the references below. Cf. also al-Māturīdī, *at-Tawḥīd*, 33, 19 f. and 53, 8 f. Cf. also the citation of al-Jubbā'ī given by abū Rašīd (*K. al-Masā'il*, fol. 150V°):

ان القديم لما جاز ان لا يفعل ما يقدر عليه في بعض الاوقات جاز ان لا يفعل أبدا

103. *M* 11, 122; cf. also pp. 153–156 and 14, 66, 11 ff.; al-Māturīdī, *op. cit.*, 30, 9 ff., 97 f. and also his formulation pp. 33, 17 ff., 47, 19 ff., *et alibi.*

104. *Ilāhīyāt aš-šifā'*, Cairo, 1960, 2: 380; *al-jūd* is also viewed by Ibn Zurʿa as one of God's chief attributes (cf. Paul Sbath, *Vingt traités philosophiques et apologétiques d'auteurs arabes chrétiens*, Cairo, 1929, 12 f.).

105. On the question, cf. *Studia Islamica* 33, 14 ff.

106. Cf. *M* 14, 56; for his treatment of the attribute *jawād*, cf. *ibid.*, 45 ff. By *aṣḥāb al-aṣlaḥ* he refers most often to the Baghdad School.

107. Cf. also *M* 11, 63, 2 ff. and 14, 1-306. Cf. also *M* 6/1, 13, 10 ff.

108. Cf., e.g., *M* 13, 419 f.; on the place of *taklīf* in relation to the nature of man, cf. *Studia Islamica* 33, 14 ff.

109. Cf. the formulation used in the *ʿaqīda* transmitted from abū Faḍl at-Tamīmī in Ibn abī Yaʿlā, *Ṭabaqāt al-Ḥanābila* 2, 295, 13 ff.

110. Cf. e.g., the citation of al-Jubbā'ī in *M* 6/2, 208, 15 ff.; for the position of abū l-Hudhayl and a patristic parallel, cf. *le Muséon* 92 (1969), 496 ff. and on the question generally see *M* 6/2, 111 ff. and 170–213 *et alibi.*

111. Cf. *de Authexusio, GCS* 27, 175, 11–179, 18. The whole discussion, both in its basic structure and in its use of the duality of ὕλη/ουσία (*al-jawhar*) and ποιότῆες (*al-aʿrāḍ*), foreshadows that of the *kalām* far more clearly and directly than do the arguments of Zealous John "the Grammarian" who has been suggested as the source of the *kalām* proofs by H. A. Davidson ("John Philoponus as a Source of Medieval Islamic and Jewish Proofs of Creation" *JAOS* 89 [1969], 357 ff.). The arguments of the mutakallimūn represents a much later and, as it were, "classical" stage of the evolution of the tradition of this argument; thus where Gregory of Nyssa (who, it should be noted, held that the ultimate unit of bodies is the atom: Τὸ αημεῖον ἀρχὴ τῆς γραμμῆ και τοῦς ὄγκου τὸ ἄτομον . . . , *PG* 44, 72A), for example, yet feels that it is extremely difficult to demonstrate rationally the createdness of bodies (cf. *PG* 46, 121B f.), it would seem that those from whom the mutakallimūn learned their proofs already accepted them as traditional. In the *kalām,* the arguments develop within an atmosphere in which the Aristotelian universe and its categories can, in large measure, be ignored. Thus when abū Hāšim and his successors find it necessary to discuss at length the question of whether matter (sc., the atom) has a contrary (cf., e.g., *M* 11, 433 ff. and abū Rašīd an-Nīsāpūrī, *K. al-Masā'il,* 18) the question is raised entirely within the framework of the *kalām*'s topology and in no wise envisions the possibility of the uncreatedness of matter. Matter (*al-jawhar*) is "something" (*ḏāt, šay'*), having known essential properties, and must be temporally created (cf. the arguments used to show this in the Pseudo-Justin Αποτροπὴ δογμάτων τινων `Αριστοελικῶν *PG* 6, 1501D f. (§5)). Cf. also below, particulary, nn. 119 and 121.

112. Cf., e.g., Basil, *Hexaemeron* (*Sources Chrétiennes,* 26), 100; Zacharias of Mytilene, *op. cit., PG* 85, 1049A f., 1105B, and 1092A ff.; and the citations given in M. Wacht, *Aeneas von Gaza als Apologet,* Bonn, 1969, 100, n. 7; the Pseudo-Justin, *op. cit., PG* 6, 1492 ff. (which contains a number of elements that clearly lie in the background of

the *kalām* arguments), esp. pp. 1497 ff., 1505 f., and 1513A f. (§8), and *Quaestiones Graecae and Christianos, PG* 6, 1476B f.

113. Cf., e.g., Maximus Confessor, *de Variis difficilibus locis, PG* 91, 1805; on Pantaenus, cf. J. Quasten, *Patrology* 2, 4 f.

114. Cf. G. Florovsky, "The Concept of Creation in St. Athanasius," *Studia Patristica* 6 = *Texte und Untersuchungen* 81 (1962): 36 ff.

115. *PG* 26, 457B: τὰ ποιῆματα βουλήσει . . . υπέστη και ἡ κτῖσις πᾶσα θελήματι γέγονιν.

116. Cf. Florovsky, *op. cit.,* 49 ff. and H. Schaeder, "Die Christianisierung der aristotelischen Logik in der byzantinischen Theologie repräsentiert durch Johannes von Damaskus und Gregor Palamas," *Kerygma and Dogma* 8 (1962), 298 ff. For the distinction in John of Damascus, cf. *PG* 95, 812 f. (*cit.* Schaeder, *op. cit.,* 304) and in terms of *kalām* usage, note the distinction between αἰτία and δύναμις ποιητική made by Zacharias of Mytilene, *PG* 85, 1112D though in order to maintain the traditional terminology he does go on to define αἰτία as an agent; *ibid.,* 1113A.

117. Cf. *Contra Arianos* I; 26 (*PG* 26, 65 f.) cited by Florovsky, *op. cit.,* 51 f.

118. Cf., e.g., *M* 8, 265 ff. as well as 149 f. and 11, 347 f. Cf., e.g., al-Māturīdī, *op. cit.,* 33, 5 ff. and my "Notes and Remarks on the *Ṭabaʿi* in the Teaching of al-Māturīdī." It is in terms of this background (i.e., that these theses are taken as common and fundamentally unchallengeable) that one understands why most frequently the *kalām* proofs for creation simply assume that the *mūjid/muḥdiṯ* is an agent (*fāʿil*) (cf. above, n. 83), the philosophical questions regarding *qudra,* freedom, etc., being taken up elsewhere.

119. *Contra Arianos* I, 29 (*PG* 26, 72A f., *cit.* Wacht, *op. cit.,* 93): τὰ ποιήματα ἔξωθεν τοῦ ποιοῦτόσ ἐστι . . . καὶ ποιητὴς μὲν ἄν εἴη και λέγοιτο κ' ἄν μήπω ᾖ τὰ ἔγα. The whole chapter is significant in terms of the *kalām*'s background.

120. Cf., e.g., John of Damascus, *de Fide orthodoxa, PG* 94, 957 f. It is interesting to note that he here argues that the act that depends upon us (i.e., that is ἐφ' ἥμιν *min jihatinā*) is recognized by the validity of the application of praise and blame (cf. also *ibid.,* 952 f.) as did al-Jubbāʾī and the early masters of the Baṣra School (cf., e.g., *M* 8, 25 f.) and so also to show that such an act is indifferent in its possibility to being and nonbeing (ἐπίσης) cites, as does ʿAbd al-Jabbār (cf. supra n. 73) our ability to move or not to move. His whole analysis of voluntary and involuntary actions and of acts that are voluntary (ἑκούσιος) but not chosen (προαιρούμενος) is to be compared to that of the Muʿtazila of Baṣra, sketched above. Generally within the Patristic tradition the most exact equivalent of *qudra* in *kalām* usage is ἐξουσία (and so, *al-qādir* = καθεξούσιος); in this connection, again, one notes that John of Damascus (cf. *op. cit.,* 957 f. and *de Duabus voluntatibus in Christo, PG* 95, 149A f.) as well as others (e.g., Maximus Confessor, *PG* 91, 17C f.) holds that ἐξουσία *qudra* entails the law νόμος *taklīf*) as do the Baṣrian Muʿtazīlites (see *Studia Islamica* 33, 14ff.; there are also parallels to be drawn with the teachings of the Ašāʿira and al-Māturīdi).

121. Probably the most common Greek equivalent in the Fathers corresponding to the term *ṣifa* is ἰδίωα; cf., e.g., the use in Gregory of Nyssa, *Opera Minora,* ed. by F. Mueller, Leiden, 1958, 1: 21, 13 and compare the *kalâm* analysis of names, attributes, etc.

122. Qurʾān 11, 107; 85, 16.

123. Cf. generally P. Labriolle, *La Réaction paienne* (Paris, 1950).

124. *PG* 95, 877A f.:

ἐπεὶ παρ' Ἀθηναίοις ἔνθα μάλιστα διεφάνη φιλοσοφία, παντελως ἄγνωοτος και εἰς τὸ μηδὲν ἀπέρριπται. . . . Ἐρώτα δὴ . . . οὐδεὶς γάρ με πολλῶν ἐτῶν ἠρώτησε καινὸν οὐδέν.

125. *PG* 85, 107B–76. Al-Māturīdī suggests (95, 3–6) that those who follow the doctrines of the philosophers in these questions base themselves not on reason but on *taqlīd*.

126. Qur'ān 26, 5.

Faith as *Taṣdīq*

WILFRED CANTWELL SMITH
Dalhousie and Harvard Universities

FAITH (*al-īmān*), some Muslims held, is overtly doing something; some, that it is saying something; most, that it is an inner act. Various combinations of the three were also canvassed. In the rhyming formulation that came to prevail:

> *al-īmān taṣdīqun bi-l-janān, wa* [*aw*] *iqrārun bi-l-lisān, wa* [*aw*] *ʿamalun bi-l-arkān.*

Our purpose in the present paper is to explore the point made concerning the inner dimension, and specifically the language used in setting it forth. *Al-īmān huwa al-taṣdīq* (or, more fully: . . . *al-taṣdīq bi-l-qalb*). If faith is indeed this movement of the heart, as the majority of Muslims came to hold, we would go on to ask: What, then, is *taṣdīq?*

This has seemed to many a simple matter. The present investigation would suggest that, on the contrary, the question is subtle, complex, and important. The meaning of the word is not so evident as most have assumed.

We leave here quite untouched the question as to what else faith might or might not be. Muslim thinkers deliberated on the relation among the three dimensions noted above; and the development of their positions has been studied by some Western scholars. That too we leave aside.[1] Into the meaning of the notion of *taṣdīq* as here engaged, however, few in modern times seem to have inquired.

In a careful and persuasive paper, Professor Wolfson several years ago showed that the word *taṣdīq* was used in classical Arabic logic, in the sense of the mind's making a judgment, in continuance of a similar notion in late Greek thinking.[2] It is the purpose of the present paper to submit that in addition to this *falsafah*[3] usage, the term served also in *kalām* in another sense. We shall suggest that, especially in the major formula *al-īmān huwa al-taṣdīq,* these additional considerations have an important, even decisive, bearing. Indeed, they are remarkably revealing, for understanding not only Islamic but general human concerns.

The present writer has been interested in this issue for some time, both philosophically and technically; and in presenting for consideration now certain observations, he hopes to illuminate the problem, and at least to show that it is more elaborate than has often been recognized. If the solutions here propounded are not themselves accepted, at least some of the ramifications will, it is hoped, have been brought to attention, and oversimplification discouraged.

Before the matter is tackled in specific detail, two general reflections are in order. The first is major: that religious faith as a virtually universal human quality or characteristic is, surely, a delicate and problematic affair. Many a profound and careful theologian in many a community has averred that this quality transcends verbal description, and rational apprehension. Many a modern student, whether in the social sciences or in history or in the humanities, recognizes that the religious faith of persons and groups eludes his easy grasp. What is this human involvement, which has inspired so much of the world's greatest art and heroism and brutality; has underlain very decisively so much of man's civilizations and humdrum life? If at the turn of our century the sophisticated intellectual could dismiss religious faith on one or another secular score, nowadays such an intellectual recognizes rather that we have not yet understood it. If the believer could accept it as relatively straightforward, he too now more openly senses mystery. The more that light is thrown upon it from various modern investigations and increasing historical awareness, the more complex and elusive it is seen to become.

Clearly faith has taken many different forms. There has been variety, both of gross forms, of which "the Islamic" form is one, overtly different from Christian or Buddhist or Hindu; and variety of subtle forms, of which there have been many within, for instance, the overall Islamic pattern, forms of which the Sunnī and the Shīʿī, or the Ṣūfī and the legalist and the philosophic, or the urban and the village, or one century's and another's, or one man's and his brother's, are variations. Along with such endless variety seems to go also, in human history, an impressive persistence.

We should be cautious, therefore, in imagining that we have understood or defined faith, either in general or in any particular case. Also, by the same token, we do well to give careful heed to any major instance in human history where a significant and intelligent group has proffered a thesis of what it considers faith, or anyway its own faith, to be.

Our second general consideration, at the introductory level, is that the concepts available to us for an understanding or interpretation of faith, and especially faith of another people or age or religious system, are themselves particular. They are both limited and specific. This is true of the concept "faith" itself, which in modern Western usage has connotations deriving from two main traditions. One is the Christian, incorporating through the Old Testament the tradition of ancient Israel, and in the course of its history much of the tradition of Greek thought, and in recent times enlarged to the Judaeo-Christian. The second is the objective-critical, the academic: especially since the Enlightenment, the tradition that considers faith from the outside, and more recently that observes it, generically but passively, in a wide variety of forms across the world. It is clear that the Islamic concept of faith, classically, is and must be formally and in principle different from both of these.[4]

Despite considerations such as these, I propose in the present article to translate *īmān* by "faith" (and this despite certain more technical and yet fundamentally important considerations also, such as that in Arabic this term is a *maṣdar,* is verbal, is the name of an act before it is the name of a quality). I do so because to do otherwise would distract us too radically from our primary subject matter here, the meaning of *īmān*'s predicate, *taṣdīq.* My procedure is to postulate that none of us adequately understands "faith," either in general or in the particular Islamic case.[5] Accordingly, we can explicitly mean by "faith" something somewhat beyond our intellectual apprehension, something toward a partial clarification of which we can hope to move. If this openness for "faith" can be maintained, then we can go on towards elucidating, if not what it is or was, at least something that Muslims classically held it to be; namely, *taṣdīq.*

Yet here also our elucidatory predicates are also particular. The English term "believe," for example, is redolent of both ambiguity and particularity. Like French *croire* and German *glauben,* the word comes into modern usage saturated with its classical Christian past and its Western intellectualist-neutralist-skepticist currency. To say that *ṣaddaqa* mean 'to believe' (as has regularly been said) can be, therefore (and regularly has been), either misleading or ambiguous or both. Even *fürwahrhalten,* an explicatory predicate of *glauben,* leaves open, of course, the notoriously problematic question of truth (*Wahrheit*)—to which is relevant the important Arabic distinction between *ḥaqq* and *ṣidq,* as we shall presently observe. And *credo,* I believe it can be shown, has changed its meaning over the centuries. . . .[6]

Part of the present thesis is that the concept *taṣdīq* signifies that for Muslims faith was discerned and interpreted in ways significantly differing from those current in the modern West.

The *object* of faith in the Islamic case has of course been explicitly different—conceptually—from its object among other communities. This is manifest enough, and many have thereupon contented themselves with specifying that difference of object, leaving then unexplored and even unasked a question as to the form of the faith that is oriented to that object. Christian faith is faith in God and Christ. . . . ; Muslim faith is faith in God and the Qur'ān and Muḥammad. . . . Our concern here is to supplement this obvious point, suggesting that the pluralism of faith around the world is not merely that faith is (and/or is conceived to be) a relationship to *x*, to *y*, to *z*, etc., in various cases. We would focus rather on the more subtle matter of attempting to ascertain the human side of those relationships in each case. On more careful consideration it turns out that, in the various religious patterns that variegate human history, faith is a P-relationship to *x*, a Q-relationship to *y*, an R-relationship to *z*, etc. (It might even then turn out that P,Q,R, are as different from each other as are *x*, *y*, *z*.)

A neglect of this personalist, or formal, quality of faith, as distinct from its object, or substantial content, has support within many traditions, where in each case the particularity tends to be taken for granted. In the Islamic instance, for example, faith was at times explicated merely in terms of its object: faith is faith in *x*, they said with formal tautology (along with substantive force). In the words of the classic *ḥadīth:*

al-īmān an tu'mina bi-llāh wa bi-malā'ikihi wa bi. . . .[7]

This tells us nothing, and assumes that we need be told nothing, as to what faith itself is; merely, where it is directed.

At other times, however, and that constitutes our interest here, Muslims did ask what faith inherently is; and their standard answer often was, it is *taṣdīq*.[8] What did they mean when they said that?

It is not surprising that Christians, and Western ex-Christians, have tended to suppose that they meant, "faith is belief." This is not surprising, given their own background and presuppositions in these matters; given their own relation to Islamic data (which, as outsiders, they themselves do not "believe," but suppose that Muslims do); and given the superficial plausibility of the translation. This last is enhanced by the fact with which we began, that the logicians in classical Arabic, as distinct from the theologians, did, as Wolfson has demonstrated, employ *taṣdīq* to mean the making of an intellectual judgment, following the Greeks. A closer examination of the texts, however, shows that for *kalām* the "believing" notion is inadequate. It is the argument of the present inquiry, at least, that this is a mistranslation. To suppose that for Muslims faith is belief, or that they themselves thought so, is, we suggest, to misunderstand.

To explore this, we must clarify certain understandings of truth. Those who interpret *taṣdīq* as "believing" arrive at that position by rendering it first as "holding to be true." Truth, however, in itself, and man's relations to it, are intricate and the subtle matters, which repay rather careful consideration.

The present thesis is that more critical awareness of what sorts of issues are at stake in this concept is needed if we are to apprehend the *taṣdīq* notion adequately, as it bears on religious life. Our proposal, accordingly, is to develop first a rather general interpretation of this term (*taṣdīq*) in the context of a comprehensive Islamic view of truth; and then with this orientation to confront specific passages of *kalām* writing that, it is submitted, illustrate and confirm the suggested rendering. The actual working method, of course, was in fact the other way around. Over the course of some years, a wrestling with particular passages which did not seem to make sense with the standard renderings pushed me to modify these, and finally to attain a new understanding of what was being said and within what framework of ideas.

What is truth?

We may begin our presentation by recalling simply that there are three roots in the Arabic language around which crystallized Muslims' concepts on this mighty question. These are *ḥaqqa, ṣadaqa,* and *ṣaḥḥa.* All three have something to do with truth. Yet the three are, of course, quite distinct—which fact in itself can serve us instructively. If I might oversimplify in order to introduce a major point, I would suggest that the first has to do with the truth of things, the second with the truth of persons, and the third with the truth of statements. But let me elaborate.

First, *ḥaqqa.*

When a Western student first learns Arabic, he is taught that *ḥaqq* sometimes means "true," sometimes means "real." He may perhaps remember that the same remark, actually, had been made to him also about the Latin term *verus,* which can mean real, genuine, authentic, and also true, valid. If he goes on to learn Sanskrit, he will meet the same point again with regard to that language's (and civilization's) term *satyam:* it too denotes both reality and truth. Eventually he may come to realize that what is happening here is not necessarily that all these peoples are somehow odd folk who have confused or converged two concepts, or used one word indiscriminately for two different notions; but that it is perhaps rather the modern West that is odd, is off the track, in having somehow dichotomized a single truth-reality, in having allowed its conception of truth to diverge from its conception of reality. At least, an important case can be made for such a view.

Even the West today harbors remnants of this earlier usage. For Western civilization, decidedly, was built upon concepts of this type. Westerners still at times can speak of true courage, or false modesty; of true marriage or a true university; even of a true note in music. I mentioned this once, however, to a professional philosopher, only to have him dismiss it as metaphorical, and not really legitimate or even significant. Only propositions, he said, are *really* true or false. And even for nonanalysts among us, whatever our residual vocabulary, there has come to be widespread today a certain discomfort, most will probably agree, with any but a very imprecise position that things, qualities, actions, can be true or false. Things are just there, somehow, many feel, and it is only what one says about them that is subject to this discriminating judgment.

However that may be, in Arabic *ḥaqq,* like *satyam* and *veritas,* refers to what is real, genuine, authentic, what is true in and of itself by dint of metaphysical or cosmic status. It is accordingly a term par excellence of God. In fact, it refers absolutely to Him, and indeed *al-Ḥaqq* is a name of God not merely in the sense of an attribute but of a denotation. *Huwa al-Ḥaqq:* He is reality as such. Yet every other thing that is genuine is also *ḥaqq*—and some of the mystics went on to say, is therefore divine. We leave this issue, however; simply noting that *ḥaqq* is truth in the sense of the real, with or without a capital R.

Secondly, *ṣadaqa.* Our excursus about *ḥaqq* was in order to make sense of the remark now that this term *ṣadaqa* refers to a truth of persons. It matches to some extent Western notions of honesty, integrity, and trustworthiness; yet it goes beyond them. It involves being true both (i) to oneself and to other persons, and (ii) to the situation with which one is dealing. Propositional truth is by no means irrelevant here. It is not ruled out or even set aside. Rather, it is subordinated, being incorporated as an element within a personalist context. For indeed the term is of course used predomininantly, although not exclusively, for "telling the truth." This is often the simplest way to translate it; yet there is something more. What that something more involves, at the personalist level, becomes apparent when one considers, in both Arabic and English, the contrasting concept of telling a lie. *Ṣadaqa* is the precise opposite of *kadhiba,* "to be a liar." This latter, as is its translation in English, is a highly revealing usage. For it denotes the saying of something that not only is untrue, but that also the speaker knows to be untrue and says with an intent to deceive. The Arabs do not normally use *kadhiba,* as English does not use "liar," in the case where a man says something inaccurate but in good faith.

It is curious, as we shall develop later, that English has the concept "lie" and "liar" corresponding more or less exactly to the Islamic concept of *kadhiba,* a personal falsity, untruth at the level of human intent and practice, and of interpersonal relations, but does not have an exact equivalent to, has not formulated a special concept for, the counterpart notion of *ṣidq:* truth of the strictly personalist focus.

This concept, then, has been a central one for Muslims, not least in their religious life, and is central too for the thesis that is being advanced in this paper. We will return to pursue it further, therefore, presently. We set it aside for a moment to consider briefly the third term, *ṣaḥḥa.*

This verb, and its adjective *ṣaḥīḥ,* although expressing important notions, have been much less spectacular in Islamic life, and especially in the realm that concerns us here. The words mean, more or less, "sound," and refer to quite a variety of matters, such as being healthy or being appropriate. One would hardly think of it right off as a term for "truth" at all, except that its usage does, indeed, overlap in part with that of that English word (especially as used in modern logic) in that it may be used in Arabic of propositions when they are what we would call true or correct. (*Hādhā ṣaḥīḥ, hādhā ghalaṭ*—or, *ḳhaṭa'*, or simply *ghayr ṣaḥīḥ.*)

Of these three Arabic concepts, it is to be noted that the first two have strongly polarized contraries. *Ḥaqq* stands in stark and even awesome contrasts to *bāṭil,* as the true and the false, or the real and the "phony." Behind the one is metaphysical power, while the other in strident dichotomy from it is ludicrously vain and vacuous. To distinguish between the two is one of man's most decisive tasks or prerogatives. Again, there is the resonant pair of *ṣidq* and *kadhib,* or to use the more concrete human terms, *ṣādiq* and *kādhib:* the honest man of truth stands sharply over against the despicable and wretched liar. At play here is the Islamic vision of man's dramatic freedom and moral choice, in a world where decisions matter.

Ṣaḥīḥ, on the other hand, has no clear opposite. One of its applications is to a man's being in sound health; possible alternatives are that he may be weak, or sick, or old, or not old enough, or missing a limb, or what not; but there is no clear other pole.[9] The only opposite of "sound" is a wide range of unsoundness, of unspecified imperfections; although as we have already noted, in the particular case of a sentence, if it is not *ṣaḥīḥ,* true, then one may perhaps call it mistaken, *ghalaṭ* or *khaṭa'*. A railway timetable that is no longer in force, or an argument that is not cogent, various sorts of things that do not come off or are not in good working order, may be characterized as not *ṣaḥīḥ;* but this designates a quality that is not a category, or at least not a cosmic one. In other Islamic languages too—Persian, Urdu, and others, as well as Arabic, those familiar with these languages will readily agree—this third notion, used for, among other things, propositional truth, has by far the feeblest moral connotations of the three.[10]

Indeed, the first and the second are saturatedly, bristlingly, moral; they and their respective pejorative contraries are highly moralistic. Human destiny is at stake with them, and human quality. And, appropriately enough, it turns out on inquiry that the third root, *ṣaḥḥa,* does not even occur in the Qur'ān. The other two reverberate in it, mightily.

It would hardly be an exaggeration to see the Qur'ān as a vibrant affirmation that the loci of significant truth are two: the world around us, and persons. The reality of the former is divine. The inner integrity of the latter, and our conformity to, and commitment to, the real, are crucial. Indeed, this is what human life is all about.[11]

Let us return, then, specifically to *ṣadaqa, yaṣduqu, ṣidqan.* Being a resonant term in the Qur'ān, for Muslims it formulates a cosmic category, constituting one of the basic points of reference in relation to which human life and society take on meaning in the Islamic complex.

If we consult the Arabic dictionaries, we find illuminating presentations and analyses of this word. In virtually all cases these are given in conjunction with the correlative *kadhiba.* And in virtually all cases, given first, or made quite basic, is the link with speech. Since the dictionary entries under *ṣadaqa* converge substantially in their understandings of the term, at least in so far as our concerns here are at issue, it is representative enough for our purposes to cite illustratively from *Lisān al-ʿArab* and *Tāj al-ʿArūs.*[12] First, we note that although *ṣadaqa* and *kadhiba* are considered in their relation to speech, they are viewed as applied there not only to what in modern logic would be called statements or propositions, but to all sorts of things that man may say—including questions and much else. Explicitly indicated is that the speech may be about the past or about the future, in the latter case whether by way of promise or otherwise; and may be indicative, but also either interrogative, or imperative, or even supplicative. Thus a question may be not *ṣidq,* truthful, if it involves something of the "Have you stopped beating your wife?" sort. Similarly a command, such as "Give me back my book," or an entreaty, "Would you please give me back my book," may be *ṣidq* or *kadhib,* truthful or lying, depending upon whether the man addressed has the book, and the person speaking genuinely wishes it back.

In general, these and other dictionaries clearly make the point that *ṣidq* applies to that sort of speech in which there is conformity of what is said simultaneously with two things: i) what is in the speaker's mind; and ii) what is actually the case.[13]

Particular discussion is given to an assertion that "Muḥummad is the Apostle of God"—which is the Muslim's paradigm of a true statement—when it is made by someone who says it insincerely. One view is that any utterance may be half *ṣidq,* in reference either to the speaker's sincerity or to the objective facts; but there is full *ṣidq* only when both are satisfied. Similarly, when there is reference to the future, then *ṣidq* demands congruity both between inner conviction and a man's words, and between the latter and his subsequent deeds.

The verb may take an indirect object of the person addressed, inasmuch as telling the truth, in this sense, and lying, are matters of personal interrelations. *Ṣadaqahu* or *kadhibahum* indicate that the truth and falsity under consideration here are attributes of a statement in its role of establishing or constituting communication between or among human beings. Here again, it may be noted that the modern West maintains in its conceptualization of lying an implication that one can hardly tell a lie alone on a desert island, but has tended to relinquish this interpersonal dimension from its conception of speaking truth.

Comparable considerations operate when the Arabic verb is used of human actions other than speaking. Transitional is a phase such as *ṣadaqahu al-naṣīḥah:* "He was true in the advice that he gave him," or "He spoke the truth to him in his advice," or "He advised him with *ṣidq.*" This implies that the counsel was both sincere, and effectively wise. Non-verbally: *ṣadaqahu al-ikhā'*. "He was true towards him in brotherliness," or "... behaved towards him with true brotherhood." Again: *ṣadaqūhum al-qitāl,* "They fought them with *ṣidq,*" or "They were true against them in battle." This means that they fought against them both with genuine zeal and with good effect.

Throughout, *ṣidq* is that quality by which a man speaks or acts with a combination of inner integrity and objective overt appropriateness. It involves saying or doing the right thing out of a genuine personal recognition of its rightness, an inner alignment with it.

In modern English, negative concepts like lying and cheating conceptualize overt performance in terms of the performers and their moral quality, inwardly, as well as in terms of the objective outward facts or rules. On the other hand, English conceptually has not developed carefully, or formulated strongly, counterpart positive concepts to assess and to interpret behavior in these trilateral[14] terms. This is what the notion *ṣadaqa* precisely does.

Human behavior, in word or deed, is the nexus between man's inner life and the surrounding world. Truth at the personalist level is that quality by which both halves of that relationship are chaste and appropriate—are true.

The Muslims were no fools when they regarded this as an important human category. In a recent philosophic paper I have attempted to argue that modern Western logic has done a radical disservice, symptomatic perhaps of a serious disruption in human life, by championing the position, nurtured by impersonalist objective science, that the locus of truth and falsity is propositions rather than the persons who use them. In that paper I explore, a little, some of the differences and their ramifications between the orientation implicit in the concept *ṣidq* and the orientation increasingly current in Western and/or "modern" intellectual and social life in its notion of truth—differences that seem crucial and ramifications that seem profound.[15]

Next let us consider the second form: *ṣaddaqa, yuṣaddiqu, taṣdīqan.* Like other *taf'īl* forms, it constitutes an intricate causative or double transitive of wide potentiality. If *ṣadaqa* means to say (or to do) something that is at the same time both inwardly honest and outwardly correct, what then does the reactivated form *taṣdīq* signify? I may enumerate four meanings.

First, of course, it can mean "to regard as true." Its primary object may be either a person, or—less usually—a sentence; so that *ṣaddaqahu* means, "He held him to be a speaker of the truth," or may mean, "He held it to be spoken truly." These might be rendered, if one liked, as "He believed him" (or: "it"); but there are two caveats. One is that in both cases, it is because he trusted the speaker. It can indicate that he held him to be *ṣādiq,* a speaker sincerely of truth on a particular occasion, or held him to be *ṣiddīq,* a habitual teller of the truth by moral character. Secondly, a rendition by "believe" is inadequate also because it omits the reference to objective validity, since "believe" in English has become so openly neutral a term. One can believe what is false. I have not checked enough passages to be able to affirm flatly that *taṣdīq* applies only to believing what is in fact true; and yet I think that there can be no question but that, even if there are some exceptions, the standard implication still is strongly one of objective truth as well as of sincerity. This is a cosmic human quality, with little room for sheer gullibility. Accordingly, one should translate, at this level, not by "believe" but by "recognize the truth of." The difference is deep.

Even this, however, takes care of only one side of the double reference, that to the correctness of what is so regarded. There is still the other side, the personal sincerity involved. This operates at least as strongly in this second form as in the first. And the personalism is of both the primary subject and the secondary: to recognize a truth as personal for others, and as personal for oneself. Thus, if I give *taṣdīq* to some statement, I not merely recognize its truth in the world outside me, and subscribe to it, but also incorporate it into my own moral integrity as a person.

A second standard usage of this form is that it means, not "He held him to be a speaker of the truth," but rather "He *found* him to be so." One may hear a man's statement, and only subsequently find reason or experience to know that that man was no liar.

Thirdly, it may indicate this sort of notion but with a more active, resolute type of finding: that is, "He *proved* him to be a speaker of truth," or confirmed or verified the matter. Thus the common phrase, *ṣaddaqa al-khabara al-khubru:* "The experience verified the report." Accordingly, *taṣdīq* has become the term for scientific experimental verification, proving something true by test, although the notion of vindicating the experimenter as well as the experiment is never far distant. A stricter translation of the phrase just quoted would be "The experiment verified the report and the reporter."

Fourthly, still more deliberately, *taṣdīq* may mean to render true, to take steps to make come true. One instance of this is one's own promise: a radically important matter. Thus, one of the meanings of *ṣiddīq* is *alladhī yuṣaddiqu qawlahu bi-l-ʿamal,*[16] "He who validates what he says in what he does"; and another, *man ṣadaqa bi qawlihi wa-ʿtiqādihi wa ḥaqqaqa ṣidqahu bi-fiʿlihi,* "He who is truthful in his speech and in his inner conviction, and who actualizes his truthfulness in his behavior."[17]

Furthermore, *muṣaddiq* is given as equivalent to *ṣiddīq*[18]—or, conversely, *ṣiddīq* as equivalent to *dhū taṣdīq*[19] or *dā'im al-taṣdīq*[20]—presumably in any or all of the senses of this adjective, including that simply of an intensive: *al-kathīr al-ṣidq*[21] and *man kathara minhu al-ṣidq.*[22]

On the other hand, when *ṣiddīq* is said to signify, rather, one who is outstanding (*mubāligh*) in both *al-ṣidq* and *al-taṣdīq,*[23] the meaning of the latter is presumably activist: *ṣidq* refers to this person's sincerely speaking the truth, and *taṣdīq* to his sincerely acting it.[24]

To summarize. *Taṣdīq* is to recognize a truth, to appropriate it, to affirm it, to confirm it, to actualize it. And the truth, in each case, is personalist, and sincere.

All of this is in general; what has been said thus far is on the basis of the medieval Arabic dictionaries. And there is legitimacy in having begun so, with ordinary language, before we turn to the specifically theological interpretations; since those men of *kalām* who promoted the thesis that faith is *taṣdīq* would habitually begin by stressing the straightforward linguistic grounds for this. *Al-īmān fī-l-lughah al-taṣdīq,*[25] they would say, referring to traditional usage. This is over against the logicians' use of the latter term,[26] behind which, as Wolfson has shown, lies a Greek rather than an Arab tradition.

When classical Muslim thinkers, then, on being asked what faith is, affirmed that it is *taṣdīq,* what did they have in mind? The historian of religion is interested in various conceptions of faith around the world, and this one not least. If we ponder this formula a little, and correlate it with the several versions that we have just noted of *taṣdīq,* we can see that it makes good sense, and can see what the men of religion meant when they said that faith is doing or making or activating truth: doing personal truth, or making truth personal.

In a quite general and preliminary way, we may list some linguistic implications. To begin with, faith is then the *recognition* of divine truth at the personal level. Faith is the ability to recognize truth as true for oneself, and to trust it. Especially in the Islamic case, with its primarily moral orientation, this includes, or makes primary, the recognition of the authenticity and moral authority of the divine commands. Thus there is the recognition of the obligatoriness of moral obligations; and the acceptance of their obligatoriness as applying to oneself, with the personal commitment then to carrying them out.

Again: it is the personal making of what is cosmically true come true on earth: the *actualization* of truth (the truth about man).

More mystically, it is the *discovery* of the truth (the personal truth) of the Islamic injunctions: the process of personal verification of them, whereby, by living them out, one proves them and finds that they do indeed become true, both for oneself and for the society and world in which one lives.

Taṣdīq is the inner appropriation and outward implementation of truth: the process of making or finding true in actual human life, in one's own personal spirit and overt behavior, what God—or Reality—intends for man.

And, with many a passage strongly insisting that faith is more than knowledge, that it is a question of how one responds to the truth, one may also render the proposition "faith is *taṣdīq*" as "Faith is the ability to trust, and to act in terms of, what one knows to be true."

All these are not bad definitions of faith, one will perhaps agree.

They are not, and are not meant to be, definitions of Islamic faith; rather, they are Islamic definitions of human faith. At issue here is not the content of faith but its form, not its object but its nature; in question is not what is true, but what one does about what is true.

Of course, the Islamic epistemological point that Muslims learn what the final truth is about man's duty and destiny through the divine disclosure of it (in their case, in the Qur'ān) was of course taken for granted in the theological treatises, and eventually colors the further discussion of faith a little, although surprisingly little. As my presentation will perhaps make clear, and as a book on which I am working will more explicitly document, a sizeable portion of many passages in Islamic theology about faith could be introduced word for word into Christian discussions of the matter almost without modification, and with considerable profit. And the same might be true, to some degree, in humanist discussions.

We are concerned, it will be recalled, with the human quality of faith, not with its object. In the past, concern with object has distracted students from discerning *either* the similarities *or* the differences among conceptions of faith's form, both of which on inquiry turn out to be striking.

For of course (still apart from any question of the object of faith), in addition to correspondences of form, there are also divergences. Between the Islamic and the Christian religious orientations, there have been certain fundamental differences of tone; and of course the differences are even more pronounced between the classical Islamic and the modern semi-skeptical Western. These have implications for the respective notions of faith, considered as a human phenomenon. We shall note two.

One has to do with an Islamic sense of clarity. Mystery, although of course for Muslims by no means absent, yet has been something that—especially outside Ṣūfī circles—they have played up deliberately and conceptually much less than have Christians. For Muslims, God's revelation is clear, *mubīn*. (This word occurs on an average more than once per *sūrah* in the Qur'ān.[27])

A second difference has to do with the fact that the Islamic orientation is in general more moralist, more practical (more "legalistic," as Christians have tended to say of it and of the comparable Jewish orientation, but this can be seriously misleading[28]). It is more dynamic, with its revelation primarily of God's will (as distinct from the Christian case, with its revelation primarily of God's person), and derivatively then with its primary stress on *figh* more than on theology. For Muslims, "the eternal Word of God is an imperative."[29]

The radical inadequacy of the standard Western understanding of Islamic notions of faith (especially as "believing") appears at least two levels, relating to these two matters. One is a divergence in relation to knowledge; the other, in relation to moral action.

For the Muslim, God's revelation being clear (*mubīn*), it leads at once to knowledge. The concept of knowledge is vividly communicated by the Qur'ān. The verb *ʿarafa* is less common, occurring about 70 times; but *ʿalima* much more so, 856 times—which, for instance in the now standard Royal Egyptian edition, means on an average of more than once per page. The concept is lavishly imprinted in Muslim consciousness, and is central to the Islamic drama: God has acted to make quite manifest to men what He would have them know. Faith is man's positive response.

In relation to knowledge, then, a major difference at once appears between faith in its typically Islamic form and in some of its Christian forms. For many Westerners, including Christians, faith has to do with something less than knowledge, so that that to which it is oriented is "taken on faith" or is "believed" (and will be *known*, perhaps, only beyond the grave); hence also, "the leap of faith." To have faith is to believe, not yet to know. For Muslims, on the other hand, faith is on the other side of knowledge, not on this side of it.

Actually, there was an early stage in the course of Muslim reflection on these matters when faith was equated with knowledge (*maʿrifah*); while others equated it rather with acting in accord with what is known. The latter position does not concern us here: besides, its inadequacy was quickly made apparent, in the Khārijī excesses at the practical level, and theoretically in its failure to make room either for the hypocrite, *munāfiq,* who had *ʿamal* without *īmān,* or for the sinner who has *īmān* without (full) *ʿamal.* The other equation, faith is knowledge, proved equally unsatisfying, and was also soon discarded; although by deprecation, it was negatively kept alive in that later writers kept recurring to it to explain how much it leaves out. It was roundly criticized, however, on the grounds that in fact faith is *more* than knowledge. Faith is not knowledge, it was agreed; yet it has to do with what is known. In Christian scholastic thought, opinion, faith, and knowledge form a series in that order;[30] in *kalām,* the order is, rather, opinion, knowledge, faith.

Al-īmān wājib fī mā ʿulima, as Taftāzānī explicitly says: man is required to have faith in those things that he knows.[31] *Al-taṣdīq,* others said, "means a binding of one's heart *ʿala mā ʿulima.*"[32] Again, it is submitting *li-mā ʿulima.*[33]

Just as faith for Muslims has to do not with believing but with knowing, so *kufr,* rejection, is not a lack of belief, not an intellectual position that holds that something is otherwise than is the case, and is certainly not mere ignorance. Rather it, too, like its correlative *īmān,* presupposes knowledge; for it is an active repudiation of what one knows to be true. This is why it is a sin, and indeed a (the) monstrous sin. It is the one final, cosmic (or some would say, the one final human) wrong: the deliberate saying of "no" to what one knows to be right. This, too, is set forth in the Qur'ān; for instance, in two passages repeatedly cited by the *mutakallimūn* in their discussions of the relation between faith and knowledge. One (coloring the perception by many Muslims of Christians to this day) sets forth the point that some to whom the Book was sent "know it as they know their own sons"[34] and yet do not respond with faith. The other speaks of men who rejected the signs of God "even though within themselves they knew full well" that they were true.[35] Cited also, if less frequently, is the reference to those who rejected after they had accepted.[36]

The Islamic scheme, then, envisages God's acting, and thereby man's knowing; so that the all-important question becomes man's response: the response to what is now known. Ideally, there are two basic reactions possible: to accept, or to reject (*īmān,* or *kufr*).[37] The object of faith being thought of as pellucid and incontrovertible, the issue is, what does one do about that which one knows?

Faith, then, is the positive response to God's initiative. It is not merely knowledge; it includes knowledge, but is something else as well. That something additional, the men of *kalām* came to agree, is *taṣdīq. Huwa* (that is, *al-taṣdīq*) *amr zā'id ʿalā al-ʿilm.*[38]

We turn, then, from faith to *taṣdīq;* for we are now in a position to address ourselves to the question with which we began, what this term means in *kalām.* We can now see that it designates not belief, but knowledge; and not merely knowledge, but knowledge of the truth plus something else. (Neither of these two components—that of knowing the truth, nor that of the something additional—is found in the current Western translations; nor quite in the logicians' *taṣdīq.*[39]) "There is no getting away from it," says al-Taftāzānī, "that the difference is manifest between knowing, being quite sure about, on the one hand, . . . and, on the other hand, *taṣdīq* and *iʿtiqād*"[40]—in that the latter include the former and add to them. Again: "There were some Qadarīs who took up the position that faith is knowledge; but our scholars are agreed that that position is wrong—since there are the People of the Book who used to know that Muḥammad . . . was a prophet 'as surely as they knew their own sons,' and yet there is no question but that they were *kāfirs* because of the absence of *taṣdīq;* and since among the *kuffār* are some who know the truth in full certainty, but simply reject it, out of 'stubbornness and haughtiness'" (and he then notes Qur'ān 27: 14 as we have done).[41] Again, the ninth-century (*hijrī*) commentator al-Kastalī writes: "*Taṣdīq* does not mean knowing that something said or the one who says it is true (*ṣidq*): otherwise, it would have to be the case that everyone who knows the truthfulness of the prophet would have *īmān* in him (be a *mu'min* of him) and this is just not so—indeed, there were many of the *kuffār* who knew that (the Prophet) was true . . . ," and he goes on to quote the same Qur'ān passages.[42]

What, then, is *taṣdīq*? Clearly, it lies in the realm of activist sincerity. *Ṣidq*, as we have seen, designates truth at the personalist level of integrity: the second form of the verb designates an activating of this.

Fundamental for understanding one of the prime meanings of *taṣdīq* in this connection is a remark such as the following of al-Ṭabarī:

> *al-qawn kānū ṣadaqū bi-alsinatihim wa-lam yuṣaddiqụ qawlahum bi-fi'lihim.*[43]

Obviously this is not "to believe" but rather to confirm, to actualize the truth. They ". . . spoke the truth with their tongues, but did not corroborate what they were saying with their deeds." Or one might use such verbs as "authenticate" or "validate." An older usage in English would legitimately appear here if one translated by: ". . . they were not faithful to what they were saying, in their deeds."

This actualizing aspect of *taṣdīq* is illuminated, again, in the oft-cited statement, *al-īmān mā waqara fī-l-qalb, wa-ṣaddaqahu al-'amal.*[44] "Faith is that about which the heart is firm, and which deeds validate (authenticate, corroborate)."

Again, and more theologically, the fact that God Himself is called *mu'min* is also explained, for instance by al-Baghdādī, as His being activatingly faithful in this sense:

> *wa-llāh mu'min li-annahu yuṣaddiqu wa'dahu bi-l-taḥqīq.*[45]

"God is 'faithful' because He gives *taṣdīq* to His promise, carrying it out in effective realization (or actualization)."

(It would be ludicrous to translate either *īmān* or *taṣdīq* as "believing" in any of these cases—and I feel, in any cases at all.)

The difference, then, between knowledge and *taṣdīq* lies in the sincerity and in the operationalist addenda denoted by the latter term. Knowledge is the perception of a truth outside oneself; *taṣdīq* is the personal appropriation of that perception. It is the inner reordering of oneself so as to act in terms of it; the interiorization and implementation of the truth in dynamic sincerity. *Taṣdīq* means not simply "to believe" a proposition, but rather to recognize a truth and to existentialize it.

The existentializing is basic; and I have come across one instance where the parallel to modern existentialists' phrasing, even, is curious and entrancing. There are many passages in, for instance, Taftāzānī's commentary on Nasafī's *'Aqā'id,* where the activating force of *taṣdīq* is conspicuous. In one such, he explicitly rejects in so many words the notion that this term means to "believe," and even to "recognize" as true. He rejects it as altogether inadequate, and goes on to make the matter the more interesting in his endeavor to set forth the notion of self-commitment that is at issue. For, just as in English modern existentialists in order to express this notion turn to French, and borrow thence the terms *engagé* and *engagement,* so this medieval writer, in struggling to express the existentialist involvement that "faith" connotes, turns to Persian and introduces into his Arabic a Persian term, *giravīdan*—which is virtually the precise counterpart of *s'engager,* since *girav* is the Persian for that for which *gage* is the French: namely, the stake of pawn or pledge that is put up as a warranty by a participant in an affair. "The true nature of *taṣdīq* is not that there should take place in the mind the attributing of veracity to what is said, or to the person who says it, unaccompanied by a yielding to it and an accepting of it for oneself. On the contrary, it is rather a yielding to and an acceptance of that, such that the term 'surrender' applies to it as Imām Ghazzālī has made clear. All in all, it is the meaning that is expressed in Persian by *giravīdan—s'engager.*"[46]

All this is especially relevant to, and leads to a consideration of, the second of the two fundamental orientations that we averred to be characteristic of Islamic life and significant for its faith: namely, the moral. For the truth to which the Muslim must respond is largely a moral truth. The knowledge conferred by revelation is largely a knowledge of moral requirements, of commands, of duties: *awāmir, aḥkām, farā'iḍ.* In the moral life especially, as all of us recognize, knowledge is not yet virtue. The recognition that something ought to be done is not yet the recognition that *I* ought to do it, not yet the resolve to do it, not yet my personal decision so to act. Involved in the moral life is a particular quality or act, more than and other than knowledge and its awareness of objective truth, which brings one to the point of committing oneself to act in terms of what one has recognized as right. This is *taṣdīq,* and to have it is to have faith.

This notion of "reaching a certain point" is brought out sharply in the following:

> *Annahu* [*sc. anna al-īmān*] *al-taṣdīq al-qalbī alladhī balagha ḥadd al-jazm wa-l-idhʿān.*[47]

This is in a discussion of the position that faith is a yes-or-no matter, rather than a more-or-less one. One either decides to act, or one does not. Hence *ḥadd,* the dividing line or boundary between two realms, here that of deliberation and that of decision. *Al-jazm,* also communicates this same idea. The basic meaning of *jazama, yajzimu, jazman* is to cut off, to cut short, to come to an end (thus it means to pronounce the final consonant of a word without a vowel); and the derived and standard meaning then is to decide, to judge, to resolve, to be positive or certain about something, to make up one's mind. The notion seems to be that of terminating that period of deliberating and pondering wherein one is mulling a thing over. More or less literally, then: "faith is that appropriation of truth by the heart that comes to the point of decision and compliance." With it, one crosses over from awareness to engagement.

One of the compelling expositions of the matter comes in the fuller elaboration of a statement by the late writer al-Kastalī, of which we have already[48] quoted the first part: "*Al-taṣdīq* does not mean knowing the truth . . . ; no, it is rather a yielding to what is known and a letting oneself be led by it, and the soul's being quiet and at peace with it and its accepting it, setting aside recalcitrance and stubbornness, and constructing one's actions in accordance with it."[49] (This is a beautiful example of a passage that Christian theology could be happy and proud to take over word for word.)

Another explication, again completing a passage already[50] introduced in part: "The distinction is inescapably clear between, on the one hand, knowing the moral injunctions, being quite sure about them, and on the other hand appropriating their truth actively to oneself and binding oneself to them."[51]

The moralist orientation of faith comes out in many passages such as this, where traditional Western translations appear altogether inept. Phrases such as *al-īmān bi-l-farḍ.*[52] *al-taṣdīq bi-l-aḥkām,*[53] and *taṣdīq (al-) ḥukm*[54] are standard; their significance is clear when our existentialist self-committing understanding is recognized, of *āmana* as "to accept" and *ṣaddaqa* as "actively to personalize for oneself the truth of." "Believe," however, will not do. One "believes" a doctrine, or "believes in" a person (as Christians have it); but when the revelation is a command, the appropriate category is other. With the object of faith injunctions, the nature of faith is a moral stance.

It may be noted that both *ṣidq* and *taṣdīq* are regularly used with *khabar* (also *mukhbir,* etc.),[55] but it must be remembered that these latter terms refer not to reports or statements in the indicative mood necessarily, or even especially, but to anything that is said, including imperatives. As an illustration:

mā akhbarahu bihi min awāmirihi wa-nawāhīhi.[56]

It may further be remembered that the *mukhbir* here is God (not Muḥammad).[57] In the Islamic orientation, faith is primarily a personal acceptance of the divine imperatives for oneself.

Turning to a statement of al-Nasafī, in his widely accepted *ʿAqāʾid,* we find the following:

al-īmān huwa al-taṣdīq bi mā jāʾ a min ʿinda-llāh taʿālā.[58]

The impulse of a Westerner is to take the last six words here as a paraphrase, or even as a technical term, for the Qurʾān. Strictly, however, it is neither; and to neglect what is actually being said can be misleading, omitting the subtleties. For at issue here is not a *taṣdīq* of the Qur'ān (outsiders are of course conscious of this "object" of faith, since it is what manifestly separates Muslims from themselves). It is, rather, a *taṣdīq* of what is from God: in principle, whatever it be. (It is true that Muslims regard the Qur'ān as this; but that is assumed here, not said.) The difference is fundamental. Faith is not to recognize something as divine revelation; it is to recognize divine revelation as—for oneself, personally—authoritative. To be a man of faith is not to accept something as from God; rather, if something is from God, then to be a man of faith is to incorporate that into your life and to act accordingly.

Some would be tempted to suspect that I am forcing the interpretation here, and reading too much into the text. Let us turn to the commentators, then. The most widely accepted of them, Taftāzānī, says that the above phrase[59] means:

> *ay, taṣdīq al-nabī, ʿalayhi al-salām, bi-l-qalb fī jamīʿ mā ʿulima bi-l-ḍarūrah majīʾuhu bihi min ʿinda-llāh taʿālá, ijmālan.*[60]

"To give *taṣdīq* in one's heart to the Prophet, on him be peace, and to all that is indubitably known as having come from God through him, in general."[61] "Believing" and "regarding as true" are ruled out here. For explicitly it is a matter of what one knows (*sic*) (the root *ʿalima* however pointed) incontrovertibly (*sic*) to be from God. Faith is a response to what one indisputably knows to be of divine origin.[62] And indeed the word *ijmālan* confirms that at issue here is the principle of *taṣdīq* of what (-ever) is transcendent: the author explicitly goes on to say that faith is not infringed by lack of knowledge as to what precisely *was* revealed. For the next sentence in his text reads:

> *wa-innahu kāfin fī-l-khurūj ʿan ʿuhdat al-īmān wa lā tanḥaṭṭu darajatuhu ʿan al-īmān al-tafṣīlī.*[63]

By *hu* here he understands *al-īmān al-ijmālī* (more exactly, *al-īmān ijmālan*). Faith in principle (faith in general) "is sufficient to enable a person to discharge his obligation to have faith; and it does not rank lower than detailed faith."

Faith, then, was understood by classical Muslims not in terms alien to modern men, nor in terms parallel to but never converging with other communities' involvements, but rather in ways deeply discerning and universally human. Admittedly, the Muslim world did, to use an infidel's term, "believe" (Muslims would say, rather, "recognize") that the Qur'ān is the word of God; within that framework of ideas they set forth their analysis of the human condition. *Kalām* is a statement within, not about, their *Weltanschauung;* and to that statement the concept of *taṣdīq* could and did make an impressive and significant contribution.

It may seem to the patient reader that in my exposition of this term I have overly belabored my point, elaborately commentating upon passages whose meaning is self-evident, being at pains to defend interpretations that hardly require elucidation, and piling up evidence that reiterates the obvious. I have been pushed to this, I suppose, in order to render it unlikely that in the future anyone will ever again translate *īmān* as "belief," or *kāfir* as "unbeliever." The question is not what one believes, but what one does about what one believes or recognizes as true. At issue, in the matter of faith, is what kind of person one is.

Notes

1. The present study is not primarily an historical one; neither by intent nor otherwise. It does not investigate development (which was intricate), nor concern itself with the earliest phases of that development. Rather, being concerned to elucidate simply the meaning of one term (*taṣdīq*) which gradually became standard in *īmān* discussions, it deals primarily with usage at a relatively mature phase of classical and even medieval development. The first to posit the equation *al-īmān huwa al-taṣdīq* was perhaps the Murji thinker Bishr al-Marīsī. (Cf. Abū al-Ḥasan al-Ashʿarī, *Kitāb Maqālāt al-īslāmīyīn*, ed. Hellmut Ritter [*Die Dogmatischen Lehren der Anhänger des Islam: Bibliotheca Islamica,* I.a.] (Istanbul/Leipzig, 1929–30) 1: 140. It was taken up by al-Ashʿarī himself (*Kitāb al-Lumaʿ*, ed. and trans. by Richard J. McCarthy, Beirut, 1953: Arabic, p. 75; English trans. p. 104.) Historically there was a pre-Ashʿarī stage when *maʿrifah,* rather than *taṣdīq,* was canvassed as the role of the heart (if any: whether along with or over against *iqrār* and *ʿamal* in *īmān*), but this gained but little lasting favor. (Cf. infra, at ref. 30 et seqq.) Once *taṣdīq* was accepted as the heart's role, it prevailed and remained virtually unchallenged until Ibn Taymīyah, who, using the conception of *ʿamal al-qalb* or *aʿmāl qalbīyah* (as distinct from external *aʿmāl*), insisted the *taṣdīq,* which at best is one of these, is not sufficient in itself to constitute *īmān.* I have accumulated some evidence to suggest, but have not weighed or sifted it enough yet to prove, that by *taṣdīq* Ibn Taymīyah may exceptionally tend to understand merely or primarily an intellectual judgment (along the lines that, on the basis of other texts than his, I am otherwise criticizing in this present paper), and that therefore he finds it an inadequate interpretation of *īmān,* even *bi-l-qalb.* Faith is not merely or even primarily belief, he would then be saying: but I here claim that the earlier writers were also saying this, inasmuch as to them, including those who were content with the *īmān*-equals-*taṣdīq* formula, the latter term can be seen to have signified a good deal more than that. (See Ibn Taymīyah, *Kitāb al-Īmān,* Damascus, 1961, passim and esp. pp. 259–60).

   If my general interpretation of *taṣdīq* be validated, an historical study of its use might then follow. If the suggested view of Ibn Taymīyah be correct (and I have found no other *kalām* writer to agree with him), then so far as an historical dimension of our problem is concerned, it could mean that the development would perhaps be that *taṣdīq* meant what I am here suggesting in the minds of most writers (with varying degrees, of course, of sensitivity and insight) for perhaps some five centuries over the classical period, from roughly the third century on, but that the meaning then began to give way, at least in certain circles (perhaps those most influenced by, or reacting against, *falsafah?*), to one closer to the logicians', and/or its presently accepted sense. I am doubtful about this, however; for against it is that Taftāzānī, who is later than Ibn Taymīyah, and even Kastalī, who is much later, are much more personalist.

   Historical presentations of the processes of *īmān* discussions, especially in their formal and especially in their early aspects, have, of course, been done, most notably by Wensinck, Izutsu, Gardet and Qanawātī; and one looks forward to a comprehensive new study of *kalām* promised by Harry Wolfson, forthcoming from Harvard University Press, Cambridge, Mass. I am taking the liberty of disagreeing, however, with all these writers in their understanding of the one word *taṣdīq*.

2. Harry A. Wolfson, "The terms *taṣawwur* and *taṣdīq* in Arabic philosophy and their Greek, latin and Hebrew equivalents." *The Muslim World* 33 (1943): pp. 114–28.

3. As his title suggests, the writers that Wolfson's article investigates are chiefly the *falāsifah* (al-Fārābī, Ibn Sīnā, Ibn Rushd), but he includes also Ghazālī's study of these (*Maqāṣid al-Falāsifah*) and Shahrastānī's treatment of them (in *al-Milal wa-l-Niḥal*).

4. The latter conceptual tradition, the academic, within which this present submission is done, might manage to apprehend the classical Islamic form of faith without managing to comprehend the classical Islamic substance of faith. Faith is precisely that element in religious life that makes the difference between insider and outsider.

5. The term *al-īmān* in Arabic is ambiguously generic or specific (human or Islamic). The ambiguity was resolved (did not appear) in a convergence by those who thought or felt that human faith normatively (ultimately; truly; divinely) is what outsiders would call faith in its Islamic form. This has been the standard Muslim position.

6. I am currently at work on a comparative study of faith concepts which includes an investigation of the Latin term *credo* and the English term *believe.*

7. *Ṣaḥīh al-Bukhārī*, "Kitāb al-Īmān". In the Cairo edition *bi-Sharḥ al-Kirmānī* of al-Maṭbaʿah al-Bahīyah al-Miṣrīyah (ʿAbd al-Raḥmān Muḥammad), 2nd ed., 1358/1939, it is Bāb 47, vol. I, p. 194. In the Muḥammad Fu'ād ʿAbd al-Bāqī edition, Cairo, Dār Iḥyā'al-Kutub al-ʿArabīyah, 1368/1949, it is Bāb 1, vol. 1, p. 2, *ḥadīth* 5.

8. It could perhaps be argued that the other types of answer—that faith is *iqrār* and/or *ʿamal*—are, like the *ḥadīth* just quoted, rather synthetic than analytic statements about Islamic faith: that they indicate what having faith means (entails) in human life rather than what the word "faith" means at the conceptual level.

9. Sometimes *s-q-m* is coupled over against *ṣ-ḥ-ḥ* as an opposite. One instance that I have happened upon is in Rāzī, *Tafsīr,* 3:19—*aḥwāl al-khalq fi-l-ḥusn wa-l-qubḥ, wa-l-ghinā wa-l-fugr, wa-l-ṣiḥḥah wa-l-suqm, wa . . . Mafātīḥ al-Ghayb,* al-Maṭbaʿah al-ʿĀmirah, Istanbul, 1307 [1889–90], vol. 2, p. 626.

10. On the matter of the classical Islamic view of the morality of truth and lies, it is perhaps not inappropriate to quote here something that I had occasion to write elsewhere, in commenting on a passage of the *Nihāyat al-Iqdām* of al-Shahrastānī, who "contends that a false sentence is not intrinsically better or worse, morally, than a true one. Some truths, he says, are not very pretty. (Keats was inspired by an urn to remind us that this view is un-Grecian.) There are some who would agree with this, holding that it is not lies themselves, but the telling of lies, that is wrong. Our author goes further: for him, the telling of lies, even, is not intrinsically moral or immoral. What is wrong, hellishly so, is for *me* to tell a lie—or for you to do so. And the reason for this is that God has created us and has commanded us not to lie." Wilfred Cantwell Smith, "The Concept of Sharīʿa Among Some Mutakallimūn," in *Arabic and Islamic Studies in Honor of Hamilton A. R. Gibb,* ed. George Maḳdisi, Leiden, Brill, 1965, p. 598.

11. And what eternity is all about, too, in a sense. The reality of the objective world, although it is prior to our personal orientation to that reality, in the end will vanish; but the way that persons have responded to that reality is of a transcending significance which, to use poetic imagery, will survive, will cosmically outlast the world. The

mundane world is independent of man and is not to be subordinated to his whimsies. Yet ultimately, in this vision, man if he relates himself truly to reality is greater than the world.

12. The remainder of this paragraph is a translation (or paraphrase: the "wife-beating" phrasing is my modern counterpart to the Zayd illustration actually used; and similarly for the book-giving) from the entry s.v. "ṣ-d-q" in Muḥibb al-Dīn Muḥammad Murtadá, *Sharḥ al-Qāmūs al-musammá Tāj al-ʿArūs,* 1304, [1886], vol. 6, pp. 403ff. See also Ibn Mukarram Ibn Manẓūr, *Lisān al-ʿArab,* Dar Sādir/Dar Bayrūt, Beirut, 1374–6/1955–6, vol. 10, p. 193.

13. *Al-ṣidq muṭābaqat al-qawli al-ḍamīra wa-l-mukhbara ʿanhu maʿan. Tāj al-ʿArūs,* p. 404, lines 5–6.

14. I say "trilateral" because in the case of, for instance, a statement three things are involved: the man who makes the statement, the statement itself, and the facts that it purports to describe. In a game, cheating similarly involves three things: the cheater, his action, and the rules of the game. I leave aside for the moment a question (in the end, perhaps exceedingly important) as to whether we should in fact include a fourth element in the complex: the person spoken to, the other player. The common view that the truth of a statement is a function of the relation between it and the overt facts may be termed a bilateral theory. A relationship cannot be unilateral.

15. Wilfred Cantwell Smith, "A Human View of Truth," *SR: Studies in Religion/Sciences religieuses,* vol. 1, no. 1, Toronto, 1971, pp. 6–24; to be published also presently in *Proceedings* of the University of Birmingham 1970 Conference on the Philosophy of Religion.

16. *Tāj al-ʿArūs,* p. 405, lines -2, -1.

17. *Ibid.,* p. 406, line 1.

18. *Lisān al-ʿArab,* p. 193, col. 2, line -3.

19. More strictly, *ṣiddīqah* (of Mary in Qur'ān 5:65) as *dhāt taṣdīq: Lisān al-ʿArab,* p. 193, col. 2, lines -2, -1; and also *Tāj al-ʿArūs,* p. 406, line 2.

20. *Lisān al-ʿArab,* p. 193, col. 2, lines -6, -5; and *Tāj al-ʿArūs,* p. 405, line -2, citing *al-Ṣiḥāḥ.*

21. *Tāj al-ʿArūs,* p. 405, line -3.

22. *Ibid.,* line -1.

23. Same ref. as for note 19 above.

24. *Taṣdīq* here, and in the previous six references, clearly has nothing to do with "believing": it is not being said that Mary or other *ṣiddīqūn* excel in credulousness or gullibility!

25. This begins from the very first time, apparently, that this explication of *īmān* is introduced into the discussions, by Bishr al-Marīsī: *Aṣḥāb Bishr al-Marīsī, yaqūlūna inna al-īmān huwa al-taṣdīq, li-anna al-īmān fī-l-lughah huwa al-taṣdīq, wa-mā laysa bi-taṣdīq fa-laysa bi-īmān* (al-Ashʿarī, *Maqālāt,* 1, 140). The point is repeated by, for instance, al-Māturīdī, and continues with virtually all subsequent *kalām* discussions of the matter. See Abū Manṣūr al-Māturīdī, *kitāb al-Tawḥīd,* ed. Fatḥ Allāh Khulayf, Bayrūt,Dār al-Mishriq, n.d., p. 375, line 7; cf. p. 377, line 11.

26. The "over against" here is my own, but there is explicit support for it in the sources. In *kalām,* some of the writers included the special logicians' use of *taṣdīq* in their interpretation of *īmān* as being *taṣdīq* (e.g., Taftāzānī, *Sharḥ al-ʿAqā'id al-Nasafīyah,* Cairo ed.,

ʿĪsā al-Bābī al-Ḥalabī [1335?], p. 125, lines -5, -6); but others had reservations or explicitly rejected this. For instance Aḥmad Mūsá al-Khayālī contrasts *al-taṣdīq al-manṭiqī* with that *fī bāb al-īmān;* and Isām al-Dīn al-Isfarā'īnī contrasts *al-taṣdīq al-madhkūr fī awā'il kutub al-mīzān* with *al-taṣdīq fī kutub al-kalām.* Al Isfarā'īnī also writes *wa-lā yakhfá alayka al-farqa bayna al-īmān, wa-l-taṣdīq alladhī yubḥathu ʿanhu fī kutub al-mīzān.* (References for these three: on the margin of the Cairo edition of al-Taftāzānī just cited, p. 125, lines 24-25 [viz., lines 7-8 of his section], 30-31, 2-3.) Cf. also Muṣliḥ al-Dīn Muṣṭafá al-Kastalī, on the margin of the istanbul edition of the same work, 1310 [1892-93], p. 152, lines -6 ff.

27. 119 times; and other forms of the verb (not counting, of course, the preposition *bayna,* but including *bayyannā*) a further 138 times.

28. On "moral" rather than "legal" as the better, more accurate, translation of *shar'ī,* and the better attribution to the Islamic outlook generally, see my article in n. 10 above.

29. Wilfred Cantwell Smith, *Islam in Modern History,* Princeton, 1957/London, 1958, p. 17; New York, 1959, p. 25 (italics in the original).

30. *Differunt secundum perfectum et imperfectum apinio, fides et scientia:* St. Thomas Aquinas, *Summa Theologica,* IIa IIae, qu. 67, a. 3. *Fides est . . . supra opinionem, infra scientiam:* Hugo of St. Victor, *De Sacramentis,* lib. 1, p. X, c. 2.

31. The passage in full reads:
wa-l-īmān wājib ijmālan fī māʿulima ijmālan wa tafṣīlan fī māʿulima tafṣīlan.
In the Cairo edition, p. 129, lines 4-5; in the Istanbul edition, p. 157, lines 11-12.

32. *Al-taṣdīq ʿibārah ʿan rabṭ al-qalb ʿalá mā ʿulima* (or: *mā ʿalima,* sc., *al-qualbu*) *min akhbār al-mukhbir.* This definition is attributed to *baʿḍ al-mashāykh* by Taftāzānī, Cairo, p. 129, lines 18-19.

33. *Huwa idhʿān li-mā ʿulima wa-nqiyād lahu wa. . . .* al-Kastalī, p. 152, lines 11-12. *Huwa* here refers to *al-taṣdīq,* which *al-īmān* has just been said to be. The passage is cited more fully in n. 42 below.

34. Qur'ān 2: 146 and 6:20. *Alladhīna ātaynāhum al-kitāba yaʿrifūnahu kamā yaʿrifūna abnā'ahum.*

35. Qur'ān 27: 14. *Wa-jaḥadū bihā wa-stayqanat-hā anfusuhum ẓulman wa-ʿulūwan.*

36. Qur'ān 9:74. *Wa-kafarū baʿda islāmihim.*

37. Once man is confronted with the truth from God, he is to choose whether to accept or to reject. *Al-ḥaqqu min rabbikum fa-man shā'a fa-l-yu'min wa-man shā'a fal-l-yakfur.* Qur'ān 18: 29.

38. Al-Kastalī, p. 152, lines 16-17.

39. Strictly, the differences between *taṣdīq* in *kalām* and *taṣdīq* in logic, although major, are of a different order from those obtaining between the former and modern Western understandings. See the references given above in n. 26. The contrast there tends to be in terms of knowledge: although the logicians themselves speak of *taṣdīq* as one of the divisions of *ʿilm,* the *mutakallimūn* interpret the logicians' *taṣdīq* as having to do with believing rather than knowing, while their own concept of *taṣdīq,* they say, excludes opinions, ignorance, and hearsay. "Logical *taṣdīq* includes mere belief": *al-taṣdīq al-mantiqī yaʿummu al-ẓannī* (al Kahayālī, p. 125, line 25 [8]). *al-taṣdīq al-mīzānī yaʿummu al-ẓunūn* (al-Isfarā'īnī, p. 125, line 32). *al-taṣdīq fī kutub al-kalām qism li-l-ʿilm al-mufassar bi-mā lā yaḥtamilu al-ẓann wa-l-jahl wa-l-taqlīd, bi-khilāf kutub al-mīzān* (id., p. 125, line 31). Kastalī, despite remarks of this kind and over against his strong preceding emphasis

on the truthfulness involved in *taṣdīq* (above, at ref. 38), does cautiously admit that this latter term may occasionally get used in its sense of sincerely acting upon one's conviction even in cases where those convictions may be invalid: *huwa amr zā'id ʿalá-l-ʿilm, bal rubbamā yataʿallaqu bi-l-maẓnūn wa-l-muʿtaqad ayḍan wa-li-hādhā yubná al-ʿamal ʿalayhimā;* but he adds, *wa-ammā, māhīyatahu mā hiya* ("nonetheless, its nature is what it is") (*op. cit.*, p. 152, lines 16-21).

40. Taftāzānī, Cairo, p. 129, lines 16-17. The passage is given in Arabic more fully below, n. 51. *Iʿtiqād,* in this and other passages, has in *kalām* thought its more or less literal meaning of "binding oneself" to an idea, not merely holding it passively. For a distinction, even in modern Arabic, between it and *ra'y,* "belief," "opinion" see Aḥmad Amīn, *Fayḍ al-Khāṭir,* vol. I, pp. 1-3. (The original of this article appeared in the journal *Al-Risālah,* Cairo, Oct. 16, 1933.)

41. Taftāzānī, Cairo, p. 129, lines 13-16:
. . . anna baʿḍ al-qadarīyah dhahaba ilá anna al-īmān huwa al-maʿrifah wa-aṭbaqa ʿulamā'unā ʿalá fisādihi li-anna ahl al-kitāb kāna yaʿrifūna nubūwat Muḥammad ṣallá Allāh ʿalayhi wa-sallam ka-mā yaʿrifūna abnā'ahum maʿa al-qa'ṭʿ bi-kufrihim li-ʿadam al-taṣdīq wa-li-anna min al-kuffār man kāna yaʿrifū al-ḥaqq yaqīnan wa-i [*nnam*] *ā kāna yunkiru ʿinādan wa-stikbāran.*
In the Istanbul edition, this passage is found p. 158, lines 8 ff.; it reads *Allāh taʿālá,* and supplies the reading *inna-mā,* which is obscured in my copy of the Cairo text.

42. Kastalī, p. 152, lines -6 ff.:
al-taṣdīq laysa ʿibārah ʿan al-ʿilm bi-ṣidq al-khabar aw al-mukhbir, wa-illā, lazima an yakūna kullu ʿālim bi-ṣidq al-nabī ʿalayhi al-salām mu'minan bihi, wa laysa ka-dhālik. Fa-inna kathīran min al-kuffār kānū ʿālimīn bi-ṣidqihi ʿalayhi al-salām, kamā dalla ʿalayhi qawluhu taʿālá.

43. Abū Jaʿfar Muḥammad ibn Jarīr al-Ṭabarī, *Jāmiʿ al-Bayān fī tafsīr al-Qur'ān,* ad 49: 14. I have used the Cairo edition of 1323-29 [1905-12], al-Maṭbaʿah al-Kubrá al-Amīrīyah, vol. 26, p. 89.

44. More fully: *laysa al-īmān bi-l-taḥallī wa-lā bi-l-tamannī wa-lākinna mā waqara. . . .* This statement is frequently attributed to al-Ḥasan al-Baṣrī, but is cited as an ḥadīth from the Prophet by Abū Manṣūr ʿAbd al-Qāhir ibn Ṭāhir al-Baghdādī, *Kitāb Uṣūl al-Dīn,* Istanbul, Ilâhiyat Fakültesi, 1346/1928, pp. 250-251.

45. Al-Baghdādī, p. 248, line 2.

46. Taftāzānī, Cairo, p. 125, lines 3 ff.:
wa-laysa [sic] *ḥaqīqat al-taṣdīq an yaqaʿa fi-l-qalb nisbat al-ṣidq ilá al-khabar aw al-mukhbir min ghayr idhʿān wa-qubūl. bal huwa idhʿān wa-qubūl li-dhālik, bi-ḥaythu yaqaʿu ʿalayhi ism al-taslīm ʿalá mā ṣaraḥa* [or: *ṣarraḥa*] *bihi al-imām al-Ghazzālī. wa-bi-l-jumlah huwa al-maʿná alladhī yuʿabbaru ʿanhu bi-l-fārisīyah bi-kirawīdan.*

47. Taftāzānī, Cairo, p. 128, lines 15-16.

48. Cf. nn. 42, 33 above.

49. Kastalī, p. 152, lines 6, 11-16:
[*inna*] *al-taṣdīq laysa ʿibārah ʿan al-ʿilm bi-ṣidq al-khabar aw al-mukhbir. . . . bal, huwa idhʿān li-mā ʿulima wa-nqiyād lahu wa-sukūn al-nafs ʿalayhi wa-ṭmi'nānuhā bihi wa-qubūluhā bi-dhālik, bi-tark al-jaḥd wa-l-ʿinād, wa-binā' al-aʿmāl ʿalayhi.*

50. Cf. n. 40.

51. Taftāzānī, Cairo, p. 129, lines 16-17:
lā budda min bayān al-farq bayna maʿrifat al-aḥkām wa-stayqānihā wa bayna al-taṣdīq bihā wa-ʿtiqādihā.

52. E.g.: *kānū āmanū fi-l-jumlah; thumma ya'fī farḍun ba'da farḍ, fa-kānū yu'minūna bi-kulli farḍ khaṣṣ*—Taftāzānī, Cairo, p. 129, lines -1, -2.

53. E.g.:
al-taṣdīq bi-hā (sc., *bi-aḥkām*) (*Ibid.*, line 17.) It may be noted that I am taking *ḥukm, aḥkām* here and usually as imperatives, signifying the command of one in authority (viz., God). This interpretation is supported by the constant parallels with *farḍ, awāmir wa nawāhin,* etc., as well as by the contexts and by the general Islamic orientation (and by the way that I have heard the word used in colloquial parlance in the Muslim world). The prevailing sense of incumbent duties that permeates the Muslim consciousness—and, more formally, the central significance of *shar', sharī'āh,*—are to be recalled here. Gardet tends rather toward "état juridique" (Louis Gardet, *Dieu et la destinée de l'homme,* Paris, 1967, p. 381).

54. E.g., *taṣdīq ḥukm al-nabī.*

55. E.g.:
al-mu'min bi-llāh huwa al-muṣaddiq li-llāh fī khabarihi, wa ka-dhālik al-mu'min bi-l-nabī muṣaddiq lahu fī khabarihi (al-Baghdādī, pp. 247–48).

56. Al-Taftāzānī, Cairo, p. 131, line 2.

57. Also in the first part of the Baghdādī passage just quoted (in n. 55).

58. Najm al-Dīn Abū Ḥafs 'Umar al-Nasafī, *'Aqīdah,* in William Cureton, ed., *Pillar of the Creed of the Sunnites . . . ,* London, Society for the Publication of Oriental Texts, 1843, appendix. Rather than simply *jā'a,* the reading *jā'a bihi* appears in both the Cairo and the Istanbul editions of the Taftāzānī *Sharḥ:* Cairo, p. 126, lines 3–4; Istanbul, p. 153, lines 8–9.

59. With *bihi:* cf. preceding note.

60. Taftāzānī, Cairo, p. 126, lines 4–5.

61. Three readings are possible:
'ulima . . . majī'uhu
'allama . . . majī'ahu
'alima . . . majī'ahu.
I have chosen the first for my transliteration and my translation. In the second, which is rather forced, the subject of the verb is the prophet. In the third, the subject of the verb is the understood subject of *al-taṣdīq.* Such a reading of *'alima,* with *al-muṣaddiq* as the understood subject, is a possibility for each of the cases considered above (cf. nn. 31, 32, 33 and elsewhere) where I have read *'ulima.* Although possible, however, I find it less cogent. It does not, in any case, affect the sense or modify our argument.

62. It might be possible to submit that, especially with the second and except with the third pointing of *'alima* (cf. preceding note), a given man's *īmān* could be envisaged as a *taṣdīq* by him of what other people know to be true. This, however, would constitute a kind of *taqlīd,* with all the ensuing problems as to whether that amounts to *īmān* or not. And in any case the force then of *ḍarūrah* would, in such an interpretation, be awkward, to say the least. So too would be *ijmālan.* And why was this clause introduced into the explications at all, if not to make the point that our own argument here is endeavoring to elucidate.

63. Taftāzānī, Cairo, p. 126, line 5. The Istanbul edition reads *yanḥaṭṭu,* presumably then *darajatahu:* "it is not less in its rank" (p. 153, line 12).

The Shiite and Khārijite Contribution to Pre-Ashʿarite *Kalām*

WILFERD MADELUNG
The University of Chicago

SHIISM AND KHĀRIJISM, the two earliest schismatic movements in Islam, arose about the problem of the legitimate leadership of the Muslim community. Their respective positions concerning the question of the imāmate, as it came to be called, has always remained constitutive for both movements and, in the case of the Shīʿa, also for most of its subdivisions. For the Khārijites the related question of the membership in the community of the faithful, which for them depended chiefly, if not exclusively, on the acceptance of their specific doctrine and of the proper attitude toward the *dār,* i.e., the Muslim community at large, became equally vital. It was mainly around this question that the movement split further into its various branches. Naturally then the most conspicuous and consistent contributions of Shiism and Khārijism to Islamic dogmatics and *kalām* consisted in the formulation and elaboration of their doctrine of the imāmate and, for the Khārijites, of their doctrine defining faith and infidelity. Yet this contribution will not primarily concern us here.

Less obvious is the role Shiism and Khārijism may have played in the elaboration of more specifically theological doctrine, particularly in respect to the two most prominent problems of *kalām:* the unity of God versus the multiplicity of his attributes, and divine determinism versus human free will. The question poses itself whether Shiism and Khārijism, having originated in a dispute over the leadership and organization of the Muslim community, developed a specific theological doctrine of their own in the early discussion of these problems. Because of the general unavailability of early Shiite and Khārijite theological works, modern studies have tended either to rely on late treatises of creeds of these movements and then have usually noted the predominance of Muʿtazilite concepts and tendencies in them, or to rely on the heresiographical works and then stressed the lack of unity of view among the representatives of both Shiism and Khārijism. A more precise definition of the time and character of the Muʿtazilite influence and a closer examination of the non-Muʿtazilite doctrines described by the heresiographers appear indispensable for an adequate assessment of the Shiite and Khārijite contribution to early *kalām*.

Shiism was represented in the early *kalām* discussions by its two major branches, the Imāmiyya and the Zaydiyya. The earliest discussions in which representatives of both groups participated evidently took place in the time of Imām Jaʿfar al-Ṣādiq (d. 148/765),[1] that is, soon after the two branches constituted themselves as well-defined movements during the revolt of Zayd b. ʿAlī in 122/740. The chief spokesmen of the Imāmiyya at this time appear in the sources as Muḥammad b. al-Nuʿmān, known among his opponents as Shayṭān al-Ṭāq; Zurāra b. Aʿyan (d. 150/767 Hishām b. Sālim al-Jawālīqī; and Hishām b. al-Ḥakam (d. 179/795–6).[2] The titles of some theological treatises of these men are mentioned by Ibn al-Nadīm and al-Ṭūsī;[3] and the heresiographers, especially al-Ashʿarī, record their views on a variety of theological topics. Only the views of Hishām b. al-Ḥakam, however, are reported with some degree of regularity. Besides their views, Al-Ashʿarī occasionally mentions those of some later Imāmī scholars, more often simply attributing doctrines to anonymous Imāmī groups.

The theological views of the Imāmiyya assembled by al-Ashʿarī may at first sight appear to vary greatly. In considering the earliest phase of Imāmī doctrine we may, however, exclude the anonymous views of a definitely Muʿtazilite character. Al-Ashʿarī himself repeatedly stresses that these views had been introduced only recently among the Imāmiyya. They are to be attributed, as has been shown elsewhere in more detail,[4] to some scholars of the second half of the 3rd/9th century. The other Imāmī views reported by al-Ashʿarī upon closer examination reveal a common core of basic concepts. The differences among them resemble those among the views of different Muʿtazilite scholars, which also revolve around a core of basic concepts common to all Muʿtazilites. The basic Imāmī concepts of God can indeed best be defined in contrast to some of the Muʿtazilite concepts.

The Muʿtazilites conceived God as transcending space and time. Transcending space, he cannot be localized on the throne or in the heavens; transcending time, he is absolutely immutable in his essence, and motion cannot be ascribed to him. This immutability is the basis of the distinction between attributes of essence and attributes of act, which was universally recognized by the Muʿtazilites already in the 2nd/8th century. Only essential attributes are immutable and can never be absent in God, like knowledge, power and life. Changeable attributes, or those which apply to God at certain times, like creation, speech, pleasure and displeasure, are attributes of act. They do not affect the immutable essence of

God, for they are logically outside of God, or, in the terminology of the *mutakallimūn*, "other than" (*ghayr*) God.

The early Imāmī theologians took a contrary position in all these matters. According to their concept, God is immanent in space, at least after the creation of space. Hishām b. al-Ḥakam is reported to have maintained that God was (originally) not in space; but when space came into being by a movement of God, he came to be in it. This space, he said, was the throne.[5] God, in the doctrine of the early Imāmī theologians, is located on his throne in accordance with the Koranic text. Al-Ashʿarī reports disagreement among them on the question of whether the bearers of the throne carry the throne only or also the Creator.[6] The spatial concept of God held by the Imāmī theologians commonly expressed itself in their defining God as a body (*jism*). Hishām b. al-Ḥakam described him specifically as having length, breadth, and depth. While he is reported to have likened God variously to a crystal or a pure ingot shining like a round pearl, his final position was that God is a body unlike bodies (*jism lā ka l-ajsām*).[7] He and probably the doctrine of his school also defined God as a body, in the meaning that he is existent (*mawjūd*).[8] Hishām al-Jawālīqī and Muḥammad b. al-Nuʿmān hold that God has the form (*ṣūra*) of a man,[9] a view specifically repudiated by Hishām b. al-Ḥakam[10] and others. Most of the Imāmī views, including those of the three prominent scholars mentioned, agreed, however, in describing God as light, no doubt with a view to the light verse of the Koran.

The Imāmī theologians did not hesitate to ascribe motion to God. As has been mentioned already, Hishām b. al-Ḥakam held that God produced space by his own motion. Specifically the will-act (*irāda*) of God was defined as a movement by Hishām b. al-Ḥakam, al-Jawālīqī, Muḥammad b. al-Nuʿmān, Abū Mālik al-Ḥaḍramī, and ʿAlī b. Mītham. If God wills a thing, he moves (*taḥarraka*), and it becomes into being.[11]

The theological concepts underlying these formulations of the early Imāmī *mutakallimūn* are the same as those of Sunnite traditionalists, although the Sunnite formulations differ in some points. God, according to Sunnite traditionalist doctrine, is also immanent in space and time. He is located above the throne and is occasionally described as light in accordance with the light verse of the Koran.[12] Although the Sunnite formulation does not describe God as a body or as having form (and sometimes expressly repudiates these terms), God is, in fact, also conceived in anthropomorphic shape. Sunnite traditionalism, too, affirmed that God moves, that he descends from the throne to the lower heavens,[13] that he walks and hastens. The doctrine that God cannot be a substratum of temporals (*ḥawādith*), by which the Muʿtazilites supported their concept of his immutability, was rejected by the Karrāmiyya,[14] whose *kalām* doctrine reflected Sunnite traditionalist views, and by Ḥanbalite scholars down to Ibn Taymiyya.[15]

While the Imāmī theologians in these aspects agreed substantially with Sunnite traditionalism, in their doctrine of the divine attributes, they went far beyond it in opposition to the Muʿtazilite view of the immutability of God. Most attention and criticism was aroused among the Muʿtazilites by their views on the divine attribute of knowledge. The early Imāmī theologians almost unanimously maintained the impossibility of the Muʿtazilite dogma that God has known all things from eternity. Hishām b. al-Ḥakam held that God does not know things eternally, for that would necessitate the eternity of the things known by him. God knows only existing things.[16] Similarly his discipline al-Sakkāk maintained that God cannot be described as knowing a thing before it comes into existence: knowledge of the nonexistent is impossible.[17] Muḥammad b. al-Nuʿmān held that God knows things when he determines (*gaddara* or *aththara*), i.e., wills (*arāda*) them.[18] Another group maintained that the meaning of God's knowing is his acting (*maʿnā anna llāha yaʿlamu annahū yafʿalu*).[19] God's knowledge thus was closely tied to the creation and like it was subject to constant change. The divine attributes of power, seeing, and hearing, which were also considered immutable attributes of essence by the Muʿtazilites, were treated by the Imāmī doctrine analogously to the attribute of knowledge. One group argued that God cannot be described as eternally having power, seeing, and hearing, for power, sight, and hearing, like knowledge, require objects. These attributes, therefore, cannot be ascribed to God before he produces the things.[20] One Imāmī group is even reported to have extended this principle to the attribute of life, affirming that God had not been living from eternity. But this view was rejected by others.[21]

God's attributes thus are essentially subject to change. Of momentous significance was this view in respect to the divine attribute of will (*irāda*). The will of God is indeed also subject to change in the view of the early Imāmī theologians. The technical term for this change of will was *badāʾ*. The doctrine of *badāʾ* was expressly sanctioned by statements of Imām Jaʿfar al-Ṣādiq[22] and therefore universally accepted among the early Imāmiyya.[23]

How is the doctrine of *badāʾ* to be understood in the context of the theological thought of the Imāmī *mutakallimūn?* The term *badāʾ* and the phrase *yabdū lahū* indicate that this change of will was not seen as an unprovoked, unilateral change of mind, but rather as a response to the emergence of a new situation. The emergence of a new situation for God is possible, of course, only if he does not have foreknowledge of all events, as the predestinarians as well as the Muʿtazilites maintained, and has not ordained them from eternity, as the predestinarians including the Sunnite traditionalists held. The Imāmī theologians in denying the eternity of God's knowledge were thinking specifically of the acts of man. Hishām b. al-Ḥakam, according to al-Khayyāṭ and al-Ashʿarī, argued that if God knew what man will do, there would be neither trial nor test.[24] Against the common view of the early Imāmī scholars, another Imāmī group upheld the divine knowledge of events before their occurrence, expressly excluding human acts, no doubt with a similar motivation.[25] In order to be put to trial, man must have a choice, as the Muʿtazilites also affirmed. That the Imāmī theologians supported the concept of freedom of choice is indeed also indicated by the fact that they generally agreed with the Muʿtazilites in affirming that capability (*istiṭāʿa*) precedes the act.[26]

Are then the acts of man determined by himself as the Muʿtazilites contended, in rejecting the notion that the acts of man are created by God? Hishām b. al-Ḥakam, according to one report, stated that human acts are created by God;[27] but according to another report, which appears more consistent with his systematic thought, he held that the acts of men belong to them and cannot be said to be created or uncreated.[28] God, however, provides the occasion for the act which alone makes it possible and necessary.[29] Others abstained from either affirming or denying that human acts are created by God.[30] Muḥammad b. al-Nuʿmān probably expressed the standard view of the Imāmiyya in maintaining that no act occurs unless God wills it.[31] God, in other words, keeps direct control over all events in the world, yet responds positively or negatively to the free choice of man. God determines the course of the world at any time, but he has not preordained it. Nor has he created man with responsibility but no choice, either as an infidel, the object of his eternal hatred; or as a believer, the object of his eternal love, as the Muslim predestinarians maintained. The doctrine of the Imāmī *mutakallimūn* thus indeed offered an intermediate position between the Jahmite thesis of constraint (*jabr*) and the Muʿtazilite thesis of empowerment (*tafwīḍ*), as supported by a famous statement of Imām Jaʿfar.

The doctrines of Hishām b. al-Ḥakam were distinguished by some concepts not shared by the other Imāmī theologians. These concepts were derived from dualist, specifically Dayṣānite, doctrine. Hishām indeed was long and closely associated with a Dayṣānite, Abū Shākir al-Dayṣānī, and was evidently, as some of the heresiographers charged, also influenced by his ideas.[32] To Dayṣānite influence can be traced his concept of man as an active and sensitive spirit consisting of light and inhering in a dead body;[33] his definitions of qualities and motions, both in God and man, as descriptive attributes neither identical with them nor other than they;[34] and probably also his concept of God as a shapless body of light. Hishām's views on physics were also derived from dualist doctrine. His theory of the interpenetration (*mudākhala*) of bodies[35] corresponds, as is known, to the dualist belief in the mixture of light and darkness.[36] And his support of this theory entailed the rejection of atomism in favor of infinite divisibility of matter,[37] and the thesis that bodies may pass from one place to another without moving through the intervening space (*ṭafra*).[38] Much of Hishām b. al-Ḥakam's world view was adopted by the Muʿtazilite al-Naẓẓām,[39] who rejected, however, those aspects of Hishām's doctrine which were in conflict with the Muʿtazilite concept of God's transcending space and time, the definition of the human spirit as consisting of light,[40] and the concept of descriptive attributes, whose role he attributed partly to accidents (as in the case of motion),[41] and partly to attributes of essence.[42]

The Dayṣānite concepts of Hishām b. al-Ḥakam stand in contrast to the views of the other contemporary Imāmī theologians, in particular Muḥammad b. al-Nuʿmān and al-Jawālīqī.[43] Some of the views of these two reported by al-Ashʿarī agree with the doctrine of Jahm b. Ṣafwān, the Murjiʾite theologian of the previous generation. Like Jahm, they held that every thing (*shay*ʾ) is a body and that God alone is incorporeal. In agreement with Jahm's view, they affirmed that motions (*ḥarakāt*), including all human acts, are bodies.[44] Moreover, the general Imāmī doctrine that God does not know things before they come into existence had been propounded by Jahm.[45] Does this agreement indicate a specific influence of the teaching of Jahm on early Imāmism?[46] The Imāmī doctrine certainly cannot have been formulated in ignorance of Jahm's doctrine. On the other hand, it is evident that the thesis of the temporality of the knowledge of God had specific roots in the system of Imāmī theology, also. And there are indications that the view of the world as consisting exclusively of corporeal beings in its extreme simplicity reflects an early stage in the development of *kalām* in general, before the introduction of the concepts of accidents, substance, atoms, etc., rather than a specific school doctrine.[47] The information of the sources on this early stage is too sparse, however, to permit us to form a definite opinion.

Zaydism was represented in the early *kalām* discussions chiefly by Sulaymān b. Jarīr. Since he appears before the death of Imām Jaʿfar, a prominent Zaydī leader,[48] he belongs to the same generation as Hishām b. al-Ḥakam and the eccentric Muʿtazilite Ḍirār b. ʿAmr. Other Zaydī views are recorded by al-Ashʿarī anonymously. Most of them are distinctly Muʿtazilite and presumably belong to later generations closer to the time of al-Ashʿarī.[49] There are also, however, occasionally anonymous views quite close to those of Sulaymān b. Jarīr, which may belong to Zaydī scholars contemporary with him.[50]

Sulaymān b. Jarīr's views as reported by al-Ashʿarī agree basically with the doctrine upheld in some extant early Zaydī works.[51] Early Zaydism adopted the Khārijite, specifically Ibāḍite, position in the doctrine of faith and infidelity.[52] It also shows a distinct affinity to the Khārijite views in theology. The Imāmī doctrine of *badā*ʾ was unanimously repudiated by the Zaydiyya. Sulaymān b. Jarīr probably represented the early Zaydī consensus in teaching that God knows and wills from eternity;[53] while the eternity of God's knowing was affirmed by both Muʿtazilites and Khārijites, the eternity of God's willing was specifically Khārijite doctrine. Of Khārijite origin also was Sulaymān's thesis that friendship (*walīya*), enmity (*ʿadāwa*), pleasure (*riḍā*), and wrath (*sukhṭ*) are attributes of the divine essence.[54] These views reflect the distinctly predestinarian outlook shared by the early Zaydīs and the Khārijites in sharp contrast to the antipredestinarian Imāmī view. That Sulaymān b. Jarīr affirmed the acts of man to be created by God, as did the Khārijites and most of the early Zaydīs,[55] is very likely, though not specifically reported by al-Ashʿarī. Sulaymān b. Jarīr also agreed with the consensus of the Khārijites against Muʿtazilite doctrine in maintaining that God cannot be described as capable of doing injustice of lying.[56]

Yet Sulaymān also manifested his independence from the Khārijite position by affirming that God from eternity hated or did not want (*lam yazal kārihan*) acts of disobedience.[57] It is not quite clear how this thesis agrees with his general system, for he evidently would not have admitted the Muʿtazilite proposition that acts of disobedience can occur against the will of God. Presumably he wanted to affirm that God does not will acts of disobedience as such and that man is fully responsible for them, even though they result from the predetermined creation of God. This emphasis on the responsibility of man is also apparent in an anonymous Zaydī view which agrees with the Khārijite predestinarian doctrine that capability occurs only simultaneously with, not before, the act, but deviates from it in affirming that the capability for faith is the same as that for infidelity.[58] The Khārijites sharpened the determinist edge of their doctrine on this point by maintaining that capability applies only to a definite act, not to its opposite.[59]

Early Zaydism, in contrast to early Imāmism, adopted the anti-anthropomorphist concept of God also supported by the Muʿtazilites and the Khārijites. Sulaymān b. Jarīr accepted, however, Hishām b. al-Ḥakam's definition of attributes as being neither identical with nor other than their substratum; moreover, he affirmed of the attributes of the divine essence, individually though not collectively, that they are "things."[60] He thus was considered as belonging to the *ṣifātiyya,*[61] those who affirmed the reality of the essential attributes of God against the Muʿtazilite and Khārijite doctrine. His formulation was consequently adopted by Sunnite *kalām* theologians like ʿAbd Allāh b. Kullāb[62] and al-Ashʿarī. The Sunnite theologians applied it, however, also to the anthropomorphic attributes of God and affirmed their reality, which Sulaymān b. Jarīr rejected.[63]

In his views on the structure of physical nature, as far as al-Ashʿarī records them, Sulaymān b. Jarīr agreed with Ḍirār b. ʿAmr and the Ibāḍiyya. Thus he considered color and taste and also capability (*istiṭāʿa*) as corporeal parts (*abʿāḍ*) of the body which adjoin each other (*mujāwara*) and mingle (*mumāzaja*) but do not interpenetrate, as Hishām b. al-Ḥakam and al-Naẓẓām maintained.[64]

Khārijite theological doctrine as presented by al-Ashʿarī was predominantly anti-anthropomorphist and strictly predestinarian. It is true that al-Ashʿarī mentions a few Khārijite groups which agreed with the Muʿtazila in affirming human free will. All of these groups arose, however, as minor splinter sects probably under Muʿtazilite influence in the 2nd/8th century,[63] when the general predestinarian attitude of Khārijism was already well established. There is no evidence that Khārijites were prominently involved in the origins and the early development of the doctrine of human free will in Islam, as has been suggested by M. Watt.[66] The Khārijite *kalām* theologians of the 2nd/8th century rather played a major role in the elaboration of the doctrine of strict predestination.

Al-Ashʿarī's summary account of the theological doctrines of the Khārijites provides hardly any details on the views of individual scholars. More often he speaks of the view of the Khārijites or of the Ibāḍiyya in general or the great majority (*jull*) of them. Among the Khārijite *mutakallimūn* listed by him,[67] the earliest ones are the Ibāḍī ʿAbd Allāh b. Yazīd, a business companion of Hishām b. al-Ḥakam;[68] and al-Yamān b. Rabāb, a Bayhasī who later turned a Thaʿlabī. Al-Yamān was the brother of a prominent Imāmī traditionist who probably also belonged to the generation of Hishām b. al-Ḥakam.[69] Both Khārijite scholars, according to Ibn al-Nadīm, composed treatises on *tawḥīd* and refutations of the Muʿtazilite doctrine of human free will.[70] One such refutation by ʿAbd Allāh b. Yazīd indeed is preserved largely in a later Zaydī refutation of it. These Khārijites evidently participated fully in the early *kalām* discussions of the 2nd/8th century, and their doctrine is most likely included in al-Ashʿariī's references to the Khārijites in general.

The Khārijite anti-anthropomorphist theology thus is to be considered the result of a parallel but not independent development in relation to the Muʿtazilite theology,[71] and not of a later adoption of it. The Khārijite *kalām* theologians agreed with the Muʿtazilites in distinguishing between divine attributes of essence and of act. Like most of the Muʿtazilites, they held that the essential attributes describe God in himself (*bi-nafsih*), not through attributes which are distinct from the essence.[72] They upheld the thesis of Jahm b. Ṣafwān and the Muʿtazila that the Koran is created.[73] In contrast to the Muʿtazilites, however, they counted the attribute of will (*irāda*) among the essential attributes of God,[74] and were perhaps the first to uphold this view consequently adopted by Sunnite *kalām* schools.

The thesis that the will is an essential, eternal attribute of God reflects the predestinarian outlook of the Khārijites. The Ibāḍiyya in particular maintained that God wills from eternity that what he knows will happen shall happen, and what he knows will not happen shall not happen.[75] They argued, then, that man cannot be capable of doing anything but what is eternally known by God; for if he were capable of doing otherwise, he would be able to vitiate the knowledge of God and turn it into ignorance.[76] God, they maintained, guides the faithful, but misleads the infidel, not in consequence of a previous free choice of man, but because of God's decree that he should be an infidel. If God were to provide guidance to all men, as the Muʿtazilites contend, all would necessarily be faithful. The Ibāḍiyya held that the capability is simultaneous only with the act and applies only to the act, not to its opposite.[77] They denied that God is able to do injustice[78] on the grounds that whatever God does is just. The concept of the injustice of God thus was deprived of any meaning in favor of the idea of his absolute sovereignty.

The views of two Ibāḍī scholars of the beginning of the 3rd/9th century, Muḥammad b. Ḥarb and Yaḥyā b. Abī Kāmil, in these matters, as described by al-Ashʿarī, are nearly identical in detail and formulation with those of the contemporary Ḥanafite Murji'ite al-Ḥusayn al-Najjār.[79] The roots of al-Najjār's doctrine have usually been traced to such Murji'ites as Bishr al-Marīsī and Ḥafṣ al-Fard and ultimately to Ḍirār b. ʿAmr.[80] In fact, however, al-Najjār in his views on predestination stands much closer to the Khārijite tradition.[81] Many of his and the contemporary Ibāḍī scholars' views were earlier upheld by ʿAbd Allāh b. Yazīd in his extant treatise. It is thus evident that al-Najjār and the contemporary Ibāḍī theologians, whatever their relationship, were both indebted to the earlier Ibāḍī tradition. Al-Najjār's predestinarian views, on the other hand, are characterized by the Ashʿarite ʿAbd al-Qāhir al-Baghdādī as agreeing with the view of the Ahl al-sunna wa l-jamāʿa.[82] The doctrine on predestination elaborated by the Ibāḍiyya was indeed adopted virtually without modification by al-Ashʿarī.

Concerning the Ibāḍī views on physical nature, al-Ashʿarī provides only scant information, which places them close to the doctrine of Ḍirār b. ʿAmr. Some of the Ibāḍiyya affirmed that the body consists of assembled accidents (*aʿrāḍ mujtamiʿa*) and that those accidents which do not form part of the body do not endure.[83] This was the doctrine probably first developed by Ḍirār and then adopted by Ḥafṣ al-Fard and al-Najjār. Most of them, however, according to a somewhat obscure statement of al-Ashʿarī, seem to have spoken only of parts (*abʿāḍ*) of the body.[84] presumably without affirming the concept of assembled accidents. This view, no doubt, also entailed a wide concept of corporeality which considered colors, tastes, and similar qualities as parts of the body. It probably reflects an early stage of thought in *kalām,* on the basis of which Ḍirār elaborated his more advanced theory.[85] His elaborations apparently were not accepted by most of the Ibāḍī scholars and the Zaydī Sulaymān b. Jarīr.[86] In agreement with Ḍirār's view, the Ibāḍī scholars also held that the atom is corporeal,[87] thus rejecting, on the one hand, the infinite divisibility of the body maintained by Hishām b. al-Ḥakam and al-Naẓẓām, and, on the other hand, the concept of atoms without volume constituting the body, which was supported by Abū l-Hudhayl and most of the Muʿtazila.[88]

Notes

1. Cf. for instance al-Ashʿarī's report of the view of an Imāmī group which maintained that the true doctrine concerning a certain question was whatever Imām Jaʿfar would say about it (Al-Ashʿarī, *Maqālāt al-Islāmiyyin,* ed. Hellmut Ritter, Istanbul, 1929, p. 36).

2. Concerning the date of his death cf. Josef van Ess, "Ibn Kullāb und die Miḥna," *Oriens* 18–19 (1967): 115; and Wilferd Madelung, s.v., "Hishām b. al-Ḥakam," in *The Encyclopaedia of Islam,* new ed.

3. Ibn al-Nadīm, *al-Fihrist,* ed. Gustav Flügel, Leipzig, 1871, pp. 175f.; and al-Ṭūsī, *Fihrist Kutub al-shīʿa,* ed. Aloys Sprenger, pp. 143 (cf. also Āghā Buzurg al-Tihrānī, *Al-dharīʿa ilā taṣānīf al-shīʿa,* 2:27 no. 105), 323, 355f. ʿAlī b. Ismāʿil al-Mīthamī al-Tammār, who is described by Ibn al-Nadīm (p. 175) as the first Imāmī *mutakallim* (*awwal man takallam fi madhhab al-imāma*), seems to belong rather to the following generation. He is nowhere associated with Imām Jaʿfar, and participated in the *kalām* discussions held in the circle of the Barmakids in the time of Hārūn al-Rashīd. He survived Imām Mūsā al-Kāẓim (d. 183/711), for he had debates with those who denied Mūsā's death (al-Nawbakhtī, *Firaq al-shīʿa,* ed. Helmut Ritter, p. 69).

4. "Imamism and Muʿtazilite Theology," in *Le Shīʿisme Imāmite,* pp. 13ff.

5. *Maqālāt,* p. 32.

6. *Maqālāt,* p. 35.

7. *Maqālāt,* pp. 32ff., 207f.

8. *Maqālāt,* pp. 208, 521. The view of the anonymous "second group of the Rāfiḍa" (p. 34, ll. 1–4) is evidently later formulation belonging to the school of Hishām b. al-Ḥakam. The view of the fifth group (p. 34, l. 13–p. 35, l. 2) may also belong to his school.

9. *Maqālāt,* pp. 34, 209, al-Shahrastānī, *al-Milal wa l-niḥal,* ed. Cureton, p. 143. ʿAlī b. Mītham evidently held the same view. According to a report quoted by al-Kulaynī (*al-Uṣūl min al-kāfī,* ed. A. A. al-Ghaffārī, I: 100 f.; Ibn Bābūya, *al-Tawḥīd,* al-Najaf 1386/1966, p. 69, quoted in al-Majlisī, *Biḥār al-anwār,* ed. J. al-ʿAlawī and M. al-Ākhūndī, 4:39f.). Imām ʿAlī al-Riḍā repudiated the identical doctrine of al-Jawālīqī, Muḥammad b. al-Nuʿmān, and Ibn Mītham that "God is hollow to the navel, and the rest is solid." This doctrine, no doubt a malevolent distortion, is ascribed by ʿAbd al-Qāhir al-Baghdādī (*al-Farq bayn al-firaq*) and al-Shahrastānī (*al-Milal* pp. 141f.) to al-Jawālīqī specifically, (Al-Ashʿarī ascribes it to the Murjiʾite Dāʾūd al-Jawāribī, *Maqālāt,* pp. 153, 209). The doctrine of Muḥammad b. al-Nuʿmān and al-Jawālīqī was based on the well-known *ḥadīths* that Muḥammad had seen God in the shape of a young man and that God had created Adam in his image.

10. *Maqālāt,* p. 33. Hishām b. al-Ḥakam's view thus was anti-anthropomorphist and was later sometimes supported as such against the anthropomorphist concept of God held

by al-Jawālīqī and others. The prominent Qumman scholar ʿAlī b. Ibrāhīm al-Qummī, who was still alive in the year 307 (914) and was an important authority of al-Kulaynī (d. 329/941), defended Hishām's doctrine. In his Koran commentary (*Tafsīr al-Qummū*, ed. al-Sayyid Ṭayyib al-Mūsawī al-Jazā'irī, 1: 20), he upholds the doctrine of the visibility of God (*ru'ya*), which was rejected by al-Kulaynī and later Imāmī doctrine, quoting Koran 53: 11–15 and a report that Imām ʿAlī al-Riḍā asked Aḥmad b. Muḥammad b. Abī Naṣr about the dispute between his associates and the followers of Hishām b. al-Ḥakam. Aḥmad answered: ". . . We affirm [that God has human] shape on the basis of the *ḥadīth* which is related that the Prophet saw his Lord in the shape of a young man, while Hishām b. al-Ḥakam affirms the negation [of anthropomorphic attributes] and corporeality (reading *bi l-mafy bi l-jism* in accordance with the quotation of the text in *biḥār* 3: 307 instead of *bi l-mafy al-mujassam*)." Al-Riḍā replied: "Oh Aḥmad, when the Messenger of God ascended to the heaven and reached the Lotus Tree of the Extremity, the veils were rent for him the size of a needle's eye, and he saw of the light of sublimity what God wanted him to see. But you want to ascribe an image to him (*aradtum antum al-tashbīh*). Leave this, oh Aḥmad, lest something dreadful befall you on account of it." Even more directly is the doctrine of Hishām b. al-Ḥakam and his disciple Yūnus b. ʿAbd al-Raḥmān endorsed as anti-anthropomorphist against that of al-Jawālīqī in a *ḥadīth* of al-Riḍā quoted by al-Kashshī (al-Kashshī, *Maʿrifat akhbār al-rijāl,* Bombay, 1317, pp. 183f., quoted in *Biḥār* 3: 305).

Other Imāmī traditions of the late 3rd/9th century equally rejected the doctrines of Hishām b. al-Ḥakam and of al-Jawālīqī and adduced statements of the imāms repudiating both. The Qumman Saʿd b. ʿAbd Allāh (d. 301/913–4) wrote a book on "the blemishes (*mathālib*) of Hishām (b. al-Ḥakam) and Yūnus (b. ʿAbd al-Raḥmān)" and another one in "refutation of ʿAlī b. Ibrāhīm al-Qummī concerning Hishām and Yūnus," ʿAlī b. Ibrāhīm apparently had written a treatise defending Hishām and Yūnus (Cf. M. Jawād Mashkūr, introd. to his edition of Saʿad b. ʿAbd Allāh's *K. al-maqālāt wa l-firaq,* pp. Yā'f.).

11. *Maqālāt,* pp. 41f., 219f., 515. It is to be noted that the concept of motion in the early Imāmī usage was essentially identical with act (*fiʿl*). Muḥammad b. al-Nuʿmān and al-Jawālīqī are expressly reported to have held that human acts are motions (*Maqālāt,* p. 346). Hishām b. al-Ḥakam probably also identified motion and act, although motions are mentioned besides acts in general (*sā'ir al-afʿāl*) in a report of his doctrine (*Maqālāt,* p. 344). The Muʿtazilite al-Naẓẓām, who adopted much of the systematic thought of Hishām, affirmed that all human acts, including acts of will (*irādāt*), of hatred (*karāhāt*), of knowledge, and of ignorance are motions (*Maqālāt,* pp. 346, 403). The concept of motion for al-Naẓẓām thus had a temporal rather than a spatial connotation. This evidently also applies to Hishām b. al-Ḥakam's concept. For the motion through which God created space could not be spatial. Hishām moreover is reported to have maintained that the motion of God consists in his "doing the thing (*fiʿluhu l-shay'a*) "while at the same time refusing to say that God departs (*yazūlu*) when he moves (*Maqālāt,* p. 215). The Imāmī *mutakallim* al-Sakkāk, who belonged to the following generation, on the other hand, admitted that God may depart (*ajāza ʿalayhi l-zawāla*). That *zawāl* is here to be understood spatially is indicated by the fact that al-Sakkāk is reported to have added a denial of *ṭafr,* i.e., motion from one place to another without passing through the intervening space, in respect to God (*Maqālāt,* p. 215).

12. Cf. for instance the doctrine of the Ahl al-sunna and the traditions quoted by al-Ashʿarī, *Maqālāt,* p. 211, 1.7.

13. The *ḥadīth al-nuzūl,* on which this affirmation is based, is quoted also by ʿAlī b. Ibrāhīm al-Qummī in his *tafsīr* (2: 204) as a *ḥadīth* of Imām Jaʿfar. In the edition, *amruhū,* God's order, is added as the subject to *yanzilu* and *ʿāda.* It is thus not God himself who

descends to the lower heavens and returns to the throne, but merely his order. This is evidently an attempt to bring the text more in conformity with the abstract concept of God of later Imāmī doctrine. The passage is quoted by al-Majlisī (*Biḥār* 3: 315) without the addition. Al-Majlisī explains the meaning of God's descent and return metaphorically.

14. Cf. Al-Juwaynī, *al-Irshād,* ed. M. Y. Mūsā and A. A. ʿAbd al-Ḥamīd, p. 44. Some Karrāmī groups also affirmed that God is body (*al-Irshād,* p. 42).

15. Cf. for instance Ibn Taymiyya, *Majmūʿat al-rasāʾil wa l-masāʾil,* ed. Rashīd Riḍā, 3: 102ff.

16. *Maqālāt,* pp. 37, 493f; al-Khayyāṭ, *K. al-intiṣār,* ed. H. Nyberg, pp. 108f. According to al-Jāḥiz, Hishām b. al-Ḥakam described the knowledge of God in quite material terms, maintaining that God knows through rays which proceed from him and touch the object of his knowledge, penetrating even the depths of the earth. *Maqālāt,* pp. 33, 221, 491.

17. *Maqālāt,* pp. 219, 490.

18. *Maqālāt,* pp. 37, 219f., 493.

19. *Maqālāt,* pp. 38, 220, 490.

20. *Maqālāt,* pp. 36, 491. The supporters of this view are reported to have also denied that God has been Lord (*rabb*) or God (*ilāh*) from eternity.

21. *Maqālāt,* pp. 37, 219, 491.

22. Goldziher, s.v. "Badāʾ," in *The Encyclopedia of Islam.*

23. *Maqālāt,* pp. 36, 39, 491f.

24. Al-Khayyāṭ, pp. 116f. *Maqālāt,* pp. 37, 494.

25. Al-Ashʿarī reports as their argument that if God knew in advance who would disobey him, he would prevent his act of disobedience. This evidently describes their argument rather than their motivation.

    While the early denial of the eternity of God's knowledge was soon abandoned by Imāmī tradition, *badāʾ* has remained a cardinal doctrine of Imāmism. Although it could no longer mean the emergence of a new situation for God, its later interpretations retained its antipredestinarian significance. In the *tafsīr* of ʿAlī b. Ibrāhīm al-Qummī (1: 37, quoted in *Biḥār* 5: 238), ʿAlī is reported to have explained that God originally created the prophets, Imāms, and their pious followers from sweet water and created the oppressors, the unjust, and "the brethren of the devils" from salt water. For the second group he stipulated, however, *badāʾ*. Their apparent condemnation was, in other words, open to revision. Imām al-Bāqir is quoted as having stated that God determines in the Night of Determination (*al-qadr*) every year whatever shall happen in the coming year, but many of his decisions concerning deaths, sustenance, calamities, and diseases remain subject to *badāʾ*. The Prophet is informed of these decisions and of which ones are open to revision. He informs ʿAlī who in turn informs the imāms down to the imām of the time (2:290, quoted in *Biḥār* 4: 101). *Badāʾ* implies here merely an apparent change of decision, which in fact had been foreseen by God. God is still viewed, however, as reacting to changed circumstances.

26. *Maqālāt,* p. 42ff. The early standard view, supported by Zurāra, al-Jawālīqī, Muḥammad b. al-Nuʿmān, and others, was that "capability precedes the act and consists in physical soundness (*ṣiḥḥa*). Everyone who is physically sound is capable." Hishām b. al-Ḥakam propounded a more complex theory. Capability according to him consisted

of five matters of which four precede the act: soundness, freedom of circumstances (*takhliyat al-shu'ūn*), space of time, and the necessary tool, like the hand or an axe. The fifth matter is the incentive occasion (*al-sabab al-muhayyij*) which is only simultaneous with the act. When this occasion is provided by God the act occurs necessarily. (Imām Jaʿfar is quoted as naming the same five matters in only slightly different terms as constituting the intermediate position between constraint (*jabr*) and empowerment (*tafwīḍ*), in a treatise ascribed to Imām ʿAlī al-Naqī, cf. *Biḥār* 5: 70).

In affirming that the act will occur necessarily in the presence of the incentive occasion, Hishām evidently presupposed that the capable actor desired the act. This is indicated by a report of the Muʿtazilite Jaʿfar b. Ḥarb quoted by al-Ashʿarī (*Maqālāt,* p. 40f.) that Hishām b. al-Ḥakam held that human acts are "his choice (*ikhtiyār*) in one respect and compulsion (*iḍṭirār*) in another. They are choice in that he wills them and acquires (*iktasaba*) them; and they are compulsion in that they do not take place unless the occasion stimulating them occurs." The will and the consequent "acquisition" result from a free choice. But given the will and the occasion the act occurs necessarily. This is further clarified by a report of al-Nāshi' (Josef van Ess, *Frühe muʿtazilitische Häresiographie,* Ar. text p. 96, no. 86) which no doubt refers to the doctrine of Hishām b. al-Ḥakam, as J. van Ess suggests (introd., p. 92), or of his school. "Others stated that man has power over the act which he brings forth by the tools, but not over the occasion (*sabab*), and also over refraining from it (*tarkih*). They said: the cause is not [part of] the capability, it is rather the stimulus of (*dāʿin ilā*) the act." Although the occasion is excluded here from the matters constituting capability, in contrast to the definition reported by al-Ashʿarī, it is obvious that essentially the same doctrine is meant.

An illustration of what is meant by *sabab* is provided by a *ḥadīth* of Imām ʿAlī al-Riḍā reported by al-Kulaynī (1: 160f.) and Ibn Bābūya (*al-Tawḥīd,* p. 283, quoted in *Biḥār* 5:37) which is obviously based on the theory of Hishām b. al-Ḥakum. Al-Riḍā is quoted as stating that there are four prerequisites for a man to be capable. He must be free to act (*mukhallā l-sarb*), possess a healthy body and sound members, and a *sabab* coming from God must be present to him (*lahū sababun wāridun min llāh*). Al-Riḍā offered the example "that a man who is free to act, of healthy body and sound limbs, wants to fornicate, but he does not find a woman, and then he finds one. Either he is restrained (*yuʿṣam,* al-Kulaynī: he restrains himself, *yaʿṣim nafsah*) and abstains as Yūsuf abstained, or free course is given to his desire (*yukhallā baynahū wa-bayna irādatih*) and he fornicates. . . ." Al-Majlisī (*Biḥār* 5:37) explains the *sabab* coming from God "as the restraining (*ʿiṣma*) or the giving free course (*takhliya*)." This interpretation, however, is probably incorrect. The "incentive occasion" of the theory of Hishām b. al-Ḥakam in this example is the woman whose presence is the "stimulant of the act." The final statement about the restraining or giving free course is evidently meant as an additional affirmation of the fact that God retains the ultimate control over human acts, and is foreign to Hishām's theory.

The doctrine of the followers of Abū Mālik al-Ḥaḍramī is described by al-Ashʿarī (*Maqālāt,* p. 43) in rather enigmatic terms. "They said that man is capable of the act at the moment of the act (*fī ḥāl al-fiʿl*) and that he is capable of it without a capability at other times (*fī ghayrih*)." According to Zurqān, Abū Mālik moreover held "that the capability before the act [is valid] for the act and for refraining from it." These formulations probably are also to be explained on the basis of Hishām's theory. The capability through which the act occurs is the occasion which is only simultaneous with the act. Before the act, man can be said to be capable of it and of refraining from it without having the actual capability, i.e., the occasion. At the moment of the act the capability is valid only for the act, no longer for refraining from it.

Zurāra's doctrine in particular was later considered as ascribing a large degree of capability to man, and statements of the imāms were cited, some repudiating and some endorsing it (cf. al-Kashshī, pp. 96 ff., quoted in *Biḥār* 5:44ff.). Imāmī traditionalist opinion of the 4th/10th century was divided concerning the question of *istiṭāʿa.* The traditions assembled by al-Kulaynī (1: 161f.) support the view that man is capable of the act only at the moment of it, and that if he refrained from an act, he cannot be said to have been capable of it. One of these traditions is quoted by al-Kulaynī on the authority of Muḥammad b. Abī ʿAbd Allāh, i.e., Muḥammad b. Jaʿfar b. Muḥammad b. ʿAwn al-Asadī (d. 312/924), who according to al-Ṭūsī wrote a "refutation of the people [affirming the doctrine] of *istiṭāʿa,*" (Al-Ṭūsī, p. 282; it is probably identical with the *K. al-jabr wa l-istiṭāʿa* mentioned by al-Najāshī, who says that Ibn ʿAwn supported the doctrines of constraint [*jabr*] and anthropomorphism [*tashbīh*], *al-Rijāl,* Tehran, n.d., p. 289). The Shaykh al-Mufī (d. 413/1022) wrote a refutation of Ibn ʿAwn's determinist views (*al-Radd ʿalā Ibn ʿAwn fī l-makhlūq,* al-Najāshī, p. 314). Some of the traditions quoted in Ibn Bābūya's *al-Tawḥīd* (pp. 281ff.) support the view that capacity exists both before and at the time of the act and does not necessitate it.

27. *Maqālāt,* p. 40.

28. Al-Nāshi', pp. 92f., no. 70. Acts, in the view of Hishām b. al-Ḥakam, are attributes (*ṣifāt*), and attributes cannot receive further attributes such as created or uncreated.

29. Al-Nāshi', pp. 92f., no. 70. Cf. above n. 26.

30. *Maqālāt,* p. 41.

31. *Maqālāt,* p. 43. Latter Imāmī traditionalist doctrine also commonly refrained from affirming that human acts are created by God, while emphasizing that they occur only in accordance with the will of God.

32. Al-Mismaʿī quoted by ʿAbd al-Jabbār, *al-Mughnī* 5, ed. M. M. al-Khuḍayrī, p. 20; al-Khayyāṭ, pp. 40f.

33. *Maqālāt,* pp. 60f., 331; O. Pretzl, "Die frühislamische Atomenlehre," *Islam,* 19 (1931), p. 129.

34. *Maqālāt,* pp. 37f., 344, 369, 493f.; al-Masʿūdī, *Murūj al-dhahab,* ed. Barbier de Meynard, 7:232f.; ʿAbd al-Jabbār, *al-Mughnī* 5:20; O. Pretzl, *Die frühislamiche Attributenlehre,* p. 49.

35. *Maqālāt,* p. 60.

36. *Maqālāt,* p. 327; al-Khayyāṭ, p. 31; Josef van Ess, "Ḍirār b. ʿAmr und die 'Cahmīya'," *Islam* 43 (1967), p. 258.

37. *Malqālāt,* p. 59.

38. *Maqālāt,* p. 61. Concerning the connection between the theory of *ṭafra* and the rejection of atomism cf. Ibn al-Murtaḍā, *Tabaqāt al-Muʿtazila,* ed. S. Diwald-Wilzer, p. 50; al-Baghdādī, *al-Farq,* pp. 123 f.; al-Shahrastānī, *al-Milal,* p. 33f.; Pretzl, "Atomenlehre," p. 126; S. Pines, *Beiträge zur Islamischen Atomenlehre,* p. 11. It is to be noted that the sources generally describe al-Naẓẓām as the originator of the theory of *ṭafra.* That Hishām b. al-Ḥakam held the doctrine of *ṭafra* was reported specifically by Zurqān, who is also named by al-Ashʿarī in several other instances as the reporter of Hishām's views. Al-Ashʿarī expresses reservation in respect to the reliability of Zurqān's report that Hishām held the doctrine of *mudākhala* (*Maqālāt,* p. 60), perhaps because this doctrine was later generally associated with al-Naẓẓām. There seems to be no strong reason, however, to doubt the reliability of Zurqān, especially since he was a student of al-Naẓẓām.

39. Various aspects of the influence of Hishām's doctrine on al-Naẓẓām have been noted by Pretzl, "Atomenlehre," pp. 125ff.; *Attributenlehre,* pp. 16, 48; Pines, *Beiträge,* p. 18,

n. 2; van Ess, *Die Erkenntnislehre des ʿAḍudaddīn al-Īcī,* pp. 136, 169, 181, "Ḍirār b. ʿAmr," p. 257. Concerning affinities of some views of al-Naẓẓām with Shiite doctrine in general, cf. Josef van Ess, "Ein unbekanntes Fragment de Naẓẓām," in *Der Orient in der Forschung,* ed. W. Höhnerbach, pp. 197 ff. The dependence of al-Naẓẓām on Hishām has been most broadly discussed, though in some points overestimated by ʿAbd Allāh Niʿma, *Hishām b. al-Ḥakam,* pp. 90–95 (summarized in his *Falāsifat al-shīʿa,* pp. 564 f.).

40. *Maqālāt,* p. 331; Pretzl, *Attributenlehre,* p. 16.

41. *Maqālāt,* pp. 358, 362, 378, 566; Pines, *Beiträge,* p. 18. As has been noted, all human acts, including will, hatred, knowledge and ignorance, were defined as motion by al-Naẓẓām (cf. n. 11).

42. Besides upholding the common Muʿtazilite doctrine concerning the essential attributes of God, al-Naẓạām treated life and capability as essential attributes of man. Man, he maintained, is living and capable by himself (*bi-nafsih*), not by a life or a capability which is other than he (*Maqālāt,* pp. 229, 487).

43. Some differences between the reported views of al-Jawālīqī and of Muḥammad b. al-Nuʿmān might suggest that the former was somewhat closer to Hishām b. al-Ḥakam than the latter. While both of them defined God as having human shape, only Muḥammad b. al-Nuʿmān is reported to have expressly repudiated Hishām's definition of God as a body (cf. n. 44). Al-Jawālīqī is moreover reported to have held the same view as Hishām b. al-Ḥakam about the will of God, defining it as motion and a descriptive attribute which is neither identical with him nor other than he (*Maqālāt,* pp. 41, 515). This view agrees with the general theory of Hishām b. al-Ḥakam on descriptive attributes. If its attribution to al-Jawālīqī is not erroneous (it might well have resulted from a mistaken identification of the name Hishāmiyya in a source as including the followers of both Hishām b. al-Ḥakam and Hishām al-Jawālīqī), it would indicate that al-Jawālīqī adopted Hishām b. al-Ḥakam's doctrine in the matter. Al-Jawālīqī did not adopt, however, Hishām b. al-Ḥakam's thesis of descriptive attributes in respect to human acts.

44. *Maqālāt,* pp. 44f., 346. On Jahm's doctrine in these points cf. *Maqālāt,* pp. 181, 346, 518, 589. Muḥammad b. al-Nuʿmān is reported to have expressly denied that God is corporeal (al-Shahrastānī, *al-milal,* p. 143. The anonymous view quoted in *Maqālāt,* p. 34, 1.5–6, p. 210, 1.1 can be identified as that of Muḥammad b. al-Nuʿmān). It is not unlikely that al-Jawālīqī did so also.

45. *Maqālāt,* pp. 272, 280, 494. The reports on Jahm's doctrine about the divine attribute of knowledge are conflicting. According to one report he held that God knows through a temporal knowledge produced by him which is other than he. He did not maintain that God cannot know things before their existence. This is disputed by another report affirming that he held that God cannot know things before they come into existence. According to this report the view that God's knowledge is produced in time was merely forced upon Jahm by his opponents (*alzamahū mukhālifūh*). The fact that his discussion according to the sources primarily concerned the attribute of knowledge seems to indicate that the latter report is correct. For if Jahm's motive had been to deny eternal attributes of God, there is no reason why he should have mentioned this particular attribute rather than others. That he considered the divine attributes as being "other than God," as the first report asserts, does not seem to agree with his systematic thought. Since he maintained that everything "other than God" is corporeal, he would have had to view the divine attributes as created bodies.

A solution to this problem is offered by the view of Richard M. Frank that Jahm's doctrine embodied a Neoplatonic system of thought (Richard M. Frank, "The Neoplatonism of Ǧahm Ibn Ṣafwân," *Muséon* 78 [1965], pp. 395ff.). Frank suggests that both reports are reliable and that the divine attributes of power and knowledge in Jahm's system were immaterial beings outside of God, corresponding to the World Soul and the Mind of the Neoplatonists (pp. 406ff.). The only textual support, however, for this view is a statement found in al-Juwaynī's *Irshād* and other late sources that the divine knowledge in the opinion of Jahm subsists in no substrate (*lā fī maḥall*). The reliability of this statement is doubtful since the concept of substrate (*maḥall*) was introduced in the thought of *kalām* together with the concept of accidents two generations after Jahm (cf. n. 47). Al-Juwaynī's statement probably represents a rationalization of the doctrine ascribed to Jahm that God's knowledge is produced in time. For according to the later thought of *kalām,* knowledge is an accident and thus should be treated analogously to the doctrine of Abu l-Hudhayl and later Muʿtazilites concerning the divine will-act (*irāda*), which is produced in time and therefore must subsist outside of God in no substrate (*lā fī maḥall*) (cf. ʿAbd al-Jabbār *Sharḥ al-uṣūl al-khamsa,* ed. ʿAbd al-Karīm ʿUthmān, p. 440. Abū l-Hudhayl seems to have used the formula *lā fī makān* [in no place], cf. *Maqālāt,* pp. 190, 363). The idea of divine attributes subsisting outside of God as spiritual beings is indeed so foreign to early *kalām,* and early Islamic thought in general, that it could not have escaped attention by the early heresiographers, and polemical repudiation in the traditionalist refutations of the Jahmiyya if Jahm had supported it.

The early Imāmī doctrine was also often described as affirming that God's knowledge is produced in time (*muḥdath,* cf. for instance al-Khayyāt, p. 6), although this formulation was evidently wrong for most of the Imāmī theologians. According to Hishām b. al-Ḥakam, knowledge was an attribute of God which could not be predicated with the further attribute "produced in time." Muḥammad b. al-Nuʿmān and others considered knowledge as an attribute of the divine essence, stating that God is "knowing in himself (*fī nafsih*), not ignorant," although he does not know the things before willing them. Even the doctrine of the followers of Zurāra, which al-Ashʿarī (*Maqālāt,* p. 36) describes with the vague formulation that "God was from eternity not hearing (*samīʿ*), nor knowing (*ʿalīm*), nor seeing (*baṣīr*), until he created that for himself (*ḥattā khalaqa dhālika li-nafsih*), is most likely to be interpreted in this sense. The choice of attributes strongly suggests that they really meant the creation of objects of hearing, knowing, and seeing rather than the attributes. The formulation is probably based on an *ilzām.*

46. An influence of Jahm's doctrine specifically on Hishām b. al-Ḥakam, who according to some sources was a follower of Jahm before becoming a Shiite, has been suggested by ʿAbd Allāh Niʿma, *Hishām b. al-Ḥakam,* pp. 51 ff.; *Falāsifat al-shīʿa,* p. 563. There is, however, less agreement with the doctrine of Jahm in the views of Hishām than in those of the other Imāmī scholars. Hishām's doctrine appears as a development of the general Imāmī doctrine, not as the basis of it.

47. The concepts of accident (*ʿaraḍ*) and atom (*jawhar, juzʾ lā yatajazzaʿ*) were evidently missing in the earliest stage of *kalām.* It has been suggested that they were introduced by the Muʿtazilite Abū-Hadhayl (Nyberg, s.v., 'Abū l-Hudhayl al-ʿAllāf," in *The Encyclopaedia of Islam,* new ed.). Abu l-Hudhayl and the other early Muʿtazilites whose views are recorded by al-Ashʿarī: al Naẓẓām, al-Muʿammar, Bishr b. al-Muʿtamir, and al-Aṣamm are a generation later than the Shiite theologians discussed here. They cannot have joined the *kalām* discussions before the caliphate of al-Mahdī (158–169/775–785), when the systematical thought of these Shiite scholars was already formed and could only secondarily be modified. Of the theologians belonging to their generation apparently only the eccentric Muʿtazilite Ḍirār b. ʿAmr used the term accident (*ʿaraḍ*). He adopted it most likely secondarily, perhaps in reaction to the views de-

veloped by the Muʿtazilites of the following generation, for it is poorly suited for his complicated system of primary and secondary accidents (cf. van Ess, "Ḍirār b. ʿAmr," pp. 261ff.). His primary accidents were indeed fully corporeal and were commonly termed parts (*abʿāḍ, ajzā'*) of the body by him and other early *mutakallimūn.* While Abū l-Hudhayl's concept and theory of accidents became the basis of the common view of most later Muʿtazilites and indeed of later *kalām* in general, the contemporary Muʿtazilites al-Naẓẓām and al-Aṣamm retained more corporealist views. Al-Naẓẓām restricted the concept of accidents to motions, considering everything else in the physical world as corporeal. Al-Aṣamm (d. 200–1/816–8) denied the existence of anything but bodies and maintained that motions, acts, color, taste, etc., were nothing other than the body (*Maqālāt,* p. 343).

48. Some supporters of Imām Jaʿfar deserted him after the death of his son Ismāʿīl and became followers of Sulaymān b. Jarīr (al-Nawbakhtī, *Firaq al-shīʿa,* pp. 57ff.).

49. This is expressly stated by al-Ashʿarī in recording the Zaydī doctrine of faith (*Maqālāt,* pp. 73f.). Some of the later Zaydīs say that faith consists of all acts of obedience, and deny that every act for which God has threatened punishment constitutes infidelity: this agrees with the Muʿtazilite doctrine. All early Zaydīs according to al-Ashʿarī held that faith consists in knowledge, affirmation, and abstaining from any act for which God has threatened punishment. Every such act constitutes infidelity through ingratitude (*kufr niʿma*): this agrees with the Ibāḍī view.

50. Probably quite early is the view attributed to an anonymous Zaydī group that God is not a thing (*Maqālāt,* p. 70). The great majority of the Zaydiyya according to al-Ashʿarī held that God is a thing (*shay'*). So did evidently Sulaymān b. Jarīr, since he considered even the divine attributes of power, knowledge, and life individually as a thing (*shay'*), though he refused to call the divine attributes collectively things (*ashyā'*) (*Maqālāt,* pp. 70, 171). The Zaydī Imām al-Qāsim b. Ibrāhīm (d. 246/860), whose theology is closer to Muʿtazilism than that of Sulaymān b. Jarīr, also expressly repudiated the view that God is not a thing (Wilferd Madelung, *Der Imam al-Qāsim b. Ibrāhīm,* p. 116). The only theologian commonly mentioned as having denied that God is a thing is Jahm. Since the early Imāmī theologians like Jahm generally considered the term *shay'* as equivalent with body (*jism*), it would have been consistent with the system of Muḥammad b. al-Nuʿmān and probably of al-Jawālīqī to hold the same doctrine, though it is not explicitly attributed to them. The motivation of the anonymous Zaydī group in denying that God is a thing was probably also to affirm that he is not corporeal.

51. Besides the works described in *Der Imam al-Qāsim,* pp. 54ff., the *tafsīr* related by Abū l-Jārūd Ziyād b. al-Mundhir, one of the founders of the Zaydiyya, from Muḥammad al-Bāqir may be cited. This *tafsīr,* which is mentioned by Ibn al-Nadīm (p. 33) and al-Ṭūsī (p. 146), is quoted frequently in the *Tafsīr al-Qummī.* These quotations were added, as the editor notes (1:134, n. 1), to the *Tafsīr al-Qummī* by its first transmitter Abu l-Faḍl al-ʿAbbās b. Muḥammad (although ʿAlī b. Ibrāhīm al-Qummī occasionally also related on the authority of Abū l-Jārūd, cf. 1: 209). The *tafsīr* of Abu l-Jārūd, in striking contrast to that of al-Qummī, is uncompromisingly predestinarian. It quotes Muḥammad al-Bāqir as interpreting Koran 6:39 as "a refutation of the Qadariyya of this community, whom God shall raise on the Day of Resurrection together with the Sabians, Christians, and Jews," and as citing the well-known *ḥadīth:* Each community has its Magians, and the Magians of this community are those who say there is no predestination (*qadar*) and claim that God (reading *li llāh* for *lahum*) has neither will nor power (*Tafsīr al-Qummī* 1: 199). In interpreting Koran 7: 29 "Such as He created you in the beginning so shall you return," it affirms that God created men as believers or infidels, predetermining them for eternal bliss or for eternal misery. In Koran 7:30

it identifies those who "took the devils as friends instead of God and think they are well-guided" as "the Qadarites who say there is no predestination (*qadar*) and claim that they have power over the right guidance and over going astray and that this belongs to them: If they want they are rightly guided, and if they want they go astray. They are the Magians of this nation. The enemies of God are lying. The will and the power belong to God." It then quotes the predestinarian *ḥadīth,* "Miserable shall be he who was (created) miserable in his mother's womb: Happy shall be he who was (created) happy in his mother's womb" (1:226). Commenting on Koran 8: 24 "God intervenes between man and his heart," it affirms that God intervenes (*yaḥūlu*) between the faithful and disobedience of God which would lead him to the fire, and between the infidel and obedience of God by which he would gain perfect faith (1: 271).

52. Cf. *Der Imam al-Qāsim,* pp. 60f.

53. *Maqālāt,* pp. 70, 514.

54. *Maqālāt,* p. 582. Among the early Khārijites, the Khāzimiyya and the Shaybāniyya, subdivisions of the ʿAjārida, are specifically reported to have held that friendship and enmity are attributes of the divine essence (*Maqālāt,* pp. 96, 99). These sects were probably earlier than Sulaymān b. Jarīr. The doctrine implied that God holds friendship towards those who die as believers, even while they act as infidels, and harbors enmity towards those who die as infidels, even while they act as believers (*Maqālāt,* pp. 96, 100). It was probably held also by other Khārijite groups, though disputed by others. In later Ibāḍism, the question whether pleasure, wrath, frienship, enmity, love (*ḥubb*), and hatred (*bughḍ*) are attributes of the divine essence or attributes of act was disputed (cf. M. M. Moreno, "Note di teologia ibāḍita," in *AIOUN* 3 [1949], p. 303; V. Cremonesi, "Un antico documento ibāḍita sul Corano creato," in *Studi Magrebini* 1 [1966], pp. 153f.). The dispute probably has old roots in Ibāḍism too.

55. *Der Iman al-Qāsim,* pp. 81, 85; *Maqālāt,* p. 72.

56. *Maqālāt,* pp. 71, 125.

57. *Maqālāt,* p. 70.

58. *Maqālāt,* pp. 72f.

59. *Maqālāt,* p. 108.

60. *Maqālāt,* pp. 70, 171. The motive for refusing to call the attributes collectively things no doubt was to avoid the inference that God is composed of things or parts.

61. Cf. for instance ʿAbd al-Jabbār, *Sharḥ al-uṣūl al-khamsa,* p. 183.

62. Cf. especially Josef van Ess, "Ibn Kullāb," pp. 113f.

63. Thus he interpreted the expression "face" (*wajh*) of God as meaning God himself (*Maqālāt,* pp. 70, 171, 522).

64. *Maqālāt,* pp. 306, 73.

65. In the account of al-Ashʿarī three of these sects are described as holding the view of the Muʿtazila on *qadar* (*Maqālāt,* p. 93: Maymūniyya; p. 104: Ḥārith al-Ibāḍī; pp. 115 f.: Aṣḥāb al-su'āl).

66. W. Montgomery Watt, *Free Will and Predestination in Early Islam* (pp. 22ff.). Watt was misled by Hellmut Ritter's identification (*Maqālāt,* index, p. 25) of Shabīb al-Najrānī with the early Khārijite leader Shabīb b. Yazīd al-Shaybānī (d. 77/696) into considering the followers of the former, the Aṣḥāb al-su'āl, as a sect of the 1st/7th century (*Free*

Will, p. 40). This identification is definitely erroneous. Shabīb al-Shaybānī did not originate from Najrān, and his followers, the Shabībiyya, are treated as a separate group (*Maqālāt,* pp. 122f.). The Aṣḥāb al-su'āl probably belong to the 2nd/8th century like the Thaʿlabiyya, whose view about the fate of children in the hereafter they shared (*Maqālāt,* p. 116). The identification of Maymūn, the follower of Ibn ʿAjarrad, with the early Ibāḍī Maymūn suggested by Watt (p. 40) is not convincing. The dispute of the followers of Ibn ʿAjarrad about the will of God in any case can be dated, as Watt states, in the years from 105–120/723–738. Watt's further identification (p. 53) of Maʿbad al-Juhanī, the reputed inaugurator of the debate on *qadar* in Basra, with Maʿbad, the founder of a subsect of the Thaʿlabiyya, is untenable.

67. *Maqālāt,* p. 120.

68. *Der Imam al-Qāsim,* pp. 243f.

69. Al-Masʿūdī states that al-Yamān b. Rabāb had a brother, ʿAlī b. Rabāb, who was a prominent Imāmī scholar (*Murūj al-dhahab,* ed. Barbier de Meynard, 7: 442). This brother is presumably identical with the Kūfan ʿAlī b. Rabāb mentioned by al-Najāshī (p. 189) as a transmitter from Imām al-Kāẓim. Al-Ṭūsī (p. 221) and most other Imāmī sources give his name as ʿAlī b. Ri'āb. Flügel in his edition of Ibn al-Nadīm's *Fihrist* chose the reading of al-Ṭūsī and some mss., while other mss. have *bā'* instead of *hamza* (cf. *al-Fihrist* 2: 95).

70. Ibn al-Nadīm, *al-Fihrist,* p. 182.

71. This has been suggested by M. M. Moreno ("Note di teologia ibāḍita," pp. 311ff.), who stressed the fact that the spiritual center of Ibāḍism was still in Baṣra at the time when the founders of Muʿtazilism were active there, and who pointed out the Khārijite affinities in the political views of the early Muʿtazila. The question of the origin of the Muʿtazilite elements in Ibāḍī doctrine in the Maghrib had been posed and left open by Carlo A. Nallino, who was the first to draw attention to them ("Rapporti fra la Dogmatica Muʿtazilita e quella degli Ibāḍiti dell' Africa Settentrionale," in *RSO* 7 [1916–18]: 459f.).

72. *Maqālāt,* pp. 124, 164.

73. Al-Ashʿarī in stating that all Khārijites affirm the creation of the Koran (*Maqālāt,* p. 124) presumably meant their *kalām* theologians. His statement is not invalidated by the fact that among the Ibāḍiyya of ʿUmān the doctrine was opposed at least until the 6th/12th century, as has been shown by V. Cremonesi ("Un antico documento Ibāḍita sul Corano creato," pp. 157ff.). According to al-Faḍl al-Ḥawārī (d. 278/892) the doctrine was first introduced there under the Imām al-Muhannā b. Jayfar (226–37/841–51) and rejected by common accord. Cremonesi suggests that the doctrine was not taught by the early Ibāḍi missionaries sent by Abū ʿUbayda Muslim b. Abī Karīma in the late Umayyad age to various parts of the Muslim world, and was introduced in the Maghrib perhaps also as late as the time of the *miḥna* in the first half of the 3rd/9th century. The fact that the Rustamid Imām Abū l-Yaqẓān (241–81/855–94) in his treatise in support of the doctrine repeatedly appeals to the authority of the early Ibāḍī scholars and pious imāms for his view indicates that the doctrine had been well established for some time among the Ibādiyya in general and presumably also in the Maghrib.

The treatise of Abū l-Yaqẓān should probably be seen more in the Ibāḍī and less in the Muʿtazilite tradition than Cremonesi suggests. The implicit repudiation of the doctrine that pleasure and wrath are attributes of God's essence (cf. above n. 54) seems to be motivated rather by the wish to take a position in the controversy within the Ibāḍiyya than by the adoption of the doctrine of al-Naẓẓām (p. 153). There would be no evident reason for a Muʿtazilite to choose these particular attributes of act as illustrations in preference to others. There is no indication that Abū l-Yaqẓān was influenced by the view of Abū ʿAlī al-Jabbāʾī, or rejected that of the Baghdad Muʿtazilite school (p. 153). The view rejected by him (pp. 167f.) that the Koran in this world is created and a reproduction of the uncreated Word of God which subsists in him as an essential attribute is substantially the doctrine of the Sunnite ʿAbd Allāh b. Kullāb. This is not to deny that Khārijites, Muʿtazilites, and other supporters of the createdness of the Koran used largely the same arguments, often borrowed from each other.

74. *Maqālāt,* p. 124. Al-Ashʿarī attributes the view specifically to the Ibāḍiyya, but it was probably held by most of the other Khārijites too.

75. *Maqālāt,* p. 180. Some of the later Ibāḍī imāms and scholars in the Maghrib affirmed that man has a choice (*ikhtiyār*) in his acts. This view was repudiated by others. Nothing is known so far about the origins of this dispute. Cf. Moreno, "Note di teologia ibāḍita," pp. 308f.

76. This argument is developed at length in ʿAbd Allāh b. Yazīd's refutation of the Qadariyya as quoted in the *K. al-najāt* of the Zaydī Imām Aḥmad al-Nāṣir.

77. *Maqālāt,* pp. 107f.

78. *Maqālāt,* p. 125.

79. Cf. Watt, *Free Will,* p. 129. The date of the third Ibāḍī scholar named by al-Ashʿarī (*Maqālāt,* p. 708) as holding the same views, Idrīs al-Ibāḍī, is unknown.

80. Watt, *Free Will,* p. 106; Carra de Vaux [A. N. Nader and J. Schacht], s.v. "Bishr b. Ghiyāth al-Marīsī" in *The Encyclopaedia of Islam,* new ed.; van Ess, "Ḍirār b. ʿAmr," pp. 56 ff.

81. Thus Ḍirār b. ʿAmr, like the Muʿtazila in general, considered the will of God as an attribute of act. Ḥafs al-Fard and Bishr al-Marīsī maintained that it is partly an attribute of essence and partly, as far as it consists of his command, an attribute of act (*Maqālāt,* p. 515). Al-Najjār's formulation is identical with that of the Ibāḍī scholars. God willed from eternity that what he knew would happen should happen and that what he knew would not happen should not happen (*Maqālāt,* p. 514). The continuation of the text l. 13f. is indeed incomplete and can be completed by comparison with the passage on the identical doctrine of the Ibāḍiyya, p. 108, l. 11 f.

82. *Al-farq,* p. 195.

83. *Maqālāt,* p. 109.

84. *Maqālāt,* p. 109, l. 5f. *wa-yaqūlu aktharuhum innahū abʿaḍun li l-jism.*

85. Cf. above n. 47.

86. Al-Ashʿarī indeed stresses that most people refused to admit that accidents can be turned (*qalb*) into bodies, as Ḍirār and his school maintained (*Maqālāt,* pp. 281, 371). There are unfortunately no reports on how the Ibāḍī scholars and Sulaymān b. Jarīr treated motion and acts in their systematic thought.

87. *Maqālāt,* p. 109. Al-Ashʿarī states that their view agreed with that of al-Ḥusayn, i.e., al-Najjār, who adopted the doctrine of Ḍirār. The formulation "the atom is a body" is not expressly ascribed by al-Ashʿarī to Ḍirār and al-Najjār, but rather to Abū-Ḥusayn al-Ṣāliḥī (*Maqālāt,* p. 301). One might be tempted to read *ʿalā madhhab Abī l-Ḥusayn,* namely al-Ṣāliḥā, instead of *ʿalā madhhab al-Ḥusayn.* The Ibāḍī views concerning bodies previously described by al-Ashʿarī are, however, clearly in agreement with those of Ḍirār and al-Najjār, and definitely at variance with those of al-Ṣāliḥī.

88. Cf. Pretzl, "Atomenlehre," pp. 119f.

III.
The Development of Philosophical and Mystical Theology

Reason and Revelation in Ibn Ḥazm's Ethical Thought

GEORGE F. HOURANI
State University of New York at Buffalo

I

NORMATIVE ETHICS (*akhlāq*) in the sense of wise advice for a good and happy life, was written about by Ibn Ḥazm in two well-known books, '*Ṭawq al-ḥamāma* and *Mudāwāt an-nufūs.* The following article, however, is not concerned with his views on ethics in that sense, but with his answers to fundamental questions of modern philosophical ethics: the meanings of ethical concepts, the sources of our knowledge of them and of values in practice, the theory of moral motivation. In the religious tradition of medieval Islam, to which Ibn Ḥazm for all his individuality belonged, these questions were not marked off as a separate field of knowledge but fell somewhere between theology and law. More precisely, theology provided the framework of doctrines from which the principles of ethics could be derived, and these principles were applied by jurists in working out Islamic law.

Accordingly, we find Ibn Ḥazm's treatment of philosophical ethics mainly in his major work on theology, the *Fiṣal,* and his major work on jurisprudence, the *Iḥkām.* Both these works were written in the later years of his life, when his theological and legal position as a Zahirite was settled, and together with other works of the same period they supply a unified theory of ethics. His last work, *Mudāwāt an-nufūs,* although of a different literary genre, also throws light on this theory and is consistent with it. All these writings, then, will be used to reconstruct his ethics. But *Ṭawq al-ḥamāma* will not generally be used, because it is a work of Ibn Ḥazm's youth, completed no doubt after he had taken up religious studies in earnest but before he had adopted Zahirism.[1] The dividing line has to be put around A.D. 1027–29, when Ibn Ḥazm was studying in the Great Mosque of Córdoba under the Zahirite Abū l-Khiyār of Santarén. By that time he had already quit politics as his main activity and gone through a few years of religious studies, first as a Shāfiʿite, then as a Zahirite. From then on he devoted his intellectual and literary life to working out the theory of Islam in its Zahirite form and combating its enemies, and it is with this phase of his thought that we shall be concerned.

In the following systematic account I shall rely on the eminent studies of Goldziher, Asín Palácios, Cruz Hernández, and Arnaldez[2] for the general lines of Ibn Ḥazm's thought, and use the texts of his own works as evidence on his ethical philosophy.[3]

II

In showing the respective roles of reason and revelation in ethical knowledge according to Ibn Ḥazm we have to start with reason, because in certain directions he regards it as prior to revelation. ("Reason" or "intellect" (*ʿaql*) is used here in a broad sense to include all natural channels of knowledge.) He is neither a fideist nor a mystic, and firmly upholds reason as the starting point of knowledge in three directions relevant to our subject: (i) in justifying revelation itself, and (ii)-(iii) in supplying us with two kinds of primary knowledge related to value—lexical and psychological—though not supplying directly any knowledge of particular ethical values, as will be shown.

(i) The first sources of all human knowledge are the soundly used senses and the intuitions of reason, combined with a correct understanding of a language. From these sources we can gain extensive further knowledge by the use of reasoning in its proper place. The most important knowledge attained by these rational methods is the preambles of revelation. These include certain provable truths about God, such as His existence, unity and eternity, His creation of the world, and the authenticity of the Qur'ān as the Word of God or (what amounts to the same thing) the genuineness of Muḥammad's prophethood (*Iḥkām,* 1: 28). In spite of his emphasis on revelation as the sole source of normative ethical knowledge, Ibn Ḥazm, like Aquinas and many other theologians, is well aware that to make revelation the first source of all religious knowledge is self-defeating, because it leaves nothing but a circular argument on which to base the authenticity of revelation itself. He says this very clearly in a context where he is stating that we must, of course, pay attention to whatever the Qur'ān says confirming the conclusions of the natural sources.

> "We are obliged to understand the Qur'ān and accept its contents. Among these, we find it drawing attention to the soundness of the means by which we arrive at knowledge of things as they are: the faculties of intellect and the senses. But I do not mean by this we can verify by the Qur'ān anything whose truth we had doubted by the

comprehension of our intellect and senses. If we did that we should be refuting realities and proceeding on a circular demonstration, by which nothing at all can be confirmed. For suppose we are challenged and asked, 'How do you know that the Qur'ān is genuine?', we can answer only on the basis of true premises attested by intellect and the senses. Then if we are asked, 'How do you know the soundness of intellect and the senses, which affirm those premises?' and we reply 'By the Qur'ān,' this is a fallacious proof that refutes realities. Rather we say: 'The Qur'ān draws the attention of ignorant and heedless people and puts an end to the contentions of the stubborn'" (*Iḥkam,* 1: 66).

(ii) The primary terms of value, such as "good," "evil" and "obligatory" are understood in the same way as we understand the rest of our vocabulary, in any language. A language was given to men by God at the time of their creation, together with the natural endowments of intelligence enabling them to speak, understand and expand language. The Qur'ān and preceding scriptures do not provide us with definitions of the primary terms of value; they simply use them, on the assumption that they have definite "correct" meanings which are already understood.[4]

Thus, there is a concept of the personal good, in the sense of what is advantageous (*ṣāliḥ*) or a benefit (*fā'ida*) for the subject, what truly satisfies him. This concept will provide the starting point for our consideration of Ibn Ḥazm's ethics.

Then there is the concept of the obligatory (*wājib*), which is taken to mean whatever is commanded by the supreme Commander, who has the power to impose sanctions for disobedience. Since the concept of *wājib* is central in Ibn Ḥazm's theory, it is important to give evidence for his use of it. He does not give a separate definition of it in his glossary of terms, *Iḥkām,* 1: 35–52. The nearest approach is his definition of *farḍ,* "duty": "that for which the omitter deserves to be blamed and called disobedient to God, the Exalted, and it is [synonymous with] *wājib* ['obligatory'], *lāzim* ['necessary'] and *ḥatm* ['imposition']" (*Iḥkām,* 1: 43). The presence of "deserves" (*istaḥaqqa*) here creates a problem since it imparts an objective quality to the definition of *farḍ* and its synonyms, which is alien to the rest of Ibn Ḥazm's theory. Indeed, the first phrase of the formula (*mā istaḥaqqa tārikuhu l-lawma*) is taken straight from the Muʿtazilite definition of *wājib.*[5] We can obtain a more accurate understanding of the meaning of *wājib* in Ibn Ḥazm from his many refutations of rationalist objectivism in ethics, which will be discussed later: but here is one example to confirm our understanding of *wājib.* In *Fiṣal* Ibn Ḥazm argues against the theory that we can know by reason our obligations of gratitude to other human beings, and he concludes by saying, "Gratitude is obligatory only toward those persons to whom God Himself has declared it obligatory for us to show ourselves grateful" (3: 109; cf. *Iḥkām,* 1: 60). But, apart from any particular quotations, the entire ethical and legal theory of Ibn Ḥazm, like those of all the more or less "traditionalist" thinkers—Shāfiʿī, Ibn Ḥanbal, Ashʿarī, etc.—is based on the assumption that obligation is intelligible only in terms of the commands of revelation.

Similarly, "evil" (*qabīḥ*) is used as equivalent to what is forbidden or disapproved by revelation, without any objective essence, and unknowable to unaided human reason (*Fiṣal,* 3: 101–15). "Virtue" (*faḍīla*) means obedience to God, and more particularly to the general injunctions to upright living (*Iḥkām,* 1: 5; *Mudāwāt,* §§ 16, 45, etc.), as contrasted with fulfilment of the specific obligations of the *sharīʿa.*

If we are to avoid hopeless confusion about the functions of reason and revelation in Ibn Ḥazm's ethics, it is essential to understand clearly the sharp contrast implicit in his thought between our knowledge of the *meanings* of value terms, which is given to us by our intellectual understanding of language, prior to revelation (although confirmed by it), and our knowledge of the specific *contents* of ethical value, such as virtues and obligations, which is given to us only through revelation, with the supplementary aid of intellect for interpretation in strictly limited ways. To test and illustrate the function of intellect, we may examine briefly a sentence about obligation, which looks like the concept most dependent on revelation.

> "It belongs to the intellect only [1] to understand the commands of God the Exalted and [to understand] the obligation [or necessity] (*wujūb*) of avoiding transgression in cases where eternal punishment is to be feared," [followed by two other kinds of rational knowledge] (*Iḥkām,* 1: 29).

Here *wujūb* is ambiguous, but on either alternative it is possible to show how it is understood by the intellect. (a) If it means "obligation," we know the obligation of avoiding transgression, etc., analytically, because the later words "avoiding transgression . . . to be feared" are part of the definition of *wujūb* in this sense. (b) If *wujūb* means "necessity," as it sometimes does in Arabic, we may rule out logical necessity or any kind of force, since it is obvious that men do not necessarily avoid transgression in these senses. What is left is "prudential necessity," i.e., the necessity that follows from an agent's rational estimate of his own interest. Now the "necessity," in this sense, of avoiding punishable transgression is known partly[6] by intellect, according to Ibn Ḥazm, because men know prior to revelation that avoidable pain, such as hellfire, not leading to any further satisfaction, is disadvantageous (*Iḥkam,* 1: 28–29). That will now be shown from the general psychology of desires outlined in *Mudāwāt an-nufūs.*

(iii) We can also know independently of revelation some general facts of human psychology which are relevant to our choices of goals. That the personal good is what satisfies a man over the long term is true by definition, as mentioned; but that everyone strives for such satisfaction (conceived in the vaguest terms) is an empirically known fact. In *Mudāwāt* Ibn Ḥazm induces the negative facet of this truth from his lifelong observation of human efforts: that all men aim at freedom from care, *qillat al-hamm,* the *ataraxia* of ancient Greek philosophers.

> "I looked for a goal that all people alike approve of and seek, and I found only one, repulsion of care. And on reflection I realized that all alike not only approve of it and seek it; I saw that, in spite of the variety of their desires and pursuits and the differences in their concerns and objectives, they make not the slightest move except in the hope of repelling care, and they speak not a word except with the intention of removing it from their souls" (*Mudāwāt,* § 5).

He describes this discovery as "exalted knowledge," "a wonderful secret" and "a great treasure," with which God has illuminated his mind (§ 6), but with no suggestion that he has acquired it from the study of scripture. This is knowledge gained by experience and reflection, as the whole passage shows (§§ 5–7). Perhaps this viewpoint classes Ibn Ḥazm's formal ethics as egoistic hedonism, but as we shall see that name is inadequate as a description of its inner spirit and contents.

He then goes on to tell how he looked for the best means to freedom from care, and how he found all activities defective for this purpose except one: working for salvation in the next life (§ 8). Here too he uses his experience, but also his religious knowledge derived from scripture, concerning the afterlife; so at this point his thought goes beyond reason.

III

After these three starting points in rational knowledge, all further religious knowledge, in theology, ethics and law, is derived mainly or partly from divinely inspired sources. These sources for Ibn Ḥazm are the Qur'ān above all, but also the Traditions of the Prophet and his Companions and the *ijmāʿ* (consensus) of these Companions. His Zahirism consists of two major elements: (1) strict literal interpretation of these sources, (2) refusal to extend the message of the sources by dependent rational procedures such as analogy. Yet both in the theoretical formulation and in the application of his Zahirite principles there are elements of reason at every step, which he does not deny. For instance, the principle of literal interpretation is based partly on explicit statements of the Qur'ān, such as the notable verses iii, 3–5, forbidding allegorical interpretation (*ta'wīl*) as a mischievous activity, partly on the simple and direct attitudes of Muḥammad and his Companions, but partly also on a comprehensive theory of human language and its purposes, which has been expounded by Arnaldez in his massive study[7] and need not be gone over here. So, too, in the detailed understanding of the meaning of the scriptural texts one must apply the rules of ordinary language in the context of the speech of Makka and Madīna in the early seventh century, with the help of the substantial philological knowledge of scholars of Arabic. Thus in writing above that further religious knowledge is derived "mainly or partly" from revelation, I meant to state precisely that from this point on revealed texts are always an indispensable element in that knowledge, but also that in spite of Ibn Ḥazm's Zahirism elements of reason are present at all levels, within strict limits.

Before we proceed to the distinctive Zahirite features of his ethical theory, we have first to explain a range of ethical doctrine which he shares, more or less, with traditionalist jurisprudence and theology of the regular Sunnite schools, but not with Muʿtazilite rationalism or with Graeco-Islamic philosophy.

IV

Ibn Ḥazm's ethics, like that of most other medieval theologians, is oriented primarily toward the good of the individual, conceived in terms of his long-range happiness. As was stated above, the good for man is defined in these terms, and its most general content, freedom from care, is known from experience to be in fact the aim of everyone. But these two pieces of general knowledge do not take us very far in making practical decisions, in ordering our lives. The more urgent questions are, (i) What kind of life constitutes a state of freedom from care? and (ii) What are the means to attain such a life?

(i) From the Qur'ān, which is known to be the Word of God, we learn that there is an eternal afterlife, in which man may either enjoy the Reward of permanent happiness and complete freedom from care in paradise or suffer permanent torment in hell. This is the first overwhelming fact about his future prospects that man learns from revelation. The afterlife must then be his foremost concern, since in comparison with it the present life is insignificant in length and intensity. Its ends in themselves are the same in their nature but transitory, and must be subordinated to any relation they may have as means to attaining eternal felicity and avoiding eternal misery.

(ii) The second overwhelming fact revealed by the Qur'ān is that every individual's salvation or damnation to the two alternative kinds of afterlife is dependent on his conduct in this present life, as judged by God on the Day of Judgment. Therefore man must learn what are the features of conduct that will be rewarded or punished by that Judgment, and his entire present life must be oriented toward fulfilling the rewardable conduct as a means to salvation as described. It is a sign of stupidity and irrationality to prefer the mixed goods of this short life, just because they are immediate, to the pure goods of eternal life. It is like the behavior of a man who would prefer a day's walk through a countryside of pleasant meadows, with some hazards, in order to arrive at a squalid cottage and live there a hundred years, to a day's walk with some sorrows, at the end of which he would arrive at a splendid palace with servants and gardens, trees and streams, and live there a hundred years (*Iḥkām,* 1: 5–6).

But the Qur'ān does not merely inform man vaguely that there is a causal relation between his conduct and his fate in the next life. It also tells him what kinds of conduct will receive Reward and Punishment. In general, the whole of rewardable conduct comes under the heading of obedience to God's commands and prohibitions. This rule is emphasized as the guiding line for all human virtue and obligation, the means to salvation (*Iḥkām,* 1: 7 and 29; *Mudāwāt,* chap. 2). But before we go into the details of obedience, three points deserve to be noticed briefly at this general level:

(a) While scripture tells us that in fact God rewards obedience and punishes disobedience, Ibn Ḥazm takes pains to declare in many ways that there are no rational limits to God's judgment in this matter. He judges as He pleases, and whatever He judges is just (*Fiṣal,* 3: 98 and 105). Human intellect cannot set rules for God's decisions, as the Muʿtazila suppose, "who by their intellects 'correct' for their Creator, Mighty and Glorious, judgments which their Lord does not make in the way they assert" (*Iḥkām,* 1: 28). Indeed, Abū Hāshim, one of the former heads of the Muʿtazila (d. 932), was shameless enough to use expressions like "God ought to do so and so." Ibn Ḥazm asks: then who obliges Him?—since, on his view (although not on Abū Hāshim's), every obligation implies the existence of an obliger (*mūjib*), otherwise there would be an effect without an agent. Only two answers are possible: that the obliger is human, which is impious, or that God obliges Himself. In the latter case, either He can change any obligation and is completely free, as we claim, or else He has committed an eternal act of obliging, which sets up a coeternal being—impious in the direction of fatalism (*Fiṣal,* 3: 102–03).

In accordance with this doctrine of God's unrestricted freedom and unquestionable justice, Ibn Ḥazm draws out some of the alternative moral orders that He might have set up for the world. He could have punished the angels, the prophets and believers everlastingly in the Fire, and rewarded the devil and unbelievers everlastingly in heaven (*Fiṣal,* 3: 105). He could have imposed on man obligations impossible to fulfil, then punished him for failing to fulfil them; that this is evil is not known by reason, since many theologians deny that they know it thus; it is evil only because it is denied by God in revelation (*Fiṣal,* 3: 107). God could justly punish a man for something that He has helped him to do; the denial of this by the Muʿtazila is sheer anthropomorphism, judging God's justice by what natural reason judges just for man (*Fiṣal,* 3: 97).

> "And if God the Exalted had informed us that He would punish us for the acts of others . . . or for our own obedience, all that would have been right and just, and we should have been obliged to accept it" (*Fiṣal,* 3: 92).

Finally, it is not unimaginable and quite possible that God would have commanded us to be unbelievers, to deny Him, to worship idols and commit wrong; however, He has told us that He does not do so in fact (*Iḥkām,* 1: 69–70). But God can do anything He wants!

(b) As early as *The Ring of the Dove, (Ṭawq),* Ibn Ḥazm had become convinced that the emotional soul (*nafs*) of man left to itself naturally counsels evil (*Ṭawq,* 316), and without the help of revelation and reason he inevitably yields to persistent sensual temptations (*Ṭawq,* 318–20, 328, 376). This conviction he gained not only from the Qur'ān (xii, 53/Cairo, Joseph's famous comment on his temptation by the governor's wife and his resistance only with the aid of God), but also from his own experience as narrated in the *Ring.* There is no reason to believe that he changed his belief on this question in his later life. On the contrary, the more deeply we study the *Ring* the more clearly we find in it the elements of personal struggle and sorrow which led its young author into the refuge of a religion that would give him security and tranquility; and this impression is confirmed by his other personal book, the *Mudāwāt,* as well as by what we know of the rest of his troubled life and passionate character. Even his choice of the Zahirite form of Islam, which may seem odd in such a brilliant and broadly educated man, may be partly explained by his desire for the security of firm textual commands and prohibitions, free from the variety of interpretations and extensions open to the other traditional schools.

(c) Concerning the relation between predestination and responsibility, Ibn Ḥazm holds as against the Muʿtazila that a man cannot choose to be either obedient or disobedient to the divine commands entirely by his own capacity (*istiṭāʿa*) at the time of action; his choice depends on the favor or disfavor of God, who gives or withholds from him the power to act at the moment of action. Thus at the decisive point Ibn Ḥazm is a predestination. Yet he thinks at the same time that man is responsible and justly burdened with obligations to obey commands and prohibitions, so long as he has capacity (*istiṭāʿa*) in another sense, that prior to the action he has "soundness of his limbs and the removal of obstacles," i.e., if he is free from external impediments (*Fiṣal,* 3: 32).

Confirmation of his view is found in several other passages, of which the following is perhaps the clearest. He starts from the Muʿtazilite use of Qur'ān, iv, 81, to support their doctrine of human free will: "If anything good happens to you, it comes from God, but if anything evil happens to you, it is from yourself." The first half of this quotation does not serve their purpose, and Ibn Ḥazm accepts it willingly. With regard to evil, he draws attention to the preceding verse, iv, 80, "Say to them that everything comes from God," and lays it down that the meaning of 81 must be consistent with this general principle. Then he explains the words on evil thus:

> "We deserve punishment for the moral evil that appears to proceed from us as its subject, by which we are guilty of rebellion against God, according to the decrees of His providence, which is justice and truth itself" (*Fiṣal,* 3: 92–94: quotation from 94; cf. also 3: 51, 104).

This explanation brings together the same elements of responsibility and predestination as were asserted in the previous statement of his doctrine. Whether he succeeds in harmonizing these two elements is open to question, but it is not my concern to discuss his position critically. The fact that concerns us in a historical account is that in all ethical contexts he regards man as responsible for his own actions and liable to Reward and Punishment accordingly. In any case, for Ibn Ḥazm God's disposition of the moral order is just, for reasons given under (a) above.

V

Since obedience to God's commands leads to salvation, and revelation specifies what obedience consists of, the most important practical tasks for man are to find out what revelation prescribes and then to do it faithfully at all times and in all circumstances. At this point, Ibn Ḥazm is not altogether consistent in his terminology. Sometimes he speaks of "the virtues" (*faḍā'il,* sing. *faḍīla*), as synonymous with all acts of obedience (*ṭāʿāt*), and the vices as synonymous with all acts of disobedience (*Mudāwāt,* §§ 16, 185; *Ṭawq,* 404). In other instances he divides the obligatory (*wājib,* coextensive with acts of obedience) into two classes, *faḍīla* and *sharīʿa* (*Mudāwāt,* § 45). This division corresponds with the division of subject matter in his two books, *Mudāwāt* and *Iḥkām.* In *Mudāwāt* he is treating the general virtues—generosity, continence, courage, justice, etc., where no specific act is commanded by scripture, but rather to behave in a certain spirit, and he speaks here about virtue and virtues. *Iḥkām* is a treatise on jurisprudence, in which he concentrates on the justifications for the specific obligations of the *sharīʿa,* such as the rules for prayer and other matters prescribed by religious legislation. So it will be more convenient to take *faḍīla* and "virtue" in the more restricted sense, in order to distinguish what is said about each of the two types of obligation.

Ibn Ḥazm expresses many value judgments on the virtues and vices in his two books of normative ethics, *Ṭawq* and *Mudāwāt.* A close study of what he has to say would be of interest in other contexts—biographical or social-historical—but would be out of place in the present outline of his ethics as a theoretical construction. Only a few general observations may be offered, for the sake of giving some body to this construction. In *Mudāwāt* (§§ 89–92) he defines and discusses four virtues, three of which are the same as those chosen by Plato in his *Republic:* courage, continence and justice, although his definitions differ from Plato's. For Plato's "wisdom" he substitutes "generosity" (*jūd*), a virtue highly esteemed among the Arabs. But wisdom, intelligence and knowledge receive plenty of commendation throughout the book, in fact it *is* primarily a book of practical wisdom.[8] In another place (§ 26) he says that all the virtues are summed up in two Traditions of the Prophet, his saying "Do not be angry" and his command to desire for others what we desire for ourselves. In *Ṭawq* he praises fidelity above all other virtues of love and friendship (2, 198–200, 208–10) and thinks this has been his own particular merit (296). He regards lying as the greatest vice (140–44). In *Mudāwāt* (§§ 96–114) he discusses his own faults and merits at length and frankly; his faults are grouped around excessive pride, and include his passion for triumphing in argument and proneness to anger (§ 97), both of which brought him into much trouble in his relations with other scholars.

"The sum of the virtues and avoidance of vices is obedience to God, Mighty and Glorious" (*Iḥkām,* 1: 5). Even in *Mudāwāt,* a book of reflective wisdom drawn from Ibn Ḥazm's own experience, he makes it clear that the supreme end is to be attained only by such obedience. In the heading of chapter 2, which he calls "an important chapter," he asserts that the whole of intelligence and tranquillity consists of "casting aside attention to the words of men and paying attention [only] to the words of the Creator, Mighty and Glorious", i.e., to revelation (before § 13). And although the spirit and style of this book make it inappropriate to quote scriptural texts at every turn, as he does in his Zahirite legal works, there is no inconsistency between the virtues emphasized in it and those emphasized in the Qur'ān, which was after all the piece of literature that had been most deeply formative of his mind during at least thirty years before the *Mudāwāt,* and perhaps also in his early childhood. We should also recall that the supreme goal of man is stated in this book to be freedom from care, and that this is to be attained mainly in the next life and worked for as the principal activity of this life (§ 4); and it is implicit in these ends and means that the specific means is practice of the religious virtues. Thus, in spite of first impressions, there is no sense in which *Mudāwāt* can be described as a "secular" book, even to the extent that *Ṭawq* can be. At the same time, Ibn Ḥazm points out in passing that the quest for salvation also brings joy in this life, through "freedom from care for what other people are concerned about, and respect from friend and enemy" (§ 4).

While the emphasis in the conception of virtue is on obedience to revelation, Ibn Ḥazm leaves a place for philosophy too in the work of cultivating virtue. In *Fiṣal* he writes that

> "in reality the meaning and result of philosophy and the aim intended in studying it are nothing other than the correction of the soul, achieved both by practicing the virtues and good conduct in this life, which lead to salvation in the other life, and by good social organization, domestic and political. Now this and nothing else is also the aim of the religious law (*sharīʿa*)."

This is admitted by all parties—philosophers and lawyers (1: 94).

Questions arise as to what he means here by philosophy, and how a theologian with such an insistence on scripture as the only authoritative source of values could find any use in philosophy, which was by definition regarded as a secular science. The answer to the question on meaning is, I believe, to be learned from the quotation, where he mentions the three *practical* branches of philosophy according to the Aristotelian tradition: personal ethics, household or family management (the original "economics"), and politics. We find them distinguished and treated as normative knowledge or wisdom in books of "ethics" such as *Tahdhīb al-akhlāq* of Miskawayh (d.c. 1030), where the original rationalistic theories of Greek ethical philosophy are in the background and the interest is rather in advice for the virtuous life; yet such books were still classed as "philosophy." We can now answer the question on the use of such philosophy. Ibn Ḥazm's own final book *Mudāwāt an-nufūs* almost fits into this type, and it is not hard to reconcile this sort of "philosophy" with his theory of the virtues. For these are viewed, as we have seen, as the more general obligations, not specified precisely by *sharīʿa* laws; therefore there is legitimate scope for human wisdom to supply guidance on the details, using all the resources of pertinent rational sciences.

> "The definition of reason (*ʿaql*) is practice of obedience and the virtues, and this definition implies avoidance of disobedience and the vices" (*Mudāwāt,* § 185).

For Ibn Ḥazm, reason when properly used is not opposed to revelation, it is simply put at its service in any useful direction.

It should further be noticed that all his advice on virtue conceives it as a means to the good of the individual. There is no idea of virtuous activity as an end in itself, done for its own sake and constituting its own reward; we are far from any Kantian notion of duty. And, although our fulfilment of virtues and other obligations may contribute in fact to the good of society, that is not their essence: it is simply obedience to the divine will, as expressed in revelation. That is not to say that Ibn Ḥazm is not concerned with the good of the *umma,* the earthly community of Muslims; indeed his own efforts in writing books to guide them show that he is. But his concern is now with the salvation of each individual member of the *umma*. In his youth he had engaged passionately and often dangerously in politics, hoping to help the restoration of a stable Umayyad dynasty such as had created the conditions for a wholesome Muslim community in Spain for so long in the past. But, like Ibn Khaldūn in North Africa three centuries later, he had given up political struggles as useless in the conditions of his environment, and directed most of his later life to intellectual efforts to help individual Muslims find their own way to the true end of life.[9] There is a maxim in *Mudāwāt* (§ 45) which, although not perfectly apposite, is worth quoting because it illustrates a general trend in his thought: "Beward of pleasing others by actions which harm your own soul, and which are not made obligatory for you by the *sharīʿa* or virtue." The imperfection in this quotation is that it probably refers to antisocial actions demanded by others for selfish ends. It therefore does not display a case of "personal" virtue being preferred before "social" virtue by Ibn Ḥazm —indeed, such a case may be hard to find in his writings, since he has no tendency to see a conflict between these two kinds of virtue or to make a problem out of it. Still, the quotation shows well enough where he places the priority in true human interests.

While *Mudāwāt* is about the general virtues, the more specific obligations of the *sharīʿa* are dealt with in *Iḥkām* in a theoretical way, in *Kitāb al-Muḥallā* in detail, and in other religious works in various controversial contexts. It should be understood that *Iḥkām* is not confined to the *sharīʿa* obligations but spans "the sources of [ethical] judgments in religion" (*uṣūl al-aḥkām fī d-diyāna*) (1: 8). But here I shall draw upon it only for some remarks on the *sharīʿa,* since the other kind of obligations (virtue) has already been discussed. In the sphere of *sharīʿa* it is even clearer that the obligations are derived from a positive divine Law exclusively. God, addressing man through the Prophet in the Qurʾān and the Traditions, imposed divine Laws (*sharāʾiʿ*) on man for his salvation and obliged us to follow them (*Iḥkām,* 1: 9–10).

> "Whatever we have said, we have not said at random. We have not uttered a word on all this subject that is not drawn from what God the Exalted has said, as a witness to its truth, and what the intellect has distinguished, (*mayyazahu l-ʿaql*), understanding its reality, praise to God, Lord of the worlds" (*Iḥkām,* 1: 6).[10]

Even while asserting emphatically the revealed source of all ethical judgments, Ibn Ḥazm does not neglect to mention the role of reason in "distinguishing," i.e., understanding accurately the meaning of the sacred text. This is a derivative but important role. For Ibn Ḥazm it consists above all of understanding the text in a literal sense wherever possible, and stopping there. This is where as a Zahirite he parts company with the majority of Sunnite traditionalists in medieval Islam. His Zahirite doctrines in law and theology have been sufficiently explained in the books of Goldziher and Arnaldez in particular (see note 2), and it will be unnecessary to elaborate them here. But a little more will be said on them in the next section, in explaining what it is that Ibn Ḥazm wants to deny, and why.

VI

The last section has expounded Ibn Ḥazm's theory of obligation in positive terms, showing its entire dependence in content on the will of God as revealed in scripture. In the present section we shall turn to his polemics against the false uses of reason in ethics and law. And we shall here divide reason into two kinds, which he attacks in different ways although holding basically the same objection against both. (i) "Independent reason" is here defined as the attempt to arrive at value judgments without any source in revelation at all. (ii) "Dependent reason" is defined as the attempt to extend the legal knowledge derived from revelation by illegitimate methods. I am using these two expressions as convenient stipulated names for two kinds of reason which he attacks, not for all possible uses of reason; for, as has been and will again be mentioned, Ibn Ḥazm allows certain uses of reason at vital points in his system.

(i) It has already been shown (in IV) that no limits can be set in terms of supposed "objective" standards of value to the general moral order that God could have set up for the world. Now the same thing has to be shown with regard to the specific obligations of man (whether virtues or *sharīʿa* laws matters little in this context). But before we come to his refutations concerning particular obligations, some theoretical statements of his position will be useful. The general position is that there are no such characters as good or evil, obligatory, just or unjust "in essence," but only as descriptions of what is commanded, approved, etc., by a judge; and that the only qualified judge is God, the Creator and Lord of the world (*Fiṣal,* 3: 100–02): this is theistic subjectivism. Consequently, the human intellect does not have the power to attribute any such characters to things, people or acts independently of the Word of God. In *Iḥkām* there is a clear statement of the limits of the human mind in this sphere:

> "The intellect only distinguishes between the qualities (*ṣifāt*) of existing things, and informs him who seeks its guidance of the facts concerning the properties (*ḥaqāʾiq kayfiyyāt*) of actual objects, and of the distinction from them of what is impossible. But whoever claims that the intellect makes lawful or forbids (*yuḥallilu aw yuḥarrimu*) or that the intellect provides obliging causes (*yūjiba ʿillalan mūjibatan*) for the existence of all acts—laws or others—manifested by God the Exalted

Creator in this world, is in the same condition as he who denies the need for the intellect altogether" (1: 27; cf. *Fiṣāl,* 1: 98; 3: 98).

Ibn Ḥazm is here drawing a distinction, accepted by many modern ethical philosophers, between "descriptive facts" and "values," although his theological explanation of the latter is not one that is acceptable to most of our Western contemporaries.

Such a statement as the one quoted above sounds dogmatic, but Ibn Ḥazm had found his reasons for reaching his conclusion in the failures, as he viewed them, of the Muʿtazila to justify the rules of morality and law by any rational arguments. His manner of disputing their claims is best shown by several examples, mostly from a few pages in *Fiṣal* (3: 105–30) where he deals directly with this problem in its detailed aspect.

(a) Enmity between animals is not condemned as evil and wrong; yet it would be, if enmity as such were evil and wrong—they would be so wherever they existed. Thus enmity has these attributes not in itself but only when declared evil by God (105; cf. 128–30 on the injustices of animal life).

(b) The golden rule that it is always evil to do to others what you would not want them to do to you is disproved by many examples, such as the laws of marriage in Islam, by which it is permitted and good for a man to marry up to four women at a time, but not for a woman to marry more than one man at a time, in spite of the feelings of jealousy that arise in women's hearts as much as in men's (106).

(c) Likewise the laws of inheritance allot to males twice the shares of females, regardless of the wealth or poverty or earning capacity of individual heirs (107).

(d) The Muʿtazila claim that it is known that ingratitude to benefactors is always evil and disapproved by reason. "We reply that God is the only real benefactor, since He has created us and every benefit we enjoy, so there is no rational obligation of gratitude to any human being. And there is no [human] benefactor except him whom God the Exalted has named as such, and gratitude to a benefactor is obligatory only after God the Exalted has made such gratitude obligatory; in that case it is obligatory and not otherwise" (107–08; quotation from 108). Another answer is given elsewhere: Suppose a beneficiary faces a former benefactor in war (presumably religious war), is it his duty to try to kill him or not? The "rule of reason" would have to deny it, but we know by *ijmāʿ* that it is his duty (*Iḥkām,* 1: 60). In another example on gratitude, a Muslim who enslaves non-Muslims and makes them work hard on menial tasks is within his rights so long as he provides for them in the minimum lawful ways; and if he then emancipates them it is for them to be grateful to him! But if another Muslim enslaves some Muslims, treats them well and gives them a good religious education, he does all this without any right, and if he abuses one of their women he is liable to death by stoning, regardless of any former benefits for which he would normally deserve gratitude (*Fiṣal,* 3: 108–09).

(e) The obligations of obedience to parents are limited and assigned by divine Law, not by any natural reasons (107–09).

(f) If it is said "Lying is always evil," we can point out cases where it is commanded by the Law: to conceal a fugitive and his possessions from an oppressive government, to mislead an enemy in war, to avoid hurting one's wife's feelings and causing her to withdraw her love. It is not that God can make lying good *against* reason; rather it is impossible for God's commands to be irrational, as the Muʿtazilite "principles of reason" seem to imply that they might be (109–10).

(g) When they claim that wrongdoing (*ẓulm*) is always evil, we ask them to define "wrongdoing," and all they can do is to produce a list of types of acts such as killing, taking another's property, suicide, allowing one's wife to other men, etc. But in every case we can show them exceptions that are lawful, without any difference in the type of act as a mere physical event (110–11).

Other examples can be found easily, but these will be enough to illustrate Ibn Ḥazm's methods of argument against Muʿtazilite rationalism in ethics. It will be apparent that the main method is to show that the ethical conclusions of their supposed reason are always overturned by some cases prescribed differently by revelation. Looking at these arguments from a detached position outside the religion and the period, we can readily point out that many of them beg a rather large question: If the laws of a religion conflict with the intuitions of ordinary morality, as they seem to do in some of the examples in (b), (c) and (d) at least, could that not be taken as evidence that these laws are not from a divine source? In face of this question, several positions can be taken. The dominant attitude of medieval Christendom was to seize upon the weaknesses of Islamic law eagerly as proofs of the falsity of the Muslim claim to a genuine revelation. Fortunately, the ferocious hostility of that era against Islam has almost disappeared, but it remains legitimate to raise the moral and religious questions involved in the international debate on world religions which is and must be increasingly a part of the intellectual life of our times. For convinced Muslims, however, the possible attitudes are more limited. In the medieval world of Islam, the revelation given to Muḥammad was beyond question. It was a fixed starting point of argument, and the only flexibility on this side came from the various possibilities of interpreting the revealed obligations. And in disputes on this issue, traditionalists like Ibn Ḥazm and Ghazālī, who had only to follow scripture closely, were in a far stronger position than the Muʿtazila, who had to reconcile scripture with a rational system based on other considerations. Modern Muslim liberals, however, have been resuming essentially the same task as the Muʿtazila in a more favorable intellectual environment, and it is doubtful that they will meet today any opponent within Islam combining the education and confidence of an Ibn Ḥazm, and willing and able to use the literal interpretation of scripture to put an end to all opposing moral argument.

There is, however, another strand in Ibn Ḥazm's method of argument, more like an undercurrent, which is powerful but not fully brought to the surface. This is illustrated by our example (f) on lying. Although he refutes the Muʿtazilite generalization "Lying is always evil" by flat assertions based on the Law of Islam, which is his "official" method, the rational ethical reasons for the Law's commands become apparent in this case. For the generalization is too sweeping to be accepted by most ethical theories, and needs refinement. ʿAbd al-Jabbār (d. 1025) in his fully developed Muʿtazilite ethics ran into difficulties with regard to lying, because he was unwilling to make concessions. On other questions he was able to be more flexible by applying the theory of prima facie obligations, which allowed for conflicting ethical considerations and differing final judgments to fit different cases.[11] Yet in the end the ethical intuitionism of the Muʿtazila did not carry conviction in most of medieval Islam, perhaps because its elaborate set of ethical intuitions had no unifying principle, such as modern utilitarianism has, and at the same time appeared dogmatic and arbitrary. To the medieval Muslim, the Qurʾān appealed as a surer basis for ethical judgments because of its divine authority; and no further unifying principle seemed necessary in the face of that outstanding source.

VII

We can turn next to consider a more technical use of independent judgment which Ibn Ḥazm rejects: the use of legal judgment known as *istiḥsān* or *ra'y*. *Istiḥsān* is literally "thinking good," and it was used as a judgment of equity where the *sharīʿa* gives no explicit guidance. This term was used more particularly by the Hanafite law school. *Ra'y* is "opinion"; it had been used in the same sense in earlier times, but had dropped out of currency by Ibn Ḥazm's day. He says that these words, as well as *istinbāṭ,* "discovery," have the same connotation: "judgment according to what the judge thinks more advantageous (*aṣlaḥ*) in its consequences and in itself" (*Iḥkām,* 6: 16). (This definition reminds us of the Malikite term *istiṣlaḥ,* "thinking in the public interest," which Ibn Ḥazm does not attack directly—perhaps out of prudence, since the school of Mālik was dominant in Andalusia).

He raises several objections to this practice in Islamic law, by whatever name it is called. Probably the most basic objection is that it does not even reach the level of rational judgment, but is nothing more than the result of following desires and fancies, without proofs (*Iḥkām,* 6: 17; *Mulakhkhaṣ,* 5, 50–51, 56). And since different judges have different natures and desires, *istiḥsān* leads to disagreements about the law, which is a deficiency in religion (*Iḥkām,* 6: 17; *Mulakhkhaṣ,* 5), Worse still, there is no way to resolve this kind of disagreement, for what difference is there in authority between what you approve and what someone else approves, or between what he approves and what you disapprove? What makes one such opinion closer to the truth than another? (*Iḥkām,* 6: 21)

The supporters of *istiḥsān* and *ra'y* claim in their support the Tradition, "Whatever the Muslims think good (*ra'āhu ḥasanan*) is good in the eyes of God." This Tradition, he retorts, does not have a sound *isnād.* And even if it did, it would only support *ijmā'*, for it does not refer to some of the Muslims rather than others. When they disagree, their opinions are on the same level of authority and contradictory, so, according to their view, we should be commanded to do contradictory acts (*Iḥkām,* 1: 18–19).

In short, Ibn Ḥazm condemns a view which looks to him like human subjectivism in ethics. "What is true is true even if people condemn it, and what is false is false even if people approve of it" (*Iḥkām,* 1: 17). But this judgment does not lead him back to the human objectivism of the rationalists, which we have seen him attacking just as strongly, but to the theory of revelation as the only valid source of value judgments. "He who gives a decision by *ra'y* does so without knowledge. There is no knowledge in religion except from the Qur'ān and the Traditions" (*Mulakhkhaṣ,* 56). I have often named this position "theistic subjectivism," because it makes values utlimately dependent on the will of God rather than on any facts in the natural order of the world. But it should be mentioned that from another point of view the position appears to a believer as objective: in the sense that, given revelation as the source of all ethical truth, he has before him something that he can know by a science (philology), namely the meaning of revelation. In other words, ethics is reduced to positive law, in which the proper object of study is texts. This is why Ibn Ḥazm can assign to reason an essential place in his ethical theory, while being antirationalist as against theories of ethical knowledge by natural reason independent of scripture.

VIII

A special problem of theodicy arises from Ibn Ḥazm's position that ethical decisions cannot be correctly made either by independent reason or any other form of independent judgment, but only by the guidance of revelation. What about people who have lived, live or will live beyond any knowledge of revelation? How are they able to make moral judgments, and how does God judge them? It will be seen that there are two questions here, but since they are closely interconnected it is possible to give a single account of Ibn Ḥazm's answers. These are somewhat complex, but not obscure.

It is fair to say that Ibn Ḥazm's first thought on any problem of this kind is that God can do what he wishes: thus He can leave men without any sound means of ethical judgment, and then He can punish them, without entitling us to call Him "unjust"—for who is man, to pass judgments on God? The only questions that arise, then, are what dispensations He has actually made, and the answers can be known only through scripture (*Iḥkām,* 1: 54).

The problem had been posed by the Muʿtazila with special reference to the state of mankind before the coming of Islam, since the people of antiquity were supposed to have been certainly beyond the reach of the true revelation. Ibn Ḥazm turns aside the force of this objection by asserting that men were never without a Law, on the basis of the Qur'ān's rhetorical question: "Does man think he would be left to wander at random?" (lxxv, 36). Adam was a prophet and received commands and prohibitions. Therefore the intelligence of mankind as a whole never had an occasion or a need to make judgments on what was disapproved or permitted before the existence of a Law (*Iḥkām,* 1: 58–59).

This particular form of the discussion, however, avoids the main issue; for there certainly have been, are and will be some people beyond the range of revelation through no fault of theirs, and Ibn Ḥazm admits this (*Iḥkām,* 1: 60). Such people's judgments of value are comparable to those of children: they simply lack the means to make anything prohibited or even permitted, for their intellects without revelation supply no valid guidance (*Iḥkām,* 1: 59). Therefore they will not be held responsible and punished for what is not in their power, as the Qur'ān proclaims (ii, 286; etc.). On the other hand, those who have heard revelation but ignored or forgotten it will certainly be held responsible (*Iḥkām,* 1: 60–65).

So far Ibn Ḥazm's answer seems "reasonable," in the sense of agreeing with common conceptions of justice. But it would not be in character for him to stop here. In at least two places he reminds us that God not only can but sometimes does make inexplicable decrees. He has favored the nations of Islam by sending them a prophet to summon them to the true religion, whereas Africans, Chinese and Europeans have heard only critics of Islam; thus He has given a better chance of paradise to some people than to others, without any difference in initial deserts. This is one of many examples that show the falsity of the Muʿtazilite claim that God's actions always accord with our notions of justice (*Fiṣal,* 3: 104). In the other passage he poses a borderline case and answers it in a way that seems shocking to a modern mind. He imagines a saintly man who seeks God and does everything good, but who lives in remote islands where he hears only distorted and malicious accounts of Muḥammad; and he dies doubting or denying his prophethood. "Then is not his course to the Fire, eternal, everlasting, endless? If anyone doubts this he is an unbeliever and a polytheist, by the *ijmāʿ* of the Community." Then he imagines a Jew or a Christian who has killed Muslims and committed every sin; after that he becomes a Muslim and dies as such. "Is he not among the people of paradise?" This too is a decision of *ijmāʿ*, to doubt which is unbelief. The intellect has no way to work out these incalculable and unexpected value judgments; the only way to know them is from scripture (*Iḥkām,* 1: 56). We may wish that Ibn Ḥazm had at least been more charitable to the saintly non-Muslim and counted him among those who had not had a chance to appreciate Islam; but he thought he had the backing of *ijmāʿ* for his judgment, and it is rather typical of his combativeness to use such an argument. (Besides, the Muʿtazila had not survived in Andalusia and made an all too easy target).

IX

(ii) If Ibn Ḥazm fiercely opposes Muʿtazilite and other uses of independent reason to make value judgments, he is no less strongly opposed to certain uses of reason by most of the law schools to make legal judgments, starting from texts of scripture. These "dependent" uses which he finds illegitimate are *qiyās,* "analogy" and *taʿlīl,* "giving reasons"; the latter is subordinate, in the sense that it supplies reasons for a *qiyās.* In this opposition he takes his stand with the Zahirites against all the other law schools. Since this is not a technical article on Islamic law, I shall only go over this question in its main lines, drawing upon *Iḥkām* and *Mulakhkhāṣ Ibṭāl Al-Qiyās.*

Qiyās is defined as "judgment on matters on which there is no text, on a level with (*bi-mithli*) those on which there is a text or *ijmāʿ*" (*Mulakhkhaṣ,* 5). Ibn Ḥazm has several objections to this practice, two of which are more fundamental than the rest, according to his way of thinking. The first is that there is no scriptural authority for *qiyās.* The Qur'ān does not prescribe it, and those Traditions which have been claimed to support it are historically unsound—he goes into the details in a few pages (*Mulakhkhaṣ,* 6–9). The second objection is that *qiyās* is not needed, because all of the Law is present in texts of scripture (*Iḥkām,* 1: 10; 8: 2–3; *Mulakhkhaṣ,* 5). This assertion may seem surprising, in view of the vast range of situations in human life that a Law claiming completeness needs to cover. However, there are several features in Ibn Ḥazm's theory of jurisprudence which make his position more tenable. (a) We can recall the distinction made in *Mudāwāt* (see V above) between the obligations of virtue and those of the *sharīʿa,* which limits greatly the range of situations that *sharīʿa* law has to cover. (b) He argues in detail for the

Zahirite position that all expressions in scripture must be interpreted in their most general sense (*ʿumūm*) without further inquiry, unless a proof can be presented requring us to restrict the meaning (*khuṣūṣ*) in a particular passage (*Iḥkām,* 3: 97–160).[12] Obviously, this principle allows the texts to cover the maximum range of cases. (c) The Traditions tell us that whatever scripture is silent about is neither a duty nor forbidden, and the Qur'ān says that everything on earth was made for man: so everything is permitted except what is expressly commanded or forbidden. The partisans of *qiyās,* Ibn Ḥazm alleges, maintain that any act that scripture is silent about is not permitted, unless it is analogous to another act that is expressly permitted; but this ruling is at variance with the Traditions (*Mulakhkhaṣ,* 44–45). *We* might also point out that it needlessly restricts human freedom; but it is against Ibn Ḥazm's principles to make this value judgment out of his own head; for him, it must come from the Prophet if it is to carry any weight, and it comes in his saying *Dharūnī mā taraktukum,* "Let me off [passing judgment] on what I have left for you [to do freely]" (*Mulakhkhaṣ,* 44).

After working out these two fundamental objections to *qiyās,* that it is unauthorized and unnecessary, Ibn Ḥazm might have been satisfied. But he was not one to give up before scoring all possible debating points. So he has to show that, even if *qiyās* were authorized and useful, the kinds of justification that have been given for particular cases are weak. He says they are two.

(a) Mere resemblance between a case mentioned in a text and the case under consideration. The trouble with this is that everything resembles everything else in some respect, so there would be no limits to what anyone could claim, and ethical judgments based on religious texts would become worthless (*Mulakhkhaṣ,* 5, 40).

(b) *Taʿlīl,* transfer of the divine reason for the decision in the textual case to another case where the application of the same reason seems fitting. (The stock example: Wine is prohibited in scripture, because it is intoxicating—the *ʿilla* or "reason." Beer is not mentioned in scripture but is also intoxicating so the same *ʿilla* applies to it; therefore beer too must be prohibited, by the argument of *qiyās*).

Among the several objections of Ibn Ḥazm to *taʿlīl,* it will be convenient to begin by dismissing one which is based on a quibble about definitions of terms. In *Iḥkām* (8: 99–101), he defines a few related terms, and he takes *ʿilla* to mean "any quality that necessitates a thing by an immediate necessity, where the cause (*ʿilla*) is not separated at all from the effect (*maʿlūl*), as fire is the cause of burning, or snow is the cause of chilling, where one of the two does not occur without the second at all, and one is neither before nor after the other at all" (99). Taking *ʿilla* in this sense of "efficient cause," Ibn Ḥazm then objects that if God had such causes for His Laws, He would be compelled to make them, which is inadmissible (102). Also, to avoid an infinite chain of such causes, God Himself must initially have taken decisions without any causes (98). Further, intoxication cannot be the *ʿilla* for the prohibition of wine, for in that case it would have caused its prohibition always, as fire causes heat (106). Now, if Ibn Ḥazm chose to restrict *ʿilla* to the meaning "efficient cause"—which is in fact one common use in *kalām*—he was perfectly able to understand that the Sunnite jurists—Shafiʿites and others, not Muʿtazilites—used it as "reason" in the purposive sense. Or he could have discussed the question in terms of *gharaḍ,* which he himself defines as that which an agent aims at by his act, and which follows after that act necessarily (100). So, in the case of alcoholic drinks, to say that the *gharaḍ* of the prohibition is avoidance of intoxication amounts to the same as saying that intoxication is the legal *ʿilla* for the prohibition of these drinks.

But in other passages Ibn Ḥazm forgets his special definition of *ʿilla* and criticizes *taʿlil* in the ordinary legal sense on the grounds that really matter to him. The basic criticism is that there is no textual proof that there is an *ʿilla* for any of God's judgments (*Mulakhkhaṣ,* 5; *Iḥkām,* 8; 102). In other places he softens his stand a little by saying that in particular cases the Qur'ān may specify a *sabab* or "cause" for a decision, e.g., theft is the *sabab* for cutting off the thief's hand. But such causes apply only to the case mentioned (*Iḥkām,* 8: 77; 102). No pattern of *taʿlīl* can be found in the divine commands (*Mulakhkhaṣ,* 47–49). The practice of *taʿlīl* is a human operation which has led to arbitrary judgments, by which lawyers have abandoned the decision of the Qur'ān and turned what was approved into something disapproved (*Mulakhkhaṣ,* 10). He gives examples of inconsistency and arbitrariness in claims of *ʿilla* (*Iḥkām,* 8: 114).

Thus all *qiyās* is arbitrary (*Iḥkām,* 8: 42 ff.). The Laws are either found in texts or they do not exist; there is no place for analogies (*Iḥkām,* 8: 2–3). The Qur'ān says: "today I have perfected for you your religion and completed for you my blessing" (v. 3). If the protagonists of *qiyās* assert that they are drawing out the particular laws (*furūʿ*) from the principles (*uṣūl*) given by scripture, Ibn Ḥazm denies that there is any such distinction; all the Laws are *uṣūl,* such as those prescribing prayer, pilgrimage, etc. (*Iḥkām,* 8: 3). Here, presumably, he means by *uṣūl* "sources" rather than "principles," for in his theory we cannot group together the Laws of God under "principles": that would only be another instance of human meddling, whereas each Law is valid in its own separate right because it is prescribed by God and for no other reason. Finally, *qiyās* has proved harmful because by its arbitrary nature it has led to many disagreements among lawyers (*Iḥkām,* 8: 48–76).

Now that everything has been said against various uses of dependent reason, we may ask whether any kind is left as legitimate. The answer is: interpretation of scripture, in accordance with the laws of logic and the evidence of philology and the senses. The rules for interpretation are set by the Zahirite method, which is itself based on both scripture and reason.

X

It can never be a simple matter to classify such an individualist as Ibn Ḥazm among the schools of thought in medieval Islam. But a few conclusions emerge from the preceding account about his place in the history of Islamic ethics. It will have become clear that the center of his concern was to uphold the autonomy of God as the sole source of value judgments, against the rationalist objectivism of the Muʿtazila. Reason cannot independently decide questions of right and wrong: this is his primary message. But reason is competent and necessary wherever description or explanation of facts is called for, and must be used actively in the service of obedience to revelation, the sole path to salvation. All this he holds in common with the main stream of Sunnite law and *kalām* that was opposed to Muʿtazilism. He is the most eminent forerunner of Ghazālī in his discriminating appreciation of human reason as a tool to be used actively within the framework of Islam as conceived in this main Sunnite tradition, although he differs from Ghazālī in many other respects.

In the religious milieu of his time, his Zahirism appeared as a sharp divergence from the methods of the other schools of law and theology. But within the total frame of his ethical system it looks to us more like a minor deviation from the main stream.

Notes

1. On the earlier life of Ibn Ḥazm see especially the introduction of E. García Gómez to *El Collar de la paloma* (Madrid, 1952); also the introductions of Asín and Tomiche to their works cited in nn. 2 and 3.

2. Ignaz Goldziher, *Die Zâhiriten, ihr Lehrsystem und ihre Geschichte* (Leipzig, 1884), pp. 116–69. Miguel Asín Palácios, *Abenházam de Córdoba y su historia crítica de las ideas religiosas,* 5 vols. (Madrid: Revista de Archivos, 1927–32), vol. 1. Miguel Cruz Hernández, *Historia de la filosofía española: Filosofía hispano-musulmana,* 2 vols. (Madrid, 1957), vol. 1, chaps. 5–6. R. Arnaldez, *Grammaire et théologie chez Ibn Ḥazm* (Paris, 1956); idem, s.v. "Ibn Ḥazm", in *The Encyclopaedia of Islam,* new ed. (Leiden and London, 1960–), vol. 3.

3. Works of Ibn Ḥazm referred to, in approximate chronological order, and editions used:

   Ṭawq al-ḥamāma, ed. and tr. by Léon Bercher as *Le Collier du pigeon: ou de l'amour et des amants* (Algiers: Carbonel, 1949). *Kitāb al Fiṣal fi-l-milal wa l-ahwā' wa n-niḥal,* with Shahrastānī, *Kitāb al-Milal wa n-nihal* in margin, 5 vols. (Cairo, 1899–1903); re-edition, 5 vols. in 2 (Baghdad, 1960?); the Spanish translation of Asín in *Abenházam,* vols. 2–5, is almost complete and gives page references to the Cairo edition. *Kitāb al-Iḥkām fī uṣūl al-aḥkām*, ed. A. M. Shakir, 8 vols. (Cairo, 1925). *Mulakhkhaṣ Ibṭāl al-qiyās wa r-ra'y wa l-istiḥsān wa t-taqlīd wa t-ta'līl*, ed. by S. al-Afghani (Damascus, 1960); used in preference to the extracts from the complete *Ibṭāl* in Goldziher, *Zâhiriten,* pp. 207–22, because the *Mulakhkhaṣ* covers the main ideas more widely than the extracts, and omits little of importance. *Kitāb al-Maḥallā,* 11 vols. (Cairo, 1929–34). *Mudāwāt an-nufūs,* ed. and tr. by N. Tomiche as *Épître morale (Kitāb al-Aḥlāq wa-l-siyar)* (Beirut, 1961); the Arabic title is a matter of opinion.

4. Arnaldez, *Grammaire et théologie,* and "Ibn Ḥazm," *Iḥkām,* 1: 29–35.

5. George F. Hourani, *Islamic rationalism: the ethics of 'Abd al-Jabbār* (Oxford, 1971), p. 39.

6. "Partly," because revelation alone gives knowledge of the after-life and its specific sanctions.

7. *Grammaire et théologie.*

8. Cruz, *Filosofía hispano-musulmana,* 1: 282, is mistaken in including wisdom among the four cardinal virtues listed by Ibn Ḥazm, and in saying that the Greek *sōphrosunē* is specified by him as "generosity." The two latter are listed separately, as *'iffa* and *jūd* respectively, and wisdom is not mentioned in §§ 89–92.

9. *Fiṣal,* 4: 87–111 and 163–71, goes over the classical questions on the caliphate (rights of succession, etc.), but with little originality and few remarks about the purpose of the institution in serving the *umma.*

10. Cf. *Iḥkām,* 1: 10 and *Mulakhkhaṣ,* 5: the whole of religion is drawn from revelation.

11. Hourani, *Islamic rationalism,* pp. 32–34, 76–81.

12. See Goldziher, *Zâhiriten,* pp. 120–23; Arnaldez, *Grammaire et théologie,* p. 131.

Avicenna's Proof of the Existence of God as a Necessarily Existent Being*

HERBERT A. DAVIDSON
University of California, Los Angeles

1. The cosmological proof of the existence of God may be characterized as a proof that begins by recognizing the actual existence of something in the universe; then it employs the principle of causality to establish that that thing and the universe as a whole have a cause. The a priori or ontological proof, in contrast, operates in the realm of thought without assuming the actual existence of anything. It begins with a concept of the nature of God,[1] such as "that than which nothing greater can be conceived";[2] the "best";[3] the "absolutely simple";[4] "most perfect being";[5] "immeasurably powerful being";[6] "infinite being";[7] or "substance" par excellence.[8] Then, as the proof is generally understood,[9] merely by analysing the concept, it undertakes to demonstrate that such a being must exist. It does their either directly, by showing that actual existence can be logically deduced from the concept;[10] or indirectly, by showing that a self-contradiction would result from assuming that the being in question does not exist.[11]

The term *necessary being* echoes through much of the history of the ontological proof.[12] This term is not defined by every writer using it, but it seems, in ontological proofs, to have been used in one of two senses:[13] (a) *Necessary being* may be understood in the sense of a being whose existence is established as a necessary truth, in the way that necessary truth is defined by Leibniz. According to Leibniz: "When a truth is necessary, its reason can be found by analysis, resolving it into more simple ideas and truths until we come to those that are primary . . . Truths of reasoning are necessary and their opposite is impossible."[14] (b) A necessary being may also be understood as that which exists "through

* The first part of this article profited considerably from discussions I had with my colleague Amos Funkenstein.

itself"[15] or "through its essence,"[16] as that "which has in its essence the sufficient reason of its existence."[17]

There have been instances of ontological proofs employing the term *necessary being* in one sense or the other, as well as instances employing the term without specifying which sense is intended or whether both are. In fact, however, whether a given argument does happen to use the term *necessary being* in one sense or the other, every ontological proof should, it would seem, make both points. That is to say, every ontological proof[18] attempts to show that the existence of God follows by logical necessity from an analysis of the concept of God's nature; such simply is what we mean by an ontological proof. And, it would further seem, an ontological proof can infer the existence of God from a concept of His nature only if the essence of God, as reflected in the concept, should somehow contain the "sufficient reason" of His existence. Thus the ontological proof assumes that the existence of God can (a) be proved by a priori, logical necessity; and by virtue of this assumption it further assumes that (b) God exists *through His essence,* that He has in His essence a *sufficient reason of His existence.*

Ontological proofs formulated with the aid of the term necessary being or necessary existence are known from the time of Descartes,[19] and that term can appear in different stages of given argument. Descartes, in the course of elucidating his ontological proof, introduces *necessary existence* as a middle term, to justify passing from the concept of God as a perfect being to the actual existence of God: "Because actual existence is *necessarily* and at all times linked to God's other attributes, it follows certainly that God exists."[20] In a number of philosophers, the thesis that God is necessarily existent is the conclusion of an ontological proof. Thus Spinoza,[21] More,[22] Leibniz,[23] perhaps Christian Wolff,[24] Baumgarten,[25] and Moses Mendelssohn[26] offer ontological proofs establishing the existence of a "necessary being," a "necessarily existent being," or a being that "necessarily exists." There also are at least two instances of proofs that start with necessary existence. That is to say, rather than beginning with a concept such as *perfect being* or *infinite being* or the like, they begin with the concept of *necessary being,* and then, by analyzing the concept, they establish that such a being does in fact exist. One of several formulations of the ontological argument in Leibniz consists in the following bare syllogism: "necessary being exists," which, Leibniz explains, is equivalent to saying that "being to whose essence existence belongs, exists; or being *per se* exists." This "is evident from the terms." "But God is such a being. . . . Therefore God exists,"[27] Mendelssohn reasoned, also as one of several formulations: "It is clear that necessary being . . . must possess all perfections in the highest degree. . . . The concept of the necessary must accordingly also include within itself the perfection of existence. Therefore the necessary must also actually exist."[28]

In addition to its role in the ontological proof, which must undertake to establish the existence of God as a necessary being in both senses of the term distinguished earlier, necessary being also plays a role in the cosmological proof. Now whatever sense the term *necessary being* may have in a given cosmological argument, the first of the two senses distinguished earlier would presumably be excluded. A cosmological proof could hardly establish the existence of a necessary being in the sense of a being whose existence is established merely by analyzing concepts: for the characteristic of this proof is precisely that it does not restrict itself to the mere analysis of concepts. On the other hand, every cosmological proof, whether or not it happens to use the term *necessary being*, must explicitly or virtually establish that God exists as a necessary being in the second sense. For the cosmological proof undertakes to establish the existence of God as an uncaused cause, consequently as a being that exists through itself, a being that has a sufficient reason of its existence in itself. Thus the cosmological proof—whether or not a given instance of the argument happens to use the term *necessary being*—cannot establish the existence of God in the first sense of necessary being affirmed by the ontological proof; and it must undertake to establish the existence of God in the second sense.

Leibniz gave perhaps the best known instance of a cosmological argument using the term *necessary being*. By the side of his ontological argument, Leibniz offered another wherein he begins by considering the actual existence of objects in the external world. Then, employing the principle of sufficient reason, a form of the principle of causality,[29] Leibniz establishes that "contingent things . . . can have their final or sufficient reason only in the necessary being," that is to say, in a being "which has the reason of its existence in itself"[30]—the second sense of necessary being. Wolff, Baumgarten, and Mendelssohn all repeat, with minor variations, Leibniz's cosmological proof, concluding in the existence of a necessary being.[31] Thus Leibniz, perhaps Wolff, Baumgarten, and Mendelssohn give parallel proofs, one ontological and the other cosmological, of the existence of a necessary being. The contention of these philosophers is that the ontological and cosmological proofs lead independently to the same result,[32] the existence of a necessary being in some such sense as that which exists "through its essence."

The two proofs were not, however, always kept distinct. At least one philosopher, Samuel Clarke, intentionally or inadvertently combined the two into a single overall demonstration. Clarke presents a cosmological argument in the spirit of Leibniz, contending that the changeable and dependent beings in the universe must have their "ground or reason of existence" in an eternal being which is "self-existent, that is, necessarily existing." But the only meaning of "self-existent" recognized by Clarke is that whose "necessity . . . must be antecedent in the natural order of our ideas to our supposition of its being"; whose necessary existence "must *antecedently* force itself upon us whether we will or no, even when we are endeavoring to suppose that no such being exists"; "the supposition of whose non-existence is an express contradiction."[33] That is to say, the cosmological argument, which begins with the actual existence of things in the external world, establishes a being which is *necessarily existent* in the sense that its existence can be discovered merely by examining its concept "antecedently" and without considering the existence of anything in the external world, a being such that assuming it not to exist gives rise to a self-contradiction. This, however, is the sense of necessary being that can be established only through an ontological argument. Thus Clarke has intentionally combined or inadvertently confused two arguments, following the reasoning of the cosmological, but giving the conclusion of the ontological.[34]

Clarke is of particular interest because he inspired Section IX of Hume's *Dialogues Concerning Natural Religion.* In Section IX of the dialogue, Hume allows the conservative participant to have his say. This participant maintains that the most effective way of establishing the existence of God is the "simple and sublime argument *a priori.*" The argument, it turns out, has three steps, the first two of which correspond to the cosmological part of Clarke's demonstration. The third step then concludes that in order to explain the existence of the world "we must . . . have recourse to a necessarily existent being who carries the reason of his existence in himself; and who cannot be supposed not to exist without an express contradiction." That is to say, we must have recourse to a first "necessary" cause—a proper conclusion of the cosmological argument—whose concept is such that a self-contradiction results from assuming it not to exist—the conclusion of an ontological argument. if there should be any doubt, Hume's critique reveals that two arguments are in fact present here. The critique begins by showing that the existence of nothing at all can be established a priori, merely by examining its concept; that is a criticism appropriately directed against the ontological method. But then Hume goes on to argue that perhaps the universe as a whole has no cause, a criticism appropriate for refuting a cosmological argument.[35]

Whereas Hume's critique blurs the distinction between the cosmological and ontological proofs of a necessarily existent being, Kant's critique, as is well known, clearly distinguishes the two, and then proceeds to establish an intrinsic connection between them. The cosmological proof, Kant argued, ultimately reduces itself to the ontological. Kant gives a concise statement of a cosmological argument establishing the existence of an "absolutely necessary being," and then contends: "What properties this being must have, the empirical premise cannot tell us." Consequently, human reason is led to "abandon experience altogether and endeavors to discover from mere concepts what properties an absolutely necessary being must have." The only means human reason can discover for pouring content into *absolutely necessary being* is to identify this being with *ens realissimum,* being possessing the fullness of perfection. But in order to show that *ens realissimum* is identical with the *necessary being* established by the cosmological argument, human reason must first analyze the concept of *ens realissimum* and derive *necessary existence* from it. Since *ens realissimum* is a necessarily existent being and in fact the only one, so human reason proceeds, it must be identical with the necessarily existent being established by the cosmological argument. Thus the absolutely *necessary being* whose existence is established through the cosmological argument acquires meaning only on the assumption that *necessary existence* can also be analyzed out of the concept of *ens realissimum*—which, according to Kant, amounts to the assumption that the concept of *ens realissimum* can serve as the basis for an ontological argument. Hence Kant concludes that the cosmological argument inevitably reduces itself to an ontological argument.[36]

The foregoing survey shows that an ontological argument, whether it explicitly says so or not, must establish the existence of God as a necessary being in two senses: as a being whose existence can be established by a prior, logical necessity; and as a being that exists *through itself,* whose essence contains sufficient reason for its existence. Individual instances of the ontological proof have used the term *necessary being* at different stages of their argument. A cosmological argument, whether explicitly or not, should establish the existence of God in the second of the two senses of necessary being. And individual instances of the cosmological proof, it was seen, did undertake to prove the existence of God as a necessary being in this sense. In at least one instance, Clarke, a cosmological and an ontological argument were combined or confused: from a cosmological argument, Clarke concludes the existence of a necessary being in the sense that can be established only by the ontological proof. Of the two best known critiques of the cosmological argument, Hume's deals with the combined or confused version, and Kant's contends that the cosmological argument for a necessary being must inevitably reduce itself to an ontological argument.

The first philosopher known to use the concept of *necessary existence* in order to construct a proof of the existence of God was Avicenna. Avicenna's proof, it will appear, neither is, nor inevitably reduces itself to, an ontological proof. It is rather a certain kind of cosmological proof.

2. The concept of necessary existence is used by Avicenna to prove the existence of God in two works, at length in the *Najāt,*[37] briefly and

somewhat obscurely in the *Ishārāt.*[38] The concept is also discussed fully in two other works, the *Shifā'*[39] and *Danesh Nameh,*[40] but there Avicenna employs it only to define the nature of God, not, as far as I can see, to establish His existence.[41]

Avicenna gave thought to the method of his proof. The proof, he explains, consists in "examining nothing but existence itself"; by "considering . . . the nature (*ḥāl*) of existence," the proof has "existence *qua* existence testify to the first [cause]."[42] This method pursued by Avicenna is contrasted by him with another whereby the existence of God is established not from a consideration of existence in general, but rather from a consideration of one segment of existence: God's "creation and effect." Although the latter method, which takes its departure from "creation and effect," is also recognized by Avicenna as legitimate, his own method, he claims, is "more certain and more exalted."[43]

The difference between the two is stated here in language that is deliberately allusive, but easily deciphered. Metaphysics was defined in the Aristotelian tradition as the science that "examines the existent *qua* existent and what belongs to it by virtue of itself."[44] Accordingly, when Avicenna claims to have constructed a proof exclusively by examining "existence itself" and by considering "existence *qua* existence," he means that he has constructed a proof using philosophic principles drawn only from the science of metaphysics. This he contrasts with the proof that begins with God's "creation and effect" and reasons back from them to the existence of God as a first cause. Avicenna cannot mean that his proof uses absolutely no data drawn from God's "creation and effect." For, as we shall see, his proof does require at least one datum from the external world;[45] and the parts of the world accessible to man are himself and physical nature, both of which belong to God's "creation and effect." Avicenna does mean that his proof considers no peculiar properties of God's creation, that is, no properties of physical nature, but instead considers the attributes belonging to physical nature or anything else solely insofar as it is existent. He is thus claiming to have constructed a metaphysical proof which is superior to proofs that do use principles drawn from physical science, such as—to take the most notable example—Aristotle's proof from motion does. Averroes was later to attack Avicenna for this presumption. At every possible opportunity, Averroes undertook to refute the claim that the existence of God can be established by nothing more than metaphysical principles; and in opposition he defended the position, represented as truly Aristotelian, that the proof of the existence of God is at least in part a subject for the science of physics.[46]

It is easy to point out advantages Avicenna could have perceived in the metaphysical proof, rendering it "more certain and more exalted" than the physical proof. Aristotle's proof from motion rested on a set of physical principles: motion in place underlies all other kinds of change;[47] everything moved has the cause of its motion outside itself;[48] nothing can maintain itself in motion unless it is continuously moved by an agent;[49] only circular motion is continuous;[50] only an infinite force can maintain the heavens in motion for an infinite time.[51] Using all these physical principles, Aristotle undertook to establish the existence of an unmoved incorporeal cause solely of the *motion* of the universe.[52] Avicenna, although not rejecting Aristotle's physical principles, dispenses with them in his metaphysical proof. And yet, without them, he is confident that he can prove the existence of a cause not merely for the motion, but for the very existence of the universe. The metaphysical proof requires fewer premises and is thus "more certain." And it is "more exalted," for it establishes a cause of the very existence of the universe. With less fuel it travels, or attempts to travel, further.

Avicenna found two passages in Aristotle especially suggestive. One of them appears in Aristotle's *Metaphysics,* Book XII. There Aristotle gives a version of his proof from motion, then adds a postscript: Since the prime mover "can in no way be otherwise than as it is," it "is an existent . . . of necessity."[53] Avicenna's proof, particularly the fuller version in the *Najāt,* can be understood as starting just where Aristotle left off. Avicenna sets aside all the physical arguments leading up to Aristotle's prime mover, which is an "existent . . . of necessity." He begins afresh by analyzing the concept "existent . . . of necessity" or, as he calls it, *necessarily existent,* working out everything contained in the concept. Then he undertakes to establish that something corresponding to the concept actually exists. He does this, however, without using the principles of physical motion employed by Aristotle, and also without relying exclusively on his analysis of the concept, as an ontological proof would.

The second Aristotelian passage underlying Avicenna's proof appears in another part of the *Metaphysics,* in Book V. *Metaphysics* V is a philosophic glossary that strikes a modern scholar as "evidently out of place" in the totality of the *Metaphysics.*[54] Avicenna, however, read Aristotle differently. The subject matter of metaphysics was after all understood to be the existent *qua* existent and its attributes,[55] and *Metaphysics* V consists precisely in an analysis of *existence* and of attributes of existence such as *unity, plurality, necessity, potentiality, actuality,* and the like. Book V can therefore be understood as a philosophic analysis of the subject matter lying at the heart of metaphysics. Avicenna must have read it that way, for he used Book V of Aristotle's *Metaphysics* as a cadre for a good half of his own *Metaphysics,* the subject of the remainder of his *Metaphysics* being the existence of God, His attributes, and the incorporeal realm.

Among the terms analyzed by Aristotle in the section in question is *necessary; necessary,* he explains, has three senses, of which the most fundamental is "what cannot be otherwise."[56] Then, Aristotle observes: "For certain things, something else is a cause of their being necessary, but for some nothing is [a cause of their being necessary]; rather it is through them that others exist of necessity."[57] That is to say, there is a class of things that are necessary without having a cause of their being necessary; and a second class of things that are necessary through a cause, this cause to be found in the former class. The Aristotelian distinction was to be mirrored in the painstaking distinction Avicenna drew between the necessarily existent by reason of itself and the necessarily existent by reason of another.

Avicenna for his part begins his analysis of metaphysical concepts by showing that primary concepts cannot truly be defined. Definitions in Aristotelian logic are framed by taking a wider and already known concept, the *genus,* and setting apart a segment of it through a *specific difference.* Accordingly, Avicenna writes, primary concepts such as *existent,* and *thing,* which are not "subsumed under anything better known," cannot be defined; they are rather "imprinted in the soul in a primary fashion."[58] And among the concepts that cannot be "made known . . . in a true sense" are *necessary, possible,* and *impossible.*[59]

Because *necessary, possible,* and *impossible* are not definable, ostensible definitions of them lead to a vicious circle. Avicenna considers two ostensible definitions of necessary: "That which can (*yumkin*) not be assumed [to be] absent (maʿdūm)";[60] "that which is such that an impossibility would result if it should be assumed to be other than it is."[61] The first of the two definitions employs the term *possible (mumkin)*—"can (*yumkin*'))—and the second uses *impossible.* But, Avicenna observes, when we consider ostensible definitions of *possible* we find that they in their turn employ either *necessary* or *impossible;* possible is defined as "that which is not necessary" or as "that which is absent (*maʿdūm*), but is such that its existence is not *impossible* if it should be assumed to occur at any time in the future."[62] Ostensible definitions of *impossible,* finally, include either *necessary* or *possible.* Thus attempts to define the triad chase one another in a circle.[63] Yet, although primary concepts are not explicable by anything wider and better known and are thus inaccessible to true definition, there is, according to Avicenna, a way of explaining them to the man who for some reason does not have them imprinted in his soul. We may "direct attention" to the primary notions and "call them to mind" through a "term or an indication."[64] On this basis, Avicenna ventures an explanation of *necessary:* "It signifies certainty of existence."[65]

When Avicenna turns from *necessary* and *possible* to "necessarily existent being" and "possibly existent being,"[66] he offers the following explications: A necessarily existent being is a being that "perforce exists"; alternatively, it is "such that when it is assumed not to exist, an impossibility results." A "possibly existent being" is a being that "contains no necessity . . . for either its existence or nonexistence (*ʿadam*)"; alternatively it is "such that whether assumed not to exist or to exist, no impossibility results."[67] These obviously are not definitions by Avicenna's standard, since they do not explain the concepts by anything wider and better known. They are in fact merely adaptations of the blatantly circular definitions of *possible* and *necessary* that Avicenna has just been seen to criticize.

The distinction between possibly existent being and necessarily existent being is supplemented by the distinction, originating in Aristotle's *Metaphysics* V, between two ways in which a thing can be necessary.[68] Reflecting Aristotle's distinction, Avicenna writes that we can conceive of a being as necessarily existent either by reason of itself or by reason of something else. The former would be something "such that because of itself and not because of anything else whatsoever, an impossibility follows from assuming its nonexistence." The latter would be a being "such that should something other than itself be assumed [to exist], then it becomes necessarily existent." The illustrations Avicenna adduces for the latter category are "combustion," which is "necessarily existent . . . when contact is assumed to take place between fire and inflammable material," and "four," which is "necessarily existent . . . when we assume two plus two."[69] If some thing is necessarily existent only by reason of something else, it must—since it will not exist by virtue of itself without that other thing—be possibly existent by reason of itself.[70] Thus Avicenna distinguishes three categories: (a) the necessarily existent by reason of itself; (b) the necessarily existent by reason of another, but possibly existent by reason of itself; and (c) the possibly existent by reason of itself, which is not rendered necessarily existent by reason of another.

What Avicenna calls *necessarily existent by reason of itself* is the same as *necessary being* in the sense of that which exists "through itself" and "has in its essence the sufficient reason of its existence."[71] What Avicenna calls *necessarily existent by reason of another* is the same as the category of things having, in the terminology of Leibniz, "physical or hypothetical necessity";[72] "physical or hypothetical necessity" consists in "things, happening in the world just as they do" because "the nature of the world is such as it is."[73] However, the necessity characterizing these two categories of necessarily existent being was already seen to be indefinable for Avicenna; it is a primary concept to be grasped by the human mind immediately.[74] As a mere "indication" of its meaning, Avicenna wrote that necessity "signifies certainty of existence."[75] The necessarily existent by reason of itself would accordingly be that which has certainty of existence by reason of itself; the necessarily existent by reason of another would be that which has certainty of existence by reason of another. And the impossibility involved in supposing such a being not to exist would consist in contradicting the certainty of its existence,[76] the fact that it does exist. If no more than this can be said about the meaning of *necessarily existent,* it is difficult to see just how necessary existence differs from actual existence; not surprisingly, Ghazālī was later to accuse Avicenna of vagueness in his use of the term.[77]

These remarks relate to the meaning of *necessity* and of *necessarily existent:* Avicenna rules out any definition of *necessarily existent* and we can only infer that its meaning amounts virtually to *actually existent.* When Avicenna subsequently comes to delimit the class of necessarily existent beings, that class turns out, in fact, to coincide exactly with the class of actually existent beings. For the two categories of necessarily existent being—that which is so by virtue of itself and that which is so by virtue of another—are, according to Avicenna, the only two conceivable categories of actual existence. To put this in another way, the possibly existent does not actually exist unless rendered necessary by something else; and conversely, everything actually existing, including whatever occurs in the physical world, such as combustion, is necessary in one sense or the other. To justify the point, Avicenna reasons that as long as something is merely possible, nothing is present to "prefer" its existence over its nonexistence. The possibly existent can enter the realm of actual existence only if a factor distinct from itself should "select out" its existence. But whenever that factor is present, the existence of the possibly existent being is rendered necessary.[78] The proper way of construing possible existence, according to Avicenna, is therefore to say that during the time the possible existent actually exists, its existence is necessary, and during the time it does not exist, its existence is impossible. but that necessity and that impossibility are both conditioned, due not to the thing itself, but only to the presence or absence of an external condtiion which necessitates its existence or nonexistence. Considered in itself, in isolation from the external conditions, the possibly existent at all times remains possible.[79]

Actual existent is thus either: (a) Necessarily existent by reason of itself; this is something "such that if assumed not to exist an impossibility results," with the proviso that it has that character "by reason of itself." Or (b) necessarily-existent by reason of another, but possibly existent by reason of itself; this is something, again, such that if assumed not to exist, an impossibility results, with the proviso that it has that character only inasmuch as "something else is assumed" to exist. In distinguishing these categories, it must be stressed, Avicenna is operating exclusively in the realm of concepts, without committing himself to the actual existence of anything:[80] He is saying that if something should be assumed to exist, then it has to be classified in one of the two categories of necessarily existent being.

3. Avicenna, it appears, rejects a true definition of (a) the necessarily existent by reason of itself, (b) the necessarily existent by reason of another but possibly existent by reason of itself, or (c) the possibly existent

by reason of itself which is not rendered necessarily existent by anything else. Still, he writes, the "properties" of these three can be set forth.[81] His proof of the existence of God consists in analyzing the concept of the *necessarily existent by reason of itself* and establishing its attributes; then analyzing the concept of the *possibly existent* and showing that if anything actually exists, something necessarily existent by reason of itself must also exist.

Avicenna's analysis of the *necessarily existent by reason of itself* was not original with him. Proclus had analyzed the concept of the "self-existent" (*qā'im bi-dhātihi*) and "self-sufficient (*mustaghnīyya bi-nafsihā*) first cause" and shown that it must be eternal, uncaused, and free of composition.[82] Alfarabi subsequently applied the same type of analysis to the concept of the "First," as he called the Deity, arriving at a wider set of attributes than did Proclus.[83] And the set of attributes deduced by Alfarabi from the concept of the "First" parallels the set Avicenna now derives from the concept of the *necessary by reason of itself.* Significantly, neither Proclus nor Alfarabi required the concept of *necessity* for their analysis. This supports the suggestion that the concept of *necessity* adds nothing to Avicenna's proof, and that his proof could have as well been based on an analysis of the *actually* existent by reason of itself instead of on an analysis of the *necessarily* existent by reason of itself.

Avicenna's analysis runs as follows: The necessarily existent by reason of itself clearly can "not have a cause." If it did have a "cause of its existence," its existence would be "by virtue of something" and therefore not solely by virtue of itself.[84] Aristotelian philosophy distinguished no less than four senses of cause, including causes internal to the effect as well as those working on the effect from without, yet Avicenna does not specify which sense he is using here.[85] However, the omission is apparently intentional, for Avicenna understands that the necessary by reason of itself is incompatible not only with an external cause—an agent upon which its existence depends—but also with internal causes—elements within itself making it what it is.

The denial of internal causes means that the necessarily existent by reason of itself can have no "principles which combine together and in which the necessarily existent consists." The full argument for this rests on a distinction between a given entity as a whole and the parts of which it is composed. Any composite entity, Avicenna contends, exists by virtue of its parts and not by virtue of itself as distinct from its parts. Accordingly, considered as a whole, it does not exist by virtue of what it is in itself but only by virtue of something else—by virtue of the components that constitute it. And it is therefore not necessarily existent by reason of itself. The implications of the thesis are far reaching. For if the necessarily existent by reason of itself can contain no parts whatsoever, it is simple in every conceivable way. It is incorporeal, inasmuch as it is not composed of matter and form. It is unextended and immaterial, inasmuch as it is free of quantitative parts. It is indefinable, inasmuch as it is not composed of genus and specific difference. And it is free of the distinction of essence and existence.[86] The argument for simplicity also gives an implied answer to a much repeated object later to be directed against the proof of the existenceof God as a necessary being. Perhaps, that objection runs, the physical world is itself the necessary being.[87] Avicenna would by implication reply that the physical world cannot be conceived as necessarily existent by reason of itself, since the physical world cannot be assigned the attributes deducible from the concept of the necessarily existent by reason of itself: The physical world is not simple, unextended, and incorporeal.[88]

There can, Avicenna further contends, be only one being necessarily existent by reason of itself. To prove this thesis, he argues basically[89] that assuming two such beings amounts to assuming two beings that are similar in one respect—their necessary existence—but different in another—the respect whereby they can be distinguished and called two. But that situation would be conceivable only if at least one of the two things should be composite, containing both the element in common with its counterpart and another element whereby it can be distinguished and by virtue of which two distinct beings can be enumerated. Thus at least one of the two would have to be composite, and consequently, as already seen, not necessarily existent by virtue of itself. It follows that not more than one being necessarily existent by reason of itself is conceivable.[90]

Avicenna derives other attributes from the concept of *necessarily existent by reason of itself.* It must be pure *intellect,* for such is the nature of beings free of matter. It must be *true,* for truth consists in the highest grade of existence, and the necessarily existent by reason of itself would have the highest grade of existence. It must be *good,* for evil consists in privation, whereas the necessary by reason of itself has fullness of being and therefore suffers no privation. It must constitute the highest *beauty,* be the highest *object of desire,* be possessed of the greatest *pleasure,* and so forth.[91] Avicenna's analysis of the concept of *necessarily existent by reason of itself* thus establishes that such a being must be uncaused, simple, incorporeal, one, pure intellect, true, good, beautiful, an object of desire, possessed of the greatest pleasure.

But is there anything in the external world corresponding to that concept? Does such a being actually exist? Its existence, Avicenna writes, is surely not self-evident.[92] Nor can its existence be established through a syllogistic "demonstration" (*burhān*). For a demonstrative syllogism must be constructed with propositions that are "prior to," and the "causes" of the conclusion,[93] whereas there is nothing prior to existence, and the cause of the presence of actual existence in the necessarily existent is accepted by reason of itself.[94] What cán be provided is an indirect "proof" (*dalīl*) of the existence of a being necessary by reason of itself,[95] and that is what Avicenna undertakes.

To accomplish his proof, Avicenna leaves the conceptual realm for a single empirical datum: "There is no doubt that something exists (*anna hunā wujūdan*)."[96] It makes no difference what it is that exists or what its peculiar properties might be; for the purpose of his proof Avicenna considers merely the "existent *qua* existent"[97] and therefore all he needs is the fact that something does indeed exist. Applying the proposition that there are only two conceivable categories of actual existing beings,[98] Avicenna proceeds: "Everything that exists is either necessary [by reason of itself] or possible [by reason of itself and necessary by reason of another]. On the first assumption, a necessarily existent [by reason of itself] has immediately been established, and that was the object of our demonstration. On the second assumption, we must show that the existence of the possible [by reason of itself but necessary by reason of another] ends at the necessarily existent [by reason of itself]."[99] If the first alternative were accepted, the proof would be complete; the being conceded to be necessarily existent by reason of itself would simply be assigned all the attributes already shown to belong to such a being. But the real issue is of course posed by the second alternative, the assumption that the random existent object with which the proof started is necessarily existent only by reason of another, and possibly existent by reason of itself. The heart of the proof therefore lies in showing that anything possibly existent by reason of itself must ultimately depend for its actual existence upon something necessary by reason of itself.

Professor Wolfson has pointed out that two philosophic principles underlie Avicenna's proof, as well as other cosmological proofs of the existence of God in the Aristotelian tradition: (a) the principle of causality, and (b) the impossibility of an infinite regress of causes.[100] Avicenna does not posit the two principles in their own right, but ingeniously derives them[101] from his analysis of *necessarily existent by reason of itself* and *possibly existent by reason of itself.*

In formulating his version of the principle of causality, Avicenna employs a distinction between the cause of the "generation" (*ḥudūth*) of an object and the cause of its "maintenance" (*thabāt*).[102] The cause of generation is more obvious since no one, Avicenna is certain, can doubt that whenever an object comes into existence, it does so by virtue of something else. But Avicenna's proof cannot pursue a first cause of the generation of every possibly existent being, both because Avicenna believed that some possible beings are eternal and not generated, and also because his proof requires causes that exist together with their effect,[103] whereas the cause of generation may perish after the effect comes into existence. Therefore Avicenna gives his attention to the *maintaining* cause.[104] If, he contends, we consider any object possible by reason of itself, irrespective of whether it is generated or eternal, we may legitimately ask what maintains it in existence. The factor maintaining the object in existence must be distinct from the object,[105] for in itself the latter is only possible and does not exist by virtue of itself. And that factor must exist as long as the object exists; for even when the object is actual, it never ceases to be possible by reason of itself and dependent on something else for its existence.[106] Thus the analysis of the concept *possibly existent by reason of itself*—or, to be more precise, merely asking what *possibly existent* means—establishes that if anything possibly existent should exist, it must at all times depend on a cause distinct from itself to maintain it in existence.[107]

The second proposition required by Avicenna is formulated by him as the impossibility that "causes go to infinity"—the impossibility of an infinite regress of causes. In fact, unlike other philosophers,[108] Avicenna does not argue that an infinite regress, specifically, is absurd. He rather argues for the more general principle that whether all actually existent possible beings are "finite or infinite," they must ultimately depend on a being necessarily existent by reason of itself; and from this more general principle he derives the impossibility of an infinite regress as a corollary.[109]

Avicenna's reasoning here too is conducted solely through an analysis of concepts, in the present instance both the *necessarily existent* and the *possibly existent*. He is considering a situation wherein Z, for example, depends for its existence upon Y, which exists simultaneously with it; Y then depends upon X, which also exists simultaneously; ad infinitum. To show that such a situation is inconceivable, he mentally collects into a single group all possible beings actually existing at a single moment. Then he reasons as follows: The totality of possibly existent beings, considered as a whole, must be either (a) necessarily existent by reason of itself or (b) possibly existent by reason of itself. The former alternative would involve the absurdity that the "necessarily existent [by virtue of itself] is composed of possibly existent beings." Avicenna does not give any reason why that thesis is absurd. He presumably means[110] that assuming the necessarily existent by reason of itself to be composed of possibly existent beings amounts to assuming that the necessarily existent is composite, whereas his earlier analysis showed that the necessary by reason of itself cannot be composite.[111]

If the totality of possibly existent beings cannot (a) constitute a group that is necessarily existent by reason of itself, there remains (b) the second alternative, according to which the totality of possibly existent beings, taken collectively, is possible by reason of itself. On this alternative, Avicenna proceeds, "whether the group is finite or infinite," it stands in need of a factor that will continually "provide [it] with existence." That factor must be either (b-1) within the group or (b-2) outside of it. Assuming (b-1) that one [or more] of the members maintains the whole group is equivalent to assuming that the member in question is a cause of itself. For to be a cause of the existence of a group is "primarily" to be the cause of the individual members, and since the supposed cause is itself one of the members, it would be a cause of itself. Yet the supposed cause has already been assumed to be possibly existent, and the possibly existent is precisely what does not exist by virtue of itself. Therefore it could not be the cause of the collection of which it is one member.

If the totality of possibly existent beings cannot form a group that is necessarily existent by reason of itself, and if, further, that totality cannot be maintained by one of its own members, the sole remaining alternative is that what does maintain the totality of possibly existent beings in existence is (b-2) outside the group. Since, by hypothesis, all possibly existent beings were included inside, anything left outside is not possibly existent; it must accordingly be necessarily existent by reason of itself. Avicenna was able to reach this result, it should be observed, through the device of considering all possibly existent beings as a single group and then asking what maintains the group in existence; and the cogency of his argument depends upon the legitimacy of that procedure. Once he has established that the series of all possibly existent beings does depend on a necessarily existent being, Avicenna infers, as a sort of corollary, that the series must be finite; for the possibly existent beings must "meet" their necessarily existent cause and "terminate" there. Thus an infinite regress of causes would be impossible—a regress, however, of only one type, that wherein all the causes exist together.[112]

Avicenna's complete proof now proceeds as follows:[113] Something clearly exists, and it must be either necessary by reason of itself, or necessary by reason of another and possible by reason of itself. On the former assumption the proof is immediately complete: There is a being necessarily existent by reason of itself, which is to be assigned all the attributes of such a being. On the other assumption, the possible by reason of itself must be maintained in existence by something else, which exists as long as it exists. That other factor, in turn, must be either necessary by reason of itself or possible by reason of itself. If it is assumed to be necessary by reason of itself, the proof is again at once complete. If, on the other hand, it is assumed to be possible by reason of itself, it too must depend on a further factor distinct from it and existing as long as it exists. Once again, Avicenna asks whether the new factor is necessary by reason of itself or possible by reason of itself. It is inconceivable, he has contended, that the series of all possible beings existing simultaneously, whether finite or infinite, should be maintained in existence by part of itself or by itself as a whole. The series must be maintained in existence by something outside, something which can only be necessarily existent by reason of itself.[114] The latter is to be assigned all the attributes shown to belong to the necessary by reason of itself, and it is the Deity in Avicenna's system.

4. Avicenna thus offers a proof of the existence of God that he characterizes as metaphysical since the proof considers the attributes of what exists solely insofar as it is existent and not insofar as it is a certain type of existent. The proof begins by distinguishing that which is *necessarily existent* from that which is *possibly existent,* and that which is necessarily existent *by reason of itself* from that which is necessarily existent *by reason of something else;* it analyzes those concepts; and it shows that the possibly existent can actually exist only if ultimately dependent on something necessarily existent by reason of itself. Necessarily existent, as far as I can see, means nothing more than actually existent for Avicenna,[115] and the proof could be executed unchanged using the distinction between what is *actually* existent by reason of itself, and what is *possibly* existent by reason of itself but actually existent by reason of something else.

Avicenna has not given an ontological proof, for although his proof depends on an analysis of the concept *necessarily existent by reason of itself,* the analysis alone is not intended to show that anything exists in the external world corresponding to the concept. In deriving various attributes from the concept of necessary existence, Avicenna in fact follows a procedure later to be sanctioned explicitly by Kant, not for necessary existence, but for the concept of *God.* The proposition "God is omnipotent," Kant granted, is a "necessary judgment," inasmuch as "omnipotence cannot be rejected if we posit a deity, that is, an infinite being; for the two concepts are identical."[116] Only the derivation of actual existence from a concept gives an ontological proof, subject to the several objections raised by critics of that proof. What Kant sanctions for the concept of *God* but rules out for the concept of *necessary being,* Avicenna does undertake with the concept *necessarily existent by reason of itself;* he derives a set of attributes from the concept, but does not pretend to derive actual existence from it.

Like other cosmological proofs of the Aristotelian type, Avicenna's proof employs the principles of causality and the impossibility of an infinite regress of causes. Avicenna's proof goes beyond Aristotle's, however, in establishing a first cause of the very existence of the universe rather than just a first cause of motion.[117] His proof, further, is original in basing even the philosophical principles needed for the argument exclusively upon an analysis of concepts. Merely by analyzing the concept *possibly existent by reason of itself,* Avicenna establishes that if such a being actually exists, it must have a cause. And merely by analyzing the concepts *possibly existent by reason of itself* and *necessarily existent by reason of itself,* Avicenna shows that actual existence cannot consist solely in a series of possibly existent beings. Since Avicenna derives the philosophic principles used in the proof from an analysis of those concepts, the only proper way of refuting the proof would be to go back and question the analysis. In other words, the critic would have to go back and question Avicenna's dichotomy of what exists by virtue of itself and what exists by virtue of something else; and, more importantly, he would have to question whether what exists by virtue of another can indeed at no time in its career be self-sufficient, and whether what exists by virtue of itself cannot be composed of internal factors. Criticisms along these lines were directed against the proof by Ghāzālī, Averroes, and Ḥasdai Crescas.[118]

Avicenna's proof was widely used, less as a whole than in parts or in adaptations. The methodological insistence that a proof of the existence of God is a subject for metaphysics, not physics, was, for example, taken up by the Latin writer Henry of Ghent, although the proof Henry gives is different from Avicenna's.[119] The analysis of necessary and possible being on which the proof rests was employed by *Kalām* writers[120] and there even appeared an adaptation of the proof as a proof of creation.[121] A watered down version of the proof is given in *ʿUyūn al-Masāʾil,* and related works;[122] these are works mistakenly attributed to Alfarabi but in fact dependent on Avicenna.[123] The proof was reformulated by Maimonides,[124] from whom it was copied by Thomas Aquinas.[125] Another reformulation was offered by Crescas.[126] Avicenna's analysis of necessary and possible existence enriched one of Spinoza's ontological arguments.[127] The proof is central for Leibniz and his followers, who—although the historical filiation is unclear—reveal striking similarities with Avicenna.[128] The two best known critiques of the cosmological proof are directed against versions of this proof as formulated by the followers of Leibniz.[129] Despite the critiques, the proof is accepted by such widely-read twentieth century writers as Mohammed Abduh[130] and F. Copleston.[131]

Notes

1. If the concept is treated as an actually existent object and its cause then sought, we would have a form of cosmological proof. Such is Descartes' argument in *Meditations,* III.

2. Anselm, *Proslogion,* chaps. 2–3.

3. Richard Fishacre, cited by P. Daniels, *Geschichte der Gottesbeweise* (Münster, 1909), p. 23; William of Auxerre, cited *ibid.,* p. 26.

4. Richard Fishacre, cited *ibid.,* p. 23.

5. R. Descartes, *Meditations,* V.

6. Descartes, *Reply to Objections,* I, transl. E. Haldane—G. Ross, *Philosophical Works of Descartes* (Cambridge, 1931), II, 21.

7. B. Spinoza, *Ethics,* I, prop. xi.

8. *Ibid.*

9. The "ontological" proofs of Anselm, Descartes, and Spinoza have been interpreted as not purely logical but as based on certain psychological assumptions concerning the source of the concept. Cf. J. Hick—A. McGill, *The Many-Faced Argument* (New York, 1967), pp. 33 ff. (on Anselm); M. Gueroult, *Nouvelles Reflexions sur la Preuve Ontologique de Descartes* (Paris, 1955); H. Wolfson, *Philosophy of Spinoza* (Cambridge, 1948), I, 165 ff.

10. E.g., Descartes as cited in n. 5.

11. E.g., Anselm as cited in n. 2.

12. Cf. D. Henrich, *Der Ontologische Gottesbeweis* (Tübingen, 1960).

13. Cf. Wolfson, *Spinoza,* I, 160; J. Hick, "God as Necessary Being," *Journal of Philosophy,* LVI (1960), 725-734.

14. G. Leibniz, *Monadology,* § 33.

15. Leibniz, *Philosophical Works,* transl. G. Duncan (New Haven, 1890), p. 50.

16. Wolfson, *Spinoza,* I, 180, and n. 5.

17. Chr. Wolff, *Philosophia Prima* (Frankfurt, 1736), § 309. Wolff bases this sense on the previous sense, cf. §§ 302, 308.

18. With the qualification made above in n. 9.

19. Cf. Henrich, *Der Ontologische Gottesbeweis.*

20. Descartes, *Philosophical Works,* transl. Haldane-Ross, II, 20. Cf. *ibid.,* p. 57; *Meditations,* V.

21. Spinoza, *Ethics,* I, xi.

22. H. More, *An Antidote against Atheism,* 2nd ed. (Cambridge, 1655), pp. 12-14.

23. Leibniz, *Monadology,* §§ 44-45.

24. Chr. Wolff, *Theologia Naturalis* (Frankfurt, 1739), II, §§ 20-21, and Henrich's interpretation, *Der Ontologische Gottesbeweis,* pp. 58-60. *Theologia Naturalis,* I, § 10, and II, §§ 20-21, scholia, seem to rule against Henrich's interpretation.

25. A. Baumgarten, *Metaphysica* (Halle, 1779), §§ 810, 823.

26. M. Mendelssohn, *Gesammelte Schriften* (Leipzig, 1843), II, 36, 39.

27. Leibniz, *Philosophical Works,* transl. Duncan, p. 50.

28. Mendelssohn, *Gesammelte Schriften,* II, 384.

29. Cf. below, n. 128.

30. Leibniz, *Monadology,* § 54.

31. Wolff, *Theologia Naturalis,* I, § 24; Baumgarten, *Metaphysica,* § 381; Mendelssohn, *Gesammelte Schriften,* II, 331-332.

32. Cf. Leibniz, *Monadology,* § 45; Baumgarten, *Metaphysica,* § 856.

33. S. Clarke, *A Demonstration of the Being and Attributes of God,* 6th ed. (London, 1725), pp. 14-17. Clarke weaves in another, truly ontological argument from the concepts of *infinity* and *eternity.*

34. There is a suggestion of this combination in Leibniz, *De rerum originatione radicali,* transl. R. Latta in *The Monadology* (Oxford, 1898), pp. 339, 342; Baumgarten, *Metaphysica,* § 381 taken together with §§ 102, 109.

35. D. Hume, *Dialogues Concerning Natural Religion,* Part IX.

36. I. Kant, *Critique of Pure Reason,* trans. N. Smith (London, 1956), pp. 508–511; N. Smith, *Commentary to Kant's Critique of Pure Reason* (London, 1923), p. 532.
The present passage in Kant should be compared to *Critique of Pure Reason,* trans. Smith, p. 418, thesis.

37. *Najāt* (Cairo, 1938), pp. 224 ff.

38. *K. al-Ishārāt wa-l-Tanbihāt,* ed. J. Forget (Leiden, 1892), pp. 140 ff.: French translation by A. Goichon (Beirut—Paris, 1951), with pages of Forget's edition indicated.

39. *Shifā': Ilāhiyyāt,* ed. G. Anawati—S. Zayed (Cairo, 1960), pp. 37 ff., 343 ff.

40. *Le Livre de Science,* trans. M. Achena—H. Massé (Paris, 1955), I, 136 ff. I am unable to use the original Persian.

41. He bases the existence of God solely on the impossibility of an infinite regress of causes; cf. Aristotle's *Metaphysics,* II, and Aquinas, *Summa Theologiae,* I, question 2, article 3 (second way).

42. The sentence continues: "whereupon He testifies concerning everything in existence after Him."

43. *Ishārāt,* p. 146.

44. Aristotle, *Metaphysics,* IV, 1, 1003a20–21, and Ross's note; cf. Alfarabi, *Aghrāḍ mā ba'd al-Ṭabī'a* (Hyderabad, 1930), p. 4; Avicenna, *Shifā': Ilāhiyyāt,* p. 13; *Najāt,* p. 198.

45. Cf. below, at n. 96.

46. Cf. H. Wolfson, "Averroes' Lost Treatise on the Prime Mover," *Hebrew Union College Annual,* XXIII/1 (1950–51), pp. 683 ff.

47. Aristotle, *Physics,* VIII, 7.

48. *Ibid.,* 5.

49. *Ibid.,* 6.

50. *Ibid.,* 8.

51. *Ibid.,* 10.

52. *Ibid.,* 267b17–26; *Metaphysics,* XII, 7.

53. *Metaphysics,* XII, 7, 1072b10–13.

54. Aristotle, *Metaphysics,* ed. W. Ross (Oxford, 1924), I, xxv.

55. Above, n. 44.

56. Cf. above at n. 53.

57. Aristotle, *Metaphysics,* V, 5.

58. *Shifā': Ilāhiyyāt,* p. 29.

59. *Ibid.,* p. 35.

60. As far as I know, this definition is not explicitly found in Aristotle. It is, however, implied in *Prior Analytics* I, 13, 32a19–20.

61. Cf. above, n. 56.

62. Cf. Aristotle, *Prior Analytics* I, 13, 32a19–20.

63. *Shifā': Ilāhiyyāt,* p. 35.

64. *Ibid.,* p. 29.

65. *Ibid.,* p. 36.

66. *Necessary* with no further qualification is wider than *necessarily existent being,* for it also includes, e.g., the conclusion of a syllogism. Cf. Aristotle, *Metaphysics,* V, 5, 1015b6.

67. *Najāt,* pp. 224–225.

68. Above at n. 57.

69. *Najāt,* p. 225.

70. *Ibid.*

71. Cf. above, at nn. 15–17.

72. Avicenna would clearly consider the "four" that follows from "two plus two" (above, at n. 69) to have this kind of necessity.

73. Leibniz, *De rerum originatione radicali,* trans. Latta, in *The Monadology,* p. 339.

74. Above, at n. 59.

75. Above, at n. 65.

76. It is not *logical* impossibility.

77. Ghazālī, *Tahāfut al-Falāsifa,* ed. M. Bouyges (Beirut, 1927), IV, § 12; translation in *Averroes' Tahafut al-Tahafut,* trans. S. van den Bergh (London, 1954), p. 164.

78. *Najāt,* p. 226.

79. *Najāt,* pp. 226, 238; *Shifā': Ilāhiyyāt,* p. 38.

80. This is clear throughout, but is stated explicitly in *Shifā': Ilāhiyyāt,* p. 37.

81. *Ibid.*

82. *Liber de causis,* ed. O. Bardenhewer (Freiburg, 1882), §§ 20, 24, 25, paralleling Proclus, *Elements of Theology,* ed. E. Dodds (Oxford, 1963), §§ 45–48, 127.

83. *Al-Madīna al-Fāḍila,* ed. F. Dieterici (Leiden, 1895), pp. 5 ff. German translation: *Der Musterstaat,* trans. F. Dieterici (Leiden, 1900), pp. 6 ff.; *al-Siyāsāt al-Madaniyya* (Hyderabad, 1926), pp. 13–15. This type of reasoning is also suggested in a text attributed to Alexander of Aphrodisias; cf. *Arisṭū ʿinda al-ʿArab,* ed. A. Badawi (Cairo, 1947), p. 266.

84. *Shifā': Ilāhiyyāt,* pp. 37–38.

85. Averroes raises this point as an objection to Avicenna's reasoning as Avicenna is reported by Ghazālī. Cf. *Tahāfut al-Tahāfut,* IV, § 8; translation in *Averroes' Tahāfut al-Tahāfut,* transl. van den Bergh, p. 158.

86. *Najāt,* pp. 228–229; *Shifā': Ilāhiyyāt,* pp. 344–348; *Ishārāt,* p. 144.

87. Cf. Hume, *Dialogues Concerning Natural Religion,* Part IX.

88. This argumentation is given in Ghazālī's account of the views of philosophy, *Tahāfut,* IV, § 4; translation in *Averroes' Tahāfut al-Tahāfut,* transl. van den Bergh, p. 160. In

van den Bergh's translation, the phrase: "the first body cannot be composite," should be corrected to: "the first principle cannot be composite."

89. The complete argument is very involved.

90. *Najāt,* pp. 229–234; *Shifā': Ilāhiyyāt,* pp. 43–47; 350–354; *Ishārāt,* p. 143.

91. *Najāt,* pp. 229, 245; *Shifā': Ilāhiyyāt,* pp. 355–356; 367–370.

92. *Shifā': Ilāhiyyāt,* p. 6.

93. Aristotle, *Posterior Analytics,* I, 2, 71b19–32.

94. *Shifā': Ilāhiyyāt,* p. 438. This was a commonplace; cf. Alexander, Commentary on *Metaphysics,* in *Commentaria in Aristotelem Graeca,* I (Berlin, 1891), 686, lines 36–37; Themistius, Paraphrase of *Metaphysics, ibid.,* V/5 (Berlin, 1902), Hebrew part, p. 11, line 24; and cf. *Liber de Causis,* § 5.

95. *Shifā': Ilāhiyyāt,* p. 6.

96. *Najāt,* p. 235.

97. Cf. above at nn. 42–45.

98. Above, at nn. 78–79.

99. *Najāt,* p. 235.

100. H. Wolfson, "Notes on Proofs of the Existence of God in Jewish Philosophy," *Hebrew Union College Annual,* I (1924), 584 ff.

101. He in fact treats the two principles as three; cf. below, n. 113.

102. Avicenna explains that the maintaining cause can either be identical with the cause of generation or it can be different. For example, a container that lends its shape to the liquid contained therein is both the cause of the generation of that shape and also the cause maintaining the shape. Thus here the two are identical. But the cause of the generation of the shape of a statue is the artisan, whereas the cause maintaining the statue's shape is the "dryness of the substance" of which the statue is made. Here the two causes are different. Cf. *Najāt,* p. 237.

The distinction Avicenna draws here was later to be expressed by Thomas Aquinas as a distinction between the cause of *fieri* and the cause of *esse; Summa Theologiae,* I, question 104, article 1.

103. To refute an infinite regress, Avicenna, as will appear, treats all possibly existent beings as a single whole. This procedure can make sense only for possible beings that exist at the same time.

104. Aristotle's proof from motion, it should be noted, is also primarily interested in the causes *maintaining* the motion of the universe.

105. This does not exclude its being a component, as in the instance of the statue, above, n. 102.

106. Cf. above, at n. 70.

107. *Najāt,* pp. 236–237.

108. E.g., Aristotle, Maimonides, Aquinas.

109. The Jewish philosopher Ḥasdai Crescas constructed his proof on the general principle without using the corollary that an infinite regress of causes is impossible. Cf. *Or ha-Shem* (Ferrara, 1555), I, iii, 2.

110. Possibly, though, he considered the thesis to be intuitively absurd; this is suggested in *Ishārāt,* p. 141.

111. Above, at n. 86.

112. *Najāt,* p. 235; *Ishārāt,* pp. 141-142.

113. Besides the principle of causality and the impossibility of an infinite regress, Avicenna writes that his proof needs a third proposition, the impossibility of a circular, as distinct from a linear, regress. A circular regress is a situation in which X, Y, and Z, for example, exist simultaneously in such a way that X is the cause maintaining Y in existence, Y is the cause of Z, but Z is the cause of X. That situation is manifestly absurd, according to Avicenna, for two reasons, for the same reason that a linear regress is impossible; and also because it would mean that X is a distant cause of itself, also a distant effect of itself, and, put another way, is dependent for its existence upon something whose existence is posterior to it. Cf. *Najāt,* p. 236; Aristotle, *Physics,* VIII, 5, 257b, 13-20.

114. *Najāt,* p. 239; *Ishārāt,* pp. 141-142.

115. Cf. above at nn. 77-78.

116. Kant *Critique of Pure Reason,* transl. Smith, p. 502.

117. Avicenna does not claim originality in this. He writes that although the "first" philosophers—i.e., Aristotle and his commentators—explicitly only proved a first cause of motion, they also alluded to a proof of a first cause of existence; cf. *Mubāḥathāt,* in *Arisṭū inda al-ʿArab,* ed. Badawi, p. 180, § 290. Such had been the position of Ammonius and Simplicius; cf. Simplicius, Commentary on *Physics,* in *Commentaria in Aristotelem Graeca,* X (Berlin, 1895), 1362-1363.

118. Ghazālī, *Tahāfut,* IV, §§ 11 ff.; Wolfson, "Averroes' Lost Treatise on the Prime Mover"; Crescas, *Or ha-Shem,* I, ii, 17.

119. A. Pegis, "Toward a New Way to God: Henry of Ghent," *Medieval Studies,* XXX (1968), 229-241.

120. Juwayni, *K. al-Irshād* (Cairo, 1950), pp. 28-29, 59; Ghazālī, *al-Iqtiṣād* (Ankara, 1962), p. 25; Fakhr al-Dīn al Rāzī, *Muḥaṣṣal* (Cairo, 1905), pp. 106-108; Ījī, *Mawāqif* (Cairo, 1907), VIII, pp. 2, 5-8.

121. Ījī, *Mawāqif,* VII, p. 227

122. *ʿUyūn al-Masāʾil,* in *Alfarabi's Philosophische Abhandlungen,* ed. F. Dieterici (Leiden, 1890), §§ 1, 3; *R. Zaynūn* (Hyderabad, 1925), pp. 3-4.

123. Cf. S. Pines, "Ibn Sina et l'Auteur de la Risālat al-Fuṣūṣ fi l-Ḥikma," *Revue des Études Islamiques,* XIX (1951), pp. 121-124; F. Rahman, *Prophecy in Islam,* p. 21.

124. Maimonides, *Moreh Nebukim,* II, 1 (3).

125. Aquinas, *Summa Theologiae,* I, question 2, article 3 (third way).

126. Above, n. 109.

127. Cf. Wolfson, *Spinoza,* I, 197 ff.; Spinoza, *Ethics,* I, xi, second proof.

128. Leibniz, *De rerum originatione radicali,* transl. Latta in *The Monadology,* pp. 337-339: "The sufficient reason of existence [=Avicenna's maintaining cause] cannot be found either in any particular thing or in the whole aggregate and series of things. . . . You may indeed suppose the world eternal; but as you suppose only a succession of states

in none of which you find the sufficient reason . . . it is evident that the reason must be sought elsewhere. . . . The series of changing things, even if it be supposed that they succeed one another from all eternity, has its reason in . . . the prevailing of inclinations, . . . in inclining reasons. . . . Accordingly the reasons of the world lie hid in something extramundane, different from the concatenation of states or the series of things, the aggregate of which constitutes the world."

Wolff, *Theologia Naturalis,* I, §§ 24, 29, 33, 47, 48, 55, 1107. Wolff explains that a necessary being is a being that exists through itself. By analyzing the concept he shows that such a being cannot be extended or composite (and therefore the physical world cannot be a necessary being), and that there cannot be two of them. To demonstrate that such a being actually exists, Wolff begins with the datum that at least something exists—the human soul. Then he argues that either this thing is itself necessarily existent or ultimately depends on something that is necessarily existent: "For everything must have a sufficient reason why it should be, rather than not be." And if the thing we start with has the reason for its existence in something other than itself, we shall arrive at the sufficient reason of its existence only when we arrive at that "which does have the sufficient reason for its existence in itself" (§ 24). Also cf. Baumgarten, *Metaphysica,* §§ 361, 375, 381.

129. Above, nn. 35, 36.

130. Mohammed Abduh, *R. al-Tawḥīd,* chapter 2. This is a brief version of Avicenna's proof.

131. Cf. the Russell and Copleston debate in B. Russell, *Why I Am Not a Christian* (London, 1957), pp. 145-146. Copleston states that he is following Leibniz.

Also cf. R. Garrigou-Lagrange, *Dieu, Son Existence* et *Sa Nature,* 11th ed. (Paris, 1950), pp. 269 ff.; R. Taylor, *Metaphysics,* Englewood Cliffs, 1963, pp. 85-93.

A Third Version of the Ontological Argument in the Ibn Sīnian Metaphysics

PARVIZ MOREWEDGE
Baruch College of the City University of New York

Introduction

IN THIS INQUIRY we shall evaluate the philosophical significance of the concept of the Necessary Existent in the context of ibn Sīnā's ontological argument for the existence of God. We shall focus especially on the so-called "mystical" aspects of the ultimate being, which are important for contemporary philosophical theology, as exemplified in the works of H. D. Lewis, R. C. Zaehner and others. The outline of our argument follows a fivefold division, presenting: (I) a clarification of two versions of the ontological argument, (II) ibn Sīnā's support of the second version of this argument, (III) the pragmatics of the experimental features of the concept of the Necessary Existent which figure in religious experience, but are not fully accounted for in the first two versions of the ontological argument, (IV) the development of a third version of this argument within ibn Sīnā's writings, a version for which analogues will be cited from the doctrines of western philosophers such as Descartes, Augustine and others, and finally (V) an assessment of the philosophical significance of our inquiry, which points out the difficulties embedded in all ontological arguments encountered as well as in the experiential approach to the concept of the Necessary Existent in religious experience.

The Two Versions of the Ontological Argument

Recently interest has mounted in the philosophical significance of the ontological argument for the existence of God—an argument traditionally associated with St. Anselm's *Proslogion.* Accordingly, in a collection of articles exclusively devoted to this argument, Hick and McGill note, "Recent decades have seen a great and growing interest in the ontological argument for the existence of God, and a considerable twentieth-century literature has grown up around it," and, moreover, "There has been an intense and many-sided investigation of the meaning of this argument for the man who first proposed it, St. Anselm of Canterbury."[1] In another collection, also devoted to this argument, R. Taylor holds that, "This argument has had a profound fascination for men since it was first so thoroughly and beautifully formulated by St. Anselm of Canterbury in the eleventh century."[2] Numerous studies relate this argument to Anselm, calling, for example, Anselm's formulation "The classical version,"[3] or naming the argument itself "his [Anselm's] proof for God's existence."[4]

Perhaps the contemporary revival of interest in this argument may have been stimulated by an essay entitled "Anselm's Ontological Argument" by a major contemporary philosopher, Norman Malcolm, who uses the following strategy to "save" the ontological argument.[5] To begin with, he distinguishes between two different versions of the same argument of Anselm, stating, "I believe that in Anselm's *Proslogion* and *Responsio editoris* there are two different pieces of reasoning which he did not distinguish from one another, and that a good deal of light may be shed on the philosophical problem of 'the ontological argument' if we do distinguish them."[6] Malcolm then agrees with the critiques of the argument, recognizing that one version is inadequate, and attempts to "prove" the so-called second version of the argument.[7] This striking attempt by a major contemporary philosopher to prove the existence of God by an a priori argument has caused an uproar in contemporary philosophy. In a recent essay, we too attempted to criticize Malcolm's "proof" in the context of our study of ibn Sīnā's philosophy, by showing that: (i) prior to Anselm (1033–1109), ibn Sīnā (980–1037) held a second version of the ontological argument, (ii) the analysis of ibn Sīnā's argument unearths some new objections to Malcolm's version, and (iii) the ibn Sīnian version is not logically adequate.[8]

Let us briefly present a formulation of these two versions, since it will be necessary to refer to them in subsequent discussions. The formulation below displays some of the key features of the first version:

(V1P1) By "God" I mean the most perfect being. (The "most perfect being" meaning that entity which has all positive properties to the maximum degree, e.g., it loves maximally.)[9]

(V1P2) "Existence" is a perfection.
(This assumes that existence is a property and furthermore, that it is a positive property. A legitimate subject of which existence would be predicated would supposedly be a concept or an idea.)[10]

∴God exists. (For every perfection Φ, God has Φ to the maximum degree; since existence is a Φ, it follows that, by the rule of Universal instantiation, God has existence, which is interpreted as God exists.)

In brief, the three types of objections to this version are the following:

(Leibniz 1) "(V1P1)" may not describe a possible entity.[11] (Naming a concept does not assure that a concept in question can be realized in any possible world.)

(Kant 1) We should reject (V1P2), since "Existence is not a predicate."[12]

(Hume 1) The entire machinery of the argument is inadequate. If the conclusion of any argument is a matter-of-fact statement, then at least one of its premises must also be a matter-of-fact statement. Since in this argument the conclusion is a matter-of-fact statement and the premises are all relations-of-ideas statements, the implication is not legitimate.[13]

(Hume 2) "(V1P1)" is inadequate, since it attempts to describe an actual entity purely by analysis of ideas. The only legitimate basis we may have for talking about an actual entity is on the basis of impressions rather than ideas.[14]

If one accepts this objection (Hume 2), then (Leibniz 1) becomes superfluous since, as will become evident, the Humean objection would not enable us to claim legitimately that it is conceivable for an entity such as God to be "necessary."

Malcolm places the first version of the ontological argument into *Prosogion 2* and rejects it in accordance with (Kant 1) as follows:

> Anselm's ontological proof of *Proslogion 2* is fallacious because it rests on the false doctrine that existence is a perfection (and therefore that existence is a "real predicate"). It would be desirable to have a rigorous refutation of the doctrine but I have not been able to provide one. I am compelled to leave the matter at the more or less intuitive level of Kant's observation.[15]

However, Malcolm attempts to prove or to support what he regards as a second variation of Anselm's argument, a version which does not assert that existence is a perfection, but rather that the "Necessary Existence" is a perfection. He affirms: "*Necessary Existence* is a property of God in the *same sense* that *necessary omnipotence* and *necessary omniscience* are His properties."[16] The second argument may be formulated as follows:

(Malcolm 1) The Necessary Being (existent) exists necessarily.

Malcolm employs many arguments to substantiate this proposition while recognizing objections like the following:[17]

(Hume 3) "Necessity" is applicable to "relations-of-ideas" types of propositions; thus, the phrase "the Necessary Existent" is not legitimate.[18]

(Kant 2) For any X and any proposition, 'X exists,' it is possible to conceive 'X does not exist' to be true; thus the second part of Malcolm's affirmation (Malcolm 1), "necessarily exists," is not supportable.[19]

Ibn Sīnā and the Ontological Argument

In this section we shall turn to some passages in the ibn Sīnian Corpus which deal with the ontological argument—especially to those passages omitted in our earlier writing on this subject.[20]

To begin with, we note that the subject matter of the Necessary Existent (*al-Wājib al-Wujūd*) is the most prominent single concept in ibn Sīnā's metaphysical writing; in fact he places as much emphasis on it as Spinoza does on his God-one-substance in *The Ethics*. For example, in the *Dānish Nāma,*[21] out of fifty-seven chapters, chapters nineteen through thirty-eight and chapter fifty-five make explicit mention of the Necessary Existent in their titles. In the *Najāt,*[22] out of fifty-seven chapters, approximately nineteen take up the subject matter of the Necessary Existent, while in the *Shifā',*[23] the sixth and the seventh sections of the first chapter, the eighth chapter, and the content of many other sections, such as the last two chapters, the ninth and the tenth, touch on the same topic. Consequently, the statements which ibn Sīnā makes about the Necessary Existent should not be viewed as standing in isolation in his system; this concept, indeed, is the most central doctrine in his metaphysics.

Let us investigate, accordingly, the logic of ibn Sīnā's argumentation and note how he would classify the truth of the conclusion about the existence of the Necessary Existent or God. We may begin with the classification of sentences in the logic of *al-Ishārāt*[24] (I, 305–310), where the discussion grows out of a context specifying the relationship between a predicate (*maḥmūl*) and its subject (*mauḍū'*) which, according to ibn Sīnā, holds between both affirmative and negative propositions. The predication leads either to a contingent proposition such as "A man is a writer," or to an impossible proposition such as "A man is a stone." Subsequently he states that the matter (*mādda*) of each proposition (as related to the predicate) results in a relation which is either necessary (*wājib*), contingent (*mumkin*), or impossible (*mumtani'*). (We note here that "*mumkin*" should be translated as "contingent," which precludes "necessary"; the usual translation of "*mumkin*" as "possible," which includes "necessary," is misleading.) Having specified the general class of necessary propositions, he subdivides them into absolute (*muṭlaq*) propositions, which are categorically necessary and are independent of any one condition (*sharṭ*), such as the realization of an essence, and those propositions which are hypothetically necessary and are based upon a condition. To illustrate the first kind, ibn Sīnā presents the proposition "God (*Allāh*)—may he be exalted—exists (*maujūd*)" (*Ishārāt,* I, 310), whereas for the second he cites "A man is necessarily a rational body," implying further that whenever there is a man, there is a rational body. Consequently, our knowledge of God's existence is not dependent on any condition, e.g., the existence of other entities, whereas the truth of a sentence which attributes a predicate (even an essential one) to a subject other than God assumes the existence of the subject. This interpretation corroborates also Rescher's analysis of ibn Sīnā's position on existential propositions and genuine predicates; Rescher's position, which is based upon his analysis of the logic of the *Dānish Nāma,* is upheld by our own reading.[25]

The next problem inviting our attention is the exploration of the meta-language status of the "Necessary Existent" in ibn Sīnā's metaphysical vocabulary. In *al-Shifā'* (pp. 5–6) ibn Sīnā notes that in each science (*ʿilm*), some entities are assumed [to exist], while their modes are investigated by the science in question.[26] In metaphysics, however, the existence (*anniyya* [*ibid.,* 5], *wujūd* [*ibid.,* 6]) of God (*Allāh*) is not an assumption but a goal to be investigated (*maṭlūb*). Here, ibn Sīnā does not affirm our knowledge of the proposition, "The Necessary Existent exists," to be either true or false; he does establish, however, that we do not begin the science of metaphysics with the concept of the Necessary Existent as our primitive term but develop this concept in the course of our inquiry. His statement should not be interpreted to assert that an empirical, matter-of-fact type of assumption is necessary for proving the existence of God. This problem becomes clear if we differentiate between Aquinas' concept of what constitutes a proof for God's existence and the ibn Sīnian method.

As noted, Anselm's version of the proof is based upon "the fool's" psychological awareness in his own ear that he understands what the most perfect being means.[27] Aquinas objects to the argument on the grounds that the ontological argument based upon something "psychologically evident to us" is inadequate. He might say, nonetheless, that "God exists" is syntactically self-evident. In this vein Aquinas argues:

> I maintain then that the proposition 'God exists' is self-evident in itself, for, as we shall see later, its subject and its predicate are identical, since God is his own existence. But, because what is to be God is not evident to us, the proposition is not self-evident to us, and needs to be made evident. This is done by means of things which, though less evident in themselves, are nevertheless more evident to us by means of, namely, God's effects.[28]

Crucial to his argument is Aquinas' insistence on a proof which has to be "evident to us." At the expense of an a priori analytical proof, such an insistence leads him to offer instead an argument based upon "God's effect" in the actual world, which might be "self-evident" to the "fool" in the psalms. In this vein Aquinas states:

> On the other hand, nobody can think (*cogitare*) the opposite of a self-evident proposition, as Aristotle's discussion of first principles

> makes clear. But the opposite of the proposition 'God exists' can be thought, for *the fool* in the psalms *said in his heart: There is no God.* That God exists is therefore not self-evident.[29]

It is for this reason that all five of the celebrated "ways" which Aquinas presents to prove God's existence are a posteriori cosmological arguments. Aquinas notes subsequently that "God exists" is not a proposition which is implanted in us by nature in any clear and specific way.[30] Thereafter, he quotes St. Paul to support the view that God's existence must be demonstrated by the "things he has made."[31] A close inspection of each of the five ways shows that his arguments are a posteriori in that they focus on the changes things in the world undergo, efficient causation in the observable world, the possibility and necessity of things "we come across" in the world, gradation observed in things, and order in nature.[32] Consequently, Aquinas insists that a proof for God's existence is needed where every premise is self-evident and every concept is psychologically intuitive. Ibn Sīnā chooses a different approach. In the first place, ibn Sīnā refrains from using ordinary language to prove explicitly the God of religion to his readers. Instead, he presents a metaphysical system in which a theory about the Necessary Existent is conceptually formulated. With the exception of the last two chapters of *al-Shifā'*, a book written prior to the *Dānish Nāma* and the *Ishārāt,* his metaphysical writings are purely abstract, especially the *Dānish Nāma,* where the entire discussion of heavens and bodies is presented in an axiomatic way. The proofs refer not to "God" but to the Necessary Existent—especially the ontological proofs, which are based purely on his analytic specification of this concept, as the following analyses should clarify.

In considering the question of the self-evident nature of God's existence, ibn Sīnā does not differentiate between that which is psychologically self-evident to us and that which is analytically self-evident, as he is constructing a rational schema. In this vein he claims that it is impossible (*maḥāl*) for us to render conjectures (*faraḍ*) about the nonexistence of the Necessary Existent. He uses this doctrine to differentiate the Necessary Existent from other existents (*al-Najāt,* p. 224). The problem, as he envisages it, is to show that, even though the Necessary Existent is not in Itself a primitive metaphysical concept, "That the Necessary Existent exists," is a categorically true proposition. Accordingly, we note in the *Dānish Nāma* an outline of such an argument, which is corroborated in his other writings.

(Ibn Sīnā 1) "Being-qua-being (*hastī*) is the most general (*ʿāmm*) concept recognized by the intelligence (*khirad, ʿaql, nous, intelligentia*)."

(Ibn Sīnā 2) "According to intelligence, 'being-qua-being' is divided into 'impossible,' 'contingent,' and 'necessary' kinds of being."

(Ibn Sīnā 3) Consequently "The Necessary Being" is "The Necessary Existent", or "The Necessary Existent is that whose essence is existence."

Let us begin our analysis by pointing out the variations with which the argument comes to the fore in ibn Sīnā's various texts. (1) First we notice that there are two different terms used by ibn Sīnā to discuss the subject matter of (ibn Sīnā 1), "*hastī*" and "*wujūd.*" Having discussed these terms extensively in our previous studies, we shall do no more than note those points which are significant to our present discussion.[33]

"*Hastī,*" meaning "being-qua-being," is equivalent to Aristotle's use of "τὸ ὄν ᾗ ὄν" in *Metaphysica* 1002a20 and Ockham's use of "*ens*" in *Summa Totius Logicae*[34] ("*wujūd*" is translated as "existence," "*mawjūd*" is translated as "existent," while "*māhiyya,*" "*dhāt*" and "*ḥaqīqa*" are translated as "essence").

(2) Ibn Sīnā has two formulations of his primary hypothese: (2a) In the *Dānish Nāma*, he asserts that "being" (*hastī*) is the most general (*ʿāmm*), well-known (*maʿrūf*) notion recognized by reason (*khirad* and intelligence, *ʿaql, nous, intelligentia*) (p. 15). In the *Najāt,* he asserts without a doubt that there is existence (*wujūd*) (p. 235). In both of these cases the following theory is proposed: there is no doubt that there is being (*Dānish Nāma*) and existence (*al-Nājat*), or furthermore that in its primary division existence is either necessary or contingent (*al-Najāt*), or that being is either necessary, contingent or impossible (*Dānish Nāma*). In the *Naiāt* the premise about the modalities follows immediately in the same sentence, whereas the modal doctrine follows fifteen chapters later in the *Dānish Nāma.* These two passages provide plausible grounds for the interpretation that ibn Sīnā regards either "being" as primary, from which it follows that "necessary being," "contingent being," and "impossible being" can be assumed to be legitimate concepts (according to the doctrine of the *Dānish Nāma*) or that he regards "existence" as primary, from which it follows that "necessary existence" and "contingent existence" are considered to be primary (according to the doctrine of *al-Najāt*). Obviously this variation is legitimate, since there can be impossible *beings,* e.g., the concept of a round square, but no impossible *existents.* These two perspectives could be aligned as follows: both "being" and "existence" are primary to the intelligence. When we consider being, we do so in three instances, "necessary being," "contingent being" and "impossible being." When we consider existence, that which is primary to our intelligence is "necessary existence" and "contingent existence." (By way of providing clarification, let us note that among contingent beings, those whose causes have been realized have an instance, e.g., particular man, while those whose causes have not been realized, e.g., "being a unicorn," are mere essences without existents.)

(2b) Now we shall turn to the second set of quotations to buttress the first two premises. In *al-Shifā'* (p. 29), it is asserted that the first ideas to be configured in the soul (*nafs*) are existents (*al-maujūd*), such as being a thing (*shai'*) and being a necessity (*al-ḍarūrī*) and, moreover, that there is no need to know of other configurations in order to know these (primary) ones. Similarly, in another passage in *al-Shifā'* (*al-Shifā'*, p. 37), ibn Sīnā notes that from the vantage point of the intelligence (*'aql*) any existence (*wujūd*) is either a necessary existent (*al-wājib al-wujūd*) or a contingent existent (*al-mumkin al-wujūd*). In *al-Ishārāt* (III, 19) it is stated that any existent in its own nature (*nafsahu*), is either a contingency (*mumkin*) or a necessity (*wājib*). In *'Uyūn al-Ḥikma,* ibn Sīnā reaffirms the thesis that that aspect by which any thing (*shai'*) has existence is either a necessity (*wājib*) or a contingency (*mumkin*) (*'Uyūn al-Ḥikma*).[35] In these passages, ibn Sīnā seems to place the primariness of the notions of "existence" on the same level accorded to the modalities of "necessity" and "contingency." Now axiomatically for our purpose, it does not matter whether ibn Sīnā considers "being" or "existence" as the first set of notions and modalities (i.e., "necessity," "contingency," and "impossibility") a second set, or whether these two sets of notions have the same primary status. It is a fact that both sets are "nonempirical" and both provide ibn Sīnā with the basis from which to deduce that the concept of "necessary existence," i.e., one combining "existence" and "necessity," is a legitimate notion. Having made this assumption a part of what may be called his "rules of formations," he goes on to note that an understanding of the concept of Necessary Existence implies the existence of exactly one Necessary Existent.[36]

(3) Next, let us ask whether or not the positions designated as (ibn Sīnā 1) and (ibn Sīnā 2) commit him to a rationalistic ontology. Before resolving this issue, let us note first that no classical philosopher doubted that there is something in the world, as the alternative would be that there is nothing, and "nothing" has been a meaningless concept in classical philosophy since Parmenides. In *al-Najāt* (p. 213) ibn Sīnā himself states explicitly that there is no doubt but that there is existence. This statement is not an assumption necessary to his proof but an assertion of a primary incorrigible truth. To assert that this particular passage makes ibn Sīnā's argument a cosmological argument is not legitimate for the following reasons. Descartes in his fifth meditation (where he states his ontological argument) and Anselm in the *Proslogion* (where he formulates a version of the ontological argument par excellence) assume that they themselves and their ideas do exist as actual entities. Consequently, if we make the criterion for the cosmological argument the assumption that at least something exists, then we shall not be able to call the arguments of Anselm or Descartes (fifth meditation) "ontological"—which is

absurd. Typical cosmological arguments, such as the ones stated by Aquinas, refer to a feature some entity possesses in the actual world—not in mere thought or in definition. Now let us clarify further what we may mean by "rationalism" before investigating whether ibn Sīnā's claim that we are acquainted with "being" commits him to a rationalistic metaphysics. Since it is beyond the scope of this paper to discuss different schools of philosophy, we shall touch on no more than one central issue: whether or not a philosopher can claim that we can know bodies by reason and not by the senses. The most celebrated case of a "rationalistic" position on this topic is found at the end of Descartes' second meditation after his so-called "wax experiment," where he states:

> I now know that even bodies are not really perceived by the senses or the imaginative faculty, but only by intellect; that they are perceived, not by being touched or seen, but by being understood; I thus clearly recognize that nothing is more easily or manifestly perceptible to me than my own mind.[37]

In contradistinction to such a view stands ibn Sīnā's position. In the logic of the *Ishārāt* (I, 189), he affirms that our ability to attribute "being a figure" and "being a triangle" to the same entity does not imply that "being a figure" and "being a triangle" are one and the same idea (*ḥaqīqa*); instead, the thing (*shai'*) in question which we name "a triangle" can also be named "a figure." Ibn Sīnā returns to this example in the metaphysics found in the same collection (*Ishārāt,* III, 13–14) when he asserts that the idea, essence (*ḥaqīqa*) of a triangle is dependent upon features, such as line formation, but that its existence (*wujūd*)—that is, the realization of a particular triangle—is due to other causes. Moreover, in the *Dānish Nāma* (p. 56), ibn Sīnā makes a distinction between the meaning of a bodily substance in whose subject an essence is realized and the act of knowing that there is actually a bodily substance, on the basis that the latter belongs to the experiencing of an actually existing subject rather than to mere relations of ideas. Consequently, ibn Sīnā's adherence to "being" or to "existence" as an a priori concept does not commit him to a rationalistic metaphysics. He would reject Descartes' view that the validity of sensations depends on God's existence. For this reason, as well as on account of his essence-existence distinction with which we have dealt elsewhere, he could not accept the second premise of the first version of the ontological argument "(V1P2)," which specifies that existence is a perfection for any entity. The sole exception is the "Necessary Existent," as defined by ibn Sīnā.

(4) Moreover, this difference between the argument assuming "(V1P2)" and the argument merely assuming "(Malcolm 1)" and not "(V1P2)" is

the means by which to differentiate between the two versions of this argument, as Malcolm points out in the following passage:

> Previously I rejected *existence* as a perfection. Anselm is maintaining in the remarks last quoted, not that existence is a perfection but *the logical impossibility of non-existence is a perfection.* In other words, *necessary existence* is a perfection. His first ontological proof uses the principle that a thing is greater if it exists than if it does not exist. His second proof employs the different principle that a thing is greater if it necessarily exists than if it does not necessarily exist.[38]

Thus, ibn Sīnā's repeated assertion that the "Necessary Existent" is a legitimate concept and that "Its essence is no other than existence" permits us to assign his and Malcolm's arguments to the second version of this argument.

Malcolm indicates that philosophers other than Anselm have called the "Necessity of existence" a perfection. For example, in his replies to objections made to his fifth meditation, Descartes asserts that existence may be a property but also that "necessary existence" is a property.

> Nay, necessary existence in the case of God is also a true property in the strictest sense of the word, because it belongs to Him and forms part of His essence alone. Hence the existence of a triangle cannot be compared with the existence of God, because existence manifestly has a different relation to essence in the case of God and in the case of a triangle.[39]

Spinoza, too, begins his treatise on *Ethics* by asserting that "By cause of itself, I understand that whose essence involves existence, or that whose nature cannot be conceived unless existing."[40] He uses his feature to clarify his notion of God by stating: "The existence of God and His essence are one and the same thing."[41] "The thesis that only in the case of God are essence and existence the same is also stated by Ockham, who asserts that God cannot not exist.[42]

This view of the ontological argument has recently found a supporter in R. Taylor, who, upon noting that the concept of the Necessary Existence has been questioned by "confused" people, attempts to clarify it in his *Metaphysics.*

> If it makes sense to speak of anything as an *impossible* being, or something which by its very nature does not exist, then it is hard to see why the idea of a necessary being, or something which in its very nature exists, should not be just as comprehensible.[43]

This argument is actually much weaker than the one presented by ibn Sīnā, for it confuses an essence with an existent. There could not be *an existent* which is an impossible being, for if it were impossible for it to have been realized, then it could not be an actual entity. Consequently, Taylor's "something which by its very nature does not exist" should be reformulated as follows: "We can conceive of various kinds of essences, e.g., being a round square, which cannot have an instance." However, from this statement it does not follow that there must be an essence which must have an instance or be equal to its own instance. The difficulty in ibn Sīnā's, Malcolm's and Taylor's (reformulated) arguments is the assumption underlying each that the concatenation of "necessity" and "existence" is legitimate. In contradistinction to these positions stand Kant's classical remarks:

> If, in an identical proposition, I reject the predicate while retaining the subject, contradiction results; and I therefore say that the former belongs necessarily to the latter. But if we reject subject and predicate alike, there is no contradiction; for nothing is then left that can be contradicted. To posit a triangle, and yet to reject its three angles is self-contradictory but there is no contradiction in rejecting the triangle together with its three angles. The same holds true of the concept of an absolutely necessary being. If its existence is rejected, we reject the thing itself with all its predicates; and no question of contradiction can then arise.[44]

Taylor must contend with still another objection. Even if we assume that the Necessary Existent makes sense, just because we use the concept of "an impossible being," it does not follow that we are also using the concept of "the necessary being" in a comprehensible way.[45]

While we cannot disagree with "(ibn Sīnā1)," we do not agree with his second premise "(ibn Sīnā 2)." It is obvious that there are certain propositions which are *necessarily false,* e.g., "There is the largest number," or "There is someone who is the mother of herself." There are also some *contingent* propositions, e.g., "It will rain tomorrow." And most philosophers have held that certain propositions are *analytically true* in one sense or another, such as "'2' is an even number" or "A white horse is a horse." Modalities as applied to propositions make sense, but as applied to entities violate Hume's principles as formulated in (Hume 2) and Kant's analysis as formulated in (Kant 2). This writer is baffled by ibn Sīnā's assumption that "necessity" can legitimately be concatenated with "being." We question the significance of "necessary being" (unless applied to propositions) and "necessary existence" for these concepts are used clearly only in the context of traditional ontology. Since ibn Sīnā and others do not present any argument for their position that modalities and "existence" or "being" can be combined, while Hume and Kant present explicit arguments against this position, we cannot assume that (ibn Sīnā 2) is an a priori truth or applicable to the actual world.

Another problem with the second version of the argument is the question of the legitimacy of the concept of an "essence." C. D. Broad's analysis of Leibniz's "Predicate-in-Notion" principle, to which we shall return subsequently, sheds some light on this issue by pointing out that in some cases (e.g., a circle), an essence may easily be determined, while in other cases (e.g., an ellipse), and any member of a family of some properties can constitute an essence.[46] Yet even in the case of the circle, one would need, in addition to its so-called essence, a set of other items (e.g., Euclid's axioms), from which to derive other properties.[47] In applying this objection to the concept of the Necessary Existent, we note that "being self-caused" and "having one's essence as one's existence" are interchangeable because in medieval terminology a cause is often that agent which is essential in the realization of the patient as an actual entity; consequently, "being self-caused" is identical to "existing due to oneself" which implies "existing at all times," and "having no agent for one's realization"; for otherwise, one would have to antedate one's own existence to actualize oneself. Consequently, all theorems about the Necessary Existent which use "its essence is no other than existence" may isomorphically use the "self-caused" feature, which shows that there is no simple way of indicating the Necessary Existent.

In sum, ibn Sīnā's ontological argument is no more successful than the others we have mentioned. Having dealt with the logic of the arguments in question, let us turn to an equally important aspect of the Necessary Existent, about which ibn Sīnā's analysis will provide great insight.

The Pragmatics of the "Necessary Existent" for Religious Experience

What is the pragmatic significance of the ontological argument? A clue is provided by Malcolm's own argument, which tries to justify the legitimacy of the notion of the Necessary Existent by showing its use in ordinary language and by appealing to religious texts, such as the Bible, and to religious practices. Toward the end of his argument Malcolm remarks,

> Here is expressed the idea of the necessary existence and eternity of God, an idea that is essential to the Jewish and Christian religions. In those complex systems of thought, those "language games," God has the status of a necessary being. Who can doubt that? Here we must say with Wittgenstein, "This language-game is played!" I believe we may rightly take the existence of those religious systems of thought in which God figures as a necessary being to be a disproof of the dogma, affirmed by Hume and others, that no existential proposition can be necessary.[48]

We have discussed Malcolm's attempt to define God as the most independent entity and have noted the logical difficulties inherent in this method. It is nevertheless true that many agree with Malcolm that the formal version of the ontological argument finds little support in ordinary religious experience; consequently, support for the existence of God must be found elsewhere. The first alternative has been to reject this argument in particular and to substitute another formal argument which is as removed from the ordinary language as the first two versions are. Such a step is taken by Plantinga, when he asserts:

> It is doubtful, I think, that any person was ever brought to a belief in God by this argument, and unlikely that it has played the sort of role in strengthening and confirming religious belief that, for example, the teleological argument has played. To the unsophisticated, Anselm's argument is (at first sight at least) remarkably unconvincing, if not downright irritating; it smacks too much of word magic.[49]

He asserts thereupon that even though many of the classical objections to the argument are invalid,[50] none of the obvious ways of stating the argument can succeed. After reviewing other types of arguments, Plantinga finally offers his own, "Hence my tentative conclusion: if my belief in other minds is rational, so is my belief in God. But obviously the former is rational; so, therefore, is the latter."[51] As this type of argumentation takes us away from the main stream of our essay, we shall not pursue it further, as numerous arguments may be offered for God's existence, each of which may be unsound.

Another alternative has been to reject the logic of any rational argument for the existence of God on the grounds that it is unsuitable for religious discourse, and to uphold instead some "ontological" feature of God, e.g., "infinity," as an essential aspect of a direct religious experience. In this vein, H. D. Lewis, a celebrated contemporary philosopher of religion, argues:

> The objections to the main arguments for the existence of God are well known. But it seems to me that what these arguments tried to express, most of all in the cases of the cosmological and the ontological ones, is the conviction of the self-subsistent supra-rational source of the world as we find it. Where the argument fails is in trying to break into a series of steps what is in fact one insight, and also in seeing to start from purely finite factors, and reason to conclusions about the infinite.[52]

Lewis clarifies his use of "the infinite" in describing the "filling" or the "content" of religious awareness:

> For it seems to me that this begins to be formed from the first onset of any properly religious life through the way the first apprehension of finite being as having a supreme and infinite source, and the emo-

> tional and other accompaniments of this awareness which we have also in mind designating it 'wonder', impress themselves into the situation which prompts them by lending to that situation something of their own quality and aura of mystery.[53]

The key notion, "the first apprehension of finite being as having a supreme and infinite source . . . ," is repeated in the conclusion of Lewis's work when he attempts to emphasize the social side of religion as follows: "Moreover the moment of wondering and still appreciation of finite facts as having an infinite or transcendental source, in deepening our sense of the unity of our natural environment, will intensify in the same way our sense of affinity and kinship with other persons."[54] The notion that the concern of religious experience is not to prove God's existence but to recognize the so-called "infinite basis of our finite being" is often encountered by a historian who attempts to point out the major features of an important thinker. For instance, after pointing out the Christian background of Hegel, Copleston, in his essay on "Hegel and the Rationalization of Mysticism," asserts: "In the second place Hegel was convinced that from the philosophical point of view the finite is not intelligible except in the light of the infinite whole, which is the ultimate reality. His philosophy is therefore concerned with exhibiting the nature of the ultimate reality rather than with trying to prove its existence."[55]

Often another transcendent term is substituted for the word "infinite," while the door is kept open to possibilities of relating this feature to other terms. For example, in the conclusion of his excellent study on *The Varieties of Religious Experience* William James notes three of the broadest characteristics of the religious life. He has found:

> 1. That the visible world is part of a more spiritual universe from which it draws its chief significance;
> 2. That union or harmonious relation with that higher universe is our true end;
> 3. That prayer or inner communion with the spirit—be that spirit "God" or "Law"—therefore is a process wherein work is really done, and spiritual energy flows in and produces effects, psychological and material, within the phenomenal world.[56]

The key point in James's account is this: the dependence of every aspect of the visible universe upon a spiritual aspect attests to the possibility of an "inner communion" with the "spirit."

At this point we shall investigate the possibility of merging the basic concepts of the ontological argument with what appears to be a major theme in religious experience, according to the writers quoted, who imply that the affinity between "the finite" and "the infinite" or an immediate dependence upon the divine is the core of religious experience and may well be a source of "ordinary logic" or of belief in a God.

Towards A Third Version of the Ontological Argument

At the outset we wish to distinguish between two different kinds of a priori awarenesses or acquaintances. For example, prima facie, I may be aware of the truth of the mathematical proposition that "2+2=4," or that I am seeing a valley, without being at the same time immediately aware of other facts, as for instance that "2" is the only even prime number, or that the sighting of a valley implies the concurrent sighting of a hillside. These two kinds of epistemic states have already been distinguished by Descartes in the passage below, which is embedded in his fifth meditation, where he presents the ontological argument for God's existence,

> Of the things I thus perceive, some are obvious to anybody; others are discovered only by those who undertake closer inspection and more careful investigation, but, when discovered are regarded as no less certain than others.[57]

The examples he provides begin with the truths of mathematics, which are certain but not immediately apparent, and continue to his notion of God. The first kind of awareness is immediate, whereas the second kind of awareness, even though it requires no empirical datum for support, requires nevertheless further conceptual analysis to make the concept in question clear; once we are aware of the first type of proposition, we are in a sense able to deduce other propositions of which we were not aware, in the first sense of "awareness." For example, once we understand the axiomatic system, i.e., the rules and the signs of a formal system, such as Euclidean geometry, we also "know," in the sense that we can generate, all theorems which can be deduced from the axioms in question. Let us, for purposes of clarity, name the first type of epistemic state, "a phenomenal a priori" state and the second "a discursive a priori" state. Having made this distinction, let us now formulate the ontological argument in question.

(V3P1) In "a phenomenal a priori" mode, I know that I exist as an agent who is acting, since my acts presuppose some agent and they are "my" acts. It is impossible for me to be nothing and act simultaneously.

(V3P2) In "a discursive a priori" state, I know that I can only coexist as an aspect of something, or as a derivative from a source of my dependence, which is a kind of X (where the value of X differs in each context, e.g., "the One Substance of Spinoza", or "the Necessary Existent of ibn Sīnā"); one case of X is the Necessary Existent. A complete notion of myself, in the Leibnizian sense of a "predicate-in-notion principle" involves the description of X.

(V3C) X exists, since X coexists as an aspect of myself.

An example of an intuitive but inadequate representation of this argument is the following: "I think, therefore there is at least a mental aspect of me. This mental aspect can exist only through the mediacy of the Necessary Existent. The Necessary Existent must coexist with me, and I in context of it." Before clarifying this thesis, let us note a fundamental difference between this argument and the cosmological argument for God's existence. For the latter at least one of the premises must be a posteriori, such as the assumption of the existence of some contingent entity outside the subject, independent of analytical consideration. But variations of "(V3P1)" and "(V3P2)" all claim to be a priori; consequently, this argument as represented in this essay has the form of the ontological argument.

Let us cite some of the many illustrations the history of philosophy offers to shed light on the first premise. As has been stated, no serious ancient or medieval philosopher has ever doubted the existence of at least something in the world, for otherwise he would have had to uphold the meaningfulness of the statement "There is nothing." This general disclaimer holds even for the most extreme skeptics. For example, in his *Lives of Eminent Philosophers,* Diogenes Laertius mentions the doctrine of the most extreme skeptic, Pyrrho, whose followers declared, "For we admit that we see, and we recognize that we think this or that, but how we see or how we think we know not."[58] In defense of the skeptics against the criticism of the dogmatists, it is said that, "[The skeptics] do not deny that we see. 'We admit the apparent fact,' they say, without admitting that it really is what it appears to be."[59] Accordingly, the problem is not whether or not there is at least one entity in the world but with what degree of certainty we know a concrete entity of a specific kind.

The first set of passages to be considered is taken from St. Augustine, who first formulates the view corresponding to "(V3P1)." In his work *On Free Choice of the Will,* he introduces the following questions:

> Augustine: Let us take up our search in the following order, if you will. First, how is it proved [*manifestum*] that God exists? Second, are all things whatsoever, insofar as they are good, from God? Finally, is free will to be counted as a good? When we have answered these questions, it will be quite clear, I think, whether free will was rightly given. Therefore, to start at the beginning with the most obvious, I will ask you first whether you yourself exist. Are you, perhaps, afraid that you are being deceived by my questioning? But if you did not exist, it would be impossible for you to be deceived.[60]

From thinking, such as doubting, which is incorrigible, he deduces the existence of an agent and a thought. Perhaps the argument supporting this rather sketchy deduction assumes that the following premises are true: (i) I cannot doubt that I am doubting, (ii) doubting must be an event, (iii) all events presuppose a substance, and a mental event (e.g., doubting) presupposes the existence of the substance, i.e., myself. In this passage the argument is used specifically to affirm God's existence; in a celebrated quotation from *The True Religion,* he notes,

> If you do not grasp what I say and doubt whether it is true, at least make up your mind whether you have any doubts. If it is certain that you indeed have doubts, inquire whence that certainty.[61]

Augustine does not explicitly assert here that there is a person who entertains doubts; he asserts however that the experience of doubting is certain. He wishes to show here that the result is a truth which we experience, as is evident from the contiguous passage:

> Every one who knows that he has doubts knows with certainty something that is true, namely that he doubts. He is certain, therefore, about a truth.[62]

The truth, however, is the fact that he doubts, which, according to the passages concerning the freedom of the will, signifies that the agent exists. Another set of passages could be cited from the *Meditations* of Descartes, where he concludes that he exists because he doubts. In this vein, Descartes asserts, "I am. I exist; that is certain.", continuing, "For the present I am admitting only what is necessarily true: so 'I am' precisely refers only to a conscious being (*cogitans*)."[63] Sufficient discussion about Descartes' position exists in the philosophical literature which shows the relevance of his philosophy for the support of "(V3P1)."[64]

Ibn Sīnā's celebrated argument of the flying man manifests the same pattern.

> Let us suppose that one of us is created in an instant, and created perfect. But his eyes are blindfolded and cannot see any external objects. He is created floating in the air, or rather in the void, so that the resistance of the air which he might feel, does not affect him. His members are separated, and therefore do not meet or touch one another. Then he reflects and asks himself if his own existence is proved. Without any hesitation he would reply that he exists, although he could not prove the existence of his feet or his hand, of his entrails, his heart or his brains, or any exterior thing; but he would nevertheless affirm that he exists, without establishing the fact that he has length, breadth or thickness.[65]

In this passage, ibn Sīnā observes that epistemically the knowledge of his existence as a nonphysical entity or the nonphysical aspect of himself as prior to the knowledge of other entities. Moreover, in every one of the passages we quoted about the priority of "existence" or of "being," ibn Sīnā assumes that either the soul (*nafs*) or the intelligence (*ʿaql, khirad*), which receives these a priori truths, exists. Consequently either ibn Sīnā assumes that the soul or the intelligence aspect of persons exists as the receiver of a priori truths or he states explicitly that we know the existence of the soul aspects of ourselves a priori. In sum we found passages in the works of Augustine, Descartes, and ibn Sīnā which shed light on the first premise. Whereas ibn Sīnā places the discussion in a context other than the argument for God's existence, Augustine and Descartes relate the argument of the self directly to God's existence. Consequently we cannot assert that ibn Sīnā uses "(V3P1)" as a direct premise of an ontological argument; however, we can assert that he knows incorrigibly his own existence in a phenomenal a priori mode.

The second premise, "(V3P2)" has been variously shaped in the writings of numerous philosophers, to whose formulation of this premise we shall attend so as to clarify our argument.

Returning to Augustine's discussion of the fact that he exists because he cannot doubt that he doubts, we observe that he buttresses his argument as follows. Conceptual analysis demonstrates that only a living agent can doubt. (The step calls obviously for an a priori mode of knowledge, because the problem concerns the meaning of the words "agent" and "being alive" as applied to an entity which can doubt.) Next, Augustine notes that of all the faculties, such as external and internal senses and the understanding, reason is the best epistemic state, as it includes other states while it is not determined by them. (Here again the analysis is a prior.) Finally, Augustine comments that the eternal truths known by reason, e.g., mathematics, are necessary, immutable, and eternal. (This step is also a priori.) From experiencing these truths, Augustine deduces that God exists. He asserts, accordingly, "You granted, moreover, that if I showed you something higher than our minds, you would admit, assuming that nothing existed which was still higher, that God exists. I accepted your condition and said that it was enough to show this. For if there is something more excellent than truth, this is God. If there is not, then truth itself is God. Whether or not truth is God, you cannot deny that God exists, and this was the question with which we agreed to deal."[66] Later in the same paragraph he notes that in addition to religious faith, the existence of God can be proved by a tenuous form of reason. The most intuitive insight Augustine reveals concerning the relationship between the self and the divine lies embedded in his celebrated assertion in his *Soliloquies,* "God and the Soul, that is what I desire to know." When asked, "Nothing more?", he answered, "Nothing whatever."[67] Augustine's inquiring mind does not fail to note a special affinity between himself and God, as is evident from *The Confessions,* especially in two chapters entitled "That the God Whom We Invoke is in Us; and We in Him," and "Everywhere God Wholly Filleth All Things, but Neither Heaven nor Earth Contain Him." Augustine asks, "And how shall I call upon my God—my God and my Lord? For when I call on Him I ask Him to come into me."[68] As he ponders further, he feels himself related to God by being uplifted and filled with the Divine.

> And when Thou art poured forth on us, Thou art not cast down, but we are uplifted; nor art Thou dissipated, but we are drawn together. But, as Thou fillest all things, dost Thou fill them with Thy whole self, or, as even all things cannot altogether contain Thee, do they contain a part; and do all at once contain the same part? Or has each its own proper part—the greater more, the smaller less? Or is it that Thou art wholly everywhere whilst nothing altogether contains Thee?[69]

Evidently, Augustine's writings contain not only clarifications of the third version of the ontological argument, but indicate also the significance of the interrelationship between the knowledge of his self-soul and God, topics embedded in the first two premises of the third version of this argument.

In turning to the most celebrated case of defense of "(V3P2)," found in Descartes' third meditation, we observe that in spite of the phenomenal a priori mode by which he knows that he exists as a mental substance, he has a better knowledge of God's existence than of his own existence by means of a discursive a priori mode, as is evinced in the passage below:

> I must not think that my conception of the infinite has come about, not through a proper idea, but by a denial of the finite—as I conceive of rest and darkness by way of the denial of motion and light; on the contrary I clearly understand that therefore in a way my primary concept (*perceptionem*) is rather of the infinite than of the finite—rather of God, than of myself. How could I understand my doubting and desiring—that is, my lacking something and not being altogether perfect—if I had no idea of a more perfect being as a standard by which to recognize my own defect?[70]

We should recall that Descartes does not use the term "infinite" loosely, for in principle XXVI of his *Principles of Philosophy,* he repeats Aristotle's objection to the notion of the actual infinite.[71] Nevertheless, in principle XXVII, he consciously departs from such strictures by permitting the application of "infinity" to God:

> "We shall use the term *indefinitely great (indefinita)* rather than *infinite* in order to confine the term *infinite* to God; only as regards to God is it a matter of our not merely failing to apprehend any limit in any respect, but positively knowing there are none. We have no such positive knowledge that other things are in some respect unlimited; we merely make the negative admission that, if they have limits, at any rate they are not discoverable by us."[72]

Consequently, Descartes distinguishes between our epistemic state of knowing God as an infinite entity, of knowing Him absolutely, and the difficulties attendant upon the application of the term "infinite" to others. The most important distinction between God and others, however, is a metaphysical distinction, stated in principle LI:

> "We can mean by *substance* nothing other than a thing existing in such a manner that it has need of no other thing in order to exist. There can indeed be only one substance conceived as needing absolutely no other thing in order to exist; namely, God. We can see that all other substances are able to exist only by means of God's cooperation."[73]

As Descartes' ontological argument as stated in the fifth meditation is well known, it is omitted here. Passages in this meditation coming after the formulation of the ontological argument specifically illustrate Descartes' sense of knowing God as a source of the world's dependence, e.g., "But now [. . .] I have discerned that God exists, and have understood at the same time that everything depends on him, and that he is not deceitful."[74] Descartes notes that the essence of God is no other than existence. That he considers this theme to be a primary discursive idea is evident from the following passage:

> For what is intrinsically more obvious than that the Supreme Being is; that God, to whose essence alone existence belongs, exists? And though it took careful consideration for me to see this, yet I am as certain of it as I am of anything else that appears most certain; not only that, but I can further see that the certainty of anything else depends on this, so that apart from this no perfect knowledge is ever possible.[75]

According to Descartes, first one knows "(V3P1)," then "(V3P2)" and finally a stronger version of "(V3C)" specifying that God exists as that infinite entity through which one's own finite aspects can be understood.

The Cartesian view of God as the only infinite entity has been taken up in various senses and from various vantage points. Leibniz, for example, comments on the idea of the absolute infinite in his critique of Locke's doctrines on "Innate Ideas," in *New Essays Concerning Human Understanding*. As vehicle he has chosen the dialogue whose first participant, "Philalethes," proceeds to discard the idea of absolute infinite, whereas the second, "Theophilus," concludes by asserting that there is an (innate) idea of an infinite which is a true idea, an idea which can be applied ". . . as an absolute or attribute without limits which exists in reference to *eternity,* in the necessity of the existence of God, without depending upon parts and without the notion of being formed by addition in time."[76]

Another set of passages is found in the works of Spinoza, who introduces the notion of God into his *Ethics,* defining God as an infinite entity, noting that "finiteness is in truth partly negation, and infinitude absolute affirmation of existence of some kind. . . ."[77] He proves, moreover, the existence of God in several ways; after giving an a priori proof based upon the notion that God's essence is existence, he proceeds to explain the matter only with an a posteriori proof, not without adding, however, that an a priori proof can be established on the same grounds, and concluding, ". . . of no existence can we be more sure than of the existence of the Being absolutely infinite or perfect, that is to say God."[78]

Before focusing on the thematic contours in terms which ibn Sīnā utilizes "(V3P2)," we shall approach the genesis of the argument by turning to the contemporary remarks of two scholars who have discussed ibn Sīnā's Corpus in the context of mysticism.

In his classic work *Mysticism Sacred and Profane,* R. C. Zaehner differentiates between two kinds of mysticism: "Monism" and "Theism." Whereas one of the essential features of "monism" is its method of "integration," the essential feature of "theism" is its method of "isolation." By way of clarifying "monism," Zaehner remarks, "The nature mystic identifies himself with the whole of Nature, and in his exalted moments sees himself as being one with Nature and as having passed beyond good and evil."[79] Of a version of isolation, Zaehner states: "It [isolation] holds that man's spirit is an immortal, immutable and passionless monad, and that neither the body nor the reason, nor what Aristotle and the Muslim philosophers call the lower soul, really belong to him. He is essentially other than they, and his eternal destiny is to rid himself for ever of the whole psycho-physical apparatus. This is the reverse of integration. There is no vision of the unity of man with Nature, nor is it a case of this vision being utilized to build up the whole man."[80] In commenting on ibn Sīnā, Zaehner points out, "Avicenna, and following him most of the Muslim writers in psychology, distinguished two distinct parts in the human soul—the higher or rational soul which naturally strives upward and whose goal is the acquisition of knowledge of God, and the lower soul usually called the *nafs* or 'self' which is tripartite, being composed of the imagination, anger, and lust. These three are indissolubly attached to the rational soul, and no escape from them is possible or even desirable during this life."[81] Subsequently Zaehner's statement is actually corroborated by *Ishārāt* (IV, 125). Zaehner quotes relevant passages from ibn Sīnā's *Ḥayy ibn Yaqẓān,* which disclose that ibn Sīnā recommends accepting the lower faculties in recognition of the disaster that may result if one attempts to suppress them altogether. Zaehner reaches the conclusion, "Thus, for Avicenna as for Jung, integration of the personality was man's first aim on earth, and his lower soul does not seem to differ greatly from Jung's collective unconscious."[82] In several representative cases of Islamic mysticism Zaehner examines, there is no question but that a person is not only essentially related to God as implied by "(V3P2)" but that the statements uttered suggest an identity of persons with God. In describing these cases, Zaehner (an adherent of religious theism), follows a roundabout interpretation of the passage in question until he finally labels the entire tradition as confusing and derivative. Nevertheless, a strong support for the presence of "(V3P2)" in the Islamic tradition, to which ibn Sīnā belongs, is offered by the quotations Zaehner selects, such as the following:

> This is probably what Junayd, the founder of the 'middle' school of Muslim mysticism, meant when he spoke of his ecstatic (one is tempted to say 'manic') predecessor, Abū Yazīd of Biṣṭām, as having reached the first stage only on the mystic's path when he made such astonishing statements as 'I am He', and 'Glory be to me, how great is my glory', implying thereby that he was actually identical with the Deity.[83]

Zaehner sides of course with Junayd who to assert that Abū Yazīd's utterances are only a way of talking about a union permissible according to religious laws, rather than the problem of identity, or about Ghazālī's designation of such states as mystical intoxications. Nevertheless, even Ghazālī acknowledges this to be a very interesting description of mysticism which corresponds closely to "(V3P2)". Ghazālī notes accordingly,

> The mystics, after their ascent to the heavens of Reality (Truth), agree that they saw nothing in existence except God. Some of them attained this state through discursive reasoning, others reached it by savouring it and experiencing it.[84]

He continues as follows,

> Nothing was left to them [the mystics] but God. They became intoxicated with an intoxication in which their reason collapsed. One of them [Hallāj] said, 'I am God (the Truth.)' Another [Abū Yazīd] said, 'Glory be to me! How great is my glory,' while another said, 'Within my robe is naught but God.'[85]

Ghazālī goes on to show how "identity" actually refers to a union in this context, disclosing at the same time that there are truths in these sayings which he was not at liberty to reveal.[86]

Evidently, according to Zaehner's scheme, ibn Sīnā's position supports "(V3P2)" in the following manner: (i) ibn Sīnā's normative psychology is the foundation of an ethical system which is remarkably similar to that of nature mystics who consider man's essential task to be the recognition of his unity with nature—God, a unity that is to be achieved by integration; and (ii) ibn Sīnā does not stand in isolation but is part of a Muslim tradition embracing many mystics who have claimed an identity with God [Zaehner would prefer "nature" to "God"] and affirmed that knowledge of one's self-soul leads to knowledge of God.

J. Houben is another scholar to claim that there is a difference between what he designates as true "religious" mysticism and the naturalistic mysticism of ibn Sīnā.[87] He points out that inherent in ibn Sīnā's depiction of the chain of being connecting God and man is a non-religious monism.[88] In relating the (mystical) knowledge of God (*maʿrifat Allāh*) to ibn Sīnā, Houben notes,

> The fact which glares into our eyes is that the highest knowledge and beatitude of man is of the same nature as the usual human knowledge, though pitched to a higher degree. The highest degree, this *maʿrifat Allāh* consists therein that the mystic firstly sees in his own soul as in a mirror the intelligibles which are traces of the Divine Truth, and further in the higher stage it perceives as reflected object, God's Truth Itself.[89]

Houben mentions that this knowledge of God, received from one's own soul, is for ibn Sīnā another case of intellectual contemplation, as the soul has no (will) for God but to be reflected like a polished mirror.[90]

It appears then that Houben's account corroborates our proposal that there is some evidence that ibn Sīnā supports "(V3P2)."

Having established the nature of the support of our position, let us now discuss a few important passages in ibn Sīnā's texts which specifically disclose his adherence to "(V3P2)."

At the outset we wish to establish that in no single passage does ibn Sīnā present one concise proof with "(V3P1)," "(V3P2)," and "(V3C)" following each other in sequence. The first premise, "(V3P1)," occurs only in his psychology, but as we have shown, nowhere does ibn Sīnā entertain doubts about the existence of at least one actual entity, for time and again he refers to the fact that existence (*wujūd*) is an obvious primary datum for the soul (*nafs*) and for the intelligence (*ʿaql*). The problem of doubting the existence of entities is not the problem of ibn Sīnā the medieval philosopher. The second premise emerges out of the fundamental metaphysical doctrines designated as (ibn Sīnā 4) and (ibn Sīnā 5) which we shall illustrate as follows: (Ibn Sīnā 4): The Necessary Existent is not a Substance (*Jawhar*).

If the knowledge of one's own existence is to be essentially related to the knowledge of the existence of the Necessary Existent, certain conditions must be absent. For instance, if the individual existent and the Necessary Existent are substances of such difference that no total description of the individual in the Leibnizian sense will involve a reference to the Necessary Existent, then the individual will need something in addition to himself to obtain knowledge of the Necessary Existent. Consequently, both the Necessary Existent and the individual could not be two substances totally independent of each other. But in his metaphysical writings, as has been shown in our previous studies, ibn Sīnā (i) asserts explicitly that the necessary Existent is not a substance (*Dānish Nāma*, pp. 56–57); (ii) affirms that certain features, e.g., "genus," "differentia," "having no subject," which apply to ordinary substances, do not apply to the Necessary Existent (e.g., *alShifā'*, p. 347; *alIshārāt,* III, 53; *al-Najāt,* pp. 226‡27); (iii) explicitly rejects the notion that the Necessary Existent is a substance proper, to which one can apply "substantiality" and merely mean thereby that it is not in a subject (*al-Shifā'*, p. 348, p. 367; *al-Najāt,* p. 231); and (iv) lists substances but never includes among such a list the Necessary Existent (*al-Najāt,* p. 208; *Dānish Nāma,* p. 16; *al-Shifā'*, p. 60). In contradistinction to this view stands that of Aristotle, who regards God (*ho theos*) as an *ousia,* a term usually translated as substance, which ibn Sīnā identifies with *jawhar.*[91]

(Ibn Sīnā 5) The Concept of the World is Essentially Contained in the Concept of the Necessary Existent.

Going beyond our attempt to ascertain how knowledge of ourselves implies knowledge of this particular nonsubstance type of entity, we note that ibn Sīnā's metaphysical system contains principles which make the specification of the concept of all actual entities dependent upon certain features of the Necessary Existent, such that our knowledge of actual entities implies concurrent knowledge of the Necessary Existent.

The essential features of reality (*ḥaqq*), particularity (*khuṣūṣiyya*), necessity (*wājibī*), and even the demonstrable reason (*burhān*) for all things are found in the notion of the Necessary Existent as it is portrayed by ibn Sīnā. For example, at the beginning of a chapter entitled, "that the Necessary Existent is a reality in all the meanings of reality," ibn Sīnā asserts that in its essence (*dhāt*) the Necessary Existent is absolute reality and truth (*ḥaqq*), for the essence of each thing (*shai'*) is the instantiation (particularization—*khuṣūṣiyya*) of its existence by the agent of its actualization (*yathbat*). There is no reality (*ḥaqq*) which is more real than the Necessary Existent, and a belief in its existence (*wujūd*) is truthful according to ibn Sīnā (*al-Shifā'*, p. 356; *al-Najāt,* p. 229).

In *al-Shifā'* (p. 356) ibn Sīnā repeats verbatim the assertion made in *al-Najāt* that the Necessary Existent is reality (*ḥaqq*) and that the reality of everything is the particularization (*khuṣūṣiyya*) which instantiates (*yathbata*) that entity; he affirms again that this is the most true belief one can hold. Prior to this assertion he lists terms related to the Necessary Existent by privation and proceeds to acknowledge that there is no demonstration (*burhān*) for the Necessary Existent, while the latter is necessary to the demonstration of other entities (*al-Shifā',* p. 354). In ensuing passages he identifies the Necessary Existent with absolute perfection (*fawq al-tamām*), for all entities flow (*fāḍil*) and emanate (*fa'iḍ*) from it. It is further identified with existence (*huw al-wujūd*) or the perfection of existence (*al-kamāl al-wujūd*). Existence is a good (*khair*) and the Necessary Existent, as the perfection of existence, is the Good of all existence (*al-Shifā'*, p. 356). The notion that the Necessary existent is the absolutely perfect entity is mentioned also in the *Dānish Nāma* (pp. 79–80) following the account of the emanation of first entities. Entities are either imperfect (*nāqiṣ*), perfect (*tamām*), or absolutely perfect (*fawq al-tamām*). While the imperfect entity cannot exist by itself, and while the perfect entity can and does exist by itself, the absolutely perfect entity alone can exist by itself and be at the same time the source of the realization of all other entities. In this sense, ibn Sīnā's argument implies that as an absolutely perfect entity, the Necessary Existent is without will, since will is analyzed by knowledge and acts as the source from which the world emanates. However, as imperfect entities (e.g., in Descartes' sense of knowing himself as a finite entity), our understanding of our own realization must be due to knowledge of the existence of an absolutely perfect entity.

This essential dependence relation is corroborated in the context of many other themes fundamental to ibn Sīnā's philosophy. Two such themes are two aspects of causality which are often overlooked when the medieval thinkers emphasize a new dimension of the notion of the final cause in their description of the relationship between persons and the ultimate being. (i) As the first sense of a cause ibn Sīnā establishes the beholder, operative for instance in the case of the house and the laws governing the element's physics as well as in the case of elements which compose the entity in question (*Dānish Nāma,* p. 50). The cause, ibn Sīnā repeats, is that which necessitates (*wājib*) the persistence (*istādan*) of the entity in question, namely, the house. Now the Necessary Existent appears repeatedly in ibn Sīnā's texts (*Dānish Nāma,* 81; *al-Shifā',* 363; *al-Najāt,* 249) as the knower of the Good universal order (*al-Niẓām al-khair kullī*) in existents, whose will for the realization of the actual world is identical with its knowledge. Consequently, in the ibn Sīnian system, through its knowledge of the laws, the Necessary Existent is the beholder and the cause of the persistence of actual entities. Consequently, a discursive a priori knowledge of ourselves, if it includes the knowledge of the cause of our persistence, includes also a knowledge of the existence of the Necessary Existent. This doctrine, moreover, is embedded in the Spinozistic axiom, "The knowledge (*cognitio*) of an effect depends upon and involves the knowledge of the cause."[92]

(ii) A cause can also be a cause of perfection (*kamāl*), depicted for instance in the *Risāla fī l-ʿishq,*[93] where all entities are specified in terms of love, which leads them to complete their own perfection; here the ultimate perfection is identified with The Good (*al-Khair*) [*ʿishq,* 21 (*khair maḥḍ*)], an absolute entity, which many passages identify with the Necessary Existent [*Dānish Nāma,* 80 (*khair*); *al-Najāt,* 229 (*khair maḥḍ*); *al-Shifā',* 355 (*khair*)]. Accordingly, in the normative sense, our own concept of the perfect self implies the notion of the absolutely perfect entity as the cause of our completion—namely the Necessary Existent.

Among the positions held on this issue is one that would make the conception of the Necessary Existent dependent on the conception of what emanates from it. Since features of the Necessary Existent include absolute perfection and being the cause of the realization of others (i.e., of the actual contingent world), a complete conception of the Necessary Existent will include the conception of entities in the actual world. Perhaps it is for this reason that Spinoza specifically begins with the following definition of substance. "By substance I understand that which is in itself and is conceived through itself; in other words, that, the conception of which does not need the conception of another being from which it must be formed."[94] Measured by this concept of substance, the ibn Sīnian version of the human soul-person is not a substance because its formulation is ultimately defined by the Necessary Existent which is its ultimate cause. On the other hand, the Necessary Existent and the entire actual realm form one substance because of their interdependence through the various features of the Necessary Existent (e.g., "Absolute perfection," "being the beholder of the world," and "being the ultimate cause of the completion or the perfection of each entity"). This position is actually upheld by Spinoza when the One substance, namely God, is identified with Nature; he asserts that a substance is necessarily infinite (Proposition VIII), and that apart from God, no substance can be conceived (Proposition XIV). As we already pointed out for Descartes, in the strictest sense of the concept of substance, there is actually one substance which Spinoza identifies with God when he asserts, "There can indeed be only one substance conceived as needing absolutely no other thing in order to exist; namely, God. We can see that all other substances are able to exist only by means of God's co-operation."[95]

Moreover, we have already had occasion to point out in another study that the Self is to be united with the Necessary Existent—a concept which appears confusing in a substance-event language interpretation of the ibn Sīnian system but becomes workable in a process-language interpretation of his system.[96] That a reference to the Necessary Existent is essentially embedded as an essential constituent of a person becomes manifest when one considers the Neoplatonic delineation of the mystical return, which is the undergirding of the ibn Sīnian system. In the *Dānish Nāma*, "*paiwand*" (union) describes how the ultimate happiness of a person lies in a union (*paiwand*) with the Necessary Existent (pp. 71–76). The term union (*ittiḥād, muttaḥid*) is used both in *al-Najāt* and in the *Risāla fi-l-ʿishq*. In the former it designates the aim of the rational soul to be united (*muttaḥid*) with the beloved (*al-Najāt,* p. 293); in the latter, *ittiḥād* is used by mystics to refer to a means of attaining perfection by approximating that of the absolute Good (The Necessary Existent) (*ʿishq,* p. 22).

(iii) In *al-Ishārāt* (III, 53) there is another striking passage in which an equally affirmative feature of the Necessary Existent emerges. Here ibn Sīnā asserts that the only way in which one can indicate or point to (*ishāra*) the Necessary Existent is by way of mystical intelligence (*al-ʾirfān al-ʿaqlī*).

But a close reading of his text fails to reveal any one passage in which he explicitly asserts that the soul does in fact preserve its individuality. In an interesting passage in *al-Ishārāt* he states that the rational soul (*al-ʿaql al-nāṭiqa*) does not become the soul of the active intelligence (*al-ʿaql al-faʿʿāl*), and notes specifically that it becomes connected (*ittiṣāl*) with the active intelligence (*al-Ishārāt,* p. 293).

In sum, it appears that a monistic system emerges in which the concept of the Necessary Existent is implied in the concept of every actual entity, that is, in the individual whose self-knowledge is phenomenal a priori, whereas the knowledge of the Necessary Existent is discursive a priori; Necessary Existence here is part of the complete description of the subject in the Leibnizian form.

Concluding Remarks

Evidently, several key passages in ibn sīnā's metaphysical texts, when carefully considered in the light of his fundamental philosophical doctrines, do in fact support the second version of the ontological argument. It is remarkable that no philosophical system which supports the ontological argument (e.g., those of Augustine, ibn Sīnā, Anselm, Descartes, Spinoza, Malcolm, and Taylor) can adequately respond to the devastating criticism by Hume and Kant of all ontological arguments. We deem these arguments logically unsatisfactory—valuable only for the pedagogical study of metaphysical concepts used in the argument itself.

Its logical inadequacy notwithstanding, a more important aspect of God's existence has yet to be "proven." We note with Augustine, and perhaps with many others, that the search for knowledge of God is closely tied to the quest for self-knowledge; both are considered to be primary objects of inquiry. Moreover, manh religiously inclined philosophers, e.g., H. D. Lewis, envision the so-called "infinite" basis of the "finite" self as the core of religious experience and reject the experiential significance of the ontological argument. In this vein Lewis notes that in religious experience ". . . wondering and stilled appreciation of finite facts . . . [have] an infinite or transcendent source. . . ."[97] Following such a train of thought, we explored the possibility of constructing an argument which takes account of the phenomena felt to be significant by those taking a religious perspective, but can be aligned, at the same time, with a systematic philosophical perspective. Accordingly, we depicted a third version of the ontological argument and clarified its premises by drawing on the works of well-known philosophers who have addressed themselves to the issues in question. We demonstrated, moreover, that ibn Sīnā's metaphysical system contains doctrines of great consequence to the depiction of the premises of the argument under consideration. In spite of its "mystical monism," which is in agreement with the views of many Muslim mystics as pointed out by Zaehner, Houben, and our own previous inquiry, ibn Sīnā's monism is unacceptable to the devout on account of its naturalistic presentation of the world which conflicts with "religion" in the sense we have specified.[98] Moreover, we have rejected the notion of essence, the assumption about the predictability of existence, and the significance attached to the application of "necessity" to "things" on the grounds that they are philosophically inadequate.

In concluding we turn once more to Augustine's quest, a quest he limited to obtaining knowledge of "God" and "his own self-soul" and to the answer given in an old Arabic proverb saying, "He who knows himself, knows his God," as well as to the answer given by the mystic Ḥallāj, "I am God-Reality." Obviously neither Augustine nor contemporary religious philosophers such as Zaehner and Lewis would find these answers acceptable.

Notwithstanding the clarification of ibn Sīnā's texts and the philosophical analysis of a few concepts proffered in this essay, we have little to offer except to note that all three forms of the ontological argument fail—the first two being at least logically inadequate, and the third being unacceptable to religious systems, its mystical insights not withstanding. But such a failure should not be viewed as a shortcoming—for a legitimate application of philosophy to theology is not to justify the dogmas of the latter, but to analyze its significant problems openly and to disclose by such probing whether a rational reconstruction of a phenomenon which is important for religious experience is found to be in conflict with traditionally approved religious maxims.

Notes

1. *The Many-Faced-Argument,* ed. by John H. Hick and Arthur C. McGill, New York: Macmillan, 1967, p. vii.

2. *The Ontological Argument,* ed. Alvin Plantinga, New York: Doubleday, 1965. (Hereinafter all references to this text will be cited as *OA* and will be preceded by the name of the individual contributor.) R. Taylor, *OA,* vii.

3. *Philosophy of Religion,* ed. George L. Abernethy and Thomas A. Lanford, New York: Macmillan, 1969, p. 170.

4. *St. Anselm: Basic Writings,* trans. S. N. Deane and intro. C. Hartshorne, La Salle: Open Court, 1963, p. 1. (Hereinafter *St. Anselm*).

5. Originally appeared in *The Philosophical Review,* LXIX, no. 1 (January 1960), 41–62. We shall make reference to its printed version in *OA.*

6. Malcolm, *OA,* 136.

7. For the rejection of the first version, see Malcolm, *OA,* 140; for his defense of the second version, see *OA,* 141–157. In a counterattack on Kant's criticism of "existence as a predicate" doctrine, Malcolm states, "To these remarks [Kant's] the reply is that when the concept of God is correctly understood one sees that one cannot 'reject the subject.' 'There is no God' is seen to be a necessary false statement" (*Ibid.,* p. 148).

8. P. Morewedge, "Ibn Sīnā (Avicenna) and Malcolm and the Ontological Argument," *The Monist* 54, no. 2 (April 1970): 234–49.

9. For example, Anselm states, "And, indeed, we believe that Thou art a being than which nothing greater can be conceived," and proceeds to argue against the objection of the fool who said in his heart that there is no God, concluding, "Hence, even the fool is convinced that something exists in understanding, at least, than which nothing greater can be conceived. For, when he hears of this, he understands it." *St. Anselm,* 7–8. Another classical occurrence of this theme is in the fifth meditation of Descartes, where he states, "I assuredly find in myself the idea of a God—of a supremely perfect being—no less than the idea of a figure or a number" (*Descartes, Philosophical Writings,* trans. and ed. E. Anscombe and P. T. Geach with intro. A. Koyre, London, 1963, p. 103). (Hereinafter quoted as *Descartes, A. and G.* followed by the page number from this text.) There are at least two forms of this first premise: a syntactical one which defines the notion of God as that which is the most perfect being and an epistemic one which states that there is an idea of God in our minds than which nothing greater can be conceived. The syntactical version assumes that the concept is not logically contradictory; the epistemic version is rather vague, for the ability to conceive an idea is a psychological matter, which varies from person to person and cannot serve as a universal a priori truth.

10. Anselm argues, "And assuredly that, than which nothing greater can be conceived, cannot exist in the understanding alone. For suppose it exists in the understanding alone: then it can be conceived to exist in reality; which is greater." *St. Anselm,* p. 8.

11. *New Essays Concerning Human Understanding by Gottfried Wilhelm Leibniz,* trans. A. Gideon Langley, La Salle: Open Court, 1949, includes one version of Leibniz' objection. He notes, "It [the ontological argument] is not a paralogism, but it is an imperfect demonstration, which assumes something that must still be proved in order to render it mathematically evident; that is, it is tacitly assumed that this idea of all-great or all-perfect being is possible, and implies no contradiction. And it is already something that by this remark it is proved that, *assuming that God is possible, he exists,* which is the privilege of the divinity alone. . . . The other argument of Descartes, which undertakes to prove the existence of God because of the idea of him in our soul, and must have come from the same origin, is still less conclusive. For in the first place this argument has this defect, in common with the preceding, that it assumes that there is in us such an idea, *i.e.* that God is possible" (p. 504.) (Hereinafter we shall quote this text by "Leibniz, *New Essays,*" followed by the appropriate page number.)

12. Kant states that, " 'being' is obviously not a real predicate; that is, it is not a concept of something which could be added to the concept of a thing. It is merely the positing of a thing, or of certain determinations, as existing in themselves. Logically, it is merely the copula of a judgment. The proposition, 'God is omnipotent' contains two concepts, each of which is its object—God and omnipotence. The small word 'is' adds no new predicate, but only serves to posit the predicate *in its relation* to the subject. If, now, we take the subject (God) with all its predicates (among which is omnipotence), and say 'God is', or 'There is a God', we attach no new predicate to the concept of God, but only posit the subject in itself with all its predicates, and indeed posit it as being an object

that stands in relation to my concept" (*Immanuel Kant's Critique of Pure Reason,* trans. N. Kemp Smith, London: Macmillan, 1953, pp. 504–505).

13. Hume's basic premise is that "all the perceptions of the mind are of two kinds, *viz.,* impressions and ideas, which differ from each other only in their different degrees of force and vivacity. Our ideas are copy'd from our impressions, and represent them in all their parts" (*A Treatise of Human Nature,* ed. L. A. Selby-Bigge, London, 1964, p. 96). A similar passage is found in *Enquiries Concerning the Human Understanding and Concerning the Principles of Morals,* ed. L. A. Selby-Bigge, London, 1955, p. 18. In the *Enquiry* he divides "all objects of human reason" into relations of ideas and matters of fact (p. 25). Subsequently he states that ". . . nor can our reason, unassisted by experience, ever draw any inference concerning real existence and matters of fact" (p. 27). Since existence types-of-statements are matters and a priori types-of-statements, e.g., "(V1P1)" and "(V1P2,)" are claimed by "reason alone," then the entire argumentation is not legitimate, according to Hume.

14. Hume states, "Our ideas reach no further than our experience: We have no experience of divine attributes and operations: I need not conclude my syllogism: You can draw the inference yourself" (*Dialogues Concerning Natural Religion,* ed. N. Kemp-Smith, New York, 1947, pp. 142–43). Consequently, Hume questions the claim that we have an idea of a most perfect being. In this vein Hume argues against Descartes' claim of calling an "innate idea" of a deity the source of power, "For if every idea be deriv'd from an impression, the idea of a deity proceeds from the same origin; and if no impression, either of sensation or reflection, implies any force or efficacy, 'tis equally impossible to discover or even imagine any such active principle in the deity" (*Treatise,* p. 160). Here Hume hints that the idea of a deity must be also derived from impressions and cannot be postulated as the source of power. The previous quotations question whether there is an impression of a divine attribute. In another passage in the *Treatise,* Hume attends to "existence" as applied to a deity, saying that, "Thus when we affirm, that God is existent, we simply form the idea of such a being, as he is represented to us; nor is the existence, which we attribute to him, conceiv'd by a particular idea, which we join to the idea of his other qualities, and can again separate and distinguish from them. But I go farther; and not content with asserting, that the conception of the existence of any object is no addition to the simple conception of it, I likewise maintain, that the belief of the existence joins no new ideas to those, which compose the idea of the object. When I think of God, when I think of him as existent, and when I believe him to be existent, my idea of him neither encreases nor diminishes" (*Treatise,* p. 94). Consequently for Hume, God cannot be defined in terms of a source of power or as any entity of which we have no impression; merely postulating that "God exists" does not add any reality to God; and, moreover, at least according to one of the three figures in *The Dialogues Concerning Natural Religion,* we have no impression of an attribute of God.

15. *Malcolm, OA,* 140.

16. *Ibid.,* 147.

17. See P. Morewedge, "Ibn Sīnā (Avicenna), Malcolm, and the Ontological Argument."

18. Hume asserts that "The contrary of every matter of fact is still possible; because it can never imply a contradiction, and is conceived by the mind with the same facility and distinctness, as if ever so conformable to reality" (*Enquiry,* p. 25).

19. Kant states, "But if, on the other hand, we admit that all existential propositions are synthetic, how can we profess to maintain that the predicate of existence cannot be

rejected without contradiction? This is a feature which is found only in analytic propositions, and is indeed precisely what constitutes their analytic character" (*Critique of Pure Reason,* p. 504).

20. See P. Morewedge, "Philosophical Analysis and ibn Sīnā's 'Essence-Existence' Distinction," *Journal of the American Oriental Society* 92: 3 (July-September 1973), 425–435.

21. The *Dānish Nāma-i ʿalʾī (Ilhāiyyāt),* ed. M. Moʿīn, Tehran, 1952. Page references to this text are taken from my own translation of this work in P. Morewedge, *The Metaphysica of Avicenna (ibn Sīnā),* London: Routledge and Kegan Paul; New York: Columbia University Press, 1973. (Hereinafter all references to this text will be cited as *Dānish Nāma,* followed by the page number taken from my text.)

22. *Al-Najāt,* Cairo: Muḥyī al-Dīn al-Kurdī Press, 1938.

23. *Al-Shifāʾ: Al-Ilahiyyāt (La Metaphysique),* ed. G. Anawati, M. Y. Mussa, S. Dunya, and S. Zayed, 2 vols., Cairo, 1960. (Hereinafter all references to this text will be cited as *Al-Shifāʾ*).

24. *Al-Ishārāt wa-l-Tanbīhāt,* ed. S. Dunya, 4 vols., Cairo, 1960.

25. N. Rescher, *Studies in Arabic Philosophy,* Pittsburgh: University of Pittsburgh Press, 1966, p. 73. An adequate symbolization of the ibn Sīnian system is difficult if not impossible to obtain. If we let "a" be any individual first substance and "Φ" a genuine predicate, then if "Φa" is true, then "E!a"—meaning that affirming a genuine predicate of a subject—implies existence of the subject. Consequently no affirmative predication can be made of nonactualized entities like unicorns or "the king of France." There is no difficulty in this part of the theory. However, then we note that no adequate symbolism for the Necessary Existent can be found, for if it is not an individual substance we must conclude that the same sign cannot be applied to individuals, such as Zayd, and The Necessary Existent. See also Aristotle, *Analytica Posteriora,* 71a20–23. All references to Aristotle will be cited from *The Works of Aristotle,* ed. W. D. Ross, 12 vols., London, 1908–52, unless differently indicated in the notes.

26. Aristotle mentions in *Analytica Posteriora* 71a10–13, "The preexistent knowledge required is of two kinds. In some cases admission of the fact must be assumed, in others comprehension of the meaning of the terms used, and sometimes both assumptions are essential." The passage cited indicates that in each science one begins with a set of assumptions concerning the existence of a subject matter for the inquiry in question. In metaphysics, it is not immediately assumed that "The Necessary Existent" is apprehended prior to any other notion, but since we comprehend "existence" (*wujūd*) and "necessity" (*wājibī*) as primary terms, metaphysical analysis teaches us that "the Necessary Existent" is a meaningful notion which has certain features—the most important of which is that the Necessary Existent exists. In modern axiomatical methods a similar procedure is adopted. For example, Carnap notes that the axioms and theorems of an axiomatic system, AS, assume certain constants (names) as "axiomatic constants." Then he continues. "Some of them [the axiomatic constants of the AS] are given without definitions; they are called *the axiomatic primitive constants of the AS.* All other axiomatic constants are introduced by definitions on the basis of the primitives" (*Introduction to Symbolic Language and Its Application,* tr. W. H. Meyer and J. Wilkinson, New York: Dover, 1958, p. 171). In the Carnapian sense, "being" or "existence" and modalities such as "necessity" are *axiomatic primitive constants.* Thereafter a rule of formation specifies that "being" and "existence" can legitimately be concatenated. Finally, theorems about "the Necessary Existent" are deduced. In this context the ontological argument in an a priori sense is deduced without the use of any nonprimitive and observable datum.

27. Gaunilon's objections to Anselm capitalize on the factual aspects of the argument (*St. Anselm,* p. 146). Accordingly on behalf of "the fool," Gaunilon makes a difference between the temporal state of "the having of an object in the understanding—and what is subsequent in time—namely, the understanding that an object exists; . . ." But an analytical formulation of the problem moves the argument into an atemporal aspect which is nonempirical, cf. the difference between an atemporal "category" and a temporal "schema" in Kant.

28. St. Thomas Aquinas, *Summa Theologiae,* vol. 2, New York: McGraw-Hill, 1964, 7.

29. *Ibid.,* pp. 5–6.

30. *Ibid.*

31. *Ibid.,* p. 9.

32. *Ibid.,* pp. 13–17.

33. P. Morewedge, "Ibn Sīnā's Concept of the Self," *Philosophical Forum,* IV, no. 1 (Fall 1972), 49–73.

34. *Ockham, Philosophical Writings,* ed. and trans. P. Boehner, London: Nelson, 1967, p. 90. Here Ockham points out that in one sense (*uno modo*), being (*ens*) is associated with a concept which is common to all things. Moody clarifies Ockham's position by pointing out that, "'being' (*ens*), and the transcendental terms convertible with it, cannot, as Aristotle proves, be a genus or in a genus." Moody continues by noting that for Ockham, ". . . the subject matter of metaphysics is "being," and there is no term or concept prior to or more universal than 'being'" (Ernest A. Moody, *The Logic of William of Ockham,* New York: Russell and Russell, 1965, p. 118).

35. *'Uyūn al-Ḥikma,* ed. A. Badawi, Cairo, 1952, p. 55.

36. The classical argument for the uniqueness of the Necessary Existent assumes that the Necessary Existent is a simple entity, for if it were a complex one, then its parts would be its causes. But it is the cause of itself; thus, it has no parts. Accordingly, if there were two different cases of the Necessary Existent, then each case would have an essential differentiating feature which would have to be accounted for in its essence. Now either each of these two differentiating features would come under the same essence, which would not make them two different features; or, each of these differentiating features would be unique and a necessary condition for the specification of each Necessary Existent—thereby the unique differentiating feature would be more necessary than the Necessary Existent as its necessary condition. Since these are the only two logical possibilities and both lead to absurdity, there cannot be two Necessary Existents. See *Dānish Nāma,* 54–55.

37. *Descartes, A. and G.,* p. 75.

38. Malcolm, *OA,* 142.

39. *The Philosophical Works of Descartes,* trans. E. S. Haldane and G. R. T. Ross, London: Cambridge University Press, 1968, II, 228.

40. *Ethics and On the Improvement of the Understanding,* ed. J. Gutmann, New York: Hafner, 1967, p. 41.

41. *Ibid.,* p. 60.

42. Ockham states, "The reason why the saints and others say that God is His very existence is this. God exists in such a manner that He cannot not exist; in fact, He exists necessarily; and He is not from something else." Ockham proceeds to show that there

is a difference between God and all other entities since only He *necessarily* exists. *Ockham,* pp. 94–95.

43. R. Taylor, *Metaphysics,* Englewood Cliffs: Prentice-Hall, 1963, p. 93.

44. *Critique of Pure Reason,* p. 502.

45. A symbolization of Taylor's argument is as follows: Let "M" be "modalities," "N" be "is necessary," "C" be "is contingent," and "I" be "is impossible." Then, using ordinary logical signs, we translate his argument as follows,
(x) (Nx v Cx v Ix)
∃xCx
~∃xIx
∴ ∃xNx
The scheme of this argument is obviously invalid. (Of course a more adequate symbolization of Taylor's argument would be in intentional logic, with modal signs which we shall not pursue here.) From the fact that "M" is divided into three classes and the second premise, it does not follow that the class corresponding to "(x) Nx" is not empty. In addition, the first premise assumes that "Necessity" can be applied to individuals—but in ibn Sīnā's system at least, the Necessary Existent is not an individual.

46. C. D. Broad, "Leibniz' *Predicate-in-Notion Principle* and Some of its Alleged Consequences," *Theoria,* XV (1949), rpt. in H. G. Frankfurt, ed., *Leibniz. A Collection of Critical Essays,* Modern Studies in Philosophy, Garden City, 1972, pp. 4–5.

47. *Ibid.*

48. Malcolm, *OA,* 153.

49. A. Plantinga, *God and Other Minds,* Ithaca: Cornell University Press, 1967, p. 26.

50. *Ibid.,* p. 64.

51. *Ibid.,* p. 271.

52. H. D. Lewis, *Our Experience of God,* London: George Allen and Unwin, 1959, p. 41.

53. *Ibid.,* p. 112.

54. *Ibid.,* p. 289.

55. *Royal Institute of Philosophy Lectures, Volume 2, 1967/8,* ed. G. N. A. Vesey et al., New York: St. Martin, 1969, p. 120.

56. *The Varieties of Religious Experience,* New York: Collier Books, 1971, p. 377.

57. *Descartes, A. and G.,* pp. 105–106.

58. *Diogenes Laertius. Lives of Great Philosophers,* ed. and trans. R. D. Hicks, vol. 2, The Loeb Classical Library, Cambridge: Harvard University Press, 1958, p. 515.

59. *Ibid.*

60. *On Free Choice of the Will,* trans. A. S. Benjamin and L. H. Hackstaff, Indianapolis, 1964, p. 40.

61. John A. Mourant, *An Introduction to the Philosophy of Saint Augustine,* University Park: Pennsylvania State University Press, 1964, p. 76.

62. *Ibid.*

63. *Descartes, A. and G.,* p. 69.

64. For example, we note a list of 3612 works on Descartes in G. Sebba, *Bibliographica Cartesiana,* Hague: Martinus Nijhoff, 1964, where only the literature from 1800 to 1960 is considered. The most illuminating modern work on the subject in question is by J. Hintikka, "*Cogito, Ergo Sum:* Inference or Performance," *The Philosophical Review,* LXXI, 1 (January 1962), 3–32.

65. See A. M. Goichon, "The Philosopher of Being," in *Avicenna Commemoration Volume,* Calcutta, 1956, 109–110.

66. Augustine, *Free Will,* p. 71.

67. *Soliloquies,* II, 7, i, in *Basic Writings of Saint Augustine,* ed. W. J. Jones, vol. 1, New York: Random House, 1948, p. 262.

68. *Ibid.*

69. *Ibid.*

70. *Descartes, A. and G.,* p. 85.

71. *Ibid.,* p. 186. Aristotle, *Physica,* Book III, B.

72. *Descartes, A. and G.,* pp. 186–87.

73. *Ibid.,* p. 192.

74. *Ibid.,* p. 107.

75. *Ibid.,* p. 106.

76. *New Essays Concerning Human Understanding,* p. 164.

77. *Ethics,* p. 45.

78. *Ibid.,* p. 50.

79. R. C. Zaehner, *Mysticism: Sacred and Profane,* London: Oxford University Press, 1967, p. 109.

80. *Ibid.,* p. 125.

81. *Ibid.,* p. 106.

82. *Ibid.*

83. *Ibid.,* p. 114.

84. *Ibid.,* p. 157.

85. *Ibid.,* pp. 157–158.

86. *Ibid.,* p. 158.

87. J. J. Houben, "Avicenna and Mysticism," in *Avicenna Commemoration Volume,* p. 207.

88. *Ibid.,* p. 217. See also George F. Hourani, "Ibn Sīnā's 'Essay on the Secret of Destiny,'" *Bulletin of the School of Oriental and African Studies* XXIX, Part 1 (1966), 25–48. In this important essay, as Hourani's penetrating analysis shows, ibn Sīnā holds adamantly to the complete determination of the world by God as due to the necessity of His nature.

89. *Ibid.,* p. 219.

90. *Ibid.,* p. 220.

91. See P. Morewedge, "Ibn Sīnā's Concept of the Self." Ibn Sīnā equates the Arabic "*jawhar*" with the Greek "ousia" when he lists the categories in *Kitāb fī l-Ḥudūd* in

Tis Rasā'il, Cairo, 1908, defs. 3, 4 and in *Ishārāt* (II, 343–450) and *Dānish Nāma,* chaps. 3, 47, and 55.

92. Spinoza, *Ethics,* p. 42.

93. "*Risāla fī l-'ishq,*" ed. M. A. von Mehren in *Traités mystiques d'Aboū Alī al-Hosain b. Abdallāh b. Sīnā ou d'Avicenne; texte arabe avec l'explication en français,* 3 vols., Leiden, 1849.

94. Spinoza, *Ethics,* p. 41.

95. *Descartes, A. and G.,* p. 192.

96. See my "Ibn Sīnā's Concept of the Self." The argument in question points out that whereas substances can never be united with each other in an ethics of process of self-realization, one process may merge into another process, e.g., a state-station (*ḥāl-maqām*) leads to another state-station (*ḥāl-maqām*) until the final unity (*tawḥīd*) is achieved, which implies both the destruction of the personal ego (*fanā'*) and the eternal persistence of what remains (*baqā'*).

97. Lewis, *Our Experience of God,* p. 289.

98. See my "The Logic of Emanationism and Ṣūfism in ibn Sīnā," *Journal of the American Oriental Society,* 91, no. 4 (1972): 467–76 and 92, no. 1 (1972): 1–18. In this essay the conflict between ibn Sīnā's philosophy and religion is discussed.

Al-Jāmī's *Treatise on Existence*

NICHOLAS HEER
University of Washington

INTRODUCTION

I. The Purpose and Argument of Author

The author of this short treatise is the famous Persian poet and Ṣūfī, Nūr al-Dīn ʿAbd al-Raḥmān ibn Aḥmad ibn Muḥammad al-Jāmī,[1] who was born in Jām in 817/1414 and died in Herat in 898/1492.[2] Al-Jāmī wrote the *Risālah fī al-Wujūd* to defend the central doctrine of the *waḥdat al-wujūd,* or unity of existence, school of Ṣūfism and to refute the arguments commonly raised against it by the rationalist theologians. This central doctrine, as developed in the seventh and eighth centuries A.H. by Ibn ʿArabī[3] and his followers,[4] asserts that God is identical with absolute existence (*al-wujūd al-muṭlaq*). Absolute existence is defined as existence as it is in itself (*min hayth huwa huwa*), that is, unconditioned by anything (*lā bi-sharṭ shay'*) and unaffected by either determination or absoluteness.[5] Most Ṣūfīs of this school, among them al-Jāmī, further asserted that absolute existence is the only real existent outside the mind, and that the universe, being merely a manifestation (*tajallī*) or individuation (*taʿayyun*) of absolute existence, has no real existence in itself apart from absolute existence. Although the universe can be said to have mental existence insofar as it is perceived by the mind, its external existence is illusory.[6]

Moreover, the Ṣufīs claimed, this doctrine is not based on knowledge gained from sense perception and reason, as are the doctrines of the theologians and philosophers, but is based instead on knowledge derived from mystical insight, usually termed *kashf* (uncovering), and in particular from the mystical experience of *fanā'*, or annihilation, in which the entire universe, including the Ṣūfī's own individuality, disappears, and only God remains as the sole truly existent Reality.[7]

Many of the rationalist theologians found this Ṣūfī position unacceptable, not only because it was based on a "subjective" experience, but more importantly because it invalidated both reason and sense perception as sources of certain knowledge. That God could be identical with absolute existence was, in their view, rationally impossible, and to say that the universe did not really exist meant that sense perception, also, could not be trusted as a source of knowledge. Moreover, if both reason and sense perception were thus invalidated as sources of certain knowledge, there would be no way to demonstrate the existence of God nor any proof for the truth of revelation. Even revelation, once it was proven true, had to be allegorically interpreted if its literal meaning contradicted reason, for otherwise reason would be invalidated, and there could be proof neither for the existence of God nor for the truth of revelation.[8]

The arguments the theologians used to refute the Ṣūfī doctrine that God is identical with absolute existence were summarized by al-Taftāzānī in his *Sharḥ al-Maqāṣid.*[9] Absolute existence cannot be God, he claims, because it has the following qualities, none of which can be predicated of God:

(1) Absolute existence is a mental predicate (*maḥmūl ʿaqlī*), that is, one of the things which require a substratum mentally but which cannot inhere in a substratum externally, such as "possibility" and "quiddity," but unlike "humanity," which does not require a substratum, or "whiteness," whose subsistence in a substratum is external.

(2) It is a universal of the second intention (*maʿqul thānī*), that is, an accident which inheres in a universal of the first intention such that there is nothing corresponding to it in the external world, like "universality," "particularity," "essentiality," or "accidentality." These are all things which subsist in the realities (*ḥaqāʾiq*) of things as they exist in the mind, and there is nothing in the external world which is existence, or essentiality, or accidentality, but only such things as humanity or blackness. One might object here, however, that what this argument shows is merely that the existences of things are mental predicates and universals of the second intention, whereas what is under discussion is absolute existence.

(3) It can be divided into necessary (*wājib*) and contingent (*mumkin*) [existence], since if it requires a cause it is contingent, otherwise it is necessary, and also into eternal (*qadīm*) and originated (*ḥādith*), since if it is preceded by another or by nonexistence it is originated; otherwise it is eternal.

(4) It multiplies with the multiplicity of its individual subjects, like the existence of Zayd and that of ʿAmr, or with its specific [subjects], like the existence of humanity and horses, or its generic [subjects] like the existence of animals and plants. . . .

(5) It is predicated of existences analogically (*bi-al-tashkīk*).

Thus, according to the theologians, if God were absolute existence, He would exist only in the mind, would be divisible into parts, would be multiple rather than one, and would be an accidental rather than an essential concept, since only accidental concepts are predicated analogically.

The defense of the Ṣūfī position against arguments such as these was taken up in the ninth century by such Ṣūfīs as Shams al-Dīn al-Fanārī[10] in his commentary on al-Qūnawī's *Miftāḥ al-Ghayb,* entitled *Miṣbāḥ al-Uns fī Sharḥ Miftāḥ Ghayb al-Jamʿ wa-al-Wujūd,* ʿAlāʾ al-Dīn al-Mahāʾimī[11] in his *Ajillat al-Taʾyīd fī Sharḥ Adillat al-Tawḥīd,* and al-Jāmī in his *al-Durrah al-Fākhirah* as well as his *Risālah fī al-Wujūd.* The arguments presented in these works are based not on *kashf,* or mystical insight, but rather on reason, for if Ṣūfī doctrine could be defended on completely rational grounds, the argument of the theologians that it contradicted reason would have no basis.

The specific purpose of al-Jāmī's *Risālah* is to refute the argument, covered in the first two points listed by al-Taftāzānī, that because absolute existence exists only in the mind, it cannot be identical with an externally existing God, and to demonstrate, on the contrary, that absolute existence not only exists externally, but that it exists necessarily and must therefore be identical with God.

His basic argument for the external existence of absolute existence takes the form of a hypothetical syllogism. If existence did not exist, he argues, then nothing would exist at all. Since the consequent is obviously false, it follows that the antecedent is also false, and that existence does in fact exist.

His argument for the truth of the hypothetical premise is based on *al-qāʿidah al-farʿīyah,* or law of dependency, which states that the subsistence of something in something else depends on the existence of that in which it subsists,[12] that is, a substratum must first exist before an accident can subsist in it. The case of existence, however, presents a problem, for if existence is considered to be an accident inhering in a quiddity, that quiddity can hardly be said to exist, at least externally, before existence comes to inhere in it. Consequently, the subsistence of existence in a quiddity cannot be said to depend on the existence of the quiddity.

Rather than make an exception to the law of dependency in the case of existence, as was often proposed,[13] al-Jāmī argues that since quiddities cannot be said to exist externally, existence must be what exists externally, since if neither quiddities nor existence can be said to exist separately, combining the two in a substratum-accident relationship will hardly produce something which exists. Existence must therefore be considered an existent substratum in which quiddities inhere as accidents.

Having shown that absolute existence exists externally, al-Jāmī proceeds to demonstrate that it exists necessarily and therefore must be identical with God, who is defined as the Necessary Existent (*al-wājib al-wujūd*). Existence, he claims, must exist through itself rather than through another existence superadded to it; otherwise an endless chain of existences would result. If it is thus shown to be self-existent and not dependent on another existence for its existence, then it necessarily exists and is identical with God. It must, moreover, be a single essence since it has been demonstrated that God is one and without composition.

Al-Jāmī then takes up two possible objections to his argument. The first is that existence is an accidental concept which cannot be predicated univocally of any self-subsistent thing, but only denominatively or by derivation (*bi-al-ishtiqāq*).[14]

In reply al-Jāmī distinguishes between two meanings of existence: absolute existence (*al-wujūd al-muṭlaq*), which he calls the reality of existence (*ḥaqīqat al-wujūd*), and existence as an accidental concept (*mafhūm ʿāriḍ*) existing only in the mind.[15] It is this latter meaning of existence which cannot be predicated univocally of self-subsistent things but only denominatively. However, since it is possible to predicate it denominatively of self-subsistent things, it is also possible to predicate it of absolute existence.

An objection is here raised that what really exists, then, is existence and that existence must be considered a substratum in which quiddities inhere as accidents rather than an accident inhering in quiddities. This is the opposite of what is usually meant when one says that a quiddity exists—namely, that the quiddity is the substratum and that existence inheres in it.

Al-Jāmī answers that if one means by existence the accidental concept, then existence is indeed an accident inhering in quiddities. If, on the other hand, one means the reality of existence, then existence is a substratum in which quiddities inhere. It is existence in this latter sense only which is identical with God.

The Ṣūfī distinction between these two meanings of existence is further clarified by al-Jāmī in one of his own glosses to his *al-Durrah al-Fākhirah:*[16]

> One should know that the meaning of existence (*al-wujūd*), being (*al-kawn*), being established (*al-thubūt*), occurring (*al-ḥuṣūl*), or being realized (*al-taḥaqquq*), if the verbal meaning (*al-maʿnā al-maṣdarī*) is intended, is a mental concept (*mafhūm iʿtibārī*) and a universal of the second intention (*min al-maʿqūlāt al-thāniyah*) to which nothing in the external world corresponds. It is superadded (*zāʾid*) in the mind to all realities (*al-ḥaqāʾiq*), whether necessary or contingent, in the sense that the intellect can first apprehend them denuded of existence and then predicate existence of them, not, however, externally in the sense of there being in the external world something which is the quiddity and something else which is existence.
>
> Existence, moreover, is not predicated of external existents or even mental existents univocally with the exception of its own portions (*ḥiṣaṣ*), which become individuated when existence is annexed to realities.[17] Moreover, the

position taken by the philosophers that the necessary particular existence (*al-wujūd al-khāṣṣ al-wājibī*), which is identical with the essence of the Necessary Existent, is one of its particulars is not correct. How can it be correct when they themselves explicitly state that it is a universal of the second intention to which, as was stated above, nothing in the external world corresponds?

The rational man does not doubt that it is impossible for existence in the sense mentioned above to exist, much less be the very essence of the Necessary Existent, who is the source of all existents. How can anyone think that the Ṣūfīs, who assert the unity and necessity of existence, mean existence in the sense mentioned above, such that objection can bb taken to their assertion of that doctrine? One can understand from studying what their verifiers have to say that there is some other entity in addition to quiddities and existence in the aforementioned sense, and that because this other entity is conjoined with quiddities and they become enveloped with it, existence in the aforementioned sense comes to inhere in them. This other entity is existence in reality. It is the reality of the Necessary Existent, whereas existence in the aforementioned sense is one of its effects and a reflection of its lights. It is self-existent, bringing into existence what is other than itself, and self-subsistent, giving subsistence to what is other than itself. It does not inhere in quiddities, but, on the contrary, quiddities inhere and subsist in it in such a manner that neither the perfection of its sanctity nor the quality of its majesty is impaired.

The second objection raised against the doctrine that absolute existence exists is that absolute existence, inasmuch as it is absolute, is a natural universal (*kullī ṭabīʿī*), and that natural universals exist only in the mind. In the standard Islamic works on logic the natural universal is commonly defined as the nature or quiddity as it is in itself (*min hayth hiya hiya*) absolute (*muṭlaq*) and unconditioned by anything (*lā bi-sharṭ shayʾ*), whether universality, particularity, existence, nonexistence, or anything else. It is distinguished from two other types of universals, the mental universal (*al-kullī al-ʿaqlī*), which is the nature insofar as it is a universal, that is, the nature conditioned by universality (*bi-sharṭ lā-shayʾ*), and the logical universal (*al-kullī al-manṭiqī*), which is the concept of universality itself.[18]

Although there was general agreement that mental and logical universals existed only in the mind, there was much controversy over the question of whether natural universals existed externally or only in the mind. There were three main positions on this question.

The first, which was generally that of the philosophers, was that natural universals existed externally as incorporeal and insensible substances within particular sensible objects. This was so, they argued, because any particular substance, such as an individual man, is made up of the universal, in this case humanity, and individuation. Since the universal, humanity, is part of the externally existent individual man, it must also exist externally, although it is not perceived by the senses except as individuated.[19]

The second position, usually adopted by the theologians, was that natural universals did not exist externally but only in the mind. Those who held this position maintained that all things existing outside the mind were individuated, sensible entities. Consequently if universals existed outside the mind they would be individuated parts of their particulars and would therefore differ from them in existence. Since unity in existence is required for predication,[20] universals could not then be predicated of their particulars, which is absurd. Moreover, if a universal as a single entity existed as a part of each of its particulars, it would have to be qualified by contradictory qualities and exist in different places at one and the same time.[21]

The third position, held by the Ishrāqīs and certain Ṣūfīs, was that universals existed externally as incorporeal substances called *muthul,* or archetypes. These, however, did not exist in their particulars but in a separate nonmaterial world of archetypes, called *ʿālam al-mithāl.*[22]

It is the second of these positions, that of the theologians, that al-Jāmī wishes to discredit in support of his doctrine that absolute existence does indeed exist externally as well as in the mind. He therefore attempts a refutation of what he considers to be the two strongest arguments against the external existence of universals, namely, those of Quṭb al-Dīn al-Rāzī as found in his *Lawāmiʿ al-Asrār fī Sharḥ Maṭāliʿ al-Anwār.*[23]

Al-Rāzī's first argument asserts that if universals existed externally they would have to be either identical with their particulars, a part of each particular, or external to their particulars. Since all of these alternatives are impossible, he concludes that universals cannot exist externally but only in the mind.

The first alternative is impossible, because if a universal were identical in every respect with its particulars, its particulars would all be identical with each other as well as with the universal and could no longer be considered individuated particulars distinct from each other.

The second alternative is also impossible, because if a universal were a part of each of its particulars, then its existence would be prior to the existence of the whole and thus differ from it, so that no predication would be possible.[24]

The third alternative is obviously impossible, because, again, the unity in existence necessary for predication would be lacking.

Al-Jāmi's refutation of this argument deals specifically with the impossibility of the second alternative. Why is it not possible, he asks, to consider the universal as the external existent and its particulars as existing solely in the mind? If this were the case, the only external existent would be the universal, and there would therefore be no lack of unity in existence between universal and particulars to make predication impossible. Just as predication is possible when particulars are said to exist externally and their universals in the mind, so also should predication be possible when the opposite is true.

Al-Rāzī's second argument is that if a natural universal existed externally, it would either exist alone or combined with some other entity.[25] The first alternative is impossible, because a universal existing alone would be individually one and distinct from everything else. As such, if it were predicated of its particulars, it would have to exist in different places and be qualified by contrary attributes at one and the same time.

The second alternative is also impossible, for if the universal were combined with some other entity, then the two would exist either with one existence subsisting in both of them, or with two existences, one existence subsisting in each. If they existed with one existence subsisting in both of them, either that one existence would subsist in both of them separately, in which case a single thing would subsist in two separate substrata, which is impossible, or it would subsist in them as a combination, in which case the two would not exist separately but the combination only would exist. On the other hand, if they existed with two existences subsisting in them, the universal could not then be predicated of the combination of the two.

To refute this second argument al-Jāmī must show either that one at least of the two alternatives which al-Rāzī claims are impossible is in fact possible, or that the alternatives are not limited to two.

He begins by pointing out that what al-Rāzī means by his two alternatives is not clear. In the case of the first alternative does he mean, by a universal existing alone, one that is not combined with any other externally existing entity, or does he mean a universal not combined with any other entity whatsoever, whether externally or mentally existent? Similarly, in the case of the second alternative, does he mean by some other entity some other externally existent entity, or some entity existing either externally or mentally? Since there are two possible meanings for each alternative, the two alternatives can be restated as follows: A universal exists either: (1) alone, that is, not combined with either: (a) any other externally existent entity, or (b) any other entity at all, whether externally or mentally existent, or (2) combined with either: (a) any other externally existent entity, or (b) any other entity at all, whether externally or mentally existent.

Assuming initially that the first alternative means that the universal is not combined with any other externally existent entity (1a), al-Jāmī asks why it would not be possible for the universal to exist externally in combination with mentally existent individuations. If such were the case, the universal could then be predicated of its mentally existing particulars without having to exist in different places or be qualified by contrary attributes at one and the same time.

On the other hand, if it is assumed that the first alternative means that the universal is not combined with any other entity at all (1b), and the second alternative means that it is combined with an externally existent entity (2a), that is, that the universal is either not combined with anything at all or combined with an external entity, then, al-Jāmī claims, the alternatives cannot be limited to two. A third alternative is possible, namely, that the universal exist in combination with a mentally existing entity.

Finally, if the second alternative means the universal combined with any other entity at all, whether externally or mentally existent (2b), then it is possible, al-Jāmī says, for the universal to exist in combination with a mentally existing entity. In this case the two exist with two existences subsisting in them, but, since the existence of the other entity is mental, the universal could still be predicated of the combination.

Turning next to al-Rāzī's statement that if a universal existed in combination with some other entity, then the two would exist either with one existence subsisting in them both, or with two existences, one existence subsisting in each, al-Jāmī claims that there is no reason to limit the alternatives to two. A third alternative is possible, namely, that one of them exist through itself, rather than through an existence subsisting in it, and that the other exist through the former. In this way it would be possible for absolute existence, for example, to exist through itself, and for everything else to exist through it.

A final objection is raised that this third alternative is really the same as the first, namely, that the two would exist with one existence, and that this has been shown to be impossible, since, as previously mentioned, that one existence would have either to subsist in them both separately, which is impossible, because a single entity cannot subsist in two different substrata, or it would have to subsist in both of them as a whole, which is also impossible, because the two would not then exist separately but only the whole would exist. To this al-Jāmī replies that, again, the alternatives are not limited to two, since a third can be added, namely, that one of the two exist through itself and the other through it. This alternative is not impossible because it does not require that a single entity subsist in two different substrata, nor does it prevent the two from existing separately.

From his refutation of these two arguments of al-Rāzī, al-Jāmī's own position on the existence of universals becomes clear. Only one universal, absolute existence, exists outside the mind. It exists through itself, not through another existence subsisting in it, and is therefore necessarily existent. All other universals and their particulars are individuations of absolute existence and exist through it. However, these individuations of absolute existence have only mental existence. Al-Jāmī's position is thus the reverse of that of the theologians, in whose view it was the universal which existed in the mind and its individuations which existed externally. Al-Jāmī's position also differs from those of the philosophers and the Ishrāqīs, since each of these groups held that both universals and their individuations existed externally.[26]

II. The Arabic Text of Risālah fī al-Wujūd

In establishing the text of *Risālah fī al-Wujūd* a total of eleven manuscripts was consulted. These are described below. A comparison of the variant readings found in these manuscripts revealed the existence of two main groups. The first of these, designated Group A, is made up of ʿAqā'id Taymūr 393, Mishkāt 1035, Yahuda 2621, Yahuda 3091, Yahuda 3872 and Yahuda 5930. Within this group Yahuda 2621 and Yahuda 3091 were found to constitute a definite subgroup, as were also ʿAqā'id Taymūr 393 and Yahuda 3872. The second group, Group B, contains the remaining five manuscripts: Majmūʿ 4819/2, Or. Oct. 1854, Sprenger 1820f, Wetzstein II 1796, and Yahuda 5373. No subgroups were found within Group B.

Of these eleven, five representative manuscripts, one from each subgroup in Group A: Yahuda 3872 and Yahuda 3091, and three from Group B: Yahuda 5373, Or. Oct. 1854 and Majmūʿ 4819/2, were chosen for final collation, and their variant readings have been cited in the notes. Because of its *isnād,* Yahuda 3872 was considered the most authoritative of the manuscripts, and its readings were generally followed in the text except on those occasions when it differed from all the other four manuscripts.

Not all of the eleven manuscripts include al-Jāmī's glosses. All three glosses are found only in Yahuda 2621 and Yahuda 3091, which together make up one of the two subgroups in Group A. Glosses two and three are found in ʿAqā'id Taymūr 393, Yahuda 3872, and Yahuda 5930 in Group A, and in Majmūʿ 4819/2 and Yahuda 5373 in Group B. The collation of glosses two and three is based on Yahuda 3872 and Yahuda 3091 in Group A, and on Yahuda 5373 and Majmūʿ 4819/2 in Group B. Since gloss one is not found in the authoritative Yahuda 3872 but only in one subgroup of Group A, its authenticity is doubtful. It has nevertheless been included in the text as edited here.

The five manuscripts whose variant readings have been collated in the footnotes are designated by the following letters:

Yahuda 3091	ك
Yahuda 3872	أ
Majmūʿ 4819/2	ل
Or. Oct. 1854	ه
Yahuda 5373	د

Yahuda 2621 has been used only for the text of gloss one, and since no variant readings are cited for it, it has not been assigned a letter. Some of the manuscripts contain variant readings and corrections written in the margins by the copyists. Such marginal variants have usually been indicated by the letter خ , standing for: *wa-fī nuskhah.* Corrections, on the other hand, have been indicated by the letters صح . Both corrections and marginal variants have been cited in the footnotes along with the other variant readings.

The following is a brief description of each of the manuscripts consulted.

Group A

ʿAqāʾid Taymūr 393. Dār al-Kutub al-Miṣrīyah. Fols. 168a–170b (*Fihris al-Khizānah al-Taymūrīyah,* IV, 122). Part of a collection which also contains al-Jāmī's *al-Durrah al-Fākhirah,* as well as the commentary on it by his disciple ʿAbd al-Ghafūr al-Lārī. The title of the work is given as *Risālah fī al-Wujūd.* The Ms is not dated nor is the name of the copyist mentioned. The margins contain glosses two and three.

Mishkāt 1035. University of Tehran Library. Pp. 93–94 (Dānish Pazhūh, *Fihrist,* Vol. III, Part 1, p. 517). Copied by Shihāb al-Dīn Dībājī about 1100 A.H. Title is given as *Wujūd al-Wujūd.*

Yahuda 2621. Robert Garrett Collection, Princeton University Library. Fols. 115b–117b. No mention of date or copyist. Margins contain glosses one, two and three. Title is given as *al-Risālah al-Wujūdīyah.*

Yahuda 3091. Robert Garrett Collection, Princeton University Library. Fols. 40a–41b. Very similar to Yahuda 2621. No mention of date or copyist. Contains glosses one, two, and three. Title is given as *al-Risālah al-Wujūdīyah.*

Yahuda 3872. Robert Garrett Collection, Princeton University Library. Fols. 24a–27b. Part of a collection which also contains *al-Durrah al-Fākhirah* (fols. 3a–23a) and the commentary on it by ʿAbd al-Ghafūr al-Lārī (fols. 28a–39a). All three works were copied by Yūsuf al-Tāj ibn ʿAbd Allāh ibn Abī al-Khayr al-Jāwī al-Maqāṣirī al-Talaqī (?) al-Manjalāwī in Medina at the *ribāṭ* of al-Imām ʿAlī al-Murtaḍā in 1075 A.H. The *Risālah* was finished on 3 Rabīʿ al-Thānī and *al-Durrah al-Fākhirah* and the commentary on 2 and 9 Rabīʿ al-Thānī respectively. At the end of *al-Durrah al-Fākhirah,* on fol. 23a, the copyist states that he wrote this copy on the order of his teacher and spiritual guide al-Muḥaqqiq al-Rabbānī al-Mullā Ibrāhīm al-Kūrānī.[27] Although there is no *ijāzah* by Ibrāhīm al-Kūrānī on the manuscript itself, it would appear from this statement that Yūsuf al-Tāj was studying these three works under him when he copied them. Ibrāhīm al-Kūrānī himself states elsewhere that his authority to teach these three goes back to al-Jāmī through Ṣafī al-Dīn Aḥmad ibn Muḥammad al-Qushāshī al-Madanī,[28]

Abū al-Mawāhib Aḥmad ibn ʿAlī al-Shinnāwī,[29] Ghaḍanfar ibn Jaʿfar al-Ḥusaynī al-Nahrawālī,[30] and Mullā Muḥammad Amīn, the nephew (*ibn ukht*) of al-Jāmī.[31]

Yūsuf al-Tāj, as his *nisbah* al-Jāwī indicates, was originally from Indonesia. His *nisbah* al-Maqṣīrī refers to Macassar on the island of Celebes. According to P. Voorhoeve[32] he is to be identified with the famous saint known as Shaykh Joseph, who was banished by the Dutch to the Cape of Good Hope in 1694. Shaykh Joseph was born in Macassar in 1036/1626, left for Mecca and Medina in 1054/1644, and died in Capetown in 1110/1699.[33]

Yahuda 5930. Robert Garrett Collection, Princeton University Library. Fols. 334b–336b. Added in the same hand at the end of a copy of *al-Durrah al-Fākhirah.* No title is given the work, nor is any mention made of copyist or date. Gloss two is incorporated into the text on fol. 335a. Gloss three is written in the margin.

Group B

Majmūʿ 4819/2. Maktabāt al-Awqāf al-ʿĀmmah, Baghdad (Ṭalas, *al-Kashshāf,* p. 332, No. 2547/2). This copy is part of a collection and bears the title *Risālat al-Wujūd.* No date or copyist is mentioned. Contains glosses two and three in the margin.

Or. Oct. 1854. Staatsbibliothek Preussischer Kulturbesitz, Marburg/Lahn. Fols. 69b–70b. An undated copy written by Muḥammad ibn Muḥammad al-Bukhārī and added to the end of a copy of *al-Durrah al-Fākhirah* in the same hand. No title is given the work, and all three glosses are omitted.

Sprenger 1820f. Staatsbibliothek Preussischer Kulturbesitz, Berlin. Fols. 99b–100b (Ahlwardt, *Verzeichnis,* II, 536, No. 2326). This copy lacks a title and makes no mention of date or copyist. All three glosses are omitted.

Wetzstein II 1796. Staatsbibliothek Preussischer Kulturbesitz, Berlin. Fols. 164b–165a (Ahlwardt, *Verzeichnis,* II, 536, No. 2327). This copy is incomplete, lacking several paragraphs in the middle. Date, name of copyist, title and all three glosses are also lacking.

Yahuda 5373. Robert Garrett Collection, Princeton University Library. Fols. 1b–4a. Part of a large collection of works and quotations on *waḥdat al-wujūd* including al-Jāmī's *al-Durrah al-Fākhirah* and al-Lārī's commentary on it. The entire collection is in the same hand, and the copyist gives his name simply as Yaḥyā. No date is given for *Risālah fī al-Wujūd,* but other works are variously dated between 1104 and 1120 A.H. Glosses two and three are written in the margin.

Notes

1. See *Takmilat Nafaḥāt al-Uns,* the biography of al-Jāmī by his disciple, ʿAbd al-Ghafūr al-Lārī, where the *Risālah fī al-Wujūd* is listed among the 45 works written by al-Jāmī during his lifetime. Ms Or. 218, British Museum, fol. 172b.

2. Biographical sources on al-Jāmī are listed in Brockelmann, *Geschichte,* II, 266, S II, 285; and in Munzawī, *Fihrist,* II, 187.

3. Brockelmann, *Geschichte,* I, 571, S I, 790.

4. Especially Ṣadr al-Dīn al-Qūnawī (d. 672, Brockelmann, *Geschichte,* I, 585, S I, 807), ʿAbd al-Razzāq al-Kāshānī (d. 730, *op. cit.,* II, 262, S II, 280), and Dāwūd al-Qayṣarī (d. 751, *op. cit.,* II, 299, S II, 323).

5. See, for example, al-Qūnawī, *Kitāb al-Nuṣūṣ,* p. 294; al-Kāshānī *Sharḥ Fuṣūṣ al-Ḥikam,* p. 3; al-Qayṣarī, *Maṭlaʿ Khuṣūṣ al-Kilam,* p. 5; *al-Muthul al-ʿAqlīyah al-Aflāṭūnīyah,* pp. 117 ff.; al-Fanārī, *Miṣbāḥ al-Uns,* p. 52. An interesting explanation of why the Ṣūfīs equated God with absolute existence is given by al-Taftāzānī in his *Sharḥ al-Maqāṣid,* Vol. I, p. 55.

6. The doctrine that the universe exists only in the mind is mentioned by al-Jāmī in his *Naqd al-Nuṣūṣ,* p. 22; in his *Lawāʾiḥ* (tr. Whinfield), pp. 19-20; as well as in *Risālah fī al-Wujūd.* See also al-Mahāʾimī, *Ajillat al-Taʾyīd,* fol. 9b; al-Nābulusī, *Īḍāḥ al-Masqṣūd,* p. 19, and *Nukhbat al-Masʾalah,* pp. 59-64; al-Suwaydī, *Kashf al-Ḥujub al-Musbalah,* pp. 68-71; al-Kalanbawī, *Risālah fī Waḥdat al-Wujūd,* fol. 10b. Non-Ṣūfīs who mention this doctrine include Ibn Khaldūn in his *Muqaddimah* (tr. Rosenthal), Vol. III, pp. 86, 90-91; and al-Taftāzānī in his *Sharḥ al-Maqāṣid,* Vol. II, p. 52.

7. For the suprarational source of Ṣūfī knowledge see, for example, Ibn ʿArabī, *al-Futūḥāt al-Makkīyah,* Vol. I, pp. 31-47; al-Qūnawī, *Iʿjāz al-Bayān,* pp. 15-22; al-Qayṣarī, *Maṭla Khuṣūṣ al-Kilam,* pp. 33-37; al-Hamadhānī, *Zubdat al-Ḥaqāʾiq,* pp. 26-27, 50-51; Ibn Khaldūn, *Muqaddimah,* Vol. III, pp. 81-83. *Fanāʾ* is described by al-Ghazālī in his *Mishkāt al-Anwār,* pp. 104-107; by al-Jāmī in *Lawāʾiḥ,* p. 10; by al-Nābulusī in *Nukhbat al-Masʾalah,* pp. 52-54; and by al-Suwaydī in *Kashf al-Ḥujub al-Musbalah,* pp. 65-66.

8. The most complete statement of the position of the theologians with respect to the doctrines of the *waḥdat al-wujūd* school of Ṣūfism is that given in the *Risālah fī Waḥdat al-Wujūd* attributed to al-Taftāzānī, especially pp. 11-12. For the necessity of interpreting allegorically passages of revelation which contradict reason see al-Ghazạlī, *Qānūn al-Taʾwīl,* p. 9; and al-Jurjānī, *Sharḥ al-Mawāqif,* Vol. II, pp. 48-51.

9. Vol. I, pp. 55-56.

10. D. 834, Brockelmann, *Geschichte,* II, 303, S II, 328.

11. D. 835, *op. cit.,* II, 286, S II, 310.

12. For this law see al-Aḥmadnagarī, *Dustūr al-ʿUlamā,* Vol. I, p. 374. A fuller discussion may be found in Kāshif al-Ghiṭāʾ, *Naqd al-Ārāʾ al-Manṭiqīyah,* pp. 352-368.

13. See al-Jāmī's second gloss to the *Risālah.*

14. That is, one can say that God exists or is existent, but not that God is existence.

15. This distinction was commonly made by Ṣūfīs of the *waḥdat al-wujūd* school. See, for example, al-Qayṣarī, *Maṭla' Khuṣūṣ al-Kilam,* p. 7; al-Mahā'imī, *Ajillat al-Ta'yīd,* fol. 6a; al-Fanārī, *Misbāḥ al-Uns,* p. 53; al-Nābulusī, *Nukhbat al-Mas'alah,* pp. 9-10; al-Suwaydī, *Kashf al-Ḥujub al-Musbalah,* pp. 26-27.

16. Ms Yahuda 3872, fol. 4b.

17. That is, if existence as an accidental concept is intended.

18. For these three types of universals see Ibn Sīnā, *al-Shifā', al-Manṭiq, al-Madkhal,* pp. 65-72; al-Kātibī, *al-Risālah al-Shamsīyah,* Arabic text: p. 6, translation: p. 11; Quṭb al-Dīn al-Rāzī, *Sharḥ al-Risālah al-Shamsīyah,* pp. 289-294; and *Lawāmi' al-Asrār,* p. 53.

19. See Ibn Sīnā, *al-Shifā', al-Ilāhīyāt,* pp. 202-212; al-Ṭūsī, *Sharḥ al-Ishārāt,* pp. 192-193; al-Kātibī, *al-Risālah al-Shamsīyah,* Arabic text: p. 6, translation: p. 11; al-Urmawī, *Maṭāli' al-Anwār,* p. 53.

20. For this requirement see al-Tahānawī, *Kashshāf Iṣṭilāḥāt al-Funūn,* under the heading *al-ḥaml,* p. 353; and al-Aḥmadnagarī, *Dustūr al-'Ulamā',* also under *al-ḥaml,* Vol. II, p. 59.

21. The most thorough presentation of this position is given by Quṭb al-Dīn al-Rāzī in his *Risālat Taḥqīq al-Kullīyāt.* See also Fakhr al-Dīn al-Rāzī, *Sharḥ al-Ishārāt,* pp. 287-289; Quṭb al-Dīn al-Rāzī, *Lawāmi' al-Asrār,* pp. 53-56; al-Taftāzānī, *Sharḥ al-Risālah al-Shamsīyah,* pp. 46-47; and al-Jurjānī, *Ḥāshiyah 'alā Sharḥ al-Maṭāli',* pp. 134-138. It should be noted that one aspect of the controversy between philosophers and theologians over the external existence of natural universals was the question of whether the natural universal was to be defined as the nature as it is in itself (*min hayth hiya hiya*) unconditioned by anything, as the philosophers claimed, or whether it was to be defined as the nature conditioned by nothing (*bi-sharṭ lā-shay'*), that is, the nature insofar as universality is predicated of it, as maintained by the theologians. It is obvious that the theologians' definition supports their claim that natural universals exist in the mind only. For this aspect of the controversy see al-Taftāzānī, *Sharḥ al-Risālah al-Shamsīyah,* pp. 44-45; Aḥmad al-Maḥallī, *Tanwīr al-Mashriq,* pp. 73-74; and Kāshif al-Ghiṭā', *Naqd al-Ārā al-Manṭiqīyah,* pp. 189-192.

22. See Shihab al-Dīn al-Suhrawardī, *Ḥikmat al-Ishrāq,* pp. 92-96, 154-164, 229-235; Muḥammad 'Alī Abū Rayyān, *Uṣūl al-Falsafah al-Ishrāqīyah,* pp. 187-208; and the work by an unknown author entitled *al-Muthul al-'Aqlīyah al-Aflāṭūnīyah.*

23. Pp. 55-56.

24. Because of a lack of unity with respect to existence. See above, note 20.

25. That is, combined with some kind of individuation to form a particular.

26. Al-Jāmī's position is similar to the position on universals ascribed to the Ṣūfīs by Muḥammad Mubīn in his *Mir'āt al-Shurūḥ,* Vol. I, pp. 165-166. According to him those Ṣūfīs who believed that individuation had only mental existence also believed that universals existed externally as sensible substances. Consequently, what the senses perceive are universals rather than their particulars. Moreover, since there is only one universal, namely the highest genus, or absolute existence, which really exists externally, it is this universal alone which is perceived by the senses. This position is said to accord with the experience of many Ṣūfīs, who report that they never saw anything without seeing God in it. If one considers this Ṣūfī position on universals together with the other three positions previously described, it becomes apparent that each position corresponds to one of the four alternative answers that can be given to Porphyry's

famous question in the beginning of his *Isagoge:* "I shall refuse to say concerning genera and species whether they subsist or whether they are placed in the naked understandings alone or whether subsisting they are corporeal or incorporeal, and whether they are separated from sensibles or placed in sensibles and in accord with them." See Adolfus Busse, *Porphyrii Isagoge et in Aristotelis Categorias Commentarium* (*Commentaria in Aristotelem Graeca,* Vol. IV, Part 1), pp. 1, 25; and Richard McKeon, *Selections from Medieval Philosophers,* Vol. I, p. 91.

27. Brockelmann, *Geschichte,* II, 505, S II, 520.

28. *Op. cit.,* II, 514, S II, 535.

29. *Op. cit.,* II, 514, S II, 534.

30. See ʿAbd al-Ḥayy al-Ḥasanī, *Nuzhat al-Khawāṭir,* Vol. V, p. 301.

31. See Ibrāhīm al-Kūrānī, *al-Amam li-Īqāẓ al-Himam,* pp. 107-108.

32. *Handlist of Arabic Manuscripts in the Library of the University of Leiden,* pp. 41, 52, 341, 354, 539.

33. Brockelmann, *Geschichte,* II, 556; G. W. J. Drewes, -'Sech Joesoep Makasar" in *Djawa,* 1926, No. 2, pp. 83-88.

TRANSLATION

In the name of God, the Merciful, the Compassionate

1. Existence (*al-wujūd*), that is, that through whose conjunction (*bi-inḍimāmihi*) with quiddities (*al-māhīyāt*) the effects proper to those quiddities (*al-āthār al-mukhtaṣṣah bihā*) result,[1] exists; for if it did not exist, then nothing would exist at all, and since the consequent is false, the antecedent is also false.
2. The explanation of this implication (*bayān al-mulāzamah*)[2] is that a quiddity, before existence is conjoined to it, is decidedly nonexistent. Thus, if existence were also nonexistent, it would be impossible for one of the two to subsist (*thubūt*) in the other, since the subsistence of something in something else depends on the existence of that in which it subsists (*thubūt shay' li-shay' farʿ li-wujūd al-muthbat lahu*).[3] Therefore, if one of the two did not subsist in the other, quiddities would be neither substrata in which existence inhered (*maʿrūḍah lil-wujūd*), as is the position of the rationalists, nor accidents inhering in existence (*ʿāriḍah lahu*), as in the position of those who assert the unity of existence (*waḥdat al-wujūd*). Consequently, they would not exist.
3. Should you say: This premise applies only to what is not existence, and its meaning is that the subsistence of something other than the attribute of existence depends on the existence of that in which it subsists. The subsistence of existence in something, however, depends only upon the existence of that in which it subsists at the time when existence subsists in it, not before. Moreover, there is no doubt that, at the time existence subsists in it, it exists by that same existence.
4. We should reply: Special cases (*al-takhṣīṣ*) and exceptions (*al-istithnā'*) may be made only in presumptive rhetorical propositions (*al-khiṭābīyāt al-ẓannīyah*), not in strictly rational propositions (*al-ʿaqlīyāt al-ṣirfah*) and especially not in necessary truths (*al-ḍarūrīyāt*). Furthermore, anyone who consults his intuition (*wijdānahu*) in an unbiased manner will by himself perceive that the conjunction of two externally nonexistent entities without the subsistence of one or both of them in an external existent is something which reason not only does not allow but testifies to be impossible.[4]
5. Should you say: Quiddities insofar as they exist mentally can be substrata for external existence (*maʿrūḍah lil-wujūd al-khārijī*), so that the subsistence of external existence in them, in the mind, depends only on their existence in the mind, not in the external world.

6. We should reply: Let us then shift the argument to their existence in the mind and say that the subsistence of mental existence in them, in the mind, depends on their having a prior existence in it, and the subsistence of this prior existence [in them] depends on yet another existence prior to it. Thus an endless chain of existences results. Moreover, this chain is unlike the chain which results in the case of purely mental entities (*al-umūr al-iʿtibārīyah*), for these terminate with the cessation of the mental activity (*al-iʿtibār*) [which gave rise to them]. Indeed, every consequent (*lāḥiq*) [in this chain] is dependent upon its antecedent (*sābiq*), as is obvious to one who reflects upon this.
7. As for the falsity of the consequent,[5] it is obvious and needs no proof. It has thus been demonstrated that existence exists.
8. Moreover, if it exists its existence must be through itself (*bi-nafsihi*), otherwise an endless chain [of existences] would result. It must consequently be necessarily existent (*wājib*) because of the impossibility of a thing's ceasing to subsist in itself.[6] It must also be a single reality (*ḥaqīqah wāḥidah*),[7] to which is appended relative multiplicity (*al-taʿaddud al-nisbī*) through its being annexed (*bi-iḍāfatihā*) to quiddities; otherwise the Necessary Existent (*al-wājib*) would become multiple, and this they have demonstrated to be impossible.
9. Should you say: There is no doubt that the term existence is an accidental concept (*mafhūm ʿaraḍī*) which, like walking, laughter, color, or blackness, etc., cannot be predicated univocally (*muwāṭaʾatan*) of any self-subsistent thing (*shayʾ qāʾim bi-nafsihi*), and that to deny this is obstinacy. How, then, can the essence of the Necessary Existent (*dhāt al-wājib*) be the same as that concept?
10. I should reply: Just as it is possible for this universal concept (*al-mafhūm al-ʿāmm*) to be superadded (*zāʾid*) to necessary particular existence (*al-wujūd al-khāṣṣ al-wājibī*) as well as to contingent particular existences (*al-wujūdāt al-khāṣṣah al-mumkinah*), assuming the latter to be separate realities as claimed by the philosopher, it is possible for it to be superadded to an existent, absolute, and single reality (*ḥaqīqah wāḥidah muṭlaqah mawjūdah*), which is the reality of necessary existence (*ḥaqīqat al-wujūd al-wājibī*). This superadded concept would then be a mental entity (*amr iʿtibārī*) nonexistent except in the mind, and its substratum an external real existent (*mawjūd ḥaqīqī khārijī*), which is the reality of existence (*ḥaqīqat al-wujūd*).
11. Should you say: If the existent (*al-mawjūd*) is in reality existence, it follows that quiddities inhere in it and are annexed to it (*ʿāriḍah lahu lāḥiqah iyyāhu*), and that existence is the substratum for this inherence and annexation (*maʿrūḍ malḥūq*). This, however, is contrary to what we understand when we say that a quiddity exists, for

we definitely understand that the quiddity is qualified by existence and is therefore the substratum, and that existence inheres in it. How, then, can what you say be true?

12. We should reply: To say that it "exists" (*mawjūd*) in the aforementioned sense[8] is only in consideration (*bi-iʿtibār*) of the derivation of this form[9] from "existence" (*al-wujūd*), if one means by existence this inseparable accidental concept (*al-mafhūm al-ʿāriḍ al-lāzim*). However, when one considers its derivation from "existence" and means by existence that reality which is a substratum, then "exists" means "possesses existence" (*dhū al-wujūd*) rather than "is qualified by it" (*muttaṣif bihi*).

13. Should you say: This reality, in view of its absoluteness (*iṭlāqihā*), is a natural universal (*kullī ṭabīʿī*), and therefore what you said in the course of proving its existence is contradicted by what has been proven to the effect that it is impossible for natural universals to exist [externally].

14. We should reply: First of all we do not admit that, in view of its aforementioned absoluteness, it is a natural universal, for what is meant by its absoluteness is that it does not have an individuation (*taʿayyun*) that is incompatible with (*lā yujāmiʿ*) the individuations adhering to it (*al-taʿayyunāt al-lāḥiqah iyyāhā*) in the [various] planes (*al-marātib*) by means of quiddities being enveloped (*talabbus*) with it. This, moreover, does not exclude its being individuated in itself, through an individuation which removes it from universality (*al-kullīyah*).

15. Should we, nevertheless concede that in this respect[10] it is a natural universal, we should not, however, admit that the existence of natural universals is impossible. Indeed, many of the philosophers have asserted their existence, and books are full [of arguments to this effect]. Moreover, what has been said by some of the more recent writers (*al-muta'-akhkhirīn*) in the course of proving the impossibility of their existing is not free from one or more varieties of defect (*al-khalal*). We shall cite here the strongest of their arguments, namely, that of the commentator on *al-Maṭāliʿ*,[11] and, with the help of God, shall point out in what way it is defective.

16. He said, may God have mercy upon him: "Natural universals have no existence in the external world. This is so for two reasons. The first is that if any natural universal existed [externally] it would be either identical with [each of] its particulars (*al-juz'īyāt*) in the external world, or a part (*juz'*) of [each of] them, or external to them. All of these alternatives are impossible. As for the first [alternative] it is [impossible] because if it were identical with [each of] its particulars, then each particular would have to be identical with every other [particular] in the external world. The reason for this is that

any given one [of the particulars] would be identical with the universal nature (*al-ṭabīʿah al-kullīyah*) which, in turn, is identical with any other. This is absurd (*hādhā khulf*)."

17. "The second [alternative is impossible] because if [the natural universal] were a part of [each of] the particulars in the external world, it would be prior to them in external existence.[12] This is so because a whole cannot come into existence (*yataḥaqqaq*) as long as its parts in the external world have not first and essentially (*bi-al-dhāt*) come into existence. Thus [the universal] would be different from its particulars in existence[12] and could not then be predicated of them. The impossibility of the third [alternative] is obvious."

18. [As for] his statement, "or a part of [each of] them," if he means by its being a part of them that there is another part besides it (*warāʾahu*) in the external world, and that the particulars are tantamount to the sum of the parts, then the alternatives are not limited to three. If, however, he means that the universal is conjoined (*munḍamm*) to something else [existing] either externally or in the mind, then the limitation [to three alternatives] is admitted.

19. In this case, however, we do not admit the invalidity of the predication, for if the thing existing externally is the nature (*al-ṭabīʿah*) only, and if its particulars are distinguished from each other by means of mental individuations (*taʿayyunāt iʿtibārīyah*) which are nonexistent [externally], then the predication is certainly valid. This is so because, except for the nature, none of the particulars exists externally in such a way that one could conceive of a lack of unity with respect to existence due to priority (*taqaddum*) or posteriority (*taʾakhkhur*).

20. "The second of these reasons is that if natural universals existed in the external world (*fī al-aʿyān*), then that which existed externally would be either the nature alone (*mujarrad al-ṭabīʿah*), or [the nature] together with some other entity (*amr ākhar*).[13] The first [alternative] is impossible, for it would require that an entity individually one (*al-amr al-wāḥid bi-al-shakhṣ*) exist in different places and be qualified by contrary attributes (*ṣifāt mutaḍāddah*) [at one and the same time], and this is clearly impossible.

21. "The second [alternative] is also impossible, for otherwise both[14] would exist either through one existence or through two existences. If they both existed through one existence, and if that existence subsisted in both of them, then this would require that a single thing subsist in two different substrata (*maḥallayn mukhtalifayn*), and that is impossible. If [that one existence] subsisted in [both of them] as a whole (*al-majmūʿ*), then neither of them would exist [separately], but rather the whole would exist. If, on the other hand, they existed through two existences, then the natural univer-

sal could not be predicated of the whole. This is a contradiction (*hādhā khulf*)."

22. [As for] his statement, "then that which existed externally would be either the nature alone or [the nature] together with some other entity," what is meant by the nature alone is either that the nature is not conjoined with any external entity, or that it is not conjoined with any entity whatsoever, whether external or mental.
23. If the first is meant,[15] as appears from what he says in refuting the second alternative,[16] then we do not admit that this requires that an entity individually one exist in different substrata or that it be qualified by contrary attributes. Why is it not possible for the nature, when considered as being determined by a certain [externally] nonexistent mental individuation (*taʿayyun iʿtibārī*), to be one particular individual (*shakhṣ muʿayyan*) and, [when determined] by another individuation, to be a different individual (*shakhṣ ākhar*), and so forth? Its localization in different places and its being qualified by contrary attributes would then be with respect to these individuals, which are differentiated and distinguished from one another by means of mental entities (*al-umūr al-iʿtibārīyah*).
24. If, however, the second is meant,[17] then we also do not admit the limitation to the two alternatives,[18] for the meaning of "another entity," as is apparent from his refutation, is something existing externally, and it is quite possible for the nature to be neither alone (*mujarradah*) nor [conjoined] with another entity existing externally, but instead [conjoined] with an [externally] nonexistent mental entity, as has been mentioned.[19]
25. If, however, you understand "another entity" in a more general sense,[20] then [our] objection would shift to his statement, "they would exist either through one existence or through two different[21] existences," for on this basis it is possible for one of them to exist externally and the other mentally.
26. [Furthermore, with respect to] his statement, "they would exist either through one existence or through two different existences," one can say: We do not admit the limitation to the two alternatives mentioned. Why is it not possible for one of them to exist through itself (*bi-nafsihi*) and for the other to exist through it, as is claimed by those who assert the unity of existence (*waḥdat al-wujūd*)? In their opinion it is the nature of existence (*ṭabīʿat al-wujūd*) which exists, and all other things such as quiddities and their inseparable accidents (*lawāzimihā*) are entities inhering in it and existing through it. Accordingly, no difficulty arises.
27. Should you say: In this case it would then be true to say that they exist through one existence, since one of them exists through itself and the other [exists] through it, and that therefore no more than

the two alternatives are possible; we should answer: Let us then shift our objection to the limitation of the one existence either to subsist in each one of them or to subsist in [both of them] as a whole, for this limitation is no longer valid.

Gloss One

That is, the effects sought from them, as heat and burning, for example, are sought from fire. As is evident, the source (*mansha'*) from which these effects result is external existence (*al-wujūd al-khārijī*), not mental existence (*al-wujūd al-dhihnī*).

Gloss Two

It is a well-known [premise] among them that the subsistence (*thubūt*) of something in something else depends on the existence of that in which it subsists (*al-muthbat lahu*), and this, they claim, is known necessarily. It has been said, however, that this [premise] is contradicted in the case of the attribute of existence (*ṣifat al-wujūd*), because if its subsistence in a quiddity depended on the existence of the quiddity, an endless chain of existences would result.

The answer was found in making a special case (*al-takhṣīṣ*) [of existence] by [saying] that what is meant is that the subsistence of something other than the attribute of existence depends on the existence of that in which it subsists. This [argument for] making a special case [of existence] was attributed to al-Imām [Fakhr al-Dīn al-Rāzī].[22]

Al-Sayyid al-Sharīf [al-Jurjānī], may God sanctify his soul, said in his glosses to the commentary on *Ḥikmat al-ʿAyn:*[23] "What determines that a special case is to be made is the intuitive knowledge of the intellect (*badīhat al-ʿaql*), which distinguishes between existence and what is not existence." He also said in his gloss to the commentary on *al-Tajrīd:*[24] "This is nothing because intuitive knowledge (*al-badīhah*) does not distinguish in that [case] one attribute from another. To be sure, it witnesses to the fact that the subsistence of the attribute of existence in its substratum cannot depend on the substratum's existence. From this need be inferred only that its subsistence in the substratum cannot be an external subsistence like the subsistence of whiteness in a body, not that an exception must be made to that intuitively known premise (*al-qāʿidah al-badīhīyah*)," because exceptions to premises are made only in the case of presumptions (*al-ẓannīyāt*), not in the case of rational propositions (*al-ʿaqlīyāt*).

Gloss Three

If two externally nonexistent mental entities (*amrān iʿtibārīyān maʿdūmān bi-ḥasab al-khārij*) subsist in an external existent (*mawjūd khārijī*), one can consider them to be conjoined in view of their coming together in that in which they subsist. Similarly, when a mental entity subsists in an external existent, and another mental entity comes to inhere in it, the two entities can then be considered to be conjoined. Except for these two cases, however, to consider two nonexistents (*al-maʿdūmayn*) to be conjoined is hardly imaginable. Indeed, to say that these two [aforementioned] conjunctions exist externally is clearly by way of concession (*al-tanazzul*) only.

Notes to the Translation

1. See gloss one.
2. That is, the implication contained in the preceding hypothetical proposition.
3. See gloss two.
4. See gloss three.
5. That is, that nothing would exist at all.
6. Since its existence is itself, it cannot cease to subsist in it.
7. *Ḥaqīqah* has been translated "reality" to distinguish it from *māhīyah,* or quiddity. *Ḥaqīqah* is a term for *māhīyah* insofar as it really exists outside the mind. See al-Juranī, *al-Taʿrīfāt,* under the heading of *al-māhīyah.*
8. That is, in the sense of its being qualified by existence.
9. That is, "exists."
10. That is, in respect to its absoluteness.
11. See Quṭub al-Dīn al-Rāzī, *Lawāmiʿ al-Asrār,* pp. 55–56.

12–12. All manuscripts omit this section except Yahuda 3872, where it has been added in the margin, and ʿAqā'id Taymūr 393, where it is incorporated into the text. It also forms part of the text of *Lawāmiʿ al-Asrār* as given in the Istanbul edition of 1303.

13. Such as individuation.
14. That is, the nature together with some other entity.
15. That is, that the nature is not conjoined with any external entity.
16. See paragraph 21.
17. That is, that the nature is not conjoined with any entity whatsoever, whether external or mental.
18. That is, that the nature would exist either alone or together with some other entity.
19. See paragraphs 19 and 23.
20. That is, that it could be a mental as well as an external entity.
21. The word "different" has been added here by al-Jāmī.
22. See, for example, *al-Mabāḥith al-Mashriqīyah,* I, 37–38; and *Kitāb al-Arbaʿīn,* p. 58.
23. The glosses of ʿAlī ibn Muḥammad al-Jurjānī to the commentary of Mīrak Shams

al-Dīn Muḥammad ibn Mubārak Shāh al-Bukhārī on *Ḥikmat al-ʿAyn* by Najm al-Dīn ʿAlī ibn Muḥammad al-Kātibī. See Brockelmann, *Geschichte,* I, 613 (467), S I, 847.

24. See al-Jurjānī, *Ḥāshiyat Sharḥ al-Tajrīd,* fol. 21b.

List of Works Cited

Abd al-Hayy ibn Fakhr al-Dīn al-Ḥasanī, *Nuzhat al-Khawāṭir wa-Bahjat al-Masāmiʿ wa-al-Nawāẓir,* 7 vols. Hyderabad, 1350/1931-1378/1959.

Abū Rayyān, Muḥammad ʿAlī, *Uṣūl al-Falsafah al-Ishrāqīyah.* Cairo, 1959.

Ahlwardt, W., *Verzeichnis der arabischen Handschriften der Königlichen Bibliothek zu Berlin.* 10 vols. Berlin, 1887-1899.

al-Aḥmadnagarī, ʿAbd al-Nabī ibn ʿAbd al-Rasūl, *Jamiʿ al-ʿUlūm al-Mulaqqab bi-Dustūr al-ʿUlamā'*. 4 vols. Hyderabad, 1329-1331.

Brockelmann, Carl, *Geschichte der arabischen Litteratur.* 2 vols. Leiden, 1943-1949. 3 suppls. Leiden, 1937-1942.

Busse, Adolfus, *Porphyrii Isagoge et in Aristotelis Categorias Commentarium* (*Commentaria in Aristotelem Graeca,* Vol. 4, Pt. 1). Berlin, 1887.

Dānish Pazhūh, Muḥammadtaqī, *Fihrist-i Kitābkhāna-yi Ihdāʿī-yi Āqā-yi Sayyid Muḥammad Mishkāt bih Kitābkhāna-yi Dānishgāh-i Tihrān.* Vol. 3. 5 pts. (Intishārāt-i Dānishgāh-i Tihrān 169, 181, 299, 303, 533). Tehran, 1332-1338.

Drewes, G. W. J., "Sech Joesoep Makasar" in *Djawa,* 1926, No. 2, pp. 83-88.

al-Fanārī, Shams al-Dīn Muḥammad ibn Ḥamzah, *Miṣbāḥ al-Uns bayn al-Maʿqūl wa-al-Mashhūd fī Sharḥ Miftāḥ Ghayb al-Jamʿ wa-al-Wujūd* (Commentary on *Miftāḥ al-Ghayb* of Ṣadr al-Dīn al-Qūnawī). Tehran, 1323.

Fihris al-Khizānah al-Taymūrīyah. 4 vols. Cairo, 1367/1948-1369/1950.

al-Ghazālī, Abū Ḥāmid Muḥammad, *Mishkāt al-Anwār.* Tr. W. H. T. Gairdner. Lahore, 1952.

———, *Qānūn al-Ta'wīl.* Ed. Muḥammad Zāhid al-Kawtharī. Cairo, 1359/1940.

al-Hamadhānī, ʿAyn al-Quḍāh ʿAbd Allāh ibn Muḥammad, *Zubdat al-Ḥaqā'iq, in Muṣannafāt-i ʿAyn al-Quḍāh Hamadhānī.* Ed. Afīf ʿUsayrān. Vol. 1 (Intishārāt-i Dānishgāh-i Tihrān 695). Tehran, 1341/1962.

Ibn ʿArabī, Muḥyī al-Dīn Muḥammad ibn ʿAlī, *al-Futūḥāt al-Makkīyah.* 4 vols. Cairo, 1329.

Ibn Khaldūn, ʿAbd al-Raḥmān ibn Muḥammad. *The Muqaddimah.* Translated by Franz Rosenthal. 3 vols. Bollingen Series no. 43. New York, 1958.

Ibn Sīnā, Abū ʿAlī al-Ḥusayn ibn ʿAbd Allāh, *al-Shifā', al-Ilāhīyāt.* Cairo, 1380/1960.

———, *al-Shifā', al-Manṭiq, al-Madkhal.* Cairo, 1371/1952.

al-Jāmī, Nūr al-Dīn ʿAbd al-Raḥmān ibn Aḥmad, *al-Durrah al-Fākhirah fī Taḥqīq Madhhab al-Ṣūfīyah wa al-Mutakallimīn wa-al-Ḥukamā' al-Mutaqaddimīn.* Printed at the end of *Asās al-Taqdīs fī ʿIlm al-Kalām* by Fakhr al-Dīn al-Rāzī. Pp. 247-296. Cairo, 1328.

———, *Ḥawāshī al-Durrah al-Fākhirah* (Glosses on the author's *al-Durrah al-Fākhirah*). Ms Yahuda 3872, Robert Garrett Collection, Princeton University Library. Fols. 3a-23a.

———, *Lawā'iḥ*, Edited and translated by E. H. Whinfield and Mīrzā Muḥammad Qazwīnī. Oriental Translation Fund, New Series, no. 16. London, 1928.

———, *Naqd al-Nuṣūṣ fī Sharḥ Naqsh al-Fuṣūṣ* (Commentary on *Naqsh al-Fuṣūṣ*, an abridgement by Ibn ʿArabī of his *Fuṣūṣ al-Ḥikam*). Bombay, 1307.

al-Jurjānī, al-Sayyid al-Sharīf ʿAlī ibn Muḥammad, *Ḥāshiyah ʿalā Sharḥ al-Maṭāli* (Gloss on *Lawāmiʿ al-Asrār fī Sharḥ Maṭāliʿ al-Anwār* of Quṭb al-Dīn al-Rāzī). Istanbul, 1303.

———, *Ḥāshiyat Sharḥ al-Tajrīd* (Gloss on the commentary of Maḥmūd al-Iṣbahānī on *Tajrīd al-ʿAqā'id* of Naṣīr al-Dīn al-Ṭūsī). Ms 865 (988H), Robert Garrett Collection, Princeton University Library.

———, *Sharḥ al-Mawāqif* (Commentary on *al-Mawāqif fī ʿIlm al-Kalām* of ʿAḍud al-Dīn al-Ījī). 8 vols. Cairo, 1325/1907.

al-Kalanbawī, Ismāʿīl ibn Muṣṭafā, *Risālah fī Waḥdat al-Wujūd* (Commentary on two passages of Qāḍī Mīr's commentary on al-Abharī's *Hidāyat al-Ḥikmah*). Ms Or. Oct. 2119, Staatsbibliothek Preussischer Kulturbesitz, Marburg/Lahn.

al-Kāshānī (al-Qāshānī, al-Kāshī), Kamāl al-Dīn ʿAbd al-Razzāq, *Sharḥ Fuṣūṣ al-Ḥikam* (Commentary on Ibn ʿArabī's *Fuṣūṣ al-Ḥikam*). Cairo, 1321.

Kāshif al-Ghiṭā', ʿAlī ibn Muḥammad Riḍā ibn Hādī, *Naqd al-Ārā al-Manṭiqīyah wa-Ḥall Mushkilātihā*. Al-Najaf, 1383.

al-Kātibī, Najm al-Dīn ʿAlī ibn ʿUmar, *al-Risālah al-Shamsīyah fī al-Qawā id al-Manṭiqīyah.* Edited and translated by A. Sprenger (Bibliotheca Indica 88, First Appendix). Calcutta, 1854.

al-Kūrānī, Ibrāhīm ibn Ḥasan, *al-Amam li-Īqāẓ al-Himam.* Hyderabad, 1328.

al-Lārī, ʿAbd al-Ghafūr, *Takmilat Nafaḥāt al-Uns.* Ms Or. 218, British Museum. Fols. 151b–175b.

al-Mahā'imī, ʿAlā al-Dīn ʿAlī ibn Aḥmad, *Ajillat al-Ta'yīd fī Sharḥ Adillat al-Tawḥīd* (Commentary by the author on his own work, *Adillat al-Tawḥīd*). Ms Yahuda 4601, Robert Garrett Collection, Princeton University Library.

al-Maḥallī, Aḥmad, *Tanwīr al-Mashriq Sharḥ Tahdhīb al-Manṭiq* (Commentary on *Tahdhīb al-Manṭiq* of Saʿd al-Dīn al-Taftāzānī). Cairo, 1331/1913.

McKeon, Richard, *Selections from Medieval Philosophers.* 2 vols. New York, 1929–1930.

Mubīn, Muḥammad, *Mir'āt al-Shurūḥ* (Commentary on *Sullam al-ʿUlūm* of Muḥibb Allāh ibn ʿAbd al-Shakūr al-Bihārī). Cairo, 1328.

Munzawī, *ʿAlīnaqī, Fihrist-i Kitābkhāna-yi Ihdā'ī-yi Sayyid Muḥammad Mishkāt bih Kitābkhāna-yi Dānishgāh-i Tihrān.* 2 vols. (Intishārāt-i Dānishgāh-i Tihrān 123, 168). Tehran, 1330–1332.

al-Muthul al-ʿAqlīyah al-Aflāṭūnīyah. Edited by ʿAbd al-Raḥmān Badawī. Cairo, 1947.

al-Nābulusī, ʿAbd al-Ghamī ibn Ismāʿīl, *Īḍāḥ al-Maqṣūd min Maʿnā Waḥdat al-Wujūd.* Damascus, 1969.

———, *Nukhbat al-Mas'alah Sharḥ al-Tuhfah al-Mursalah* (Commentary on *al-Tuhfah al-Mursalah ilā al-Nabī* of Muḥammad ibn Faḍl Allāh al-Burhānpūrī). Cairo, 1344/1926.

al-Qayṣarī, Dāwūd ibn Maḥmūd, *Maṭlaʿ Khuṣūṣ al-Kilam fī Maʿānī Fuṣūṣ al-Ḥikam* (Commentary on Ibn ʿArabī's *Fuṣūṣ al-Ḥikam*). Tehran, 1299.

al-Qūnawī, Ṣadr al-Dīn Muḥammad ibn Isḥāq, *Iʿjāz al-Bayān fī Ta'wīl Umm al-Qur'ān.* Hyderabad, 1358/1949.

———, *Kitāb al-Nuṣūṣ*. Printed at the end of al-Kāshānī's *Sharḥ Manāzil al-Sā'irīn*. Tehran, 1315.

al-Rāzī, Fakhr al-Dīn, Muḥammad ibn ʿUmar, *Kitāb al-Arbaʿīn fī Uṣūl al-Dīn*. Hyderabad, 1353.

———, *al-Mabāḥith al-Mashriqīyah*. 2 vols. Hyderabad, 1343.

———, *Sharḥ al-Ishārāt* (Commentary on *al-Ishārāt wa-al-Tanbīhāt* of Ibn Sīnā). Printed in the margin of al-Ṭūsī's *Sharḥ al-Ishārāt*. Istanbul, 1290.

al-Rāzī, Quṭb al-Dīn Muḥammad, *Lawāmiʿ al-Asrār fī Sharḥ Maṭāli al-Anwār* (Commentary on *Maṭāliʿ al-Anwār* of Sirāj al-Dīn al-Urmawī). Istanbul, 1303.

———, *Risālat Taḥqīq al-Kullīyāt*. Ms Warner Or. 958 (21), fols. 67b–71b, University of Leiden Library.

———, *Taḥrīr al-Qawāʿid al-Manṭiqīyah fī Sharḥ al-Risālah al-Shamsīyah* (Commentary on *al-Risālah al-Shamsīyah fī al-Qawāʿid al-Manṭiqiyah* of Najm al-Dīn al-Kātibī). 2 vols. Cairo, 1323/1905.

al-Suhrawardī, Shihāb al-Dīn Yaḥyā ibn Ḥabash, *Ḥikmat al-Ishrāq,* in Henry Corbin, *Oeuvres philosophiques et mystiques de Shihâboddîn Yahyâ Sohrawardî* (Bibliothèque Iranienne II). Tehran/Paris, 1952.

al-Suwaydī, Abū al-Khayr ʿAbd al-Raḥmān ibn ʿAbd Allāh, *Kashf al-Ḥujub al-Musbalah alā Kharā'id al-Tuhfah al-Mursalah* (Commentary on *al-Tuhfah al-Mursalah ilā al-Nabī* of Muḥammad ibn Faḍl Allāh al-Burhānpūrī). Cairo, n.d.

al-Taftāzānī, Saʿd al-Dīn Masʿūd ibn ʿUmar, *Risālah fī Waḥdat al-Wujūd,* in *Majmū at Rasā'il fī Waḥdat al-Wujūd,* pp. 2–47, Istanbul, 1294. This same work, under the title *Fāḍiḥat al-Mulhidīn wa-Nāṣiḥat al-Muwaḥḥidīn,* is attributed to ʿAlā al-Dīn Muḥammad ibn Muḥammad al-Bukhārī (Brockelmann, *Geschichte,* 1, 573, Suppl. 1: 794).

———, *Sharḥ al-Maqāṣid* (Commentary of the author on his *al-Maqāṣid fī ʿIlm al-Kalām*). 2 vols. Istanbul, 1277.

———, *Sharḥ al-Risālah al-Shamsīyah* (Commentary on *al-Risālah al-Shamsīyah* of Najm al-Dīn al-Kātibī). Istanbul, 1312.

al-Tahānawī, Muḥammad ʿAlī ibn ʿAlī ibn Muḥammad Ḥāmid, *Kashshāf Iṣṭlāḥāt al-Funūn*. Ed. A. Sprenger. Calcutta, 1278/1861.

Ṭalas, Muḥammad Asʿad, *al-Kashshāf ʿan Makhṭūṭāt Khazā'in Kutub al-Awqāf*. Baghdad, 1372/1953.

al-Ṭūsī, Naṣīr al-Dīn Muḥammad ibn Muḥammad, *Sharḥ al-Ishārāt* (Commentary on Ibn Sīnā's *al-Ishārāt wa-al-Tanbīhāt*). Istanbul, 1290.

al-Urmawī, Sirāj al-Dīn Maḥmūd ibn Bakr, *Maṭāliʿ al-Anwār*. Printed in the margin of Quṭb al-Dīn al-Rāzī's commentary on it entitled *Lawāmiʿ al-Asrār fī Sharḥ Maṭāli al-Anwār*. Istanbul, 1303.

Voorhoeve, P., *Handlist of Arabic Manuscripts in the Library of the University of Leiden and Other Collections in the Netherlands*. Leiden, 1957.

ARABIC TEXT

رسالة في الوجود
تأليف

نور الدين عبد الرحمن بن احمد الجامي

تحقيق

نقولا هير

وما يأتيهم من ذكر من الرحمن محدث الا كانوا عنه معرضين

[1] بسم الله الرحمن الرحيم [1]

(١) الوجود ، أي ما بانضمامه الى الماهيات[2] يترتب[3] عليها آثارها المختصة بها[4] ، موجود. فإنه لو لم يكن موجوداً لم يوجد شيء أصلًا ، والتالي باطل فالمقدَّم مثله.

(٢) بيان الملازمة أن الماهية قبل انضمام الوجود اليها غير موجودة قطعاً ، فلو كان الوجود أيضاً غير موجود لا يمكن ثبوت أحدها للآخر ، فإن ثبوت شيء لشيء فرعٌ لوجود المُثْبَت له[5] ، واذا لم يُثْبَت أحدهما للآخر لم تكن[6] الماهية معروضة للوجود كما ذهب اليه أهل النظر ، ولا عارضة له كما ذهب اليه القائلون بوحدة الوجود ، فلا تكون[7] موجودة.

(٣) فإن قلت : هذه المقدمة مخصوصة بما عدا الوجود ، والمراد بها أن ثبوت شيء هو غير صفة الوجود فرع لوجود المثبت له ، وأما ثبوت الوجود لشيء فإنما[8] هو مشروط بوجود[9] المثبت له حين ثبوت الوجود له[10] لا قبله ، ولا شك أنه ،[11] حين ثبوت الوجود له ، موجود بنفس ذلك الوجود.

(٤) قلنا[12] : التخصيص والاستثناء إنما يجريان في الخطابيات الظنية لا العقليات الصرفة لا سيما الضروريات ، وأيضاً مَن راجع وجدانه وأنصف ، من نفسه أدرك أن انضمام أمرين

(١ – ١) أ : + الحمد لله وحده ، ك : + وعليه اتكائي في كل الامور ، ل : – بسم .... الرحيم

(٢) د : الماهية

(٣) ك ل : ترتب

(٤) انظر الحاشية الاولى

(٥) انظر الحاشية الثانية

(٦) ك : يكن

(٧) هك : يكون

(٨) دل : انما

(٩) دل : لوجود

(١٠) دل : – له

(١١) د ل : ان

(١٢) أ : قلت

معدومين في الخارج من غير قيامهما أو قيام أحدهما بموجود خارجي لا يجوّزه العقل بل يشهد بامتناعه[١].

(٥) فإن قلت : الماهية باعتبار وجودها العقلي معروضة للوجود الخارجي فيكون ثبوت[٢] الوجود الخارجي لها في العقل فرعاً لوجودها فيه لا في الخارج.

(٦) قلنا[٣] : ننقل الكلام الى وجودها[٤] العقلي بأن نقول[٥] : ثبوت الوجود العقلي لها في العقل موقوف على وجود سابق لها فيه ،[٦] وثبوت الوجود السابق على[٧] وجود سابق[٨] آخر ، فيتسلسل[٩] الوجودات ، وليس هذا من قبيل التسلسل في الامور الاعتبارية التي تنقطع[١٠] بانقطاع الاعتبار ، فإن كل لاحق موقوف على سابقه كما لا يخفى على المتدبر.

(٧) وأما بطلان التالي فظاهر لا يحتاج الى البيان ، فثبت أن الوجود موجود.

(٨) وإذا كان موجوداً وجب أن يكون وجوده بنفسه وإلا تسلسل[١١] ، فيكون واجباً لامتناع زوال الشيء عن نفسه ، ويلزم[١٢] أن يكون حقيقةً واحدة يلحقها[١٣] التعدد النسبيّ بإضافتها الى الماهيات وإلا تعدد الواجب[١٤] ، وقد برهنوا على امتناعه.

(٩) فإنْ قلت : لا شك أن معنى الوجود مفهوم عرضيّ لا يصدق على شيء قائم بنفسه مواطأةً كالمشي والضحك واللون والسواد وأمثال ذلك ، وإنكار ذلك مكابرة ، [١٥]فكيف يكون[١٥] ذات الواجب نفس ذلك المفهوم؟

قلت[١٦] : كما أنه يجوز أن يكون هذا المفهوم العامّ زائداً على الوجود الخاصّ الواجبيّ

---

(١) انظر الحاشية الثالثة
(٢) د : عروض ، هامش د : ثبوت
(٣) أ : قلت
(٤) د : الوجود
(٥) د ه : – نقول ، ك : يقول
(٦) د : في العقل ، هامش د : فيه
(٧) د ل : + ثبوت
(٨) ل : – سابق
(٩) أ : فتسلسل
(١٠) د ك ل : ينقطع
(١١) دك : يتسلسل
(١٢) د ه ل : فيلزم
(١٣) ك : تلحقها
(١٤) أ : + تعالى
(١٥–١٥) ك : فيكون
(١٦) ك : قلنا

وعلى الموجودات الخاصّة[١] الممكنة على تقدير كونها حقائق مختلفة على ما قال به الحكماء يجوز أن يكون زائداً على حقيقة واحدة مطلقة موجودة هي حقيقة الوجود الواجبي[٦]، ويكون هذا المفهوم الزائد أمراً اعتبارياً غير موجود إلا في العقل، ويكون معروضه موجوداً حقيقياً خارجياً هو حقيقة الوجود.

(١١) فإنْ قلت: إذا كان الموجود حقيقةً[٣] هو الوجود ينبغي أن يكون الماهية عارضة له[٤] لاحقة إياه والوجود معروضاً ملحوقاً، وهذا خلاف ما نفهمه[٥] من قولنا الماهية موجودة، فإنّا نفهم قطعاً أن الماهية متصفة بالوجود فهي معروضة والوجود عارض، فكيف يصح ما قلت؟

(١٢) قلنا: إطلاق الموجود[٦] عليها بالمعنى المذكور إنما هو باعتبار اشتقاق هذه الصيغة من الوجود إذا أُريد به هذا المفهوم العارض اللازم، وأما إذا اعتُبِر اشتقاقه منه، إذا أُريد به تلك الحقيقة المعروضة، فمعناه حينئذ ذو الوجود لا المتصف[٧] به.

(١٣) فإنْ قلت: هذه الحقيقة باعتبار إطلاقها كلّيّ طبيعيّ، فما ذكرتم في معرض الاستدلال على وجودها معارض بما استُدلّ به على امتناع[٨] وجود الكلي الطبيعي[٨].

(١٤) قلنا: لا نسلّم أوّلاً أنها[٩] باعتبار إطلاقها[٩] المذكور كلي طبيعي، فإن المراد بإطلاقها أن لا يكون لها تعيّن لا يجامع[١٠] التعينات اللاحقة إياها في المراتب بواسطة تلبّس الماهيات

---

(١) ك: الخارجية، هامش ك: الخاصة
(٢) أ ك: الواجب
(٣) ك: حقيقته
(٤) د: — له
(٥) د: يفهم، ه ل: نفهم
(٦) دل: الوجود
(٧) ه: المتصفة
(٨-٨) د: الوجود الكلي، ل: الوجود الكلي الطبيعي
(٩-٩) أ: باطلاقها
(١٠) هامش د: + مع (خ)

بها ، ولا يستلزم ذلك عدم تعينها في نفسها بتعين يُخرِجها عن الكلية[1] .

(١٥) سلّمنا أنها بهذا الاعتبار كلي طبيعي ، لكن لا نسلّم امتناع وجوده ، كيف وكثير من الحكماء صرّحوا بوجوده والكتب مشحونة به ، وما ذكره بعض المتأخرين في معرض الاستدلال على امتناع وجوده لا يخلو عن وجه أو وجوه [2]من الخلل[2] ، ولنذكر أقوى ما ذكروه[3] ، وهو ما أورده شارح المطالع ، [4]ونبيّن وجه الخلل فيه[4] بعون الله سبحانه[5] .

(١٦) قال رحمه الله : (الكلي الطبيعي لا وجود له[6] في الخارج ، وذلك لوجهين : أحدهما أنه لو وُجِد الكلي الطبيعي[7] لكان إما نفس الجزئيات في الخارج أو جزءًا منها أو خارجاً عنها ، والأقسام بأسرها باطلة ، أما الأول فلأنه لو كان نفس الجزئيات لزم[8] أن يكون كل واحد من الجزئيات عين الآخر في الخارج ضرورة[3] [10]أن كل واحد فُرِض منها[10] عين الطبيعة الكلية وهي عين الجزئي الآخر وعين العين عين ، فيكون كل وحد فُرِض عين الآخر ، هذا خُلْف) .

(١٧) (وأما الثاني فلأنه لو كان جزءًا في الخارج لتقدّم عليها[11] في الوجود[12] فلا يصح حمله[13] عليها ، وأما الثالث فبين الاستحالة) .

---

(١) هـ ل : الكليتين

(٢ – ٢) د هـ : خلل

(٣) ل : ذكره

(٤ – ٤) ك : ونبين فيه وجه الخلل

(٥) د ل : تعالى

(٦) د : لها

(٧) أ : – الطبيعي

(٢) هـ ك ل : يلزم

(٩) د هـ : حتى

(١٠–١٠) د : ان وجد فرد فرض ، هامش د : اي واحد فرض (خ) ، هـ : ان واحداً فرض ، ل : ان كل واحد منها فرض

(١١) هامش أ : + في الخارج ضرورة ان الجزء الخارجي ما لم يتحقق اولا وبالذات لم يتحقق الكل وحينئذ يكون مغايراً لها (صح)

(١٢) د هـ ل : + الخارجي

(١٣) د : الحمل ، هامش د : حمله (خ)

(١٨) قوله: (أو جزءًا منها) إنْ أراد بكونه[١] جزءًا منها أن يكون وراءه جزء آخر في الخارج ويكون الجزئيات عبارة عن مجموع الأجزاء لم ينحصر القسمة في الأقسام الثلاثة، وإن أراد[٢] به[٣] كونه منضماً مع أمر آخر خارجياً كان أو اعتبارياً فالحصر مسلَّم.

(١٩) لكن لا نسلّم عدم صحة الحمل، فإنه إذا كان الموجود في الخارج هو الطبيعة فقط ويكون التمايز بين جزئياتها بتعينات اعتبارية غير موجودة لا شك أنه يصحّ الحمل حينئذ، فإنه[٤] لا يوجد من الجزئيات في الخارج سوى الطبيعة[٥] حتى يُتصوَّر عدم الاتحاد في الوجود لتقدم أو تأخر.

(٢٠) (وثانيهما أن الطبيعة الكلية لو وُجِدت في الأعيان لكان الموجود في الأعيان إما مجرَّد الطبيعة أو مع أمر آخر، لا سبيل إلى الأول وإلا لزم وجود الأمر الواحد بالشخص في أمكنة مختلفة واتصافه بصفات متضادّة، ومن البيّن بطلانه[٦]).

(٢١) (ولا الى الثاني، وإلا لم يَخْلُ من أن يكونا موجودين بوجود واحد أو بوجودين، فإن كانا موجودين بوجود واحد فذلك[٧] الوجود، إن قام بكل واحد منهما، يلزم قيام الشيء الواحد بمحلّين مختلفين، وإنه مُحال، وإن قام بالمجموع لم يكن كل منهما موجوداً بل المجموع هو الموجود[٨]، وإن كانا موجودين بوجودين فلا يمكن حمل الطبيعة على المجموع، هذا خُلْف).

---

(١) هـ: بكونها
(٢) هـ: اريد
(٣) ك: – به
(٤) أ: لانه، هامش أ: فانه (خ)
(٥) ك: الطبيعية
(٦) ك: لبطلانه
(٧) هـ ل: وذلك
(٨) ل: الوجود

(٢٢) قوله : (لكان الموجود في الأعيان إما مجرَّد الطبيعة أو مع أمر آخر) المراد بمجرد الطبيعة إما أن يكون الطبيعة من غير انضمام أمر خارجي [١] أو من غير انضمام أمر [٢] مطلقاً خارجياً كان أو اعتبارياً.

(٢٣) فإن كان المراد الأول كما هو الظاهر من كلامه في إبطال الشق الأخير فلا نسلّم أنه يلزم وجود الأمر الواحد بالشخص في أمكنة مختلفة وكونه متصفاً بصفات متضادّة ، لِمَ لا يجوز أن يكون الطبيعة باعتبار تقيّدها بتعيّن اعتباري عدمي شخصاً معيَّناً وبتعين آخر كذلك شخصاً آخر الى غير ذلك ويكون تمكّنه في أمكنة مختلفة واتصافه بصفات متضادّة باعتبار هذه الأشخاص المتمايزة المتغايرة بالأمور الاعتبارية.

(٢٤) وإن كان المراد الثاني فلا نسلّم أيضاً الانحصار في القسمين ، [٣]فإن المراد[٣] من أمر آخر ما يكون موجوداً [٤]في الخارج[٤] كما يظهر من وجه إبطاله ، فيجوز أن لا يكون الطبيعة مجردة ولا مع أمرٍ آخر موجود في الخارج بل مع أمر عدمي اعتباري كما مرّ.

(٢٥) وإن حملْتَ الأمر على معنى أعمّ انتقل المنع الى قوله : (لم يَخْلُ من أن يكونا[٥] موجودين بوجود واحد أو بوجودين مختلفين) فإنه على ذلك التقدير يجوز أن يكون أحدهما موجوداً خارجياً والآخر أمراً اعتبارياً.

(٢٦) قوله : (يكونان موجودين بوجود واحد او بوجودين مختلفين) لقائل أن يقول : لا نسلّم الحصر في الصورتين المذكورتين ، لِمَ لا يجوز أن يكون أحدهما موجوداً بنفسه

---

(١) د ه ل : خارج
(٢) د : - أمر
(٣-٣) د : فان كان المراد ، هامش د : فان المراد (خ صح)
(٤-٤) د ه ل : - في الخارج
(٥) ك : يكون

والآخر موجوداً به كما يقول[١] به القائلون بوحدة الوجود؟ فإن طبيعة الوجود هو الموجود عندهم وما عداها من الماهيات ولوازمها أمور عارضة لها[٢] موجودة بها[٣] ، فلا يلزم محذور .

(٢٧) فإن قلت : صدق في هذه الصورة أنهما موجودان بوجود واحد ، فإن أحدهما موجود بنفسه والآخر به ، فلا يخرج عن القسمة ، قلنا : ننقل[٤] المنع حينئذ[٥] الى انحصار الوجود[٦] الواحد في كونه قائماً بكل واحد منهما وكونه قائماً[٧] بالمجموع ، فلا يُجْدي نفعاً .

الحاشية الاولى

أي آثارها المطلوبة منها [٨] كالنار مثلًا فإن المطلوب منها[٨] الحرارة والإحراق وأمثالهما وما هو منشأ لترتّب هذه الآثار عليها هو الوجود الخارجي لا الوجود الذهني وهو ظاهر .

---

(١) د : يقولون
(٢) د : له
(٣) د : به
(٤) د : ينقل ، ك : ينتقل
(٥) ك : – حينئذ
(٦) د ه ل : – الوجود
(٧) د ه : – قائماً
(٨–٨) ك : – كالنار .... منها

الحاشية الثانية

قد اشتهر فيما بينهم أن ثبوت شيء لشيء فرعٌ لوجود[1] المُثْبَت له ، [2]وادّعوا فيه الضرورة[2] ، قيل : ينتقض [3]هذا بصفة[3] الوجود ، فإن ثبوتها للماهية[4] لو كان فرعاً[5] لوجود الماهية[6] لتسلسلت[7] الوجودات ، وأُجيب بالتخصيص بأن المراد[8] : ثبوت شيء هو غير صفة الوجود فرع لوجود المثبت له ، وأُسند هذا التخصيص الى الإمام ، وقال السيد الشريف قدس سره في حواشيه[9] على شرح[10] حَكمة العين : (والحاكم[11] بالتخصيص بديهة[12] العقل الفارقة[13] بين الوجود وغيره) وقال[14] في حاشيته[15] [16]على شرح التجريد[16] : (وهذا[17] ليس بشيء لأن البديهة[18] لا تفرق[19] في ذلك بين صفة وصفة[19] ، نعم تشهد[20] بأن قيام صفة الوجود بموصوفها لا يجوز أن يتوقف على وجوده ، فوجب أن لا يكون قيامها به قياماً خارجياً على نحو قيام[21] البياض بالجسم ، لا[22] أن يستثنى[22] من تلك القاعدة البديهية) لأن الاستثناء من القاعدة إنما يكون في الظنيات[23] لا في العقليات .

---

(١) ك : + الشيء
(٢ – ٢) د : – وادعوا فيه الضرورة
(٣ – ٣) ك : – هذا بصفة ، ل : هنا صفة
(٤) د ل : للمثبت ، هامش د : للماهية (خ)
(٥) ل : قديماً
(٦) د ل : المثبت ، هامش د : الماهية (خ)
(٧) أ : بسلسلة ، ل : تسلسلت
(٨) ك : + ان
(٩) أ : حاشيته
(١٠) أ : – شرح
(١١) ل : والحكم
(١٢) د : بداهة
(١٣) ل : الفارق
(١٤) ل : قال
(١٥) ك : حواشيه
(١٦–١٦) أ : للتجريد ، هامش أ : على شرح (صح)
(١٧) أ : وهذا
(١٨) د ل : البداهة
(١٩–١٩) د ل : بين صفة وصفة في ذلك
(٢٠) ل : يشهد
(٢١) د : + صفة
(٢٢–٢٢) أ : انا نستثني
(٢٣) ل : الطبيعيات

الحاشية الثالثة

إذا قام أمران اعتباريان معدومان بحسب الخارج بموجود خارجي يمكن أن يُعتبر الانضمام بينهما باعتبار اجتماعهما[1] فيما قاما[2] به ، وكذا إذا قام أمر اعتباري بموجود خارجي وعرض له أمر اعتباري آخر يمكن أيضاً اعتبار معنى[3] الانضمام بين هذين الامرين ، وأما فيما [4]عدا هتين[4] الصورتين فاعتبار [5] الانضمام بين المعدومين غير متصوَّر ، بل القول بكون هذين الانضمامين أيضاً[6] خارجياً إنما هو على سبيل التنزّل كما لا يخفى .

---

(١) ك : اجتماع
(٢) ل : قام
(٣) د : – معنى ، ل : مع
(٤ – ٤) د : عداهما بين
(٥) ك : فباعتبار
(٦) ل : بل هذا الانضمام

Index